URBAN CHANGE AND POVERTY

Michael G. H. McGeary and Laurence E. Lynn, Jr., Editors

Committee on National Urban Policy
Commission on Behavioral and Social Sciences and Education
National Research Council

NATIONAL ACADEMY PRESS
Washington, D.C.   1988

National Academy Press • 2101 Constitution Avenue, N.W. • Washington, D. C. 20418

NOTICE: The project that is the subject of this report was approved by the Governing Board of the National Research Council, whose members are drawn from the councils of the National Academy of Sciences, the National Academy of Engineering, and the Institute of Medicine. The members of the committee responsible for the report were chosen for their special competences and with regard for appropriate balance.

This report has been reviewed by a group other than the authors according to procedures approved by a Report Review Committee consisting of members of the National Academy of Sciences, the National Academy of Engineering, and the Institute of Medicine.

The National Academy of Sciences is a private, nonprofit, self-perpetuating society of distinguished scholars engaged in scientific and engineering research, dedicated to the furtherance of science and technology and to their use for the general welfare. Upon the authority of the charter granted to it by the Congress in 1863, the Academy has a mandate that requires it to advise the federal government on scientific and technical matters. Dr. Frank Press is president of the National Academy of Sciences.

The National Academy of Engineering was established in 1964, under the charter of the National Academy of Sciences, as a parallel organization of outstanding engineers. It is autonomous in its administration and in the selection of its members, sharing with the National Academy of Sciences the responsibility for advising the federal government. The National Academy of Engineering also sponsors engineering programs aimed at meeting national needs, encourages education and research, and recognizes the superior achievements of engineers. Dr. Robert M. White is president of the National Academy of Engineering.

The Institute of Medicine was established in 1970 by the National Academy of Sciences to secure the services of eminent members of appropriate professions in the examination of policy matters pertaining to the health of the public. The Institute acts under the responsibility given to the National Academy of Sciences by its congressional charter to be an adviser to the federal government and, upon its own initiative, to identify issues of medical care, research, and education. Dr. Samuel O. Thier is president of the Institute of Medicine.

The National Research Council was organized by the National Academy of Sciences in 1916 to associate the broad community of science and technology with the Academy's purposes of furthering knowledge and advising the federal government. Functioning in accordance with general policies determined by the Academy, the Council has become the principal operating agency of both the National Academy of Sciences and the National Academy of Engineering in providing services to the government, the public, and the scientific and engineering communities. The Council is administered jointly by both Academies and the Institute of Medicine. Dr. Frank Press and Dr. Robert M. White are chairman and vice chairman, respectively, of the National Research Council.

The work that provided the basis for this document was supported by funding under a contract with the U.S. Department of Housing and Urban Development. The substance and findings of that contract work are dedicated to the public. The author and publisher are solely responsible for the accuracy of statements or interpretations in this document. Such interpretations do not necessarily reflect the views of the government.

Cover Photograph: © THE STUDIO INC./UNIPHOTO.

Library of Congress Cataloging-in-Publication Data
Urban change and poverty / [edited by] Michael G.H. McGeary and
    Laurence E. Lynn, Jr., editors ; Committee on National Urban Policy,
    Commission on Behavioral and Social Sciences and Education, National
    Research Council.
      p.   cm.
    Bibliography: p.
    Includes index.
    ISBN 0-309-03837-5
    1. Urban policy—United States—Congresses. 2. Urban poor—United States—Congresses.
3. Urban economics—Congresses. I. McGeary, Michael G. H. II. Lynn, Laurence E. III. National Research Council (U.S.). Committee on National Urban Policy. IV. National Research Council (U.S.). Commission on Behavioral and Social Sciences and Education.
HT123.U7425 1988   88-1556
362.5'0973—dc19   CIP

Printed in the United States of America

First Printing, May 1988
Second Printing, December 1989

iii

Preface

The Committee on National Urban Policy was established by the National Research Council at the end of 1985 at the request of the U.S. Department of Housing and Urban Development and the other federal agencies that contribute to the biennial President's Report on National Urban Policy: the U.S. Department of Health and Human Services, the U.S. Department of Labor, the Urban Mass Transportation Administration, and the Economic Development Administration. Over a 3-year period, the committee has been asked to describe the uncertainties facing cities and their economies and populations; identify the urban policy issues facing state, local, and federal policy makers; and assess possible policy responses at each level of the intergovernmental system.

When the committee met for the first time in January 1986, it identified in a preliminary way a number of emerging and persisting urban problems that seemed to be facing national, state, and local policy makers (National Research Council, 1986). These problems included growing poverty in central cities, the lack of response of some urban economies to national economic recovery, the potential adverse effects of "creative" capital finance techniques, the capacity of state governments to increase their responsibility for urban problems, and inadequate data for assessing urban conditions. The committee decided, however, that it was necessary to examine closely and carefully the most recent information on the underlying demographic, social,

v

economic, and political trends shaping urban conditions before deciding which urban policy issues to explore in depth in subsequent years.

This volume includes a set of background papers commissioned in the spring of 1986 to address these issues, which were the basis of a 2-day workshop held by the committee in July 1986. The volume also contains the committee's report summarizing its assessment of the workshop discussions and findings and their implications for policy makers and researchers. The committee concluded that the most serious trend deserving special attention from policy makers and researchers is the increase in concentrated urban poverty in large central cities. With the concurrence of its federal sponsors, the committee has embarked in its second year on a study of urban poverty, which will be completed later in 1988.

On behalf of the committee, I would like to thank the federal officials who have supported and worked with us during the first year, including June Q. Koch, Kenneth J. Beirne, John P. Ross, and George Wright of the U.S. Department of Housing and Urban Development; Beverly Milkman, Brandon Roberts, and Mary Kate Smith of the Economic Development Administration; Patrick J. Cleary and Gary Reed of the U.S. Department of Labor; Kenneth W. Butler, Larry Schulman, Kenneth Bolton, and Fred Williams of the Urban Mass Transportation Administration; and Richard Shute, Marlys Gustafson, and Michael Fishman of the U.S. Department of Health and Human Services.

The committee is also deeply appreciative of the efforts of the authors of the workshop papers, which were commissioned on very short notice but nevertheless were of high quality and usefulness to the committee in assessing current socioeconomic conditions in urban areas. The committee would like to thank those who attended the workshop and lent their experience and expertise by participating in the discussions; workshop attendees are listed in the appendix to the report.

The committee is grateful for the support of the staff of the Commission on Behavioral and Social Sciences and Education, including executive director David A. Goslin, associate executive director P. Brett Hammond, and associate director for reports Eugenia Grohman, who edited the report. Shelly Westebbe took care of the many administrative details of committee meetings and workshops with unfailing good cheer, and Barbara Darr, Michelle Daniels, and Ann Tasseff assisted in the production of the report and papers.

I would especially like to acknowledge the hard and able work of Michael G. H. McGeary, the study director, who was primarily responsible for organizing the workshop, commissioning the background papers, and preparing this volume for publication.

Finally, I would like to thank the other committee members for their invaluable contributions in planning and participating in the workshop and producing the report contained in this volume. John C. Weicher, who resigned to take a position in the federal government, was an especially active member of the committee who will be missed.

LAURENCE E. LYNN, JR., *Chair*
Committee on National Urban Policy

Contents

**PART I
COMMITTEE REPORT**

PART II
BACKGROUND PAPERS

URBAN CHANGE
AND POVERTY

PART I

COMMITTEE REPORT

Overview

Historically, cities have been the centers of culture and civilization. Even today, they contain the major museums, symphonies, and other cultural resources of metropolitan areas. But cities are fundamentally economic entities, places where people gather to work and live. And for more than 100 years, American cities have been places where the poor and unskilled from rural areas and abroad come to seek economic opportunity and social assimilation. As economic entities, however, cities are not static. They change constantly in response to demographic shifts, the evolving structure of the national economy, emerging transportation and communications technologies, and state and federal policy decisions.

For most of this century, metropolitan areas have grown more quickly than nonmetropolitan areas. Yet within metropolitan areas, the location of people and jobs has decentralized steadily since at least the 1920s. As suburbanization has increased, central cities, older suburbs, and industrial satellite cities have declined. At the same time, at the regional level, there has been a shift of economic activity and population from the Northeast and Midwest to the South and West.

Although central cities in the older regions have been steadily losing manufacturing and other traditional blue-collar jobs, some have been able to attract new types of industries that are revitalizing their downtown economies. These new industries provide mostly white-collar jobs in communications, finance, and business services and in cultural, leisure, and tourist services.

The demographic and economic changes affecting major American cities have also affected the socioeconomic composition of their populations. White middle-income groups, followed more recently by middle-income blacks and other minorities, have moved to the suburbs. This exodus from the cities has been only partially offset by reverse migration: despite much talk about gentrification, only a few urban professionals have returned, and then only to specific neighborhoods in particular cities. Most of those moving into cities have been low-income minorities. As a result, central-city populations have declined (except in fast-growing areas of the West and South), average personal income levels have dropped, and the proportion of residents who are low income, low skilled, poorly educated, and minority has increased. Unemployment in central cities has been increasing, especially among minorities.

3

Although central-city residents have lower levels of educational skills in comparison with suburban residents, most of the growth in entry-level service sector jobs is taking place in the suburbs. There are controversies as to whether or not there is a spatial mismatch between low-skilled workers and low-skilled jobs and over the quality of those jobs: are they dead ends or stepping-stones to better and higher paying opportunities?

The Committee on National Urban Policy, which was formed to examine emerging urban policy issues, decided to begin with a careful empirical examination of fundamental economic and demographic trends to provide a sound basis for selecting specific policy issues to study in depth. The committee first of all wanted to look at the structure of urban economies and the composition of urban populations and how they are changing. Have events of the late 1970s and early 1980s—especially large cutbacks in federal aid to cities, a severe recession in 1981–1982, and a long-lasting economic recovery since 1982—affected urban areas and their central cities in new ways? Are basic urban economic and demographic trends different from or the same as those of the past 40 years or more?

The committee was also interested in empirical analyses of two closely related topics that are important to understand in assessing emerging urban policy issues: urban social structure and the economic well-being of urban residents. An analysis of economic and demographic trends should reveal any new patterns, or the continuation of old patterns, that might concern policy makers, such as the growth of families with children headed by poor women in central cities. Another topic, the fiscal conditions of local and state governments, is important because those conditions affect the capacity of the governments to respond to urban social and economic problems.

The committee proceeded by commissioning the series of papers published in this volume and holding a workshop in July 1986 to discuss them and their implications for research and policy. Although committee members are vitally concerned about such social issues as education, health, and crime and related issues such as housing and transportation, they decided it was important first to document basic economic and demographic trends affecting urban areas and their central cities to establish a baseline from which to identify emerging urban policy issues. Accordingly, the focus of the papers and the workshop was mostly economic. They reviewed and evaluated data in five topic areas: the economic well-being of residents and the statuses of urban economies, finance, governance, and infrastructure.

The committee was primarily interested in comparing central cities and suburbs; metropolitan and nonmetropolitan areas; the older regions of the Northeast and Midwest and the newer regions of the South and West; and minority and white residents. It was particularly concerned about trends affecting central cities in the older regions and their minority populations, compared with their suburbs and with central cities and metropolitan areas in the newer, growing regions.[1]

The committee found that cyclical economic forces, specifically, the 1981–1982 recession, have had surprisingly little effect on urban economies and big-city finances, at least according to available data. Federal aid cuts in social and training and employment programs have also had little direct effect on local government finances because such programs are mostly operated by private nonprofit organizations. The cuts in human capital programs may, however, reduce the ability of cities to upgrade their work forces in the long run.

At the same time the data show that long-term economic and demographic trends affecting urban areas have been continuing and are working to the disadvantage of most central cities, especially in the older regions of the country. Some central cities, blessed with high concentrations of business and government headquarters, producer services, and cultural and higher education institutions, are developing a new economic base as regional and even national "command-and-control" centers. Yet others, in particular those historically dependent on manufacturing, continue to decline.

The committee's main finding, which is detailed in this report, is the growing concentration of poverty in certain areas of central cities, especially cities in the older regions of the country. A comparison of decennial census data on poverty areas of major cities in 1970 and 1980 shows that both the number and the percentage of poor people living in census tracts with high concentrations of poor people (40 percent or more) are increasing. This growing poverty is occurring

---

[1]The report and papers in this volume use demographic and economic data from the Bureau of the Census and the Bureau of Economic Analysis (BEA). The Census Bureau and BEA use different regional classifications of the country. Generally, discussions of individual-level demographic, social, and income characteristics refer to data classified by Census Bureau regions, and the discussions of regional, metropolitan, and local economic changes refer to BEA regions; see Appendix A for a detailed comparison of the Census Bureau and BEA classifications.

even in command-and-control cities with improving economies, like New York and Boston, indicating that economic growth alone is not sufficient to improve the situation. Urban poverty appears to be a major by-product of the changing economic functions of large cities, yet little is known about its fundamental causes and dynamics after many years of research. Urban poverty, always a serious problem, appears to be getting worse, and it is being compounded by long-term changes in the structure of the national economy and in metropolitan and regional demographic patterns.

SUMMARY FINDINGS

Well-Being and Poverty

The committee found that income and earnings are growing at a faster rate in metropolitan than in nonmetropolitan areas, reversing the trend of the 1970s. Residents of large central cities, however, especially in the Northeast and Midwest, are still the poorest in the nation; suburbanites are the richest. Minorities and members of female-headed households are particularly poor, and black female-headed households in central cities are the poorest of all in metropolitan areas. Moreover, more affluent central-city residents— including middle-class minorities—are moving to the suburbs while poorer and less-educated migrants continue to arrive in the central cities. The often-noted reverse migration by middle-class whites into certain neighborhoods of central cities has not been large enough to counter the general out-migration of whites and more affluent minorities or to make much of an impact on the economic fortunes of those central cities. The result, as seen in statistics about the poorest census tracts over time, is increasing concentration of central-city poverty.

The education levels and employment rates of residents of large central cities are also lower, and the unemployment rates higher, than those of the rest of urban area residents, particularly among minorities. Even as some cities are adding jobs, unemployment remains high among the less educated because many of the new jobs require higher skill levels.

These unfavorable statistics about central-city poverty and unemployment exist in the face of generally encouraging urban economic and fiscal trends, which are detailed in this report. These trends are least favorable, however, in the regions in which poverty and unemployment tend to be highest: the Northeast and Midwest. In addition, hard-core poverty and unemployment may be growing in certain cities, like New York, despite overall economic growth in those same cities.

These two dimensions of urban poverty—concentration and isolation—are worrisome, especially where they occur together. They affect the 3.7 million residents of the high-poverty areas of the 100 largest cities, areas in which 40 percent or more of the population is below the poverty line. More than 1.8 million of these residents, 0.8 million of them children, were classified as poor by the 1980 census. Central-city governments pay a disproportionate share of the costs of this poverty, although these costs are caused by fundamental economic and demographic changes affecting entire metropolitan areas. Concentrated poverty calls for higher levels of services and taxes at the same time it reduces a city's physical and human capital. Social ills related to poverty, such as crime, poor health, and homelessness, degrade the quality of personal and community life. Higher taxes and social problems constrain economic growth because they make an affected city a less desirable place to do business. When poverty disproportionately involves particular racial and ethnic groups, it violates civic norms of equality and increases the possibilities of social and political conflict. The isolation of concentrated poverty populations from new job opportunities that are being dispersed throughout metropolitan areas only makes that poverty more difficult to reverse.

Urban Economies

The committee found that manufacturing is continuing to disperse geographically and to decline as a share of the nation's employment and that cities with manufacturing economies, which are prominent in the Mideast and Great Lakes regions, are still losing the most jobs and population overall. Metropolitan areas have regained their lead in population, income, and employment growth nationally, but people and jobs are still being redistributed from the Snowbelt to the Sunbelt.

There is evidence that large cities, especially national and regional centers, are becoming the primary locations for certain kinds of high-status service jobs—especially white-collar producer services in fields such as finance, insurance, law, advertising, and accounting— and these jobs are the basis for transformed but smaller urban economies. This trend began with the loss of manufacturing jobs in New England in the 1950s and 1960s, in the Mideast in the 1960s and 1970s, and more recently in the Great Lakes region. The latter lost nearly a million factory jobs in the early 1980s and has regained very few of them in the ensuing economic recovery. Meanwhile, New England has been transformed into an economy based on services and light manufacturing (for example, computers) and is now enjoying strong economic growth and very low unemployment rates. However, this economic success followed a long period of adjustment and relative population decline, which continues. In Boston, for example, the share of white-collar service jobs increased from 21.7 percent in 1953 to 58 percent in 1983. There are signs of a similar transformation in the Mideast, although there are many smaller cities with industrial economies that are still declining. The Great Lakes region, however, has captured very few of the 8 million new service jobs created nationally since the 1981–1982 recession; the region still had less employment of all kinds in 1984 than in 1979.

Central cities continue to grow more slowly than their suburbs, and central cities in the older regions have experienced large-scale losses of white residents. These losses have been offset in part by in-migration and natural increase of minority residents. As a result, minorities constitute a growing share of central-city populations. Racial differences in the populations of central cities and suburbs are especially sharp in the Northeast and Midwest.

Urban Finance

The committee found that the largest cities generally have been doing well, according to various accounting measures of fiscal health. There are fewer cities exhibiting signs of fiscal problems, such as same-year revenue-expenditure deficiencies for 2 or more consecutive years or deficiencies greater than 5 percent. Nevertheless, some cities still have problems, particularly those in the older declining regions.

Large cities apparently have been following conservative fiscal practices. But many have achieved their current relatively favorable positions by raising taxes and cutting services. There is also some evidence that cities in growing areas, although fiscally solvent, are not expanding their infrastructure and services fast enough to keep up with population growth.

There is no necessary relationship, however, between trends in a city's economy and in its fiscal condition or between a city's fiscal health and its social health. A city with a balanced budget can have a poor educational system, high unemployment rates, increasing poverty rates, and other social ills that might, in the long run, reduce that city's revenue growth and retard its economic development.

The ability of states to provide aid to their local governments depends on state fiscal conditions. Although most states are significantly better off now than immediately after the recessions of the early 1980s, their fiscal condition is not as strong as it was in the 1970s. This is particularly true of the economically depressed farm and energy-producing states. Many states are also constrained by legacies of the tax revolt that limit tax increases and the reserves states may maintain. States are also affected by federal aid cuts.

Urban Governance

The committee found that city officials have coped with recessions and federal aid cuts by raising taxes, diversifying their revenue sources, promoting entrepreneurial economic development, and, in some cases, cutting services and the number of city workers. At the same time, voters have not been unhappy enough with service cuts and tax increases to turn mayors and other local elected officials out of office on a large scale. New groups—minorities and women—continue to be incorporated in local political processes. Yet the longer term effects of conservative budgeting and aggressive economic development efforts—in particular, the effects of such efforts on a city's attempts to maintain and increase its human capital base—are not yet known. Local policy makers are also faced with the consequences of entrenched and apparently growing urban poverty.

Infrastructure

The committee found that the urban infrastructure is not on the verge of collapse, but it is wearing out faster than it is being replaced. Although new government capital investment has declined relative to the gross national product (GNP) and to population growth, expenditures for operations and maintenance have increased rapidly. As a result, overall expenditures for infrastructure have been keeping up with population growth. There is evidence, however, that the capital stock is not being replaced fast enough to prevent deterioration. There is also evidence that the largest cities have not been spending as much of their budgets on capital improvements in the past few years as they did previously. This reduced capital investment may result in part from high interest rates and in part from cuts in federal capital grants. Recent federal tax law changes restricting the issuance of private-purpose bonds will probably reduce capital investment, but this reduction in volume may lower the interest rates cities need to offer to sell their tax-backed general obligation bonds.

SUMMARY CONCLUSIONS

The committee concluded that there is not now a major crisis in the condition of urban economies and urban finance. There are, however, some significant causes for concern, particularly in relation to the existence and consequences of entrenched urban poverty and other social ills, problems that are now concentrated in central cities. In addition, some cities, especially those in the Great Lakes and some in the Mideast regions, have economies that have not responded to the national economic recovery and are facing fiscal problems.

Urban Economies: Long-Term Transformation and Regional Disparities

Contrary to expectations, the economies of metropolitan areas, or even their central cities, generally did not suffer disproportionately from recent recessions, even in the slow-growing older regions. There are exceptions, however, especially among cities with manufacturing economies in the Mideast and Midwest: unemployment in Pittsburgh, for example, was higher in 1984 than in 1980.

Although older urban areas and their central cities are less cyclically sensitive than previously believed, they are still undergoing fundamental long-term economic restructuring. Many central-city and entire metropolitan area economies are in the process of transformation from centers of goods production to centers of information processing and other white-collar service employment. This transformation entails painful demographic adjustments. New England, for example, is now economically healthy, but only after three decades of adjustment during which there was high structural unemployment and slow population growth. Indeed, Boston still faces fiscal problems despite its booming economy.

Metropolitan areas in the Midwest are not responding favorably to economic recovery as they always have in the past. They are continuing to decline, and some of their central cities are facing fiscal problems. The Midwest's manufacturing sector has not rebounded from the 1981–1982 recession as it did from previous recessions, and the region's economy is facing the beginning of a long process of adjustment. That process will be taking place in the face of unprecedented foreign competition.

Urban Finances: Healthier Than in the Recent Past

The finances of large central cities generally emerged from recent recessions and federal aid reductions in a better condition than had been anticipated, indicating that cities have more capacity to adjust their revenues to expenditures than is commonly believed, at least in the short run. Most of the federal aid cuts did not take effect until fiscal 1983, however, and their full impact may not have been felt yet. The impact of the termination of the revenue-sharing program, which will reduce the revenues of most large cities by 2 or 3 percent (and of some cities by more), will not be felt until the late 1980s.

The committee concluded that the maintenance and replacement of the urban infrastructure bear monitoring to ensure that U.S. economic competitiveness is not constrained. Total spending for public works in the United States (construction plus operations and maintenance) grew very slowly during 1972–1984 and fell greatly as a percentage of GNP and total public expenditures. There does not appear to be a shortage of capital, but high interest costs in the late 1970s and early 1980s made cities reluctant to issue long-term debt, which reinforced the decline in capital investment during this period.

Although recent low interest rates have revived the bond market, the recent federal tax changes will probably constrain the tax-exempt bond market. The use of tax-exempt bonds for private activities has been restricted, and, in addition, they have been subjected to stricter volume limitations. State and local governments that wish to continue to issue bonds to finance private activities, such as multifamily housing, convention and sports facilities, or waste disposal and pollution control facilities, will have to issue them as general obligation or taxable bonds. Because general obligation bonds are backed by tax revenues, the risk is borne by taxpayers.

Urban Poverty: Growing More Concentrated

The most troublesome trend identified by the committee is the growing concentration of poor people in central cities. Better educated and more highly skilled residents, including minorities, are moving out of the central cities, leaving behind a concentration of disadvantaged residents isolated in poverty neighborhoods. This group of persistently poor central-city residents, called an "underclass" by some, does not participate in expanding economic opportunities—even in those cities that have successfully made the transition from manufacturing to service-based economies. And the number of such poor people seems to be growing.

Although city economies generally are improving by shifting to a service industry base, the new jobs are being filled by white-collar workers who live—and spend and are taxed—in the suburbs. At the same time, much of the growth in jobs requiring little education is occurring in the suburbs, and central-city residents must incur the expense of commuting if they want those jobs. The committee concluded that this apparent mismatch between the educational requirements of the new information- and service-based urban economies and the educational qualifications of many urban residents needs further study.

Well-Being and Poverty

The economic well-being of an area's residents is usually measured by average family and individual incomes, employment and unemployment rates, and the poverty rate. The poverty rate refers to the percentage of people whose income does not provide an adequate standard of living, as defined by the Office of Management and Budget. The Census Bureau has identified census tracts in large central cities where 20, 30, and 40 percent of the area's residents were below the official poverty line in 1970 and 1980 (Bureau of the Census, 1973, 1985b).

Although income and earnings are growing more quickly in metropolitan than in nonmetropolitan areas in the 1980s (Garnick, in this volume), as they have throughout this century (except in the 1970s), they have not become more evenly distributed within metropolitan areas. The residents of large central cities generally, and especially residents in the Northeast and Midwest, are the poorest in the country; suburban residents are the wealthiest, in comparison with those in central cities, nonmetropolitan areas, or smaller metropolitan areas. Minorities and members of female-headed households in large central cities are even poorer than other central-city residents, and black female-headed households in central cities are the poorest group in metropolitan areas. In addition, unemployment is higher and employment and educational levels lower in large central cities than in the suburbs of the metropolitan areas of older regions, especially among minorities (Berger and Blomquist, in this volume).

Out-migration from the Northeast and Midwest (Census Bureau) regions is continuing but with the South rather than the West showing a net population gain. Since 1970 this out-migration, mostly to the South, of nearly 3 million people, most of them white, has had an impact on the racial and ethnic composition of central cities in the regions they left. In Northeast central cities, for example, the minority population grew from 33 percent to 42.3 percent between 1975 and 1985, in part because of modest increases in the minority population and in part because of the out-migration of whites. In the Midwest, the central-city minority population increased from 28.3 percent to 35.5 percent between 1975 and 1985 (Kasarda, in this volume:Table 5).

In the face of these migration trends, central cities have developed a very high poverty rate: 19 percent in 1985, compared with the national poverty rate of 14 percent (and compared with 15 percent in central cities in 1975). In central-city poverty areas, the poverty rate was 37.5 percent in 1985, up from 34.9 percent in 1975 (Bureau of the Census, 1986b:Table 8; 1984:Table 4). These poverty areas are census tracts in which 20 percent of the population was below the poverty level in the most recent decennial census.

At the same time, unemployment in central cities also has soared, especially among minorities. There is evidence that the new employment structure of the postindustrial city, in which manufacturing and other entry-level and low-skill jobs are disappearing while white-collar service jobs are taking their place as the basis for economic growth, can no longer employ migrants with low education levels, few skills, and little experience (Kasarda, in this volume).

There have been concomitant changes in social conditions and family structure in central-city poverty areas. Rates of crime, drug abuse, teenage pregnancy, female-headed families, and welfare dependency have increased steadily in recent years (Wilson, 1985). In 1984, about 43 of every 1,000 central-city residents were victims of crimes of violence, compared with fewer than 30 in the suburbs and

22 outside metropolitan areas (U.S. Department of Justice, 1986:Table 20). Between 40 and 45 percent of city residents have reported they are afraid to walk alone at night in their own neighborhoods (Garofalo, 1977), and those fears have led people to take a wide variety of protective actions (Lavrakas, 1982). Such changes in the social conditions and family structure of the poor may not cause poverty, but they may prolong or reinforce it or have a major effect on the later life prospects of poor children (McLanahan et al., in this volume).

Some analysts, including an earlier urban policy committee of the National Research Council (1982:Ch. 3), have argued that a permanent urban underclass is developing in central cities that is resistant to change through income maintenance strategies (see also Nathan, 1986; and Wilson, 1985). The committee believes that this issue and its policy implications require careful research and analysis.

ECONOMIC STATUS

Berger and Blomquist (in this volume) analyze 1980 census data on the economic status of residents of large central cities compared with residents of suburbs, small metropolitan areas, and rural areas. They first review traditional measures of economic well-being (e.g., household income, poverty rate, and unemployment and employment rates), although they point out that these measures do not take into account other aspects of well-being including quality-of-life factors such as crime, air quality, and climate. They then present a model to measure the extent to which these quality-of-life factors help explain the wide variations in traditional measures across urban areas. Their results indicate that quality-of-life factors can explain some of the differences in wage rates among residents in different cities. The Berger-Blomquist model also measures the negative effects of living in a central city and of being minority or female, and the positive effects on hourly wages of schooling and employment experience (in this volume:Tables 6 and 7).

Nationally in 1980, average household income was highest in the suburbs of large metropolitan areas (those with at least 1.5 million residents). It was lowest in the central cities of large metropolitan areas, although at the regional level, nonmetropolitan areas of the South and West had the lowest household incomes. Household incomes in the suburbs of large metropolitan areas were 34 percent higher than in their central cities (Berger and Blomquist, in this volume:Table 2). The income differentials between suburbs and central cities were largest in the Northeast (45 percent) and Midwest (47 percent), compared with only 24 percent in the South and 21 percent in the West. The differentials were less in the South and West because central-city incomes were $2,500 to $3,000 higher there than in the Northeast and Midwest.[2]

Nationally, poverty rates were highest in 1980 in the central cities of large metropolitan areas, although in the South and West they were higher in nonmetropolitan areas than in central cities. The national poverty rate was 16.8 percent in central cities, 15.3 percent in nonmetropolitan areas, 12.2 percent in smaller metropolitan areas (those with less than 1.5 million population), and 6.9 percent in suburbs. Central-city poverty rates were highest in the Northeast (19.2 percent) and Midwest (18.3 percent) and lowest in the West (12.7 percent).

There were similar national and regional patterns in unemployment rates. Unemployment rates were highest in large metropolitan area central cities: 7.4 percent nationally, 8.1 percent in the Northeast, and 10 percent in the Midwest. In the West and South, however, unemployment rates were highest in nonmetropolitan areas: 7.3 percent and 6.8 percent, respectively (Berger and Blomquist, in this volume:Table 2).

Berger and Blomquist found a strong correlation between a city's reliance on manufacturing employment and its unemployment rate, a trend that reflects the shift away from goods-producing jobs in central cities. There was little correlation between poverty and unemployment rates in the central cities of large metropolitan areas in 1980. Employment rates were negatively associated with poverty and unemployment rates and positively associated with household income. These associations suggest that because unemployment rates do not count people who have stopped looking for work, they do not adequately measure the relationship between poverty and work (Berger and Blomquist, in this volume:Table 1, part B).[3]

---

[2] These regional income differentials are not adjusted by cost-of-living factors because the comparisons are being made between central cities and suburbs within each region and the other rates of comparative interest—poverty and unemployment—cannot be adjusted regionally.

[3] Both Wilson (1985:153–156) and Kasarda (1985:58) discuss the usefulness of employment-population ratios rather than unemployment rates in gauging minority labor force participation.

Household income is much lower and poverty rates much higher for black and Hispanic households than white households in every location—central cities, suburbs, small metropolitan areas, and non-metropolitan areas. Female-headed households of all races had much higher poverty rates than married couples with or without children, and the rates were even higher among black and Hispanic female-headed households in all locations. The poverty rate among white female-headed families was highest in central cities; among similar black and Hispanic households, it was highest in nonmetropolitan areas (Berger and Blomquist, in this volume:Table 3).

CENTRAL-CITY POVERTY

Central-city residents have developed the highest poverty rate in the country (Wilson and Aponte, 1985:238). In 1975, for example, the poverty rate in central cities was 15 percent (affecting 9.1 million people), compared with a rate of 15.4 percent in nonmetropolitan areas. In 1985, the poverty rate in central cities was 19 percent (14.2 million poor people), compared with 18.3 percent in nonmetropolitan areas (Table 1).

Poverty was concentrated in particular areas of central cities. In 1985, 7.8 million of the 14.2 million central-city poor lived in poverty areas, which are defined by the Census Bureau as census tracts in which 20 percent or more of the residents were below the poverty level in 1979. The poverty rate in these areas averaged 37.5 percent (up from 34.9 percent in 1975).

The poverty rate among central-city blacks was 32.1 percent in 1985, compared with 14.9 percent among whites and 33.6 percent among Hispanics. In central-city poverty areas, 41.2 percent of black residents were poor, compared with 34.2 percent of whites and 44.8 percent of those of Spanish origin (see Table 1; for Spanish-origin data: Bureau of the Census, 1986b:Table 18).

CHANGES IN FAMILY STRUCTURE

In 1983 about 20 percent of white families in central cities were female-headed households; among black families, the corresponding figure was 58 percent. The growth of these figures has been quite dramatic, increasing from 5 percent of white families and 16 percent

TABLE 1 Number (in thousands) and Percentage of Persons Below the Poverty
Level by Type of Area and Race: 1975, 1980, and 1985

Residence	1975		1980		1985	
	Number	Percentage	Number	Percentage	Number	Percentage
All Races						
Central cities	9,090	15.0	10,644	17.2	14,177	19.0
Central-city						
poverty areas	4,446	34.9	4,284	38.1	7,837	37.5
Suburbs	6,259	7.6	7,377	8.2	9,097	8.4
Nonmetropolitan						
areas	10,529	15.4	11,251	15.4	9,789	18.3
Blacks						
Central cities	4,033	29.1	4,831	32.3	5,437	32.1
Central-city						
poverty areas	2,826	39.6	2,843	43.8	4,071	41.2
Suburbs	934	22.5	1,341	24.3	1,481	21.7
Nonmetropolitan						
areas	2,578	42.4	2,406	40.6	2,008	42.6

NOTE: Poverty areas are census tracts in which 20 percent or more of the residents are
below the poverty level. The standard errors for the figures in the table are high:
300,000 to 400,000, or 0.2-0.7 points in the rates.

SOURCE: Data for 1975 and 1980 are from the Bureau of the Census (1984:Table 4); data
for 1985 are also from the Bureau of the Census (1986b:Table 18).

of black families in 1950. Growth was especially fast during the
1970s. As a result, about 64 percent of black female-headed families
in 1983 were located in central cities (McLanahan et al., in this
volume:Figure 1).

Feminization of Poverty

The growth of female-headed households, especially among black
families, has major implications for urban policy design because children in such families are more likely than those from two-parent
families to drop out of school, work in low-status jobs, marry as
teenagers, have children as teenagers, have a premarital birth, and
divorce. According to an analysis of data from the Michigan Panel
Study of Income Dynamics (PSID) by McLanahan (1985), daughters
from female-headed households are more likely themselves to become
female heads of families and to receive welfare than the daughters of

TABLE 2 Characteristics of Female-Headed Central-City Households
(number in thousands), 1983

Family Characteristics	White			Black		
	Total	Below Poverty Line		Total	Below Poverty Line	
		Number	Percentage		Number	Percentage
All persons	5,912	2,096	35.5	6,090	3,601	59.1
Related children under 18 years	2,289	1,228	53.6	2,878	2,017	70.1
Mean family size	2.85	3.25	--	3.50	3.73	--
Mean family income	$16,203	$4,530	--	$10,986	$5,008	--

NOTE: These figures are based on city boundaries as of 1969. The Current
Population Survey (CPS) data from 1985 will be the first based on 1979 boundaries.
Unfortunately, the advance report of the March 1985 CPS does not have data on
female-headed households by place of residence.

SOURCE: Bureau of the Census (1985a:Table 9).

two-parent families. Some of the differences, for example, in educational attainment, can be explained mostly by differences in income,
but low income explains little of the higher likelihood of single parenthood or welfare dependence among daughters from female-headed
households (McLanahan et al., in this volume).

According to the 1983 Current Population Survey, the poverty
rate among individuals in central-city households headed by women
in 1983 was 47.3 percent. Of the 6.1 million black members of female-
headed households in central cities, 3.6 million, or 59.1 percent, were
poor. Among the 5.9 million whites in central-city female-headed
households, 2.1 million, or 35.5 percent, were poor (Table 2).

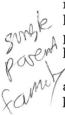

There are at least three reasons for the higher poverty rates
among these households. First, single mothers work less and earn
less. Second, the fathers of these families are not fulfilling their
child-support obligations. If they were, according to one simulation
study, the poverty gap—that is, the difference between the incomes
of poor families headed by women and the poverty level—could be
reduced by at least a quarter. Third, welfare benefits are low and
have declined in real terms in recent years (McLanahan et al., in this
volume).

It does not appear that poverty is caused, at least in the short run, by the growth of female-headed families. Recent research has found that much of the poverty among black female-headed families is not new at the individual level but results from changes in household status: for example, when a young woman with children living with her mother in a poor household moves out to set up her own poor household. In the longer run, however, it is possible that childhood in a poor, inner-city, female-headed household itself perpetuates poverty and related problems among children of female-headed households when they become adults (McLanahan et al., in this volume). Central-city poverty among families headed by never-married women is also probably not caused by lack of marriage by itself. Given the low and declining levels of employment among young black males, it is not clear that marriage to the fathers would have prevented poverty among these families (Bane, 1986).

Growth of Female-Headed Families

McLanahan et al. (in this volume) point out that common sense and economic theory suggest that increases in welfare benefits would increase the number of female-headed families. Recent empirical research indicates the presence of a modest positive relationship. A review of the most careful studies shows that increases in benefits accounted for perhaps one-seventh of the growth in female-headed families in the 1960–1975 period (McLanahan et al., in this volume); the number of female-headed families also grew in the late 1970s when the real growth in welfare benefits was declining. Most of the growth in female-headed families that is related to increases in welfare benefits probably comes from the effect that increased means have on the ability of a young mother and her children to live independently rather than remain in her mother's home.

Research also shows that increases in the labor force participation of women, especially of married women with children, account for part of the growth of female-headed families, but this effect occurs primarily among whites (McLanahan et al., in this volume). As more and more women work, the prevalence of divorce and separation increases, especially among white women. The percentage of wives in the labor force has increased steadily from 20 percent in 1947 to more than 50 percent in 1981. The percentage of wives among full-time, year-round workers increased from 15 percent in 1961 to 26 percent in 1981. Wives only earn 42 percent as much as husbands overall, however, and they earn only 63 percent as much as all full-time, year-round workers (Bianchi and Spain, 1986:200–202).

Some researchers hypothesize a relationship between decreased employment among black men and the growth of female-headed black families. For example, the number of employed black men, aged 20–24, dropped from 59.1 to 48.1 per 100 black women of the same age between 1960 and 1980; the comparable figures among whites were 77.9 and 74.1, respectively (Aponte et al., 1985:Table 4). Research shows that joblessness is clearly related to marital instability, leading some researchers to argue that black joblessness, once considered the prime factor in the dissolution of black family structure (see Clark, 1965; Moynihan, 1965), should supersede the recent interest in the effect of welfare benefits in the study of urban family structure (Wilson and Neckerman, 1986).

The reasons for the decrease in employment among central-city minorities require further study. One reason probably involves the long-term structural changes in central-city economies that are discussed in the next section. These changes have resulted in the massive loss, in central cities, of blue-collar and other jobs requiring little education. Although some of these jobs have been replaced by information-processing jobs (which may or may not be higher paying), they also require substantially higher educational and skill levels (Table 3). At the same time, especially in the Midwest and Northeast, the cities that have lost low-skilled jobs have experienced the greatest increases in the number of minority residents with limited education. Kasarda (in this volume) argues that, as a result, a potential mismatch has developed between the educational qualifications of minority residents in central cities and the educational requirements of a transforming urban economic base. This mismatch might account for the high unemployment rates among central-city blacks, compared with central-city whites, and might help explain why black unemployment rates have not responded to the economic recovery that has occurred in many of these cities.

THE URBAN UNDERCLASS

Recent scholarly work (e.g., Wilson, 1985) has examined whether or not there is an "urban underclass." The term has been defined in various ways, but generally it is considered to cover people who depend on welfare rather than earnings for income, whose dependence on welfare lasts a long time and is passed on to their children, and who

TABLE 3 Central-City Jobs in Industries by Mean Level of Education of Employees, 1970 and 1985

Educational Mean of Industry by City	Number of Jobs (in thousands)		Percentage Change 1970-1985
	1970	1985	
New York			
Less than high school	1,552	1,048	-32.5
More than high school	1,002	1,270	26.7
Philadelphia			
Less than high school	430	243	-43.5
More than high school	205	256	24.9
Baltimore			
Less than high school	207	132	-36.2
More than high school	90	124	37.8
Boston			
Less than high school	189	137	-27.8
More than high school	185	261	41.1
St. Louis			
Less than high school	210	117	-44.3
More than high school	98	97	1.0
Atlanta			
Less than high school	179	182	1.7
More than high school	92	143	55.4
Houston			
Less than high school	348	567	62.9
More than high school	144	368	155.6
Denver			
Less than high school	120	130	8.3
More than high school	72	132	83.3
San Francisco			
Less than high school	155	174	12.3
More than high school	138	218	58.0

SOURCE: Kasarda (in this volume:Table 11).

are concentrated in poverty areas of central cities that are becoming increasingly isolated from mainstream society.

McLanahan et al. (in this volume) have reviewed the research literature on the links between female-headed families and underclass status. Data on the work history of female-headed families are not readily available, but census data show that in 1979, in the 100 largest central cities, 65.1 percent of the poor female-headed families in poverty areas received public assistance income, in comparison with about 26.7 percent of such families nationally. Only 37.6 percent of those female family heads were in the labor force, and just 29.3 percent actually worked during 1979 (Bureau of the Census,

TABLE 4 Central-City Population (in millions) Under 18 Years of Age,
1970 and 1980

	1970[a]		1980[b]	
City Area	Number (in thousands)	Percentage of Area Population	Number (in thousands)	Percentage of Area Population
Poverty areas	3,961	37.5	4,834	31.2
Rest of central city	8,680	29.7	7,690	24.0
Total, central city	12,641	31.7	12,524	26.4

[a]In the 50 largest U.S. cities.
[b]In the 100 largest central cities.

SOURCE: Data for 1970 are from the Bureau of the Census (1973:Table 6);
1980 data are from the Bureau of the Census (1985b:Table 2).

1985b:Tables 4 and 6). The rate of growth in both the numbers and
the average length of time that these central-city families spent on
the welfare rolls are not known because of the lack of longitudinal
data.

To what extent are the children in female-headed families likely
to become part of the underclass? Research shows that children from
female-headed families are more likely to drop out of school, to have
low-status jobs, and to have out-of-wedlock births, but there are no
longitudinal data on the incidence of these factors in central-city
areas, let alone in poor central-city neighborhoods.

As for the social isolation or "ghettoization" of female-headed
families, the picture is complex. The absolute number of both black
and white children living in central-city poverty areas has apparently
declined greatly, but the proportion of poverty-area residents who
are children is still relatively high. In 1980 in the 100 largest central
cities, 31.2 percent of the population of poverty areas were children
under 18 years old, compared with 24 percent in the rest of the central
cities; in 1970 in the 50 largest cities, the corresponding percentages
were 37.5 and 29.7 (Table 4). In central-city poverty areas in 1980, 47
percent of the children were in female-headed families, and 75 percent
of those children were poor (Bureau of the Census, 1985b:Table 1).

As noted earlier, the poverty rates in central-city poverty areas have gone up, as have the concentrations of female-headed families, especially among blacks: in 1980, 37.6 percent of families were headed by women, compared with 29.1 percent in 1970. Among black families, those headed by women increased from 35.4 percent in 1970 to 48.1 percent in 1980 (Bureau of the Census, 1973, 1985b).

Although the overall decline in population in poverty areas leaves smaller absolute numbers of people in those areas, the increased proportion of female-headed families among those left behind and the increase in their poverty rates indicate a serious set of problems that may be getting worse. There may be less crowding, but there are also fewer social institutions and fewer middle-class role models left for children and young people to emulate. Research also reveals the extent of unemployment in central cities among men, especially among minority men, who are usually considered to be another part of the underclass (Wilson, 1985:142). In central cities the proportion of unemployed black youth aged 16–24 increased from 13 percent in 1969 to 29 percent in 1980 and 37.1 percent in 1985; the figures for white central-city male youth were 7.3, 12.1, and 13.5 percent, respectively. Unemployment among black central-city adult men was 3.4 percent in 1969, 10.9 percent in 1980, and 14.6 percent in 1985; for white central-city men, unemployment was 1.6, 5.2, and 6.2 percent, respectively, for those years (Kasarda, in this volume:Table 16).

SUMMARY

Despite recent urban economic growth and the fiscal health of many cities in the United States, the committee believes urban poverty to be a persistent major national problem because it is concentrated, isolated, and entrenched. Over the past two decades the national poverty rate first declined and then increased, moving from 17.3 percent in 1965 (33.2 million) to 11.1 percent in 1973 (23.4 million) and 14.4 percent in 1984 (33.7 million) (Bureau of the Census, 1986a:Table 1). But if transfer payments (public assistance payments, Social Security benefits, food stamps, etc.) are subtracted from income, the underlying poverty rate has stayed remarkably stable: 21.3 percent in 1965, 19 percent in 1973, and 22.9 percent in 1984 (Danziger and Plotnick, 1986:Table 1). In other words, federal income maintenance programs have reduced poverty, but they do not seem to have affected the roots of poverty.

Urban Economic Trends

Urban economies continue to be transformed by long-run structural changes in the postindustrial economy of the nation. These changes, which involve the shift from an economy based on manufacturing to one based on services, and the shift from blue-collar to white-collar jobs (even in the manufacturing sector), result from powerful technological, institutional, and demographic forces and are reinforced by developments in the international economy (Hanson, 1983:Ch. 2; Noyelle and Stanback, 1984; Stanback et al., 1981). These national and international economic changes are influencing the location as well as the nature of economic activities in the United States. They are changing the size and density of urban areas. Suburbanization has led to an overall decentralization of employment and population within metropolitan areas since at least 1920 (Hawley, 1956). More recently, the movement of jobs and population has gone to the exurbs and beyond, within regions and across regions (Long, 1981).

These metropolitan and regional shifts in economic activity and population have affected individual local areas in different ways and at different times, resulting in uneven development and differential growth patterns across regions and areas. With the suburbanization of jobs and people, large central cities have been declining relative to the remainder of their metropolitan areas for decades, except in the West and South where some cities have been able to annex the suburbs as they developed. As a result, older cities in the Northeast and Midwest have relatively static tax bases. They are also left with a larger share of the core poverty areas than newer growing cities in the South and West.

As manufacturing moved out into the exurbs and beyond, metropolitan areas actually grew more slowly than nonmetropolitan areas for a time in the 1970s. Over the long run, there has been a redistribution of employment and population to the West and South and a decline in the older Northeast and Midwest regions. Theoretically, a region or area that loses one source of industrial employment and income may eventually gain another. For example, New England, which was the first area to experience the exodus of manufacturing, has finally achieved a high-technology and service-based economy that is supporting its slowly growing population (New England's population grew only 37 percent between 1940 and 1980, compared

with 71 percent nationally [Bureau of the Census, 1986c:Table 24]).
This process of adjustment may be more complicated for the Midwest
because of increased international economic competition (Garnick,
in this volume).

URBAN GROWTH

The 1960s witnessed metropolitan growth and central-city decline. In the 1970s nonmetropolitan areas grew more quickly than
metropolitan areas, and major regional shifts in population and economic activity accelerated. In the late 1970s and early 1980s media
coverage of the phenomenon of gentrification led some to say that
the old cities were reviving. The most recent data from the U.S.
Department of Commerce's Bureau of Economic Analysis indicate
that metropolitan areas as a whole have reassumed their lead in economic growth in the 1980s, although some central cities, and even
entire metropolitan areas in the Mideast and North Central regions,
continue to lose population and employment (see Garnick, in this
volume).

In the 1960s metropolitan areas grew faster than nonmetropolitan areas nationally (Table 5) in population, total personal income,
and earnings. Nonmetropolitan areas experienced declining farm
employment and large-scale out-migration of population. Manufacturing employment began to grow in nonmetropolitan areas, however, and out-migration slowed in the late 1960s. In metropolitan
areas, central cities, especially in the Mideast region, lost population
in the 1960s, but generally this was more than compensated for by
suburban growth.

In the 1970s the trends were reversed. Nonmetropolitan areas
grew faster than metropolitan areas nationally for a variety of reasons, most of which turned out to be temporary. Manufacturing
enterprises looking for campus-type locations and lower cost settings
than central cities or even metropolitan suburbs were attracted to
nonmetropolitan areas. Other, more temporary factors that favored
nonmetropolitan areas included a slowing of the decline in the agricultural sector, the declining U.S. dollar in international trade in
the 1970s (which favored the kind of labor-intensive manufacturing
activities that were often found in nonmetropolitan areas), the boom
in recreation and retirement areas, and the development of natural
resources and oil during the energy crisis. In the metropolitan areas,

where growth was slower, there was a continued reduction in industrial activity. In particular, the old regions of the North grew more slowly.

In the 1980s the trends that favored nonmetropolitan areas have reversed: farm prices have declined, mining declined, and competition from foreign manufacturers has increased. More recently, oil prices have plummeted. In general, there has been a shift back toward metropolitan growth relative to nonmetropolitan growth. Not all metropolitan areas have recovered, however, especially in the Mideast and Great Lakes regions. Regional shifts from the North, mostly in the Mideast and Great Lakes regions, have continued into the 1980s; metropolitan areas in these regions continue to grow more slowly in population, income, and earnings (Table 6). The main reason for the continued decline of these regions, and of their metropolitan areas in particular, is the continuing loss of jobs in the manufacturing sector.

Growth rates still favored the regions in the West and South over the older regions in the early 1980s. Despite a large decline in oil prices, the annual growth rates in the Southwest and Rocky Mountain regions still exceeded the national average and were half again as large as growth in the Great Lakes region during 1979–1984 (Garnick, in this volume:Table 3).

The economic success story of the 1980s is one of growth in the service sectors, even in the declining regions (Table 7). According

TABLE 5 Average Annual Growth Rates (percentage) of Personal Income, Population, and Earnings, 1959-1984

Time and Area	Average Annual Growth Rate		
	Personal Income	Population	Earnings
1959-1969			
Metropolitan	6.98	1.60	6.83
Nonmetropolitan	6.71	0.35	6.16
1969-1979			
Metropolitan	9.81	1.04	9.21
Nonmetropolitan	10.98	1.29	10.01
1979-1984			
Metropolitan	9.37	1.07	8.26
Nonmetropolitan	8.46	0.84	6.08

SOURCE: Garnick (in this volume:Tables 1, 2, and 3).

TABLE 6 Average Annual Growth Rates (percentages) of Total
Personal Income, Population, and Earnings in Metropolitan
Statistical Areas (MSAs), 1979-1984

Metropolitan Statistical Area, by Region	Average Annual Growth Rate		
	Personal Income	Population	Total Earnings
New England	10.44	0.29	9.90
Mideast	9.20	0.17	8.26
Great Lakes	6.93	-0.05	5.23
Plains	8.73	0.71	7.55
Southeast	10.58	1.70	9.55
Southwest	11.46	2.96	10.70
Rocky Mountains	10.62	2.32	9.67
Far West	9.57	1.86	8.45
Total United States	9.37	1.07	8.26

NOTE: Data are for Bureau of Economic Analysis regions.

SOURCE: Garnick (in this volume:Table 3).

to Garnick (in this volume), the growth in "producer" services in
particular, which tend to concentrate in major metropolitan areas,
has accounted for much of the increase in metropolitan area growth,
relative to nonmetropolitan area growth. Producer services include
the areas of finance, insurance, real estate, and professional and
business services such as accounting, law, advertising, and consulting (Noyelle and Stanback, 1984). For example, the growth of the
producer service sector accounts for the remarkable transformation
of the New England economy in the 1980s, in which the growth in
personal income and earnings exceeds the national averages.[4] Even
in the Great Lakes region, where metropolitan population growth is
negative and growth in personal income is lower than nonmetropolitan income growth, metropolitan area earnings (which are measured
by place of work and not residence) are higher than nonmetropolitan
earnings; they are highest in metropolitan areas with populations of
1 million or more.

---

[4]The average annual growth in personal income in New England between
1979 and 1984 was 10.41 percent, compared with 9.2 percent nationally in the
same period and with 8.82 percent in New England in the 1970s (Garnick, in
this volume:Tables 2 and 3).

TABLE 7 Percentage of Change in Nonagricultural Employment by
Region and Major Industry Groups, 1980-1986

| Region | Change in Employment | | | |
	Production	Trade	Service	Total
Northeast	-8.4	16.5	14.8	8.5
North Central	-12.8	6.2	8.0	1.2
South	-1.0	21.7	18.0	13.3
West	1.2	16.9	15.5	12.4

NOTE: Data are for Census Bureau regions.

SOURCE: Kasarda (in this volume:Table 7).

Despite the revival of some central-city economies in declining
regions through the growth of the white-collar service sector, middle-
class people are not moving back into central-city neighborhoods in
numbers large enough to have much effect. Reverse migration by
middle-class whites has occurred in a few neighborhoods of some
central cities but not on a large enough scale to counter the general
out-migration of whites and more affluent minorities or to make much
of an impact on the economic fortunes of those central cities (Berry,
1985; Frey, 1985; Laska and Spain, 1980).

THE LARGEST CITIES

In the 1960s the populations of the 50 largest metropolitan areas
grew faster than the national average by a wide margin, and personal income and earnings were slightly higher in those areas than
nationally (Table 8). Only the Pittsburgh metropolitan statistical
area (MSA) lost population, and the loss was 0.01 percent (Garnick,
in this volume:Table 4). By contrast, in the 1970s population growth
in the 50 largest metropolitan areas was well below the U.S. average.
In fact, the population declined in 11 of the 50 MSAs; all 11 were
located in the older regions in the Northeast quadrant: New York,
Philadelphia, Detroit, Boston, St. Louis, Pittsburgh, Newark, Cleveland, Bergen-Passaic, Buffalo, and Dayton-Springfield. Employment
growth was also lower than the national average, again due to low
growth in the older regions. Employment growth in the largest MSAs

averaged 1.94 percent a year in the 1970s, compared with 2.16 percent nationally, and was especially slow in the Mideast, Great Lakes, and Plains regions (Garnick, in this volume:Table 5).

In the 1980s the average population growth in the 50 largest metropolitan areas was still slightly less than in the United States as a whole. There were eight declining metropolitan areas, all of them in the older regions of the country: Detroit, Pittsburgh, Newark, Cleveland, Milwaukee, Bergen-Passaic, Buffalo, and Dayton-Springfield. Although four of the areas that had declined in previous decades showed population growth in the early 1980s, it was very slow growth; New York, Philadelphia, Boston, and St. Louis, which lost population in the 1960s and the 1970s, gained 0.2 percent a year or less in the 1980s (Garnick, in this volume:Table 6).

The employment picture has been similar. Average employment in the largest metropolitan areas grew faster than the U.S. average in the early 1980s, but the disparities have been large and employment growth in the older regions has been slow. Employment

TABLE 8 Average Annual Growth Rates (percentage) of Total Personal Income, Population, Earnings, and Employment in the 50 Largest Metropolitan Statistical Areas (MSAs), 1959-1984

| | Average Annual Growth Rate | | | |
Time and Area	Total Personal Income	Popu-lation	Total Earnings	Total Employment
1959-1969				
Nationally	6.93	1.29	6.72	--
50 Largest MSAs	6.97	1.66	6.87	--
1969-1979				
Nationally	10.03	1.10	9.35	2.16
50 Largest MSAs	9.38	0.76	8.86	1.94
1979-1984				
Nationally	9.20	1.01	7.89	1.38
50 Largest MSAs	9.46	1.00	8.61	1.73

NOTE: These data are for primary, not consolidated, MSAs, which may underestimate the extent of economic activity taking place in some large urban areas. In the case of New York, for example, the primary MSA does not include northern New Jersey or Long Island.

SOURCE: Data from Garnick (in this volume:Tables 4, 5, 6, and 7).

grew more slowly than the national average in New York, Philadelphia, St. Louis, Baltimore, Kansas City, Cincinnati, New Orleans, Columbus, Indianapolis, Portland (Oregon), Rochester (New York), and Memphis; employment declined in Chicago, Detroit, Pittsburgh, Cleveland, Milwaukee, Buffalo, Louisville, and Dayton-Springfield (Garnick, in this volume:Table 6). Overall, large metropolitan areas have been doing well in the 1980s as compared to the 1970s, except in the older urban areas.

COMPARISONS AMONG METROPOLITAN COUNTIES

Unfortunately, economic data are collected at the county level rather than for smaller areas. It is therefore difficult to directly compare income, employment, and other economic trends in central cities, suburbs, and nonmetropolitan areas. It is possible, however, to compare "core" MSA counties, which contain the central cities, with contiguous MSA counties, which are suburbs, and so forth.[5] Data on population, income, earnings, and employment by type of county generally show that all types of counties in a growing region tend to grow. But the data also indicate that core counties have been growing slowly overall, even in the 1980s (Garnick, in this volume:Table 9). In terms of population, the MSA core counties grew more slowly than their regions and contiguous suburban counties both nationally and in the New England, Mideast, Great Lakes, Plains, and Rocky Mountain regions. They grew more slowly in income nationally and in the Mideast, Great Lakes, Southwest, and Rocky Mountain regions (but in earnings only in the Mideast and Great Lakes). Employment growth has increased in the core counties, a different pattern from that of the 1970s, for all but the Great Lakes and Plains regions.

The composition of income has also been changing over time. The wage and salary share of personal income nationally has been decreasing, dropping from 66 percent in 1959 and 1969 to 61 percent in 1979 and 54 percent in 1984 (Garnick, in this volume:Tables 10–13). The transfer payment share has been rising, increasing from 7 percent in 1959 to 8.6 percent in 1969, 12.4 percent in 1979, and 13.2 percent in 1984. The share of proprietorships has been declining

---

[5] Garnick (in this volume:Tables 7, 8, and 9) defines eight types of counties and presents data by time period; MSA boundaries are held constant at their 1972 boundaries.

as farms disappear. And the share of income earned from capital—
interest, dividends, rents, and royalties—has been increasing.

In general, a great deal of regional homogeneity has developed
over time in the composition of income, but there remain differences between core counties and suburban counties in the shares
of income from each source. In 1984 income maintenance transfers
(mostly public assistance payments) constituted 1.54 percent of total personal income in MSA core counties and only 0.79 percent
in contiguous counties. Other transfers (primarily unemployment
insurance and Social Security, government, and railroad retirement
benefits) accounted for 9.59 percent of total personal income in MSA
core counties and 11.32 percent in contiguous counties (Garnick, in
this volume:Table 13).

SUMMARY

Long-term regional shifts are continuing. Population and economic activities are still moving out of the declining regions of the
country, although the main source of the out-migration has shifted
from the Mideast in the 1970s to the Great Lakes in the 1980s.[6]
This movement is caused by continuing technological, economic, and
demographic forces that make it more efficient and less costly to do
business in the West and South. Drastically declining oil prices may
affect this trend by depressing growth in energy-producing regions
of the South and West. Thus far in the 1980s, these regions have
grown faster than the national average (although they are growing
more slowly than they did in the 1970s).

The earnings statistics of the Bureau of Economic Analysis suggest that growth in earnings may be occurring more rapidly in the
declining regions than in some of the growing regions. This seemingly
paradoxical situation may arise because of the higher productivity of
the professional services sector developing in some of the older central cities. Nevertheless, the statistics suggest that economic activity
will continue to shift to the South and West.

The urban core areas in the declining regions are not gaining a
proportionate share of recent increases in national prosperity. Even
in New England, central-city fortunes have been aided greatly by
growth in counties adjacent to the core. The slower growth in core

---

[6]See Sternlieb and Hughes (1978) for data on the movement of people and
jobs from the Mideast region in the 1970s.

counties that is indicated by the data may be an understatement of relative well-being. If there are substantial shifts in the demographic composition of the poor in core counties accompanying the slower growth in population, and if there are regional biases to this process, then the relative position of poor areas in the declining regions may be even worse than the data show.

All of these economic trends have long-term implications for the fiscal health of cities. The ability of local and state governments to finance the services they need to deliver—both currently and prospectively—is an issue, given the increased need for fiscal self-sufficiency of those governments in the face of federal aid cutbacks. Although the central cities that are declining will have fewer people to serve, few governments have found a way to reduce expenditures, in part, probably, because the remaining populations have lower incomes and use more government services. These facts have revenue implications as well as expenditure implications, especially for local governments that rely heavily on the property tax. There will be more old people in cities who will probably increase the expenditures of local governments. At the same time the school-age population is declining, although the costs of educating a smaller but poorer population may not decline. State and local governments will have to find a way to adjust to these continuing patterns in the 1980s.

Commuter patterns are continuing to change in the 1980s. More service sector activity, especially in professional or producer services, will continue to increase the tax base of cities. But more and more higher income central-city workers live in the suburbs, and few cities are able to tax commuters. Cities will also find it difficult to tax the health sector, another area experiencing great growth in employment and economic activity.

The shift in the composition of personal income has implications for urban finance. Wage and salary income, which is a more accessible tax base, constituted a smaller share of personal income in core urban counties in 1984, when it was 63 percent, than it did in 1959, when it was 71 percent (Garnick, in this volume:Tables 10 and 13). There has been an increase in nonlabor income in the form of fringe benefits, which are much harder to tax. There has also been a substantial increase in transfer payments and capital income. If capital income comes more from interest income than from dividends and royalties (as it did in the past), the recent federal tax changes that lower marginal tax rates will make it possible for state and local governments to capture a greater share of such income if they choose.

The changing economic structure of central cities thus has a number of fiscal implications, and not all of them are gloomy. There are some opportunities for revenue growth, although state and local governments have not been especially innovative in adjusting their fiscal structure in the past.

Urban Fiscal Conditions

Long-term structural economic and demographic changes continue to transform regional and local economies, but not in the same ways or at the same rates. These changes have differing fiscal and managerial implications for an urban government, depending on its location, the demographic makeup of its population, and the local economic base. Many central cities, except those in the fastest growing areas of the South and West, face the revenue and expenditure consequences of slowly growing or shrinking economic bases and populations. Some older suburbs, and even entire metropolitan areas in the Midwest and Northeast regions, face the same problems. In contrast, some metropolitan areas in the South and West have to adjust to the fiscal and political consequences of fast growth, which calls for expanding services and infrastructure.

Urban areas suffered with the rest of the country through several recessions in the early 1980s. It is common wisdom that older metropolitan areas, and especially their central cities, suffer disproportionately from business recessions, which in turn cause fiscal distress. The same period (the early 1980s) has also witnessed significant reductions in federal aid for cities. Have fiscal conditions in central cities worsened as a result?

RECENT FISCAL TRENDS

A city's fiscal health depends on the balance between the costs of the services it provides and its ability to raise revenues.[7] The ability of a city to raise revenues through taxes and user charges in turn depends on the level of economic activity taking place within

---

[7] The complexities of defining and measuring local government fiscal capacity are discussed in Ladd et al. (1985:Ch. 4) and U.S. Department of the Treasury (1985:Ch. 8).

its boundaries. A city government also relies on state and federal aid for some of its budget.

Older urban areas, especially in older regions, have in the past been affected adversely by recessions. The 1974 fiscal crisis in New York City and subsequent fiscal problems in some other older cities coincided with a recession and seemed to confirm this pattern. Also, metropolitan areas in general, and central cities in older regions in particular, performed relatively poorly during the 1970s (Garnick, in this volume:Tables 2 and 5). As George Peterson (1986) has pointed out, these trends led to attempts to explain why older cities might be more vulnerable to economic cycles. The leading explanation has been that slow-growth or shrinking urban areas, and especially their central cities, have higher proportions of obsolete and worn-out capital facilities and high-cost union labor, which are first to be abandoned when a recession reduces demand. Also, central cities tend to be more closely linked to national rather than to local or regional markets, a factor that could make the cities more sensitive to national business cycles. This analysis has led some researchers to predict that metropolitan areas generally would be more sensitive to recessions than nonmetropolitan areas, that slow-growth or no-growth metropolitan areas would be more vulnerable than fast-growth areas, and that central cities would suffer more than suburbs. Finally, "the cyclical instability of city economies was expected to spill over to city finances, making them especially precarious during recessions" (G. Peterson, 1986:13).

These beliefs in urban fiscal vulnerability were consistent with intergovernmental fiscal policy during the 1960s and 1970s. Local governments became increasingly dependent on aid from the federal and state governments until federal aid peaked in 1978. Between 1960 and 1980, federal aid grew nearly 12.6 percent per year (after adjustment for inflation). The biggest increases (31 percent per year) occurred during 1970–1974, when federal grants to local governments grew from $2.93 billion to $8.64 billion (in 1972 dollars). More than half the increase came from general revenue sharing (U.S. Department of the Treasury, 1985:64, Table III.10). In response to the 1974–1975 recession (the worst since the Depression up to that time) and the belief that urban economies were cyclically unstable, several anticyclical aid programs were adopted; the Antirecession Fiscal Assistance Program, the Local Public Works Program, and the Public Service Employment Program of the Comprehensive Employment and Training Act (CETA) provided more than $13 billion to state and local governments between 1976 and 1978 (U.S. Department of the Treasury, 1985:371–372).

By 1980 intergovernmental aid accounted for 44 percent of local government general revenues, compared with 31 percent in 1960. Within 3 years, however, federal and state aid dropped to 40 percent of local general revenues (U.S. Department of the Treasury, 1985:61–64). The decline in federal aid to localities that began after 1978 accelerated after 1981 as the new administration succeeded in making major cuts in outlays for urban programs. In an examination of nine urban programs, G. Peterson (1986:31) found that 1982 federal outlays were $5.8 billion less (23 percent) than they would have been on the basis of 1980 policies. (Most of the reduction—$3.7 billion—was accounted for by the ending of the CETA Public Service Employment Program.)

The recessions and federal aid cuts led many observers to predict that cities in general, and especially large central cities in the older regions with their declining economies and higher dependence on federal aid, would experience fiscal crises. In fact, cities currently are not only in a fairly favorable economic position (although some central cities and entire metropolitan areas in the Mideast and Great Lakes regions are still declining), but they are in better fiscal condition than at any time during the 1970s, at least as measured by balance-sheet indicators. Of course, these favorable fiscal measures may result from tax increases or service cutbacks or both, which may have adverse economic and political effects, as well as from tax-base growth or more efficient operations.

Measuring the fiscal condition of cities is difficult because cities differ in their scope of services and in their ability to "export" taxes—for example, to make commuters and out-of-area buyers assume part of the tax burden. One approach to measuring the fiscal conditions of cities, a method that does not adjust for differences among localities, is to use national income accounts figures giving the balance between general revenues and expenditures. Analyzing the state-local sector of the national income accounts as a whole, the U.S. Department of the Treasury, for example, recently concluded that "the fiscal outlook for the States and localities is more favorable today than it has been at virtually any other time in recent history" (U.S. Department of the Treasury, 1985:420–421). George Peterson (1986:25–26) found that the annual and quarterly movements of the state-local fiscal surplus have matched the expansions and contractions of the economic cycle since at least 1969, with some interesting exceptions.

In the aftermath of the 1974 recession, the state-local sector posted its largest and longest deficits since World War II, despite the $13 billion in federal countercyclical aid that was made available. In contrast, the deficits resulting from the 1981–1982 recession were smaller than expected and lasted only three quarters, despite cuts in federal aid. Peterson suggests that the prospect of federal aid in the 1974 recession, most of which was not approved until 1976, led states and localities to wait for federal help instead of moving quickly to raise taxes and cut expenditures. In 1981 they did not expect countercyclical aid and anticipated additional federal aid cuts; therefore, they moved quickly to balance their budgets through local actions. The general surplus figure in the national income accounts may indicate the state-local sector's overall financial condition, but it cannot measure the fiscal conditions of individual cities or a group of cities.

Philip Dearborn has been analyzing the financial statements of 30 large cities since 1971 and has assessed their fiscal conditions in a series of reports (Advisory Commission on Intergovernmental Relations, 1973, 1985; Dearborn, 1978, 1979), the latest of which is contained in this volume.[8]

Over the period 1971–1984, the 30 large cities (excluding New York) had current-year general budget revenues that were larger than their current-year expenditures in 9 years of the period; they had revenues that were smaller than expenditures 5 years of the period (Table 9). All but one of the deficiencies took place in years following national recessions (1971, 1975–1976, 1983), indicating a lagged effect on tax revenues (the deficiency took place in the year of the recession in 1980). The current-year surpluses amounted to 1.5 and 1.2 percent of expenditures in 1981 and 1982 and 2.4 percent in 1984, the highest percentage since 1977 (and the highest ever in nominal terms). Although revenue growth (in constant dollars) went down in previous recessions, it actually increased during the 1981–1982 recession (Table 10).

Most of the cities (18 to 20 of the 21 cities Dearborn examined in detail) purposefully budgeted a general fund deficiency in 1982, 1983, and 1984, but actual expenditures were, as usual, below budget. The

---

[8]The 30 cities were the largest U.S. cities in 1970, except for Washington, D.C., Honolulu, and San Jose, which were excluded. Dearborn analyzed only general fund budgets through 1980, but added restricted operating funds and capital improvement funds to the analysis of conditions in 1981–1984.

TABLE 9 Current-Year General Fund Revenues and Current-Year Expenditures in Selected Major Cities, 1971-1984

Year	Number of Cities in Which Expenditures Exceeded Revenues	Excess or Deficiency of Revenues, All Cities[a]	
		Amount (in millions of dollars)	Percentage
1971	16	-23.1	-0.5
1972	12	16.1	0.3
1973	8	175.1	3.5
1974	9	156.1	2.9
1975	16	-28.4	-0.4
1976	13	-154.2	-2.2
1977	6	230.6	3.1
1978	12	73.6	1.0
1979	9	98.8	1.2
1980	19	-188.7	-2.2
1981	10	212.6	1.5
1982	12	168.9	1.2
1983	16	-164.4	-1.3
1984	6	309.9	2.4

NOTE: The selected major cities were the 30 largest cities in 1970 (except Honolulu, the District of Columbia, and San Jose). New York is excluded from this table because its size tends to dominate the totals; other cities are excluded for some years in which information was not available.

[a]Cities did not necessarily have a deficit on their general fund balance sheet because they could use carryover surpluses to make up for the gap between current-year revenues and expenditures.

SOURCE: Dearborn (in this volume:Table 2).

1983 deficiency resulted when actual revenues also fell well below budget estimates in 11, mostly larger cities. Fortunately, there were relatively large surpluses in 1982 ($336 million), which most cities used to help fund their 1983 budgets (Table 11). Although the revenue shortfall in 1983 reduced the accumulated surplus somewhat, to $247 million, most cities budgeted surpluses again in 1984. General fund revenue was greater in 1984 than expected, and the overall surplus was larger at the end of 1984 than in 1982—$364.7 million.

Not all cities, however, were blessed with general fund surpluses. Some cities had end-of-the-year surpluses of greater than 5 percent of their spending budgets; others had trouble balancing their

TABLE 10   Annual Revenue Increases in Selected Major Cities, 1972-1984

Year	Type of Period	Percentage Increase In Annual Revenues (in constant dollars)
1972	Expansion	8.0
1973	Recession	3.6
1974	Recession	-2.7
1975	Expansion	1.3
1976	Expansion	2.2
1977	Expansion	5.0
1978	Expansion	1.1
1979	Expansion	-2.9
1980	Recession	-4.4
1981	Recession	0.0
1982	Recession	0.3
1983	Expansion	1.3
1984	Expansion	3.4

NOTE: The selected major cities were the 30 largest cities in 1970 (except Honolulu, the District of Columbia, and San Jose).

SOURCE: Estimated from Dearborn (in this volume:Figure 2).

TABLE 11   General Fund Unreserved Surpluses in Selected Major Cities: 1982, 1983, and 1984

Year	Surplus (in millions of dollars)	Percentage of Revenues
1982	336.1	1.1
1983	247.1	0.9
1984	364.7	1.2

NOTE: The selected major cities were the 30 largest cities in 1970 (except Honolulu, the District of Columbia, and San Jose). Data for this table include New York and exclude Los Angeles.

SOURCE: Dearborn (in this volume:Table 6).

revenues and expenditures. At the end of 1984, 25 cities accounted for the $365 million in surpluses, and 4 (San Francisco, Atlanta, Minneapolis, and Seattle) had surpluses of more than 10 percent of their previous year's expenditures. Meanwhile, 5 cities had persistent deficits on their general fund balance sheets: Chicago, Detroit, Cleveland, Boston, and Buffalo. Chicago necessarily has a deficit because, under state law, it collects property taxes the year after expenditures are incurred; Cleveland and Buffalo had deficits of less than 1 percent; only Boston's (6 percent) and Detroit's (3.1 percent) deficits were worrisome (Dearborn, in this volume:Table 7).

Dearborn also reviewed the financial condition of the same 30 cities for 1981–1984 using information on all governmental operating and capital funds and not just the general fund as in his previous reports.[9] He found that aggregate operating revenues were larger than expenditures in all 4 years, although the difference was very small in 1983 when the general funds showed deficiencies. Liquidity, the ratio of cash or cash equivalents on hand to total operating fund expenditures, was about 35 percent from 1981 to 1983 and increased to 47 percent in 1984. The liquidity of only one city was less than 15 percent in 1984, compared with six cities in 1982.

One analyst (G. Peterson, 1986) has suggested that one reason federal aid cuts in 1982 and 1983 did not have a greater impact on city finances was because federally assisted programs were segregated from general fund budgets (G. Peterson, 1986:31–32):

> Since the termination of Carter's antirecession federal aid, federal categorical assistance in most cities has not been used to support basic services like police or fire protection, sanitation, financial management, or even schools to a great extent. Federal grants typically were handled through separate funds and were used to finance auxiliary activities whose spending could be adjusted upward or downward to reflect federal assistance levels. By 1981, for example, almost all cities had moved their Public Service Employment workers out of general government services, in anticipation that federal funding for the program would be terminated at some point.

When federal aid was reduced or eliminated, the cuts were passed through to specific programs, most of which city officials considered

---

[9] Operating funds include general, debt service, and special-revenue funds. Special-revenue funds contain proceeds of specific revenue sources that are legally restricted to expenditure on specified purposes. Capital-improvement funds use receipts from bond sales and federal grants. Enterprise funds for local utilities, airports, and the like are not included in the analysis because such activities are supposed to be self-supporting.

low priority, according to a survey done for the Urban Institute (G. Peterson, 1986:31–33). Meanwhile, Congress prevented high-priority federal programs such as wastewater treatment, general revenue sharing, and mass transit from receiving major cuts. States, however, increased local aid. For example, many states acted to restore at least some of the federal funding cuts in most of the block grants created in 1981 (G. Peterson et al., 1986:13–15). State aid to local governments increased from $82.8 billion in 1980 to $99.5 billion in 1983, a 20 percent increase; but state aid as a percentage of local revenues decreased from 35 percent in 1980 and 1981 to 34 percent in 1982 and 33 percent in 1983 (U.S. Department of the Treasury, 1985:Tables V.13 and V.14). Yet municipalities receive only 16 percent of state aid to local governments. Most such aid goes to school districts (52 percent); the rest goes to counties, townships, special districts, and other recipients (Gold, in this volume:Table 9).

Federal aid cuts apparently did not require general budget adjustments, except in a few cities.[10] Moreover, in the cities examined by Dearborn, special-revenue funds, for which intergovernmental aid is usually received, did not shrink in the early 1980s. In fact, special-revenue funds as a percentage of total operating revenues were slightly higher in 1984 than in 1981 (27.1 percent compared with 26.4 percent). The elimination of general revenue sharing (GRS), however, may show more of an effect. The 30 large cities (excluding Los Angeles because of a lack of data) received $730 million in GRS in 1984, which amounted to 2.2 percent of their overall operating revenues. (The percentage of GRS received by individual cities ranged from 1.2 percent in Buffalo to 5 percent in New Orleans.) Most of the cities include some GRS in their financing of current operations and will have to adjust for its loss. For example, the cities' surpluses of nearly $365 million at the end of 1984 represented only half of the $730 million in GRS aid that year. But some cities had less of a surplus than others. Unless cities without enough surplus funds had cut services, 15 cities instead of 5 would have had general fund balance sheet deficits in 1984 without GRS. Dearborn estimates that, with the loss of GRS, most cities will have to make a 2 percent or 3 percent adjustment in revenues or expenditures or both, which will

---

[10]Detroit, for example, still had more than 1,800 public service employment workers in general city positions when CETA was terminated in 1981. This figure constitutes more than 10 percent of that city's workers (G. Peterson, 1986:32).

cause problems for those cities already experiencing fiscal problems (Dearborn, in this volume:274–276).

Finally, whereas the 30 cities as a group have had their ups and downs, reflecting fluctuations in the business cycle, at least until the 1981–1982 recession, some cities have had consistently good fiscal conditions during 1971–1984. Others have had problems for most of the period. The cities that have consistently enjoyed good fiscal conditions are San Francisco, Minneapolis, Indianapolis, Jacksonville, Milwaukee, Atlanta, and San Diego (and probably Los Angeles, although its financial reports cannot be analyzed well enough to find out). Cities that had problems for extended periods were New York, Chicago, Philadelphia, Detroit, Boston, Cleveland, St. Louis, and Buffalo. Over time, however, it appears that fewer cities have shown indicators of fiscal problems, such as expenditures greater than revenues for 2 or more consecutive years, accumulated deficits, and low liquidity (see, e.g., Advisory Commission on Intergovernmental Relations, 1985). Only Detroit and Boston had major deficits in 1984.

SUMMARY

City finances survived recent recessions and federal aid cuts remarkably well for reasons that are not entirely understood. They now have relatively large general fund surpluses to cushion future revenue shortfalls. But there are individual exceptions to this rosy picture in the Midwest and Northeast.

One likely factor has been the resilience of urban economies during recent recessions. Another has been the cities' ability to pass program cuts directly on to recipients without affecting their budget balances. George Peterson (1986) reviews the evidence on both these factors for the recessions of the 1970s and discusses possible reasons. New theories and more research are needed to understand this unexpected situation in which urban economies appear to be mildly countercyclical in recessions.

It is important to note that the fiscal situations of most older central cities in the Northeast and Midwest may not have been greatly affected by recent recessions, but their underlying economies continue to decline in response to long-term trends, as discussed in the previous section of this report. It is also important to realize that good fiscal conditions do not necessarily mean that a city's social conditions are healthy. In fact, a balanced budget may result from cutbacks in social programs and human capital investments in education and training programs that are important to a city's long-term economic growth.

Trends in Urban Governance

Kirlin and Marshall (in this volume:362–363) observe that cities, in the face of federal cutbacks, have turned to a new entrepreneurial politics of growth and development that has supplanted the politics of social service delivery that predominated in the 1960s and 1970s:

> The national government is focusing its resources more tightly upon direct service delivery and income redistribution, while cities are expanding beyond traditional delivery of municipal services to a wide range of entrepreneurial activities designed to stimulate economic activities, to create jobs, and to generate revenues, much of which are used to support the traditional service delivery.

Other urban scholars (Judd and Ready, 1986:210, 215–215) have also noted this trend:

> Over time, the municipal development agenda has been transformed. Economic development strategies have become much more elaborate and complex. Growth cities as well as cities in decline have turned to the national market and scrambled to make themselves attractive to footloose private firms. All cities are engaged in aggressive campaigns to secure their share of national economic growth. Well before the 1980 election, cities were actively trying to gain more control over their own economic destinies. They have been pushed further in this direction by the policies of the Reagan administration.
>   The federal mandate is clear: cities must make themselves more attractive to private firms and must provide fertile ground for local entrepreneurship. To accomplish these objectives, HUD suggests that localities form public-private partnerships. . . . Nearly all cities have created public-private partnerships to promote economic growth. Some 15,000 local nonprofit and quasi-public organizations currently administer much of the economic development activity that is occurring.

Usually there is general consensus on the desirability of economic development projects that will create jobs and increase tax revenues, especially in large cities. Disagreements can arise, however, over whether or not a particular project is beneficial, over the distribution of benefits, and also over the location, size, and environmental effects of a project (P. Peterson, 1981:Ch.7; Stone and Sanders, 1987).

Public opinion polls indicate that black urban residents desire a higher level of social welfare spending and government services than do whites. Black municipal leaders emphasize issues of housing inequality, health care, employment and poverty, and education. Greater proportions of the budgets in cities with black mayors and council members are devoted to health, education, and housing than are devoted to these purposes in cities with white elected officials (Karnig and Welch, and Welch and Combs, cited in Judd and Ready, 1986:211–212). By 1985 there were nearly 3,000 black municipal officials, nearly double the number of officials in 1975; most are in the South. There are 17 black mayors in cities with populations of over 100,000. Chicago, Detroit, Los Angeles, and Philadelphia have black mayors, and Denver and San Antonio have Hispanic mayors. Yet minority success in city politics relies on electoral organizing and coalition formation, even in predominantly black cities (Browning et al., 1984). Black and Hispanic officials have worked to gain the support of business interests in Los Angeles, Atlanta, Detroit, Philadelphia, Denver, and Miami, even though sometimes they have been criticized by minority groups (Browning and Marshall, 1986).

It is difficult to document the extent of local entrepreneurial activities because fiscal data are not always included in the statistical data series that are available. Kirlin and Marshall (in this volume) point to some indirect and impressionistic evidence. They show, for example, that localities are relying relatively more on user charges and utility revenues and less on taxes and intergovernmental grants than previously (Kirlin and Marshall, in this volume:Table 4). They note that the major associations representing cities and their managers have been busy sponsoring programs, workshops, and publications concerning entrepreneurship. There are also a number of case studies of local public entrepreneurship. Judd and Ready (1986) describe "the new politics of economic development" in Denver, Chicago, and St. Paul. Sonenshein (1986) looks at public–private development coalitions fostered by the mayor of Los Angeles. Frieden and Sagalyn (1984) found that public–private endeavors were more successful in completing downtown shopping centers than old style grants-oriented redevelopment efforts.

The governance of cities evidently has not been seriously threatened by recent changes in their external environment. Mayors' offices and those of other elected officials have not become notably more precarious because voters have been blaming them for cuts in city services and other social services. Cities have responded to reductions in federal aid and earlier restraints from state fiscal limit initiatives by diversifying their revenue sources and aggressively promoting economic development projects. At the same time, they have continued to incorporate new groups into local politics.

Although these moves toward greater self-sufficiency by local governments are positive, some potential problems remain. Some older city services, such as primary and secondary education, are vitally linked to a city's capacity for economic growth. Fear of crime is still a major factor in locational decisions of new businesses. These older problems are not necessarily going to be solved by successful economic development. In fact, high crime rates, a poorly educated work force, and other social problems may inhibit economic development. In addition, the bargaining between public officials and the private sector that is required in public–private ventures creates more opportunities for corruption.

Not all cities are equally endowed with entrepreneurial opportunities. Long-term structural economic shifts work to the advantage of cities in the South and West over those in the Midwest and Northeast, regardless of entrepreneurial strategies or efforts. At the same time, there is little evidence that the efforts of cities to attract development projects have any real effect in the locational decisions of firms. And even if they did, the result of such efforts may be just to deny jobs to other places rather than to create new ones (see the discussions in Judd and Ready, 1986:216–218; and Leonard, 1986:Ch. 5).

Finally, local economic growth does not necessarily reduce poverty. Most economic development projects that are encouraged by city officials are aimed at increasing downtown business activities. These activities tend to involve white-collar service and information-processing jobs and not entry-level jobs for low-skilled poor residents of central cities.

Urban Infrastructure

Public infrastructure has been suffering for many years from problems of deterioration, technological obsolescence, and insufficient capacity to serve future growth, although the nature and extent of these problems vary widely among types of infrastructure and across states and localities (Congressional Budget Office, 1983; G. Peterson et al., 1984). Only a few years ago a series of studies documented declining public investment in infrastructure; those studies, together with some highly publicized infrastructure failures—such as the collapsed Mianus River Bridge on the Connecticut Turnpike that killed three motorists, and the broken water main in New York's garment district that interrupted power to businesses there for a week—created the impression that there is an infrastructure "crisis" of enormous proportions. Estimates of the costs of bringing the nation's infrastructure up to date have ranged as high as $3 trillion. The 1982 national urban policy report, also noting the downward trend in real state and local infrastructure spending, expressed concern about "signs of erosion in the condition and performance of the urban capital plant . . . especially in the oldest urban areas" (U.S. Department of Housing and Urban Development, 1982:3–11).

The sense of crisis, however, disappeared as it became obvious that the nation's infrastructure was not in a state of imminent collapse—although it is deteriorating. The 1984 national urban policy report reviewed recent studies that indicated that the infrastructure problem was manageable (U.S. Department of Housing and Urban Development, 1984:68–69). These studies included a survey of mayors and city managers by the National League of Cities and United States Conference of Mayors (1983) and a report of the Advisory Commission on Intergovernmental Relations (1984).

Concern about the condition of public infrastructure has continued among affected groups, and in 1984 Congress established the National Council on Public Works Improvement to study the problem. The council is issuing a series of three reports by 1988 on the state of the nation's infrastructure; the first report has already been published (National Council on Public Works Improvement, 1986). The Public Sector Advisory Council for Financing Public Infrastructure also has been set up by private sector groups to report to the Senate Finance Committee.

Urban infrastructure is important for economic development, and it is not being replaced at a fast enough rate to prevent its continued deterioration. Mudge and Rubin (in this volume:308) point out that infrastructure projects are not ends in themselves:

> Rather, their importance to the economy and to society as a whole derives from the services they offer: the opportunity to improve productivity or reduce costs. Although most easily thought of in a physical form—a bridge, a wastewater treatment plant, a subway train—the real output of infrastructure is service: the movement of people and goods; the provision of adequate clean water.

Infrastructure projects also promote additional economic development through a multiplier effect.

If infrastructure is not adequate—because it is deteriorated, obsolete, or too small—it imposes costs on users, and it may ultimately constrain the economic development of the locality, the region, or even the nation. Although there is agreement that infrastructure is a critical factor in economic development, the relationship is complex, and empirical studies have had mixed findings (McGuire, 1986). New construction, which is needed in fast-growing areas, may be too small, too distant, or lacking altogether and thus hurt the competitiveness of the area. Existing capital stock, especially in older areas, may become obsolete and reduce economic activity. Maintenance of existing capital stock may be inadequate or deferred in times of fiscal stress—practices that increase lifetime costs, impose costs on private users, and even threaten safety (Advisory Commission on Intergovernmental Relations, 1984:8–9).

The committee considered several aspects of the urban infrastructure issue, which are detailed in the sections that follow. It did not examine other important local infrastructure questions, such as the possible overcapitalization of projects induced by federal subsidies, creating higher than necessary operating costs for localities; the cost-effectiveness of some types of projects (such as rail transit) that are federally financed; or the effects of infrastructure policies on urban growth patterns.

NATIONAL EXPENDITURE TRENDS

Although federal, state, and local capital outlays nearly quadrupled from 1960 to 1984 to $40 billion a year (in 1984 dollars), this investment was actually a decline when measured on a per capita basis or as a fraction of GNP (Mudge and Rubin, in this volume:Figures 1 and 2). Capital spending declined from 2.3 percent of GNP in 1960 to 1.1 percent in 1984. Capital investment on a per capita basis peaked in 1967 at $260 (in 1984 dollars) and declined to $160 in 1982 before rising slowly to $170 in 1984.

The picture looks very different when spending for infrastructure maintenance and operations is added to capital investment. Maintenance and operations spending has increased steadily from $800 million in 1960 to $55 billion in 1984 (in 1984 dollars), surpassing capital spending after 1977 (Apogee Research, 1986). In fact, operating outlays have outgrown population growth and remained fairly steady as a percentage of GNP at about 1.4 percent. Infrastructure operations are relatively labor intensive, and public sector wages have historically increased faster than the consumer price index. Total infrastructure spending—capital and operating—has been about $400 per capita (in 1984 dollars) since the mid-1960s (Mudge and Rubin, in this volume:Figures 1 and 2).

While overall infrastructure expenditures were rising steadily, the composition of the projects involved has changed dramatically over time, primarily due to demographic trends and federal priorities (Mudge and Rubin, in this volume:Table 3). In the 1960s highway spending was predominant, accounting for 60 percent of all spending. In the 1970s highway spending began to fall and wastewater treatment and water supply projects began to increase. By 1980 the interstate highway system was 97 percent complete, and highway spending had dropped to 45 percent of all spending; spending on wastewater treatment and water supply continued to grow, and mass transit spending doubled. The three programs accounted for 41 percent of all government infrastructure spending.

An analysis by the Advisory Commission on Intergovernmental Relations (1984:Table 1) of the growth rates of state and local capital outlays (including federal aid but not maintenance and operations) shows that new investment in school buildings was highest in the early 1950s; highway spending also grew quickly in the 1950s and continued in the 1960s. Although spending for these functions fell greatly after 1970, spending for conservation and development projects and water supply expanded rapidly in the early 1960s and again in the late 1970s. Sewer investment expanded in the early 1970s in response to federal clean water mandates and federal grants for wastewater treatment.

The federal and state contributions to infrastructure spending have been about $22 billion per year since 1960 (in 1984 dollars). It is the increase in local spending, from about $25 billion in 1960 to $48 billion in 1984, that has been responsible for overall growth (Apogee Research, 1986). Federal spending on public works increased from 27 percent of the total in 1970 to 32 percent in 1980 but then declined to 27 percent again in 1984. State spending fell from 32 percent of total public infrastructure spending in 1970 to 24 percent in 1980 and 23 percent in 1984, reflecting large cutbacks in highway spending. Local spending increased from 41 percent of the total in 1970 to 44 percent in 1980 and 50 percent in 1984 (Mudge and Rubin, in this volume:Table 4).

The 30 large cities studied by Dearborn (in this volume) were not spending as much on capital improvements in 1984 as in previous years. Capital expenditures as a percentage of total operating expenditures fell from 11.6 percent in 1981 to 7.6 percent in 1984. This decline probably resulted from cuts in federal capital grants (state capital grants were steady during this period) and reductions in bond sales as a result of high interest rates. Capital-fund revenues, which consist mostly of federal and state capital grants, fell from 7.6 percent of operating revenues in 1981 to 3.9 percent in 1984. Debt service costs as a percentage of operating expenditures went from 7.8 percent in 1981 to 8.8 percent in 1984 (Dearborn, in this volume).

INFRASTRUCTURE CONDITION

There is evidence that many infrastructure facilities are aging and have reached or surpassed the end of their design life. Some are deteriorating for lack of maintenance (Congressional Budget Office, 1983:6–8, 21–22, 39, 55–56; see also Advisory Commission on Intergovernmental Relations, 1984:12–15). In a 1980 Urban Institute study of 62 cities, 32 of which were large (populations of more than 250,000), G. Peterson et al. (1984:3) summarized their findings as follows:

1. Federal condition ratings for urban roads and highways over the 1970s have a declining trend . . . few cities replaced or resurfaced their street networks at a sufficient rate to avoid deterioration.
2. . . . federal condition ratings show two divergent patterns: (a) a concentration of structurally deficient bridges in the Northeast and North Central regions and in fiscally stressed, large, and declining cities and (b) a concentration of functionally obsolescent bridges in the South and North Central regions and in growing cities.
3. . . . a downward trend in the number of miles traveled by vehicles between breakdowns, despite the fact that on average bus fleets are younger because of the replacement of older vehicles.
4. Overall measures of condition for water and sewer systems have not been developed, but specific indicators of condition and maintenance practices suggest that the cities most vulnerable to problems are doing the least to correct them.

The Urban Institute data revealed some regional patterns (G. Peterson et al., 1984:3). For example:

Cities in the Northeast have higher rates of unaccounted-for water, have a greater number of deficient bridges, and appear to have deferred the largest amount of street maintenance. Cities in the South and West have capital needs more associated with growth, such as narrow bridges and roads that are inadequate to meet increased traffic levels and water and sewer systems that need expansion.

Certain kinds of infrastructure problems, such as water and sewer system breaks, were more prevalent in younger, growing cities in the South and West. In fact, Peterson and colleagues found that city or system age was not a good indicator of system condition, especially of transit systems and water and sewer pipelines. Other factors, including local maintenance practices, were more important.

By the 1970s the major postwar investment for an expanding population—schools, streets, water and sewer services, and the interstate highway system—was nearly complete except in fast-growing areas of the South and West. Wastewater treatment facilities and mass transit systems were largely completed in the 1970s. These projects have a long life, which helps to explain the trends in financing toward declining capital investment and increased spending on operations and maintenance. Also in keeping with the maturation of the public infrastructure system, the overall depreciated value of public infrastructure, which increased steadily in the 1950s and 1960s, has remained stable since the late 1970s. In fact, it has declined slightly since its peak in 1979 (by 0.8 percent for 1979–1982), consistent with a situation in which depreciation is outpacing investment (Advisory Commission on Intergovernmental Relations, 1984:Graph 3).

Data on the average age of state and local capital stock also indicate that new construction is not offsetting the aging of existing facilities. The average age of capital stock, which dropped from more than 21 years to under 19 years during 1950–1970, has increased steadily since 1970 to nearly 22 years in 1985 (Mudge and Rubin, in this volume:Figure 10).

TAX-EXEMPT BOND MARKETS

Trends in the bond market have affected infrastructure financing (Advisory Commission on Intergovernmental Relations, 1984:6–7; Petersen and Hough, 1983:13–17; Government Finance Research Center, 1983:Ch. 3). Traditionally, state and local governments have financed more than half of their capital investments by issuing long-term bonds (which mature in 20 or 30 years). Tax-exempt interest rates have been cyclical, with high points occurring in 1974–1975 and 1980–1982; in 1970 they averaged 6.2 percent, and in January

1982 they reached more than 13 percent. As a result, long-term borrowing by state and local governments almost dried up in 1980 and 1981 when long-term borrowing accounted only for 18 percent and 24 percent, respectively, of total capital investment (G. Peterson, 1984:Table 3-3). More recently, long-term debt has accounted for about 40 percent of total state and local public works expenditures (National Council on Public Works Improvement, 1986:65).

This reduced reliance of state and local governments on long-term bonds was reinforced by several other trends. The difference between taxable and tax-exempt rates has narrowed, making it less advantageous and more costly for state and local governments to use tax-exempt bonds. The increase in interest rates on tax-exempt bonds from 6 percent to 13 percent between 1978 and 1982 was an increase from 66 percent to 81 percent of the rates for taxable bonds. Although the increase in tax-exempt rates allows lower-income taxpayers to take advantage of tax-exempt bonds, the wastefulness of the federal tax subsidy has increased accordingly (Leonard, 1986:159). There has also been increased competition in the municipal bond market from nontraditional borrowers; by 1981 between 25 and 50 percent (depending on the definition used) of all long-term bonds were for private purposes—for example, industrial and commercial development, hospitals, housing mortgages, and student loans (Petersen and Hough, 1983:17). The situation has also led to the use of a wide variety of so-called "creative financing" techniques that may or may not be sound practices.

It is too early to determine the effects of recent tax law changes that tighten requirements for private-use tax-exempt bonds and lower tax rates. It will probably be harder to finance private-purpose projects, but some of them may be financed by general obligation bonds. If this happens, such projects may be cheaper initially, but the increased demand for financing may push interest rates up in the longer run. Also, because general obligation bonds are backed by state or local tax revenues, taxpayers will be assuming greater risks.

SUMMARY

Contrary to fears at the beginning of the decade, the urban infrastructure is not collapsing, but it is wearing out. The problems vary by system and by region and locality. They are particularly severe in older, fiscally stressed cities in the Northeast and Midwest regions and in some fast-growing cities in the South and West. Infrastructure condition is also affected by local maintenance practices and other factors.

Overall, rates of new capital investment have been declining, but this was to be expected given the completion of most of the nation's capital stock by 1980. Spending for operations and maintenance has increased steadily, and total expenditures—capital plus operations and maintenance—have stayed at about $400 per capita (in 1984 dollars) since the 1960s.

The withdrawal of federal capital aid does not necessarily cause local capital expenditures to drop. The latter already were declining through the late 1970s, a time when federal aid was rapidly increasing. The declines in state and local expenditures in the early 1980s probably came as much from soaring interest costs and lower state expenditures (resulting from the recession) as they did from changes in federal policy. In other words, lower levels of long-term borrowing were probably a cyclical response rather than a long-term trend. State and local borrowing has recovered, and it has reached new heights since 1982. The biggest constraint on state and local borrowing is cost; the interest rates that local government bond issuers have to pay have remained somewhat high by historical standards. These high rates affect fiscally constrained cities the most and would help explain the apparent decline in capital expenditures observed by Dearborn (in this volume) in the largest cities.

Problems remain in the tax-exempt bond market. The new tax law will probably keep the difference between tax-exempt and taxable bond interest rates small, although new restrictions on nontraditional borrowing for private purposes may ease the demand for tax-exempt bond issues and thus lower interest rates.

Policy Implications

After a careful review of recent data on demographic, economic, and governmental conditions and trends in urban areas, the committee identified three sets of issues with major policy implications.

URBAN POVERTY

The evidence that poverty is increasing in central cities in the midst of economic recovery raises the issue that is most troubling in the committee's view. The economic restructuring of American cities is creating a service economy in many urban centers that requires high levels of education and skills. This restructuring is occurring at the same time better-educated residents—whites and minorities—are leaving central cities for the suburbs and beyond, and new immigrants, mostly minorities, are still moving into central cities looking for economic opportunity. Unemployment rates are very high among central-city residents and especially among minority residents who tend to have less education and work experience. This bifurcation of jobs and residents, if it is confirmed by further research, would have major implications for public policy because cities would not be able to carry out one of their traditional functions, that of assimilating poor immigrants into the economy.

One policy approach to the problem of increasing urban poverty would be to encourage, or at least not discourage, the migration of unemployed individuals to areas with job opportunities, although the history of past attempts to relocate workers indicates that this may not be promising. The eligibility requirements and benefit levels in public assistance programs could be made more uniform, for example, so that differences in welfare generosity do not affect migration decisions. This macro-level approach, however, will not help those who do not have the education and skills for the available jobs. Another policy approach would be to improve human capital investment programs, such as early childhood, elementary, and secondary education and job training and retraining programs. These micro-level programs, which aim to intervene in the lives of individuals, are also very difficult to implement, and knowledge about how to improve them is limited.

There is a need for further research on changing urban labor markets and on the causes of urban unemployment and poverty to help policy makers design effective programs. Such research also depends on the amount and quality of local area economic statistics. These statistics should be better designed to compare economic trends and conditions in central cities and their suburbs.

Policy makers and researchers should examine approaches to reducing urban poverty that have worked in different places and with different types of poverty. Such approaches should include federal and state experiments and demonstrations, such as workfare, as well as self-help and neighborhood-level development efforts. Finally, government antipoverty policies should be concerned with the performance of the institutions constituting a central city's social infrastructure, especially the schools.

REGIONAL DECLINE

The second major set of issues with policy implications that troubles the committee concerns the effects of population and economic decline in the Great Lakes and Mideast regions. These areas are not rebounding in response to national economic recovery, and long-term trends affecting them point to continuing decline. Although metropolitan areas and many major cities are doing better overall, there are individual exceptions. The central cities with fiscal problems also tend to be in declining metropolitan areas in the older regions. There may be long-run equilibrating forces that will improve the situation in the Mideast and Great Lakes regions, as they have in New England. Unfortunately, the adjustment process may be complicated by changes in the international economy that are making it more difficult for American industry to compete.

The committee does not think it possible to reverse this fundamental economic restructuring, but public policies could ease the transformation. Although urban economic transformation may be beneficial for national efficiency and competitiveness over the long run, there are short-term costs that include high rates of structural unemployment and poverty among people not equipped to participate in the new urban economy. The decline in the tax base, even if temporary, may also worsen the fiscal position of affected localities. They may not in all cases be able to reduce expenditures as quickly as revenues, especially if the needed decline in population is slow in coming or the remaining population includes more poor, or both, which is usually the case. In addition, worsened fiscal conditions may mean that local jurisdictions will provide less than optimal levels of such public goods as local human capital investment in education and training.

Although much has been done already, more research is necessary to understand the nature and processes of economic transformations in American cities and how such transformations are operating in specific cities. This research should not be limited to the nation's older regions; it should also encompass developments in fast-growing metropolitan areas in the South and West, especially to try to understand how urban areas in the South were able to overcome the disadvantages of a relatively less-educated work force.

URBAN CAPITAL INVESTMENT

The third area of concern to the committee is urban capital investment. The urban infrastructure is not now in critical condition, but much of the stock is old and deteriorating. Replacement programs may not be keeping up with long-term needs. Growing areas also have infrastructure problems. They may not be able to build it as quickly as needed to sustain the level of economic growth that would otherwise be possible. The main barrier appears to be the high and fluctuating cost of capital, compared with historically low interest rate levels. As with human capital investment, there is more than a local interest in achieving optimal levels of local infrastructure. Policy makers should be concerned that the nation's infrastructure, including urban infrastructure, is adequate to sustain national economic growth.

Local physical infrastructure vital to human capital development is especially important, yet the data on school and other local public facilities are very poor compared with those on so-called national infrastructure systems, such as streets and mass transit. More research is needed regarding the adequacy of local capital facilities. Research is also needed on the factors affecting the cost of capital financing, such as the criteria used in decision-making by financial institutions involved in the bond market.

The impact of federal infrastructure investment policies on patterns of urban growth, including economic development, labor markets, and land use, should also be studied. The extent of the geographical mismatch between the central-city poor and unemployed and the growing number of entry-level jobs in the suburbs, and the possible ways to remedy this situation, are one set of important research topics. Another set concerns growing traffic congestion in the suburbs, where most journeys to work now begin and end. To what extent do or should federal policies ease or contribute to the separation of home and work, within the suburbs as well as between central cities and suburbs?

References

Advisory Commission on Intergovernmental Relations
  1973 *City Financial Emergencies: The Intergovernmental Dimension.* Report
         A-42. Washington, D.C.: Advisory Commission on Intergovernmental
         Relations.
  1984 *Financing Public Physical Infrastructure.* Report A-96. Washington, D.C.:
         Advisory Commission on Intergovernmental Relations.
  1985 *Bankruptcies, Defaults, and Other Government Financial Emergencies.* Re-
         port A-99. Washington, D.C.: Advisory Commission on Intergovern-
         mental Relations.
Apogee Research
  1986 Trends in Public Works Expenditures, 1960–1984. Paper prepared
         for the National Council on Public Works Improvement. Washington,
         D.C.
Aponte, Robert, Kathryn M. Neckerman, and William Julius Wilson
  1985 Race, family structure and social policy. Chap. 2 of *Working Paper
         7: Race and Policy.* Project on the Federal Social Role. Washington,
         D.C.: National Conference on Social Welfare.
Bane, Mary Jo
  1986 Household composition and poverty. Pp. 209–231 in Sheldon H.
         Danziger and Daniel H. Weinberg, eds., *Fighting Poverty: What Works
         and What Doesn't.* Cambridge, Mass.: Harvard University Press.
Berry, Brian J. L.
  1985 Islands of renewal in seas of decay. Pp. 69–96 in Paul E. Peterson,
         ed., *The New Urban Reality.* Washington, D.C.: Brookings Institution.
Bianchi, Suzanne M., and Daphne Spain
  1986 *American Women in Transition.* New York: Russell Sage.
Browning, Rufus P., and Dale Rogers Marshall, eds.
  1986 Minority power in city politics: A forum. *PS* 19(Summer):573–640.
Browning, Rufus P., Dale Rogers Marshall, and David H. Tabb
  1984 *Protest is Not Enough: The Struggle of Blacks and Hispanics for Equality in
         Urban Politics.* Berkeley: University of California Press.
Bureau of the Census
  1973 *Low-Income Areas in Large Cities.* 1970 Census of Population, Subject
         Report PC(2)-9B. Washington, D.C.: U.S. Department of Commerce.
  1984 *Characteristics of the Population Below the Poverty Level: 1982.* Current
         Population Reports, Series P-60, No. 144. Washington, D.C.: U.S.
         Department of Commerce.
  1985a *Characteristics of the Population Below the Poverty Level: 1983.* Current
         Population Reports, Series P-60, No. 147. Washington, D.C.: U.S.
         Department of Commerce.
  1985b *Poverty Areas in Large Cities.* 1980 Census of Population, Subject Report
         PC80-2-8D. Washington, D.C.: U.S. Department of Commerce.
  1986a *Characteristics of the Population Below the Poverty Level: 1984.* Current
         Population Reports, Series P-60, No. 152. Washington, D.C.: U.S.
         Department of Commerce.
  1986b *Money Income and Poverty Status of Families and Persons in the United
         States: 1985.* Advance Data from the March 1986 Current Popu-
         lation Survey. Current Population Reports, Series P-60, No. 154.
         Washington, D.C.: U.S. Department of Commerce.

   1986c   *Statistical Abstract of the United States: 1987.* 107th Edition. Washington,
           D.C.: U.S. Department of Commerce.
Clark, Kenneth B.
   1965   *Dark Ghetto.* New York: Harper & Row.
Congressional Budget Office
   1983   *Public Works Infrastructure: Policy Considerations for the 1980s.* Washing-
           ton, D.C.: U.S. Government Printing Office.
Danziger, Sheldon, and Robert D. Plotnick
   1986   Poverty and policy: Lessons of the past two decades. *Social Service
           Review* 60(March):34–51.
Dearborn, Philip M.
   1978   *The Financial Health of Major U.S. Cities in Fiscal 1977.* New York: First
           Boston Corporation.
   1979   *The Financial Health of Major U.S. Cities in 1978.* Washington, D.C.:
           Urban Institute Press.
Frey, William H.
   1985   Mover destination selectivity and the changing suburbanization of
           metropolitan whites and blacks. *Demography* 22(May):223–243.
Frieden, Bernard J., and Lynne B. Sagalyn
   1984   Downtown Shopping Malls and the New Public-Private Strategy.
           Department of Urban Studies and Planning, Massachusetts Institute
           of Technology.
   1986   Downtown shopping malls and the new public–private strategy. Pp.
           130–147 in Marshall Kaplan and Peggy L. Cuciti, eds., *The Great
           Society and Its Legacy: Twenty Years of U.S. Social Policy.* Durham, N.C.:
           Duke University Press.
Garofalo, J.
   1977   *Public Opinion About Crime.* Washington, D.C.: Law Enforcement
           Assistance Administration, U.S. Department of Justice.
Government Finance Research Center
   1983   *Building Prosperity: Financing Public Infrastructure for Economic Develop-
           ment.* Washington, D.C.: Government Finance Research Center.
Hanson, Royce, ed.
   1983   *Rethinking Urban Policy: Urban Development in an Advanced Economy.*
           Washington, D.C.: National Academy Press.
Hawley, Amos H.
   1956   *The Changing Shape of Metropolitan America: Deconcentration Since 1920.*
           Glencoe, Ill.: Free Press.
Judd, Dennis R., and Randy L. Ready
   1986   Entrepreneurial cities and the new politics of economic development.
           Pp. 209–247 in George E. Peterson and Carol W. Lewis, eds., *Reagan
           and the Cities.* Washington, D.C.: Urban Institute Press.
Kasarda, John D.
   1985   Urban change and minority opportunities. Pp. 33–67 in Paul E.
           Peterson, ed., *The New Urban Reality.* Washington, D.C.: Brookings
           Institution.
Ladd, Helen F., John Yinger, Katherine L. Bradbury, Ronald Ferguson, and
Avis Vidal
   1985   The Changing Economic and Fiscal Conditions of Cities. Draft Final
           Report to the U.S. Department of Housing and Urban Development.

State, Local, and Intergovernmental Center, Kennedy School of Government, Harvard University.

Laska, Shirley B., and Daphne Spain, eds.
1980 *Back to the City: Issues in Neighborhood Renovation.* New York: Pergamon.

Lavrakas, P. J.
1982 Fear of crime and behavioral restrictions in urban and suburban neighborhoods. *Population and Environment* 5:242–264.

Leonard, Herman B.
1986 *Checks Unbalanced: The Quiet Side of Public Spending.* New York: Basic Books.

Long, John F.
1981 *Population Deconcentration in the United States.* Special Demographic Analyses, CDS-81-5. Bureau of the Census. Washington, D.C.: U.S. Department of Commerce.

McGuire, Therese J.
1986 On the Relationship between Infrastructure Investment and Economic Development. Paper prepared for the National Council on Public Works Improvement, Washington, D.C.

McLanahan, Sara
1985 Family Structure and Dependency: Early Transitions to Female Household Headship. Discussion Paper No. 807-86. Institute for Research on Poverty, University of Wisconsin.

Moynihan, Daniel Patrick
1965 *The Negro Family: The Case for National Action.* Washington, D.C.: U.S. Department of Labor.

Nathan, Richard R.
1986 The Underclass—Will It Always Be with Us? Paper presented at a symposium of the New School for Social Research, New York.

National Council on Public Works Improvement
1986 *The Nation's Public Works: Defining the Issues.* Report to the President and Congress. Washington, D.C.: National Council on Public Works Improvement.

National League of Cities and United States Conference of Mayors
1983 *Capital Budgeting and Infrastructure in American Cities: An Initial Assessment.* Washington, D.C.: National League of Cities and United States Conference of Mayors.

National Research Council
1982 *Critical Issues for National Urban Policy: A Reconnaissance and Agenda for Future Study.* Committee on National Urban Policy, Commission on Sociotechnical Systems. Washington, D.C.: National Academy Press.
1986 *Emerging Issues in National Urban Policy: Report of a Seminar.* Committee on National Urban Policy, Commission on Behavioral and Social Sciences and Education. Washington, D.C.: National Academy Press.

Noyelle, Thierry J., and Thomas M. Stanback, Jr.
1984 *The Economic Transformation of American Cities.* Totowa, N.J.: Rowman & Allanheld.

Petersen, John E., and Wesley C. Hough
1983 *Creative Capital Financing for State and Local Governments.* Washington, D.C.: Government Finance Research Center.

Peterson, George E.
    1984   Financing the nation's infrastructure requirements. Pp. 110–142 in
            Royce Hanson, ed., *Perspectives on Urban Infrastructure*. Washington,
            D.C.: National Academy Press.
    1986   Urban policy and the cyclical behavior of cities. Pp. 11–35 in George
            E. Peterson and Carol W. Lewis, eds., *Reagan and the Cities*. Washing-
            ton, D.C.: Urban Institute Press.
Peterson, George E., Mary John Miller, Stephen R. Godwin, and Carol Shapiro
    1984   *Guide to Benchmarks of Urban Capital Condition*. Washington, D.C.:
            Urban Institute Press.
Peterson, George E., Randall R. Bovbjerg, Barbara A. Davis, Walter G. Davis,
Euguene C. Durman, and Theresa A. Gullo
    1986   *The Reagan Block Grants: What Have We Learned?* Washington, D.C.:
            Urban Institute Press.
Peterson, Paul E.
    1981   *City Limits*. Chicago: University of Chicago Press.
Sonenshein, Raphe
    1986   Biracial coalition politics in Los Angeles. *PS* 19(Summer):582–590.
Stanback, Thomas M., Jr., Peter J. Bearse, Thierry J. Noyelle, and Robert A.
Karasek
    1981   *Services: The New Economy*. Totowa, N.J.: Allanheld, Osmun.
Sternlieb, George, and James W. Hughes, eds.
    1978   *Revitalizing the Northeast: Prelude to an Agenda*. Center for Urban Policy
            Research. New Brunswick, N.J.: Rutgers University Press.
Stone, Clarence N., and Heywood T. Sanders, eds.
    1987   *The Politics of Urban Development*. Lawrence: University Press of
            Kansas.
U.S. Department of Housing and Urban Development
    1982   *The President's National Urban Policy Report, 1982*. Office of Policy
            Development and Research. Washington, D.C.: U.S. Department of
            Housing and Urban Development.
    1984   *The President's National Urban Policy Report, 1984*. Office of Policy
            Development and Research. Washington, D.C.: U.S. Department of
            Housing and Urban Development.
U.S. Department of Justice
    1986   *Criminal Victimization in the United States, 1984*. Bureau of Justice
            Statistics. May. Washington, D.C.: U.S. Department of Justice.
U.S. Department of the Treasury
    1985   *Federal-State-Local Fiscal Relations: Report to the President and the Congress*.
            Office of State and Local Finance. September. Washington, D.C.:
            U.S. Department of the Treasury.
Wilson, William Julius
    1985   The urban underclass in advanced industrial society. Pp. 129–160
            in Paul E. Peterson, ed., *The New Urban Reality*. Washington, D.C.:
            Brookings Institution.
Wilson, William Julius, and Robert Aponte
    1985   Urban poverty. *Annual Review of Sociology* 11:231–258.
Wilson, William Julius, and Kathryn M. Neckerman
    1986   Poverty and family structure: The widening gap between evidence
            and public policy issues. Pp. 232–259 in Sheldon H. Danziger and
            Daniel H. Weinberg, eds., *Fighting Poverty: What Works and What
            Doesn't*. Cambridge, Mass.: Harvard University Press.

Appendix A: Regional Classifications

The Census Bureau divides the country into four regions: Northeast, Midwest, South, and West, each of which has two or three divisions. The Northeast, for example, consists of the New England and Middle Atlantic divisions. The Bureau of Economic Analysis (BEA), however, divides the country into eight regions and lists Alaska and Hawaii separately. Three Census Bureau divisions—New England, East North Central, and West North Central—correspond to BEA regions—New England, Great Lakes, and Plains, respectively. But the remainder of the divisions and regions diverge in varying ways. For example, BEA's Mideast region combines the Census Bureau's Middle Atlantic region—New York, New Jersey, and Pennsylvania—with some of the states from the bureau's South Atlantic region—Delaware, District of Columbia, and Maryland. Figure 1 lists and compares the Census Bureau and BEA classification schemes for the reader's convenience.

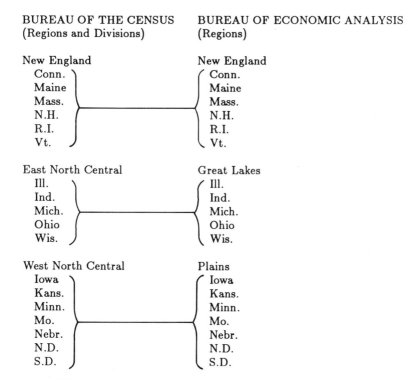

BUREAU OF THE CENSUS
(Regions and Divisions)

BUREAU OF ECONOMIC ANALYSIS
(Regions)

New England
  Conn.
  Maine
  Mass.
  N.H.
  R.I.
  Vt.

New England
  Conn.
  Maine
  Mass.
  N.H.
  R.I.
  Vt.

East North Central
  Ill.
  Ind.
  Mich.
  Ohio
  Wis.

Great Lakes
  Ill.
  Ind.
  Mich.
  Ohio
  Wis.

West North Central
  Iowa
  Kans.
  Minn.
  Mo.
  Nebr.
  N.D.
  S.D.

Plains
  Iowa
  Kans.
  Minn.
  Mo.
  Nebr.
  N.D.
  S.D.

FIGURE 1

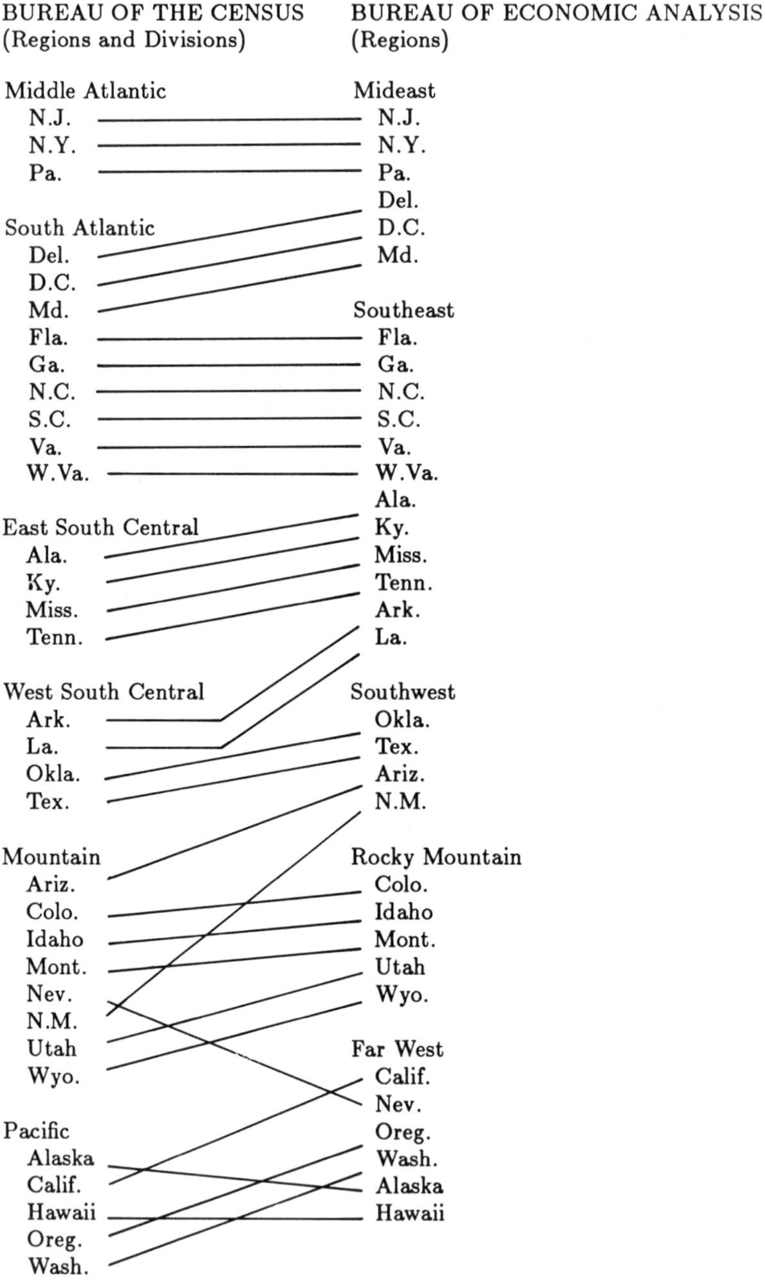

BUREAU OF THE CENSUS   BUREAU OF ECONOMIC ANALYSIS
(Regions and Divisions)   (Regions)

FIGURE 1   *Continued*

Appendix B: Workshop Participants

The following people attended the workshop held at the National Academy of Sciences, Washington, D.C., on July 16–17, 1986:

Roy W. Bahl,* Maxwell Professor of Political Economy, Maxwell School, Syracuse University

Mary Jo Bane,* Professor of Public Policy and Director, Center for Health and Human Resources Policy, John F. Kennedy School of Government, Harvard University

Mark C. Berger, Associate Professor, Department of Economics, University of Kentucky

Glenn C. Blomquist, Associate Professor, Department of Economics and James W. Martin School of Public Administration, University of Kentucky

Kenneth Bolton, Director, Office of Policy, Urban Mass Transportation Administration, U.S. Department of Transportation

Eugene P. Boyd, Government Division, Congressional Research Service

Steve Brennan, Deputy Assistant Secretary for Finance, Economic Development Administration, U.S. Department of Commerce

Luis Bueso, Planning Division, Economic Development Administration, U.S. Department of Commerce

Ross Campbell, Technical Assistance and Research Division, Economic Development Administration, U.S. Department of Commerce

Robert B. Cervero,* Associate Professor, Department of City and Regional Planning, University of California, Berkeley

Patrick Cleary, Special Assistant to the Assistant Secretary for Policy, U.S. Department of Labor

Gregory L. Coler,* Secretary, Florida Department of Health and Rehabilitative Services, Tallahassee

Cynthia Costello, Study Director, Committee on Women's Employment and Related Social Issues, National Research Council

Donald C. Dahmann, Population Division, Bureau of the Census, U.S. Department of Commerce

Philip M. Dearborn, Vice President, Greater Washington Research Center

---

*Member, Committee on National Urban Policy.

John P. Eberhard, Director, Building Research Board, National Research Council

Michael Fishman, Office of Human Development Services, U.S. Department of Health and Human Services

Doug Fitzgerald, Office of Intergovernmental Affairs, U.S. Department of Labor

Irwin Garfinkel, Professor, School of Social Work, University of Wisconsin-Madison

Daniel H. Garnick, Associate Director for Regional Economics, Bureau of Economic Analysis, U.S. Department of Commerce

Paul Gatons, Office of Policy Development and Research, U.S. Department of Housing and Urban Development

David Geddes, Division of Technical Assistance and Research, Economic Development Administration, U.S. Department of Commerce

John Gist, Office of Policy Development and Research, U.S. Department of Housing and Urban Development

Steven D. Gold, Director of Fiscal Studies, National Conference of State Legislatures

Margaret T. Gordon,* Director, Center for Urban Affairs and Policy Research, and Professor, Medill School of Journalism, Northwestern School of Journalism, Northwestern University

Bob Gray, Office of Policy Development and Research, U.S. Department of Housing and Urban Development

Edward Griswold, Office of Intergovernmental Affairs, U.S. Department of Labor

Marlys Gustafson, Office of Human Development Services, U.S. Department of Health and Human Services

Tom Hammer, Council for Urban Economic Development Research Institute, Northwestern University

Brett Hammond, Associate Executive Director, Commission on Behavioral and Social Sciences and Education, National Research Council

Heidi I. Hartmann, Committee on Women's Employment and Related Social Issues, National Research Council

Marie Howland, Institute for Urban Studies, University of Maryland at College Park

Everson Hull, Deputy Assistant Secretary for Policy, U.S. Department of Labor

John D. Kasarda, Chairman, Sociology Department, University of North Carolina

Jill Khadduri, Director, Policy Development Division, Office of Policy Development and Research, U.S. Department of Housing and Urban Development

John J. Kirlin, Professor of Public Administration, Sacramento Public Affairs Center, University of Southern California

Thomas J. Klutznick,* Co-Managing Partner, Miller-Klutznick-Davis-Gray Co., Chicago

Herman B. Leonard,* George F. Baker, Jr., Professor of Public Management, John F. Kennedy School of Government, Harvard University

Laurence E. Lynn, Jr.,* Dean, School of Social Service Administration, University of Chicago

Dale Rogers Marshall, Dean, Wellesley College

William C. McCready,* Associate Director, Public Opinion Laboratory, and Professor, Department of Sociology, Northern Illinois University

Sara McLanahan, Associate Professor, Department of Sociology, University of Wisconsin-Madison

Beverly Milkman, Deputy Director for Grant Programs, Economic Development Administration, U.S. Department of Commerce

Richard R. Mudge, President, Apogee Research, Inc., Washington, D.C.

Sylvester Murray,* Manager, State and Local Government Consulting Division, Coopers & Lybrand, Columbus, Ohio

Sandra S. Osbourn, Government Division, Congressional Research Service

Elinor Ostrom,* Co-Director, Workshop in Political Theory and Policy Analysis, and Professor, Department of Political Science, Indiana University

Diana Pearce, Director, Women and Poverty Project, American University

Carla Pedone, Human Resources and Community Development Division, Congressional Budget Office

John E. Petersen, Director, Government Finance Research Center

James E. Peterson, Executive Director, Council for Urban Economic Development Research Institute, Northwestern University

Paul E. Peterson,* Director, Center for the Study of American Government and Benjamin H. Griswold III Professor of Public Policy, Graduate School of Public Policy, Johns Hopkins University, Washington, D.C.

Milton Pikarsky, Director of Engineering Studies, National Council
    on Public Works Improvement
John M. Quigley,* Professor of Economics and Public Policy,
    Graduate School of Public Policy and Department of
    Economics, University of California, Berkeley
Franklin D. Raines,* General Partner, Lazard Frères & Co., New
    York
Steve Redburne, Office of Policy Development and Research, U.S.
    Department of Housing and Urban Development
Gary Reed, Director, Office of Program Economics, U.S.
    Department of Labor
Robert Reischauer, Senior Fellow, Economic Studies, Brookings
    Institution
Brandon Roberts, Technical Assistance and Research Division,
    Economic Development Administration, U.S. Department of
    Commerce
Elliott Rock, Office of Policy Development, The White House
John P. Ross, Director, Economic Development and Public Finance
    Division, Office of Policy Development and Research, U.S.
    Department of Housing and Urban Development
Beverly Selby, Office of Policy Development, The White House
Mary Kate Smith, Planning Division, Economic Development
    Administration, U.S. Department of Commerce
Michael Springer, Office of State and Local Finance, U.S.
    Department of the Treasury
Jennifer Stucker, Office of Policy Development and Research, U.S.
    Department of Housing and Urban Development
Dorothy Watson, Department of Sociology, University of
    Wisconsin-Madison
John C. Weicher,* American Enterprise Institute, Washington, D.C.
Fred L. Williams, Office of Policy, Urban Mass Transportation
    Administration, U.S. Department of Transportation
George Wright, Economic Development and Public Finance
    Division, Office of Policy Development and Research, U.S.
    Department of Housing and Urban Development

Michael G. H. McGeary, *Study Director,* Committee on National
    Urban Policy
Shelly Westebbe, *Staff Consultant,* Committee on National Urban
    Policy
Ann Tasseff, *Administrative Secretary*

PART II

BACKGROUND PAPERS

Income, Opportunities, and the Quality of Life of Urban Residents

MARK C. BERGER and GLENN C. BLOMQUIST

This paper reports on the economic well-being of urban residents, using estimates of quality of life as well as traditional measures. Traditional measures include household income, the poverty rate, and the unemployment rate, which are reported for residents of central cities, suburbs, small metropolitan areas, and rural areas. These measures are also disaggregated by demographic group for each residential category. Earnings differences across individuals are explained by observable differences in workers, jobs, and locations. Location-specific amenities are shown to give rise to compensating differences in wages and housing prices. Estimating values for such amenities permits comparisons of the quality of life across areas and the augmentation of traditional measures of well-being. Estimates are based on public-use microdata from the 1980 Census of Population and Housing.

CITIES AND ECONOMIC WELL-BEING

Cities are monuments to the possibilities of civilized cooperation. The benefits that can be realized by common use of sizable production resources and synergistic interactions are a powerful force that

The authors gratefully acknowledge the helpful comments of John Weicher on an earlier draft of this paper.

draws people together (Mills and Hamilton, 1984:Ch. 1). The standard of living in the United States is due in part to the clustering of economic activity. Workers and residents in cities share in these benefits. Nevertheless, there is concern about the economic status of people who live in cities (Tolley et al., 1979). The concentration of poverty in ghettos and the haunting appearance of abandoned factories are particularly striking. To provide some empirical evidence on the advantages and disadvantages of city life, this study focuses on the well-being of people who work and live in cities, compared with people outside of cities.

This paper reviews what is known about the economic status of residents of large central cities compared with residents of suburbs, small metropolitan areas, and rural areas. An ideal measure of economic status would take into account several factors: the future, distinguishing between permanent and temporary situations; the actual decision-making unit, whether independent individuals or close-knit groups; the full resources available, recognizing transactions in kind; the cost of living; and the amenities available, incorporating quality-of-life values (Danziger et al., 1981). In the absence of an ideal measure, we use a set of measures of economic status to reflect the urban situation.

Measures of well-being for metropolitan areas with populations exceeding 1.5 million are computed from the public-use microdata of the 1980 Census of Population and Housing. Comparisons are made across and within metropolitan areas and across demographic groups by type of area. Emphasis is given to annual money income. A hedonic framework of wage determination is offered as an explanation for differences in labor earnings, which account for 70 percent of total national income (Bureau of the Census, 1984:Table 728). Earnings differences can be attributed to observable differences in the characteristics of workers and jobs. Earnings differences also arise because of differences in the amenities available in the area in which the job is located. When these premiums from the labor market are combined with the compensation reflected elsewhere, we can estimate differences in the quality of life in various locations. Quality-of-life differences are then used to augment income differences to provide a better measure of differences in the well-being of urban residents.

TRADITIONAL MEASURES OF WELL-BEING

This section provides an overview of some traditional measures of well-being: household income, the poverty rate, the unemployment and employment rates, the manufacturing employment share, and individual income and annual hours worked. These summary measures are all computed from the 1980 Census 1-in-1,000 Public Use A Sample. In Tables 1-5, the measures are presented by metropolitan area, location of residence within metropolitan areas, region, family composition, race, and age.

Traditional measures of well-being are useful for describing urban conditions. Household income indicates the amount that can be spent on food, housing, and other categories of consumption. The poverty rate indicates the relative size of the group of people whose money incomes are not adequate to meet basic consumption requirements.[1] The unemployment rate shows the relative size of the group of people who are not earning income but are looking for work. The employment rate gives the relative size of the group of people who are working. The manufacturing employment share shows the relative size of the local economic base composed of traditional industry. Urban residents are usually considered to be better off when their incomes and local employment rates are higher and poverty and unemployment rates are lower. In the past, a high share of manufacturing employment was considered a good sign, but recent shifts in the economic structure away from manufacturing and toward the service and information sectors have had a negative effect on urban economies based on manufacturing.

Large Metropolitan Areas

Part A of Table 1 shows traditional measures for the 26 metropolitan areas in the United States with populations of 1.5 million or more, according to the 1980 Census. Part B gives summary statistics and correlation coefficients among the various measures. It is apparent

---

[1] Families and unrelated individuals are classified as being above or below the poverty level using an index developed by the Social Security Administration in 1964 and revised by federal interagency committees in 1969 and 1980. The poverty index is based on money income and does not take into account noncash benefits such as food stamps and public housing. The povery thresholds are revised annually to reflect the change in the consumer price index. The average poverty threshold for a family of four was $7,412 in 1979.

TABLE 1 Measures of Economic Status for Residents of Large Metropolitan Areas, 1979-1980

Part A

Metropolitan Area (1980 SMSAs)	Population Rank 1980	Population, April 1980 (000s)	Household Income, 1979 ($)	Poverty Rate, 1979 (%)	Unemployment Rate, April 1980 (%)	Employment Rate, April 1980 (%)	Manufacturing Employment Share, April 1980 (%)
New York, N.Y.-N.J.	1	9,120	19,142	15.8	6.9	54.7	15.7
Los Angeles-Long Beach, Calif.	2	7,478	21,639	11.5	6.0	60.9	23.5
Chicago, Ill.	3	7,104	23,017	11.0	6.8	61.4	24.1
Philadelphia, Pa.-N.J.	4	4,717	20,239	12.1	8.6	54.6	22.1
Detroit, Mich.	5	4,353	23,288	9.1	11.6	55.2	29.6
San Francisco-Oakland, Calif.	6	3,251	23,151	10.3	5.6	63.4	13.6
Washington, D.C.-Md.-Va.	7	3,061	27,295	6.9	3.7	69.6	5.1
Dallas-Ft. Worth, Tex.	8	2,975	21,318	11.1	3.2	65.9	20.5
Houston, Tex.	9	2,905	24,607	10.3	3.2	69.6	18.3
Boston, Mass.	10	2,763	20,518	12.2	3.7	60.6	17.0
Nassau-Suffolk, N.Y.	11	2,606	25,997	6.7	5.6	59.5	15.8
St. Louis, Mo.-Ill.	12	2,356	21,225	10.2	7.6	58.0	21.1
Pittsburgh, Pa.	13	2,264	20,275	9.6	8.2	52.1	24.6
Baltimore, Md.	14	2,174	21,657	11.4	6.1	59.9	17.3
Minneapolis-St. Paul, Minn.-Wis.	15	2,114	23,032	8.5	3.7	67.9	20.0
Atlanta, Ga.	16	2,030	21,189	12.2	4.9	64.4	11.6
Newark, N.J.	17	1,966	23,251	10.4	7.1	57.8	24.9
Anaheim-Santa Ana-Garden Grove, Calif.	18	1,933	26,434	5.1	3.2	68.6	22.6

1980 SMSAs		Population	Household Income	Poverty Rate	Unemployment Rate	Employment Rate	Manufacturing Employment Share
Cleveland, Ohio	19	1,899	21,461	8.8	8.1	55.6	30.1
San Diego, Calif.	20	1,862	21,114	10.3	4.7	60.9	16.5
Miami, Fla.	21	1,626	18,106	15.8	5.4	56.5	10.8
Denver-Boulder, Colo.	22	1,621	22,664	9.1	4.1	66.7	14.3
Seattle-Everett, Wash.	23	1,607	23,075	5.8	7.5	63.2	22.4
Tampa-St. Petersburg, Fla.	24	1,569	16,812	11.9	5.1	49.2	12.8
Riverside-San Bernardino-Ontario, Calif.	25	1,558	19,504	11.3	10.1	55.5	15.8
Phoenix, Ariz.	26	1,509	20,874	9.6	6.0	57.9	16.7

Part B

1980 SMSAs	Population	Household Income	Poverty Rate	Unemployment Rate	Employment Rate	Manufacturing Employment Share
Summary statistics						
Mean	3,017	21,957	10.3	6.0	60.4	18.7
Standard deviation	1,995	2,431	2.5	2.2	5.5	5.8
Minimum	1,509	16,812	5.1	3.2	49.2	5.1
Maximum	9,120	27,295	15.8	11.6	69.6	30.1
Correlation coefficients						
Population		−0.032	0.384	0.181	−0.105	0.183
Household income			−0.766	−0.270	0.715	0.055
Poverty rate				0.094	−0.447	−0.227
Unemployment rate					−0.688	0.512
Manufacturing employment share					−0.245	

SOURCE: Computed from Bureau of the Census (1983b). Population figures were obtained from Bureau of the Census (1983a).

from the summary statistics that the measures vary widely across metropolitan areas.[2] Somewhat surprisingly, population size is not highly correlated with any of the measures of economic status. Although there are several significant correlations among household income, the poverty rate, the unemployment rate, and the employment rate, the poverty rate-unemployment rate correlation is not among them. Metropolitan areas with high unemployment rates do not necessarily have high poverty rates. The unemployment rate, however, is significantly correlated with the manufacturing employment share. This probably reflects the long-term structural shift away from goods-producing jobs and the resulting displacement of workers.

Central-City, Suburban, Small Metropolitan, and Rural Areas

Table 2 presents the measures of economic status for households and persons in and out of metropolitan areas for the entire United States and for the four main Census Bureau regions. Residents of metropolitan areas are broken down further into three groups: residents living in the central city of large (greater than 1.5 million persons) metropolitan areas; those living in the surrounding suburbs; and residents of small (less than 1.5 million persons) metropolitan areas. Looking at averages for the entire United States, nonmetropolitan residents have the lowest incomes and employment rate of the four groups, whereas central-city residents of large metropolitan areas have the lowest manufacturing employment share and the highest unemployment and poverty rates. In contrast, suburban residents of large metropolitan areas have the highest household incomes, employment rate, and manufacturing employment share, as well as the lowest poverty and unemployment rates.

---

[2] The household income figures reported in Table 1 are not adjusted for differences in the cost of living because of problems in constructing an acceptable index. Consumer price indexes (CPIs) are reported for 22 of the 26 areas by the Bureau of the Census (1984), and household income can be deflated by multiplying it by the average CPI for all areas and dividing by the CPI for the area in question. The cost-of-living factors range from 0.925 for Houston to 1.025 for Atlanta. The correlation between household income and deflated household income is 0.95. However, the CPIs by city are only appropriate for comparisons over time within cities and not across cities at a point in time.

In all four regions, suburban residents are more affluent according to these traditional measures. Yet the lowest incomes and employment rates and the highest unemployment and poverty rates vary from region to region. In the Northeast and Midwest, central-city residents of large metropolitan areas are the poorest, whereas in the South and West the poorest individuals are those living outside metropolitan areas.

Residential Area, Family, and Race

Table 3 gives average household incomes and poverty rates in the different residential locations by family composition and race. In every case, suburban residents again have the highest incomes and lowest poverty rates. Nonmetropolitan residents have the lowest incomes and, except for households headed by white females, they also have the highest poverty rates. Married couples with children have somewhat higher incomes than their counterparts without children, but they also have higher poverty rates. Income levels are substantially lower and poverty rates higher for female householders with children than for married couples with children. For perspective, however, it should be noted that there are more than six times as many white married-couple households with children than female-headed households with children. Among blacks the ratio is more than four to one.

Summary measures of economic status by race and location of residence are shown in Table 4. White household incomes and employment rates are higher and unemployment and poverty rates lower than those of blacks, regardless of location of residence. In virtually every case the measures for Hispanics fall somewhere between those for blacks and whites.

Residential Area, Age, Earnings, and Transfers

In Table 5, household income and poverty rates are given by age of the householder and location of residence. Among 25- to 39-year-old householders, central-city residents have the lowest incomes and highest poverty rates. For householders aged 40 and over, it is rural residents who are the least affluent. Again, suburban residents have higher incomes and lower poverty rates than other groups. There does appear to be some tendency toward higher poverty rates and lower incomes among the elderly, but this is not a universal trend.

TABLE 2 Measures of Economic Status by Size and Location of Area of Residence, 1979-1980

Location of Residence	Percentage of U.S. Households April 1980	Household Income, 1979 ($)	Poverty Rate, 1979 (%)	Unemployment Rate, April 1980 (%)	Employment Rate, April 1980 (%)	Manufacturing Employment Share, April 1980 (%)
Northeast						
Metro. area > 1.5 mil.						
Central city	4.9	16,661	19.2	8.1	51.9	16.0
Suburbs	5.4	24,173	6.9	6.1	58.9	20.7
Metro. area < 1.5 mil.	6.7	19,737	10.8	6.5	57.4	26.2
Nonmetro. area	4.7	18,829	10.1	6.8	56.7	27.5
Midwest						
Metro. area > 1.5 mil.						
Central city	2.7	17,357	18.3	10.0	53.9	23.3
Suburbs	5.0	25,571	5.4	6.6	62.6	25.8
Metro. area < 1.5 mil.	9.5	20,538	10.5	7.4	59.2	25.0
Nonmetro. area	8.7	17,627	12.5	7.2	55.2	21.2

South						
Metro. area > 1.5 mil.						
Central city	2.7	19,354	16.4	5.3	61.0	14.6
Suburbs	4.5	23,948	7.6	3.7	65.1	13.6
Metro. area < 1.5 mil.	12.9	18,447	14.8	5.9	58.6	15.3
Nonmetro. area	12.8	16,031	19.7	6.8	52.6	19.9
West						
Metro. area > 1.5 mil.						
Central city	3.8	19,802	12.7	6.3	60.2	17.9
Suburbs	5.6	24,024	7.8	5.3	63.4	20.4
Metro. area < 1.5 mil.	6.3	20,621	10.7	6.8	59.8	13.1
Nonmetro. area	3.7	18,263	13.4	7.3	55.4	8.7
United States						
Metro. area > 1.5 mil.						
Central city	14.0	18,149	16.8	7.4	56.3	17.6
Suburbs	20.4	24,383	6.9	5.5	62.3	20.3
Metro. area < 1.5 mil.	35.6	19,574	12.2	6.6	58.7	19.6
Nonmetro. area	30.0	17,165	15.3	7.0	54.3	20.1

SOURCE: Computed from Bureau of the Census (1983b).

TABLE 3 Income and Poverty by Family Composition, Race, and Area of Residence, 1979

Race of Householder	Married Couple Without Children			Married Couple With Children			Female Householder With Children		
	Percentage of U.S. Households[a]	Household Income ($)	Poverty Rate (%)	Percentage of U.S. Households	Household Income ($)	Poverty Rate (%)	Percentage of U.S. Households	Household Income ($)	Poverty Rate (%)
Whites									
Metro. area > 1.5 mil.									
Central city	2.6	25,897	3.4	1.7	26,471	7.2	0.4	11,965	37.4
Suburbs	5.9	28,669	2.0	6.0	30,850	2.6	0.8	13,876	25.3
Metro. area < 1.5 mil.	9.8	23,962	3.8	9.5	25,860	5.5	1.6	11,692	31.4
Nonmetro. area	9.1	20,064	6.1	9.2	21,982	8.5	1.1	10,876	34.9
Blacks									
Metro. area > 1.5 mil.									
Central city	0.6	20,062	10.7	0.7	22,286	12.2	0.2	9,583	51.5
Suburbs	0.2	24,279	6.3	0.4	25,730	6.3	0.1	10,488	40.9
Metro. area < 1.5 mil.	0.6	16,934	13.1	0.9	20,425	11.0	0.2	8,989	54.0
Nonmetro. area	0.4	12,514	22.2	0.6	16,282	23.6	0.1	7,493	64.1
Hispanics									
Metro. area > 1.5 mil.									
Central city	0.2	18,767	12.5	0.5	17,375	17.8	0.2	7,636	65.3
Suburbs	0.2	22,230	6.6	0.5	22,925	8.8	0.1	11,225	43.0
Metro. area < 1.5 mil.	0.3	17,304	15.6	0.7	18,301	18.4	0.2	8,200	53.1
Nonmetro. area	0.1	14,610	16.9	0.3	16,557	23.8	0.5	7,310	70.2

[a]Percentage of total U.S. households. Because the categories shown are not exhaustive or mutually exclusive, the percentages do not sum to 100.

SOURCE: Computed from Bureau of the Census (1983b).

TABLE 4 Economic Status by Race and Area of Residence, 1979-1980

Part A

Area	White Householder			Black Householder			Hispanic Householder		
	Percentage of U.S. Households April 1980	Household Income, 1979 ($)	Poverty Rate, 1979 (%)	Percentage of U.S. Households April 1980	Household Income, 1979 ($)	Poverty Rate, 1979 (%)	Percentage of U.S. Households April 1980	Household Income 1979 ($)	Poverty Rate, 1979 (%)
Metro. area > 1.5 mil.									
Central city	9.2	20,135	11.4	3.6	14,193	27.6	1.6	14,112	27.2
Suburbs	18.4	24,891	5.9	1.2	18,427	18.3	1.1	19,628	14.3
Metro. area < 1.5 mil.	30.8	20,349	9.9	3.5	13,592	28.7	1.5	14,967	25.1
Nonmetro. area	27.3	17,673	13.4	2.0	10,939	39.0	7.3	14,142	27.7

Part B

Area	Whites			Blacks			Hispanics		
	Percentage of Persons,[a] April 1980	Unemployment Rate, April 1980 (%)	Employment Rate, April 1980 (%)	Percentage of Persons, April 1980 (%)	Unemployment Rate, April 1980	Employment Rate, April 1980 (%)	Percentage of Persons, April 1980 (%)	Unemployment Rate, April 1980 (%)	Employment Rate April 1980 (%)
Metro. area > 1.5 mil.									
Central city	8.5	5.3	58.2	3.5	12.3	51.4	1.6	8.8	55.6
Suburbs	18.8	5.1	62.3	1.3	10.7	61.7	1.3	7.0	61.5
Metro. area > 1.5 mil.	30.5	5.8	59.4	3.6	12.2	53.1	1.8	10.0	56.9
Nonmetro. area	27.2	6.5	54.9	2.3	12.4	47.2	0.8	7.6	54.8

[a]Percentage of persons aged 16 and over in the United States. Because the categories shown are not exhaustive or mutually exclusive, the percentages do not sum to 100.

SOURCE: Computed from Bureau of the Census (1983b).

TABLE 5 Economic Status by Age and Area of Residence, 1979

Part A: By Household

Area	Householders Aged 25-39			Householders Aged 40-64		
	Percentage of U.S. Households, April 1980 (%)	Household Income, 1979 ($)	Poverty Rate, 1979 (%)	Percentage of U.S. Households, April 1980 (%)	Household Income, 1979 ($)	Poverty Rate, 1979 (%)
Metro. area > 1.5 mil.						
Central City	4.8	18,338	17.0	5.3	22,308	13.7
Suburbs	7.0	24,291	6.7	8.5	30,022	4.4
Metro. area < 1.5 mil.	11.7	20,422	10.6	13.8	24,393	8.6
Nonmetro. area	8.9	18,912	11.6	11.6	20,929	11.9

Area	Householders Aged 65-71			Householders Aged 72+		
	Percentage of U.S. Households, April 1980 (%)	Household Income, 1979 ($)	Poverty Rate, 1979 (%)	Percentage of U.S. Households, April 1980 (%)	Household Income, 1979 ($)	Poverty Rate, 1979 (%)
Metro. area > 1.5 mil.						
Central City	1.3	14,406	14.4	1.6	11,437	18.4
Suburbs	1.7	16,954	8.1	1.8	12,602	12.7
Metro. area < 1.5 mil.	3.2	13,945	13.1	3.6	10,611	19.0
Nonmetro. area	3.2	12,205	18.0	3.8	9,216	27.3

Part B: By Individual

Area	Individuals Aged 25-39				Individuals Aged 40-64			
	Earnings 1979[a] ($)	Transfers, 1979[b] ($)	Other Income, 1979[c] ($)	Annual Hours Worked 1979	Earnings 1979 ($)	Transfers 1979 ($)	Other Income 1979 ($)	Annual Hours Worked 1979
Metro. area > 1.5 mil.								
Central city	10,116	270	461	1421	10,365	467	1,297	1244
Suburbs	12,488	103	488	1536	13,603	284	1,571	1386
Metro. area < 1.5 mil.	10,608	125	424	1506	10,962	370	1,411	1329
Nonmetro. area	9,502	115	383	1496	9,005	408	1,170	1308

TABLE 5 (Continued)

Area	Individuals Aged 65-71				Individuals Aged 72+			
	Earnings 1979[a] ($)	Transfers, 1979[b] ($)	Other Income, 1979[c] ($)	Annual Hours Worked 1979	Earnings 1979 ($)	Transfers 1979 ($)	Other Income 1979 ($)	Annual Hours Worked 1979
Metro. area > 1.5 mil.								
Central city	2,826	2,644	2,515	348	1,119	3,008	2,866	107
Suburbs	3,309	2,777	3,695	364	701	2,949	3,415	82
Metro. area < 1.5 mil.	2,266	2,761	2,934	312	637	2,866	2,768	94
Nonmetro. area	1,970	2,668	2,341	319	795	2,661	2,087	127

[a] Earnings include wage and salary and self-employment income.
[b] Transfers include social security and public assistance income.
[c] Other income includes interest, dividend, and net rental income, and income from all other sources.

SOURCE: Computed from Bureau of the Census (1983b).

Among central-city residents the poverty rate is higher for 25- to 39-year-old householders than for 65- to 71-year-old householders.

The rest of Table 5 is devoted to a breakdown of individual income into earnings, transfers, and other income, along with information on annual hours worked. In general, suburbanites have the highest earnings (annual and hourly), other income, and hours worked, whereas transfer income appears to be greatest in the central city. To the extent that, nationally, the poverty rate is highest for central-city residents, there is some evidence that transfer payments are going to those who need them most. As individuals age, it is apparent that transfers and other income partly replace earnings. Among 25- to 39-year-old central-city residents, earnings are 93 percent of total income. This percentage drops to 85 percent for 40- to 64-year-olds, 35 percent for 65- to 71-year-olds, and 16 percent for those aged 72 and older.

Tables 1–5 present traditional measures of economic well-being by metropolitan area, location of residence, region, family composition, race, and age. By looking at several traditional measures and disaggregating them in various ways, it is possible to obtain an overview of the economic well-being of urban residents. Yet, the traditional measures ignore quality-of-life factors, which can be important components in well-being. As a first step toward incorporating quality of life into the analysis, the next section develops a framework for explaining earnings differences among urban residents. With this framework, and the estimates that can be obtained, it is also possible to examine the specific factors that contribute to earnings and income differences across individuals. The framework and estimates further our ability to explain differences in the economic status of different groups in the urban population.

EARNINGS DETERMINATION

Framework

Individuals earn different amounts in the labor market for a variety of reasons. Perhaps the most important cause of observed earnings differences is differences in skills or training. When individuals invest in themselves to enhance their future earnings, they are investing in human capital. These investments may take the form of formal schooling, on-the-job training, job searches, or even diet and exercise to improve or maintain health (Becker, 1975; Mincer, 1974).

Controlling for other factors, individuals with greater investments in human capital should have higher earnings. Those with more schooling or job experience, for example, should earn more than those with less.

Even among individuals with the same investments in human capital, however, earnings may differ. For example, employers may find it necessary to pay workers a premium in dangerous or unpleasant jobs. These premiums are compensating wage differentials. They exist because jobs have different sets of characteristics, some of which workers find more valuable than others. Workers pay for pleasant job characteristics, such as flexible hours, and receive premiums for unpleasant ones. The magnitude of observed earnings differences because of compensating wage differentials is determined by the tastes of workers, their ability to move from one job to another, and the range of job characteristics offered by employers in the labor market (R. Smith, 1979).

In addition to the characteristics of a job, characteristics associated with the area of a worker's residence may produce compensating wage differentials if enough workers are mobile across areas. Examples of these types of quality-of-life factors are crime, air quality, and climate. If it were assumed that compensation for these amenities and disamenities takes place only in the labor market, then workers in desirable areas would pay for their quality of life through lower earnings. How much compensation of this type occurs in the labor market is determined by the distribution of quality-of-life factors across areas, the tastes and mobility of workers, and the existence of other markets for which compensation may occur (V. Smith, 1983).

Earnings differences may also be caused by other factors. For example, an observed difference in the earnings of two groups may be attributable in part to discrimination in the labor market instead of being explained fully by differences in investment in human capital or other factors. Earnings may differ across jobs because of unionization, which may alter the workings of the market. Variations in earnings may exist across geographic areas because of cost-of-living differences. These other factors must also be kept in mind when interpreting differences in earnings across the population.

Empirical Model and Results

In this section, we estimate a regression model that explains average hourly earnings as a function of a number of variables designed to capture the effects of human capital investments, job characteristics, and quality-of-life factors. The data on individuals that have been used to estimate the model are obtained from the 1-in-1,000 Public Use A Sample of the 1980 Census. Data on job and location characteristics are obtained from a variety of sources and are merged with the census data by county, metropolitan area, or industry. Included in the sample are 46,004 individuals living in 253 urban counties in 185 metropolitan areas from which complete data to estimate the model are available. These individuals are at least 16 years of age or older; they all reported their 1979 earnings, hours, and weeks; had some wage and salary earnings; and had positive total earnings.

The individual characteristics that are incorporated into the estimated wage equation are years of labor market experience (age − schooling − 6); experience squared; years of schooling; number of children; and dummy variables for race, gender, enrollment in school, marital status, and the presence of health limitations. These variables are included in the model alone and are made to interact with one another as appropriate. For example, gender can be made to interact with experience and with experience squared to capture differences between men and women in their profiles of earnings over the life cycle. The variables measuring individual characteristics control for differences in human capital investments and possibly some other factors such as discrimination.

The variables designed to capture the effects of differences in job characteristics are five dummies that control for six broad occupational categories and the unionization rate in the worker's industry.

Sixteen quality-of-life factors are also included in the model. Six of these variables control for climatic differences, and six capture differences in environmental quality. Others are dummies for the location of the worker's residence in the central city of the metropolitan area or in a county bordering a seacoast or the Great Lakes, the violent crime rate, and the teacher/pupil ratio in the county of residence. The teacher/pupil ratio is designed to be a measure of the quality of local publicly provided services.

Table 6 presents the wage-equation regression estimates, standard errors, and means of the independent variables. The exact functional form that was used was chosen on the basis of the results of a Box-Cox maximum likelihood search procedure. It consisted of transforming the hourly wage (W) to $(W^{.1} - 1)/.1$ and entering the independent variables in linear form. The parameter estimates presented in Table 6 have been linearized so that they are estimates of

TABLE 6 Regression Estimates of the Hedonic Wage Equation, 1980

Independent Variable	Units	Mean	Linearized Coefficient[a]	Linearized Standard Error
Experience	Age - schooling - 6, years	17.44	0.310	0.008
Experience squared		513.90	-0.005	0.0002
Schooling	Years	12.76	0.442	0.010
Race	Nonwhite=1, white=0	0.153	-0.959	0.091
Gender	Female=1, male=0	0.452	-0.312	0.100
Enrolled in school	Yes=1, no=0	0.149	-0.600	0.073
Marital status	Married=1, unmarried=0	0.586	1.441	0.077
Health limitations	Yes=1, no=0	0.048	-0.885	0.108
Gender x experience		7.598	-0.132	0.012
Gender x experience squared		221.30	0.0023	0.0002
Gender x race		0.075	1.102	0.128
Gender x marital status		0.237	-1.392	0.106
Gender x children		1.118	-0.254	0.025
Professional or managerial	Yes=1, no=0	0.232	2.499	0.088
Technical or sales	Yes=1, no=0	0.336	1.214	0.076
Farming	Yes=1, no=0	0.012	0.129	0.219
Craft	Yes=1, no=0	0.113	1.437	0.098
Operator or laborer[b]	Yes=1, no=0	0.173	0.690	0.088
Industry unionization	Percent	23.35	0.038	0.001
Precipitation	Inches/year	32.01	-0.014	0.004

Humidity	Percent	68.27	0.0072	0.006
Heating degree days	Degree days/year	4,326.0	-0.000035	0.000025
Cooling degree days	Degree days/year	1,162.0	-0.00022	0.00005
Windspeed	Miles/hour	8.895	0.096	0.022
Sunshine	Percent of days	61.12	-0.0092	0.006
Coast	Yes=1,no=0	0.330	-0.031	0.063
Central city	Yes=1, no=0	0.290	-0.454	0.065
Violent crime	Crimes/100,000 pop./year	646.80	0.00062	0.0001
Teacher/pupil ratio		0.080	-5.45	1.848
Visibility	Miles	15.80	-0.0026	0.0028
Total suspended particulates	Micrograms/cubic meter	73.24	-0.0024	0.0015
Water effluent dischargers	Number/county	1.513	-0.0051	0.012
Landfill waste	Hundred million metric tons/county	477.50	0.00009	0.00002
Superfund sites	Number/county	0.883	0.107	0.017
Treatment, storage and disposal sites	Number/county	46.44	0.0013	0.0006
Intercept		--	2.76	0.867

NOTE: $R^2 = .3138$; $F = 601$; and $n = 46,004$. The dependent variable is the hourly wage, which is estimated by dividing 1979 annual earnings by the product of 1979 weeks worked and 1979 usual hours worked per week. The sample mean for the hourly wage is $8.04.

[a] The hedonic wage equation is estimated with the dependent variable (W) as $(W^{.1} - 1)/.1$ and the independent variables in the usual arithmetic units. The choice was based on a Box-Cox maximum likelihood search for functional form. The coefficients are linearized by multiplying each coefficient by $(W^{.9})$ where W is average hourly wage.
[b] The omitted occupation is service.

the effects on hourly wages of one-unit changes in each variable. For example, the schooling coefficient is .442. It indicates that an extra year of schooling increases the hourly wage by 44 cents, consistent with greater investments in human capital as schooling increases.

The experience coefficient is .310; the experience-squared coefficient is −.005, implying that male earnings rise at a decreasing rate over the career and eventually turn downward at about 31 years of experience. This same pattern is observed in Table 5 if hourly earnings are calculated for the various age groups shown. On-the-job training is accumulated toward the beginning of the career and eventually depreciates. For women, the gender–experience interactions must be taken into account to determine the experience–earnings profile. The negative gender–experience and positive gender–experience squared coefficients indicate that female earnings rise less quickly with experience and are flatter over the life cycle. Women appear to accumulate human capital more slowly than men because of intermittent work histories or discrimination in the provision of on-the-job training opportunities and promotions.

To determine the total estimated difference by gender, after controlling for other characteristics, one must account for the gender coefficient and the gender interactions. The gender coefficient is −.312, which is the estimated difference in hourly earnings between white, unmarried men and women with no labor market experience. The gender difference for nonwhites and married individuals at various levels of experience can be determined by summing across the appropriate estimated coefficients.

Table 3 shows that female-headed households with children had lower income than other types of households. The estimated earnings equation illustrates the adverse effect of children on female earnings. The gender–children coefficient is −.254; that is, each child reduces a woman's wage by 25 cents per hour on average, presumably by restricting the range of accessible jobs in the labor market.

Table 4 reveals that white household incomes exceed those of nonwhites. The estimates in Table 6 imply that nonwhite men earn approximately 96 cents per hour less than white men, but nonwhite women earn about 15 cents more (1.102 − .959) per hour than white women. Apparently the higher household income of whites does not exist because white women actually receive higher hourly wages than nonwhite women with similar characteristics.

The estimates in Table 6 also illustrate the existence of wage differences that are the result of differences in job characteristics.

The included occupational categories all earn more than the excluded service occupations category; the differences range from 13 cents per hour for farmers to $2.50 per hour for professionals and managers. Workers in industries that are more extensively unionized also receive higher wages.

The coefficients for the quality-of-life factors show the compensation that takes place in the labor market for differences across urban areas in climate, environmental quality, crime, and so forth. To obtain estimates of the full compensation for these amenity differences, the housing market must be taken into account (see the next section). But labor-market compensation alone is of some interest. According to the estimates for location-specific amenities, shown as the regression coefficients for the last 16 variables in Table 6, lower wages are received in sunny areas, a finding consistent with workers considering sunshine an amenity; higher wages are received in humid and windy areas. Workers also pay implicitly in the labor market for central-city locations, high teacher/pupil ratios, and greater levels of visibility. Compensation is provided for living with more crime and greater quantities of toxic waste.

Given the emphasis on the location of a worker's residence, the differences in the wages of workers who reside in the central city and those who reside outside it bear further examination. The central-city coefficient is −.454, which is the estimated effect of living in the central city when the effects of other characteristics are held constant. Thus, workers living in the central city pay for their location through lower wages.[3] But the observed characteristics of residents and nonresidents of central cities differ as well. Accordingly, one can estimate the implied difference in the wages of the typical central-city resident and the noncentral-city resident that is due to differences in characteristics, in addition to the "pure" effect of holding characteristics constant. Table 7 presents such estimates, which account for differences in characteristics. The total estimated wage difference produced by differences in characteristics is quite small (6 cents) compared to the pure effect (45 cents); however, some of the effects of differences in individual characteristics are quite sizable. For instance, central-city residents face much higher crime rates and earn higher wages as a result (33 cents per hour). Other noticeable differences include those attributable to race, gender, and

---

[3] An alternative explanation is that unmeasured characteristics of the workers living in central cities or of the jobs they hold lead to lower wages.

TABLE 7 Factors Explaining the Difference in Central and Noncentral-City Wages

Factor	Mean Values		Difference	Implied Wage Difference	Percentage of Predicted Difference
	Central City (n = 13,358)	Non-Central City (n = 32,646)			
Experience (years)	17.39	17.46	-0.07	-0.02	-4
Experience squared (years²)	523.24	510.12	13.12	-0.07	-13
Schooling (years)	12.70	12.79	-0.09	-0.04	-8
Race	0.281	0.447	0.18	-0.17	-34
Gender	0.465	0.100	0.02	-0.01	-1
Enrolled in school	0.158	0.146	0.01	-0.01	-1
Marital status	0.498	0.621	-0.12	-0.18	-35
Health limitations	0.053	0.046	0.01	-0.01	-2
Gender x experience	7.905	7.472	0.43	-0.06	-11
Gender x experience squared	235.800	215.30	20.50	0.05	9
Gender x race	0.138	0.049	0.09	0.10	19
Gender x marital status	0.206	0.250	-0.04	0.06	11
Gender x children	1.116	1.119	-0.003	0.00	0
Professional or managerial	0.225	0.235	-0.01	-0.02	-5
Technical or sales	0.336	0.337	-0.001	-0.00	-0
Farming	0.008	0.014	-0.01	-0.00	-0
Craft	0.097	0.119	-0.02	-0.03	-6
Operator or laborer	0.181	0.169	0.01	0.01	1
Industry unionization	22.72	23.61	-0.89	-0.03	-7
Precipitation (inches/year)	30.99	32.42	-1.43	0.02	4

Humidity (percentage)	67.96	68.39	-0.43	-0.00	-1
Heating degree days	4,034.00	4,445.00	-411.00	0.01	3
Cooling degree days	1,179.00	1,155.00	24.00	-0.01	-1
Windspeed (miles/hour)	8.67	8.99	-0.32	-0.03	-6
Sunshine (percent of days)	61.70	60.88	0.82	-0.01	-1
Coast	0.404	0.300	0.10	-0.00	-1
Violent crime	1,026.00	492.00	534.00	0.33	65
Teacher/pupil ratio	0.076	0.082	-0.006	0.03	6
Visibility (miles)	15.42	15.95	-0.53	0.00	0
Total suspended particulates	78.53	71.08	7.45	-0.02	4
Water effluent dischargers	1.874	1.366	0.51	-0.00	1
Landfill waste	733.9	372.6	361.3	0.03	7
Superfund sites	0.794	0.919	-0.125	-0.01	3
Treatment, storage, and disposal sites	64.80	38.92	25.88	0.03	7
Sum of non-central-city factors				-0.06	12
Central city location	1	0	1	-0.45	88
Total predicted wage difference[a]				-0.51	100

[a]This table shows how much of the predicted difference between average central-city wages and average non-central-city wages ($-0.51) can be attributed to various factors. The actual difference between the sample average central city wage ($8.34) and the sample average non-central-city wage ($7.92) is $0.42.

marital status, a pattern that reflects differences in the demographic makeup of the central-city and noncentral-city populations.

QUALITY-OF-LIFE COMPARISONS

Economic Status and Quality of Life

In the preceding sections, we presented an economic model of wage determination that explains differences in wages. Schooling, experience, occupation, unionization, and other job-related characteristics were shown to be determining factors of wage differences. In addition, we found that wages are also affected by sunshine, the crime rate, the teacher/pupil ratio, and other amenities of the area in which the job is located. Taken as a group these results demonstrate that workers pay attention to amenities and that amenity levels affect labor earnings and thus income.[4] The results suggest that we can infer from the relationship between wages and amenities the values people place on amenities. These quality-of-life values can then be used, along with traditional measures of economic status, to reflect more fully the well-being of urban residents in various locations. Our measure of quality of life thus augments traditional measures such as household money income.

Labor Markets, Housing Markets, and Quality of Life

Our approach to measuring the value of the quality of life in different locations is based on the notion that people choose the amenity "bundle" they desire by locating in areas with the amenities they want. They also pay for those amenities in observable markets. If the trade-off were solely between wages and amenities, one would expect workers who live in areas with high amenity levels to earn less. In other words, those workers pay for amenities through a corresponding reduction in wages. The difference in wages for similar workers in similar jobs but in different locations could be attributed to the difference in amenities. These wage differences would measure the value of the quality of life in different locations.

In Hoehn et al. (1987), we develop a more comprehensive frame-

---

[4]In their book on urban amenities, Diamond and Tolley (1982) conclude that amenities strongly shape economic activity. One impact is their effect on wages.

work that incorporates this notion of implicit markets for amenities. The framework is a hedonic model of interregional wages, rents, and amenity values. The model expands the principle of compensating differences to allow for trade-offs between housing prices (or rents) and amenities, as well as between wages and amenities. The results of the housing hedonic regression for the areas and amenities corresponding to those in the wage hedonic regression reported in Table 6 are shown in Table 8.

Housing prices are also affected by amenities factors such as sunshine, violent crime, and the teacher/pupil ratio. In the context of the housing market alone, one might expect to find a trade-off in the form of higher housing prices for more amenities. Our more comprehensive model, which allows for compensation in multiple markets, shows that the value of amenities is the sum of partial compensations in the housing and labor markets. For an amenity, even though the sum must be positive, it is not necessary that the housing price differential be positive and the wage differential be negative. The requirement is only that the sum of the housing price differential and the (negative of the) wage differential be positive. Because the model considers geographic city size, population city size, agglomeration effects, and the costs of production for firms, as well as residential location and utility for individuals, one differential may be negative as long as it is offset by the compensation implied by the other differential. The full amenity values, based on the impact of amenities on both wages and housing prices, are used to calculate a quality-of-life index for metropolitan areas.

Quality of Life in Metropolitan Areas

There are noticeable differences in amenities across urban areas, as there are in income and employment. The mean, standard deviation, minimum, and maximum for each of the 16 amenities in our model are shown in Table 9. Considerable variation is evident; for example, precipitation ranges from 4 to 67 inches per year, violent crime ranges from 63 to 1,650 crimes per 100,000 people per year, and the number of Superfund sites ranges from 0 to 9 per county.

We can sum the impacts on wages and housing prices to obtain the full amenity values after the linearized amenity coefficients in the wage and hedonic regressions are converted to annual values per household. The amenity values are calculated as follows:

TABLE 8 Regression Estimates of the Hedonic Housing Expenditure Equation, 1980

Independent Variable	Units	Mean	Linearized Coefficient[a]	Linearized Standard Error
Units at address		2.667	1.375	1.533
Age of structure	Years	23.73	-2.363	0.099
Height of structure	Stories	2.433	16.52	1.663
Rooms		5.395	40.33	0.921
Bedrooms		3.510	6.485	1.523
Bathrooms		1.486	119.80	2.174
Condominium	Yes=1, no=0	0.032	-84.82	8.011
Central Air	Yes=1, no=0	0.313	55.68	2.877
Sewer	Yes=1, no=0	0.886	10.84	3.547
Lot larger than an acre	Yes=1, no=0	0.062	78.80	4.734
Renter	Yes=1, no=0	0.410	-58.64	12.35
Renter x unit		1.992	-2.580	1.587
Renter x age		9.964	0.899	0.144
Renter x height		1.220	-17.19	1.740
Renter x rooms		1.622	-7.189	1.932
Renter x bedrooms		1.112	2.014	3.070
Renter x bathrooms		0.479	-30.85	4.045
Renter x condominium		0.008	126.87	12.76
Renter x central Air		0.130	50.95	4.592
Renter x sewer		0.395	-39.19	8.468
Renter x acre lot		0.014	-95.75	9.167
Precipitation	Inches/year	32.02	-1.047	0.149

Humidity	Percentage	68.22	-2.127	0.251
Heating degree days	Degree days/year	4,223.0	-0.014	0.001
Cooling degree days	Degree days/year	1,185.0	-0.076	0.002
Windspeed	Miles/hour	8.872	11.88	0.867
Sunshine	Percentage of days	61.36	2.135	0.235
Coast	Yes=1, no=0	0.345	32.52	2.469
Central city	Yes=1, no=0	0.329	-40.75	2.535
Violent crime	Crimes/100,000 pop./year	681.60	0.043	0.003
Teacher/pupil ratio		0.080	635.30	71.58
Visibility	Miles	15.66	-0.831	0.110
Total suspended particulates	Micrograms/cubic meter	73.72	-0.535	0.058
Water effluent dischargers	Number/county	1.564	-7.458	0.461
Landfill Waste	Hundred million metric tons/county	467.20	0.010	0.001
Superfund sites	Number/county	0.858	13.43	0.693
Treatment, storage and disposal sites	Number/county	47.59	0.218	0.693
Intercept		--	1,256.0	33.80

NOTE: $R^2 = .6624$; $F = 1823$; and $n = 34,414$. The dependent variable is the monthly housing expenditures. The sample mean of monthly housing expenditures is $462.93.

[a] The hedonic housing expenditure equation is estimated with the dependent variable (p) as (p^2-1)/.2 and the independent variables in the usual arithmetic units. The choice was based on a Box-Cox maximum likelihood search for functional form. The Box-Cox coefficients are linearized by multiplying each coefficient by ($p^{.8}$) where p is average housing expenditure.

TABLE 9 Amenity Values and Variation in Amenities Across Metropolitan Areas

Amenity (unit)	Mean	Standard Deviation	Minimum	Maximum	Amenity Value[a]
Precipitation (inches/year)	34.51	13.38	3.76	67.00	23.50
Humidity (percent)	69.01	6.75	31.50	78.25	-43.42
Heating degree days (degree days/year)	4,469.00	2,223.00	206.00	9,756.00	-0.08
Cooling degree days (degree days/year)	1,342.00	976.00	76.00	4,095.00	-0.36
Windspeed (miles/hour)	8.98	1.47	6.10	12.40	-97.51
Sunshine (percent)	60.71	7.96	45.00	86.00	48.52
Coast (1 if on coast)	0.249	0.428	0.000	1.000	467.72
Central city (1 if in city)	0.188	0.261	0.000	1.000	645.02
Violent crime (crimes/100,000 pop./year)	535.80	268.60	62.80	1,650.30	-1.03
Teacher/pupil ratio	0.084	0.017	0.035	0.211	21,250
Visibility (miles)	18.14	15.36	8.00	80.00	-3.41
Total suspended particulates (micrograms/cubic meter)	69.5	18.9	36.0	166.30	-0.36
Water effluent dischargers (number/county)	1.02	1.80	0.00	11.00	-76.68
Landfill waste (hundred million metric tons/county)	132.3	631.40	0.0	5,608.80	-0.11
Superfund sites (sites/county)	0.566	1.158	0.000	9.000	106.07
Treatment, storage and disposal sites (sites/county)	15.20	26.0	0.0	230.00	-0.58
Quality-of-life index[b] (1980 $/year/household)	$270.00	$623.00	-$1,539.00	$3,289.00	--

[a]Dollars per unit per household per year.
[b]The values given here are for the 185 metropolitan areas included in our sample.

$$AV_i = (HC_i)(12) - (WC_i)(1.54)(37.85)(42.79),$$

where AV_i is the amenity value for amenity i, HC_i is the linearized housing coefficient, 12 is the number of months per year, WC_i is the linearized wage coefficient, and 1.54, 37.85, and 42.79 are the sample means for workers per household, hours per week, and weeks per year, respectively. The marginal amenity values for each amenity are shown in the last column of Table 9. The interpretation is that people value a change in an amenity at the amount shown. For example, a reduction in violent crime from 536 to 535 crimes per 100,000 people per year is valued at $1.03 per household per year.

The aggregate value of all amenities in an urban area forms the quality-of-life index (QOLI). The index values are calculated as follows:

$$\text{QOLI}_j = \sum_{i=1}^{16} AV_i S_{ij} \quad j = 1, \ldots, m,$$

where QOLI_j is the quality-of-life index for area j, AV_i is the amenity value for amenity i, S_{ij} is the quantity of amenity i in area j, and m is the number of areas being ranked. Quality-of-life index values for 24 selected large metropolitan areas are shown in Table 10. All of the metropolitan areas for which the traditional measures of economic status were given in Table 1 are included, except for Boston and Miami, which were excluded because of incomplete data. The values are taken from a study by Berger et al. (1987) that estimates the quality of life for 185 metropolitan areas.

Given that our bundle of climatic, urban, and environmental amenities represents quality of life, the QOLI measures the value of differences in quality of life among urban areas. The difference between the quality of life in Denver and the quality of life in St. Louis is valued at $2,188 (1,197.96 + 990.10) per year per household. This value is approximately 10 percent of the average household income for the metropolitan areas covered in Table 1.

Table 11 reports the rankings of the 24 large metropolitan areas based on quality of life, household income, poverty rate, and unemployment rate. There is no strong relationship between quality of life and any of the other measures. In fact, quality-of-life considerations can change our comparisons of areas based on traditional economic measures. In Table 12, the QOLI is added to household income to produce a quality-of-life adjusted household income for the 24 metropolitan areas included in Table 10. Although the rankings

TABLE 10   Quality-of-Life Index Values for Large Metropolitan Areas

Metropolitan Area[a] (1980 SMSAs)	Quality-of-Life Index (1979 dollars)[b]
Denver-Boulder, Colo.	1,197.96
San Diego, Calif.	980.83
Phoenix, Ariz.	870.69
Anaheim-Santa Ana-Garden Grove, Calif.	803.49
Nassau-Suffolk, N.Y.	687.80
Los Angeles-Long Beach, Calif.	667.64
Tampa-St. Petersburg, Fla.	191.57
San Francisco-Oakland, Calif.	139.55
Riverside-San Bernardino-Ontario, Calif.	135.46
Philadelphia, Pa.-N.J.	9.21
Washington, D.C.-Md.-Va.	5.08
Newark, N.J.	-11.48
Atlanta, Ga.	-25.74
Seattle-Everett, Wash.	-124.18
Cleveland, Ohio	-190.62
Pittsburgh, Pa.	-330.90
New York, N.Y.-N.J.	-369.20
Minneapolis-St. Paul, Minn.-Wis.	-372.20
Dallas-Fort Worth, Tex.	-399.70
Baltimore, Md.	-422.70
Chicago, Ill.	-822.80
Houston, Tex.	-948.40
Detroit, Mich.	-968.00
St. Louis, Mo.-Ill.	-990.10

[a]Listed are 24 standard metropolitan statistical areas (SMSAs) with a 1980 population exceeding 1.5 million. The 1980 definition of an SMSA is used. Boston, Mass., and Miami, Fla., are omitted because sufficient data were not available to estimate the parameters for the quality-of-life index (QOLI). The mean QOLI for the 24 SMSAs is -11.95.
[b]The differences in index values represent the annual premiums households are willing to pay for differences in amenities in different metropolitan areas. The values reported are taken from a study by Berger et al. (1987) that ranks 185 metropolitan areas by quality of life.

produced by household income and quality-of-life adjusted household income are similar, there are noticeable differences for cities with extreme QOLI values. For instance, Denver-Boulder has the 11th highest household income, but the 4th highest QOLI-adjusted household income because of its high quality of life. San Diego and Phoenix also move up the ladder from 18th and 19th to 13th and 14th, respectively, after adjusting for their QOLI values. On the other hand, Detroit and St. Louis drop from 5th and 16th to 10th

TABLE 11 Comparisons of Rankings of Metropolitan Areas by Alternative
Measures of Economic Status

Metropolitan Area (1980 SMSAs)	Quality of Life (ranked highest to lowest)	Household Income (ranked highest to lowest)	Poverty Rate (ranked lowest to highest)	Unemployment Rate (ranked lowest to highest)
Denver-Boulder, Colo.	1	11	7	6
San Diego, Calif.	2	18	12	7
Phoenix, Ariz.	3	19	9	12
Anaheim-Santa Ana-Garden Grove, Calif.	4	2	1	1
Nassau-Suffolk, N.Y.	5	3	3	10
Los Angeles-Long Beach, Calif.	6	13	20	12
Tampa-St. Petersburg, Fla.	7	24	21	9
San Francisco-Oakland, Calif.	8	7	12	10
Riverside-San Bernardino-Ontario, Calif.	9	22	18	23
Philadelphia, Pa.-N.J.	10	21	22	22
Washington, D.C.-Md.-Va.	11	1	4	4
Newark, N.J.	12	6	15	17
Atlanta, Ga.	13	17	23	8
Seattle-Everett, Wash.	14	8	2	18
Cleveland, Ohio	15	14	6	20
Pittsburgh, Pa.	16	20	9	21
New York, N.Y.-N.J.	17	23	24	16
Minneapolis-St. Paul, Minn.-Wis.	18	9	5	4
Dallas-Ft. Worth, Tex.	19	15	17	1
Baltimore, Md.	20	12	19	14
Chicago, Ill.	21	10	16	15
Houston, Tex.	22	4	12	1
Detroit, Mich.	23	5	7	24
St. Louis, Mo.-Ill.	24	16	11	19

NOTE: SMSAs = standard metropolitan statistical areas.

and 20th, respectively, after adjusting their household incomes for
low measured quality-of-life values.

Similar quality-of-life adjusted household incomes could be calculated for those living in the central city or suburbs, in large or small
metropolitan areas, or outside metropolitan areas. As an illustration,
the household income figures in Table 2 for those living in metropolitan areas with populations greater or less than 1.5 million can be
adjusted using QOLI figures from Table 10 and the study by Berger
et al. (1987). The average household income of those living in large
(greater than 1.5 million population) metropolitan areas is $21,846,
whereas for small (less than 1.5 million population) metropolitan
areas it is $19,574. The average QOLI for large metropolitan areas
is −$12; for small areas, it is $308, thus producing quality-of-life
adjusted household incomes of $21,834 in large areas and $19,882 in

small areas. On average, the quality-of-life value is higher in small areas, and although this offsets somewhat the income advantage of large areas, quality-of-life adjusted income is still higher in large metropolitan areas.

Finally, in Table 13 we present rank correlations between the alternative measures of economic status. The quality-of-life index is not highly correlated with any of the alternative measures of economic status, including quality-of-life income. Quality-of-life adjusted income and household income are highly correlated as expected. The poverty and unemployment rates are more highly correlated with quality-of-life adjusted income than with unadjusted income. From the observed correlations, it is apparent that quality of life adds another dimension to comparisons of the economic well-being of urban residents.

TABLE 12 Comparison of Metropolitan Areas Based on Income and Quality of Life

Metropolitan Area	Household Income, 1979 ($)	QOLI, 1979 ($)	QOLI + Household Income, 1979 ($)
Washington, D.C.-Md.-Va.	27,295	5	27,300
Anaheim-Santa Ana-Garden Grove, Calif.	26,434	803	27,237
Nassau-Suffolk, N.Y.	25,997	688	26,685
Denver-Boulder, Colo.	22,664	1,198	23,862
Houston, Tex.	24,607	-948	23,659
San Francisco-Oakland, Calif.	23,151	140	23,291
Newark, N.J.	23,251	-11	23,240
Seattle-Everett, Wash.	23,075	-124	22,951
Minneapolis-St. Paul, Minn-Wis.	23,032	-372	22,660
Detroit, Mich.	23,288	-968	22,320
Los Angeles-Long Beach, Calif.	21,639	668	22,307
Chicago, Ill.	23,017	-823	22,194
San Diego, Calif.	21,114	981	22,095
Phoenix, Ariz.	20,874	871	21,745
Cleveland, Ohio	21,461	-191	21,270
Baltimore, Md.	21,657	-423	21,234
Atlanta, Ga.	21,189	-26	21,163
Dallas-Ft. Worth, Tex.	21,318	-400	20,918
Philadelphia, Pa.-N.J.	20,239	9	20,248
St. Louis, Mo.-Ill.	21,225	-990	20,235
Pittsburgh, Pa.	20,275	-331	19,944
Riverside-San Bernardino-Ontario, Calif.	19,504	135	19,639
New York, N.Y.-N.J.	19,142	-369	18,773
Tampa-St. Petersburg, Fla.	16,812	192	17,004

NOTE: QOLI = quality-of-life index.

TABLE 13 Rank Correlations of Rankings by Alternative Measures of Economic Status

Measure	Quality of Life	Household Income	Poverty Rate	Unemploy- ment Rate	Quality- of-Life Adjusted Income
Quality of life	--	-.080	.119	.262	.253
Household income		--	.654	.357	.921
Poverty rate			--	.162	.673
Unemployment rate				--	.469
Quality-of-life adjusted income					--

CONCLUSIONS

The focus of this paper has been on the economic well-being of urban residents. We have compared the economic status of people living in large central cities to that of people living in suburbs, small metropolitan areas, and rural areas. Data from the 1980 Census of Population and Housing facilitated an in-depth inquiry for various subnational categories and groups, but it precluded a longitudinal study that might identify trends. The use of several measures of well-being somewhat mitigates the shortcomings of each, but such measures as annual household income fail to reflect relevant noncash transfers, wealth, and quality of life. In this paper, we develop a methodology to adjust for differences in quality of life.

Using the 1980 Census, we compute for metropolitan areas with more than 1.5 million residents the average household income, poverty rate, unemployment rate, employment rate, and manufacturing employment share. These measures range from $16,812 to $27,295, from 5.1 percent to 15.8 percent, from 3.2 percent to 11.6 percent, from 49.2 percent to 69.6 percent, and from 5.1 percent to 30.1 percent, respectively. The findings were several: (1) population is not correlated with any of the other measures; (2) the poverty rate and the unemployment rate are not significantly correlated; and (3) the manufacturing employment share of an area and its unemployment rate are positively correlated.

Further computations were made for traditional measures by population size of area of residence and by demographic group. Nationally, suburbanites in large metropolitan areas are more affluent than residents of large central cities, small metropolitan areas (less than 1.5 million population), or rural areas, and this dominance pervades all measures and groups. Which area's residents are the poorest, according to traditional measures, depends on the region being considered. Central-city residents are the poorest group in the Northeast and Midwest, but rural residents are the poorest in the South and West. Poverty is not peculiar to New York or Detroit inner-city neighborhoods. Among white, black, and Hispanic married-couple households, those living in rural areas are the least affluent. The same is true among black and Hispanic households headed by women. When grouped by age, central-city residents who are 25 to 39 years of age are the poorest of all age groups, but for those people over 40 years of age, rural residents are again the poorest.

Analysis based on a hedonic framework of wage determination demonstrates that differences in a major source of income—wages— can be explained by observable differences in the characteristics of workers, jobs, and job locations. For example, the higher central-city crime rate is a factor that has increased wages in the central city relative to wages outside it. On average, however, central-city residents earn less. Indeed, the crime rate and other amenity factors induce compensating differences in wages across urban areas and also compensating differences in housing prices. The compensating differences can be combined to obtain a full amenity value that, in turn, can be used to create a quality-of-life index. Comparisons across large metropolitan areas show that rankings based on quality of life are not correlated with rankings based on traditional measures of well-being. The quality-of-life premium is added to household income for each of the large metropolitan areas to obtain a quality-of-life adjusted income. The adjustment changes the ranking for areas with extremely high or extremely low quality-of-life values. The adjustment also illustrates how traditional measures can be modified to reflect well-being more comprehensively.

REFERENCES

Becker, Gary S.
   1975   *Human Capital*, 2d ed. Chicago: University of Chicago Press.
Berger, Mark C., Glenn C. Blomquist, and Werner Waldner
   1987   A revealed-preference ranking of quality of life for metropolitan areas.
          Social Science Quarterly 68(Dec.):761–778.
Bureau of the Census
   1983a *Census of Population, 1980. General Population Characteristics: United
          States Summary* (PC80-1-B1). Washington, D.C.: U.S. Department of
          Commerce.

1983b *Census of Population and Housing, 1980*: Public-Use Microdata Sample A. Washington, D.C.: U.S. Department of Commerce.

1984 *Statistical Abstract of the United States: 1985*. 105th ed. Washington, D.C.: U.S. Department of Commerce.

Danziger, Sheldon, Robert Haveman, and Robert Plotnick

1981 How income transfer programs affect work, savings, and the income distribution: A critical review. *Journal of Economic Literature* 19:975–1028.

Diamond, Douglas B., and George S. Tolley, eds.

1982 *The Economics of Urban Amenities*. New York: Academic Press.

Hoehn, John P., Mark C. Berger, and Glenn C. Blomquist

1987 A hedonic model of interregional wages, rents, and amenity values. *Journal of Regional Science* 27:605–620.

Mills, Edwin S., and Bruce W. Hamilton

1984 *Urban Economics*, 3rd ed. Glenview, Ill.: Scott, Foresman & Co.

Mincer, Jacob

1974 *Schooling, Experience, and Earnings*. New York: National Bureau of Economic Research.

Smith, Robert S.

1979 Compensating wage differentials and public policy: A review. *Industrial and Labor Relations Review* 32:339–352.

Smith, V. Kerry

1983 The role of site and job characteristics in hedonic wage models. *Journal of Urban Economics* 13:296–321.

Tolley, George S., Philip E. Graves, and John L. Gardner

1979 *Urban Growth in a Market Economy*. New York: Academic Press.

Family Structure, Poverty, and the Underclass

SARA MCLANAHAN, IRWIN GARFINKEL, and
DOROTHY WATSON

INTRODUCTION AND CONCLUSIONS

Family structure and household composition have changed dramatically during the past two decades. Young adults are more likely to live apart from their parents today than they were 20 years ago, the aged are less likely to live with relatives, and children are more likely to live in households headed by single women (Bureau of the Census, 1984). Of all these changes, the growth of mother-only families is perhaps the most striking and has certainly stimulated the most concern. This concern arises in part because of the economic insecurity of these families—nearly half are poor, and most of these poor families are dependent on welfare—and in part because mother-only families may be linked to the growth of an underclass. Over half of all children born today will spend some time in a mother-only family, which means that this family form is playing a major role in shaping the next generation of Americans (Bumpass, 1984).

This paper begins by describing the increase in the number of families headed by single women over the past several decades. We examine both overall trends and trends in central cities to determine whether the change in family structure is more or less prominent in urban areas than in suburban and nonmetropolitan areas. Following the description of trends, we discuss the causes of the growth in such families, including the effects of increases in income transfer programs and of changes in men's and women's employment opportunities. We conclude that for whites the major cause of growth has been the increase in women's employment opportunities; for blacks it has been the decline in male employment. Increases in welfare benefits accounted for about 10 to 15 percent of the growth in mother-only families between 1960 and 1975.

Some analysts have equated the growth of families headed by women with the "feminization of poverty" and the emergence of an "underclass." In the second section of the paper, we examine these claims and attempt to clarify the relationships among single motherhood, poverty, and economic dependence. We conclude that the feminization of poverty is not a particularly useful concept for understanding the economic status of mother-only families inasmuch as it implies an increase in poverty during a time when rates actually declined. Moreover, a large proportion of mother-only families are not poor, even though they may have experienced large drops in income as a consequence of marital disruption. This is not to say that poverty is not a serious problem. Mother-only families are more likely to be poor than any other major demographic group, and they stay poor longer than other groups.

An empirical analysis of the sources of income for mother-only families indicates that a major cause of poverty is the low earnings of single mothers. Despite their status as family head, single mothers earn an average income that is between 30 and 40 percent of the earnings of married fathers. The absence of child support from noncustodial parents and low welfare benefits in most states also contribute to income insecurity and poverty.

Have mother-only families contributed to the growth of an underclass? This question is addressed in the third section of the paper. Although the term *underclass* has been used in a variety of ways, we define it as a group that is both persistently detached from the legitimate work force and socially isolated. Persistence must include intergenerational persistence as well as a long-term condition for the individual.

We find that only a small minority of white mother-only families fits any of the criteria for an underclass. The picture for blacks is somewhat cloudier. A substantial proportion of black single mothers exhibit persistent nonattachment to the labor force as measured by long-term welfare dependence, and a substantial proportion of their daughters become single mothers and dependent on welfare. On the other hand, only a small proportion of the black children living in mother-only families are socially isolated in severely poor urban black neighborhoods. Furthermore, although this proportion increased during the 1970s, it is ironic that the deteriorating condition of poor black neighborhoods resulted from economic and social gains made by the black population in general. On balance, we conclude that the growth of mother-only families is not associated with the growth of an underclass among whites, but it may be among some blacks. The extent to which the growth of a black underclass threatens to undermine the more general progress of blacks in America is worthy of further research.

Government has always played some role in reducing the poverty and economic insecurity of mother-only families. As a consequence, policy-makers have continually faced and sought to resolve the dilemma over whether to give priority to reducing the poverty of single mothers or to reducing their prevalence and dependence. In the last section of the paper, we examine three recent developments in American federal income transfer policy and their effect on the economic well-being, self-reliance, and prevalence of mother-only families. The three policies are: (1) the reduction in the real value of transfer benefits, (2) the increase in the public enforcement of private child-support obligations, and (3) the increase in the public enforcement of work requirements for welfare recipients.

We find that the falling level of benefits for single mothers brought about by a combination of inflation and budget cuts has had a substantial impact on the extent of their welfare dependence and only a trivial impact on prevalence. The work requirement legislation has the potential to increase the earnings of single mothers if training is provided and jobs are available or guaranteed. It has not yet been implemented on a large scale, however, and questions remain as to whether its potential will ever be realized. Child-support legislation, as currently enforced, will probably not have a big impact on poverty, welfare dependence, or prevalence. It does have the potential to substantially reduce poverty and dependence if higher awards are secured and enforced in many more cases.

PREVALENCE, GROWTH, AND CAUSES OF MOTHER-ONLY FAMILIES

In 1983 there were over 5.7 million families headed by single mothers in the United States, representing about 19 percent of all families (Bureau of the Census, 1984). Among whites, these families accounted for 14.3 percent of all families; among blacks, for about 48 percent. Altogether, mother-only families were fairly evenly distributed across residential areas: about 42 percent lived in central cities, 32 percent lived in surrounding suburbs, and the remaining 27 percent lived in nonmetropolitan areas. The concentration among blacks was much greater, however, with about 64 percent living in central cities compared with 18 percent each in suburban and nonmetropolitan areas. For blacks, then, the experiences (and problems) of mother-only families are closely related to the experiences of urban life.

These figures on prevalence are based on cross-sectional data and offer only a snapshot of the proportion of families headed by single mothers at one point in time. This view understates the proportion of women and children who will ever live in a mother-only family because it misses all families in which the mother has remarried (or the children have grown and gone) and all families in which a marital disruption (or premarital birth) has not yet occurred. Demographers estimate that about 42 percent of the white children and about 84 percent of the black children born in the late 1970s will live for some time with a single mother before they reach the age of 18. The median duration in a mother-only family is 6 years for children of formerly married mothers and even longer for children born to never-married mothers (Bumpass, 1984; Hofferth, 1985).

Trends in the proportion of families headed by single women are depicted in Figure 1 for 1940–1983. Trends for blacks and whites are quite similar, although single motherhood has always been more common among blacks. For whites, the proportion of mother-only families grew 37 percent during the 1960s and 40 percent during the 1970s; for blacks, the proportions were 37 percent and 35 percent, respectively. Figure 1 also presents the trends since 1960 for black and white families living in central cities. The upper lines for each group show that the trend in central cities tends to parallel that of the entire group, although the absolute level is higher in the former. During the 1970s, however, the trend lines for both races appear to rise faster in central cities than in the general population.

Numerous explanations have been put forward to account for the growth of families headed by single mothers during the past few decades, and there is a vast literature of empirical studies that attempt to test many of these arguments. In the following sections, we briefly review and evaluate three major explanations for the increases in single motherhood: (1) increases in welfare benefits, (2)

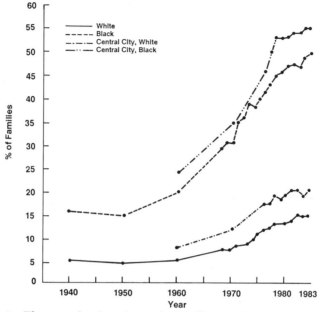

FIGURE 1   The growth of mother-only families, 1940–1983.   SOURCE: Garfinkel and McLanahan (1986).

increases in women's employment opportunities and marital conflict, and (3) declines in men's employment opportunities, especially those of young black men.

Increases in Welfare Benefits

Both common sense and economic theory suggest that raising public benefits to single mothers and their children will increase the number of mother-only families. Higher benefits increase the financial ability of single mothers to establish their own households and thereby to become household heads. They enable a single mother to choose to keep her baby or have the baby adopted rather than have an abortion. Higher benefits also increase the ability of poor married mothers to choose divorce rather than remain in an undesirable relationship. In short, increases in benefits should increase the prevalence of single motherhood, all else being equal. Neither economic theory nor common sense, however, tells us how big any of these effects will be.

The relationship between welfare and single motherhood has

been examined in numerous studies, including time-series analyses, longitudinal studies, and cross-sectional comparisons. Some researchers have compared welfare benefits across states with the proportion or "stock" of families headed by women; others have compared benefit levels with the "flows in and out" of single motherhood—for example, marital disruption and remarriage rates, illegitimacy rates, and the propensity to establish independent households.

Not surprisingly, studies that examine the correlation between welfare benefits and the stock of mother-only families are more likely to find effects than are studies that examine the effects of benefit levels on particular flows in and out of single motherhood. Studies of stocks conducted by Honig (1973), by Ross and Sawhill (1975), and most recently by Danziger and his colleagues (1982) all find an association of benefit levels with the number of female-headed households. Studies of flows, on the other hand, suggest that the association is due primarily to effects on living arrangements and rates of remarriage (Cherlin, 1976; Hoffman and Holmes, 1976; Hutchens, 1969; Moore and Waite, 1976). In response to the Honig study, Cutwright and Madras (1976) demonstrated that benefit levels were associated with the proportion of single mothers who head their own households but not with the percentage of women who were divorced or separated.

A more recent study by Ellwood and Bane (1984) confirmed these findings. After examining the effect of benefit levels on living arrangements, marital breakup, and premarital births, they concluded that the major consequence of welfare is that it allows single mothers to establish independent households. Furthermore, Ellwood and Bane also found that benefit levels are related to the proportion of divorced and separated mothers in the population but not to divorce rates. These results are consistent with an earlier finding by Hutchens (1969) and suggest that welfare affects the "flow out" of female headship (remarriage) but not the "flow in" (divorce).

The empirical studies can be used to estimate the effects of increases in welfare benefits on the prevalence of single mothers. Because some of the studies find no effect, a lower-bound estimate would be that the increase in benefits had no effect on prevalence between 1960 and 1975. If we use the highest estimate in the literature—Honig's estimate for blacks in 1960—we estimate that the 1960–1975 increase in welfare led to a 42 percent increase in single motherhood.

In our judgment, however, the studies by Ellwood and Bane (1984) and by Danziger and his colleagues (1982) provide the most reliable sources from which to estimate the effect of increased government benefits on the formation of mother-only families: the Ellwood and Bane study because it is comprehensive and distinguishes between effects on prevalence and effects on living arrangements, and the Danziger study because it models the effects of alternative opportunities. Using these studies, we estimate that the growth in benefits increased the prevalence of single motherhood by between 9 percent and 14 percent from 1960 to 1975. In view of the fact that the prevalence increased approximately 100 percent during this period, increases in welfare benefits account for no more than one-seventh of the overall growth. In short, although increased benefits may have led to a measurable increase in prevalence, they account for only a small portion of the total growth in mother-only families.[1]

That the increase in government benefits played only a small role in the overall growth in families headed by single women does not mean that the effects of benefits on single motherhood should be ignored. It seems reasonable to assume that welfare benefits played little or no role in the marital decisions of women in the top half of the income distribution. If so, welfare must have played a bigger role in the decisions of those in the lower half. Thus, if the growth in benefits accounted for 15 percent of the total growth in single motherhood, it could possibly account for 30 percent of the growth within the bottom part of the income distribution. Moreover, as documented later in this paper, women who have grown up in mother-only families are more likely to become single parents themselves, illustrating how the effects can mushroom over time. Finally, the effects of increased welfare benefits on living arrangements are a cause for concern because there is some evidence that children in families with

---

[1] The much publicized results from the Seattle-Denver income maintenance experiment (SIME/DIME) have been interpreted to show that the effect of welfare benefits on divorce is much greater than the foregoing summary indicates (Groeneveld et al., 1983). The SIME/DIME results, however, say nothing about the effects of raising or lowering the welfare benefits available to single mothers. The experiment was implemented in a world that already had a welfare system, and families in both the experimental and control groups retained whatever eligibility they would have had in the absence of the experiment. Many single mothers in the control group and some in the experimental group received welfare. Consequently, whatever effect the experiment had on behavior, it cannot be attributed to the availability of additional income to women who became single heads of households. If divorce rates were higher in the experimental groups, this was due to something about the treatment other than an "independence" effect.

other adults do better than children in families in which the mother is the only adult.

Changes in Women's Employment

Many people believe that the growth of mother-only families is due to greater participation in the labor force by women and, in particular, by married women with children. Some point to an "independence effect" that arises from increases in women's employment opportunities; others emphasize the "role conflict" that accompanies the renegotiation of the traditional roles of husband and wife. Clearly, employment provides women with an alternative means of gaining financial security and thus competes with marriage and economic dependence on husbands. It also competes with traditional ideas about husband/wife roles by reducing the amount of time available for women to spend on housework and child care.

The body of published empirical research in this area is nearly as large as the literature on welfare. It is also based on a variety of approaches, including analyses of time series, aggregate-level data, and survey data. For example, Preston and Richards (1975) examined the 100 largest standard metropolitan statistical areas (SMSAs) in the United States in 1960 and found that job opportunities, women's earnings, and unemployment were all good predictors of the marital status of women in the population. These researchers concluded that changes in job opportunities for men and women between 1960 and 1970 could account for about half of the decline in marriage during this period, or about half of the increase in single women. In her replication of the Preston and Richards study, however, White (1981) did not find a similar relationship for blacks.

Another way to look at the question is to follow married women over time to see if working mothers are more likely to divorce and less likely to remarry than nonworking mothers. Several studies based on data from the Michigan Panel Study of Income Dynamics (PSID) and the National Longitudinal Survey of Labor Market Experience (NLS) have found that married women who work or who have higher earnings potential are more likely to divorce than more dependent women. Ross and Sawhill (1975) found that, controlling for husband's income and other factors, an increase of $1,000 in a wife's earnings was associated with a 7 percent increase in separation rates. Similarly, Cherlin (1976) found that a higher ratio of wife's earnings capacity to husband's earnings was a strong predictor of marital disruption. Taken together, these studies indicate that the increase in economic opportunities for women can account for a substantial part of the increase in single motherhood among whites. For black women, the change in employment is much smaller, and the overall effect appears to be much weaker.

Changes in Men's Employment

The most widely discussed hypothesis concerning male employment comes from Moynihan (1965), who argued in the early 1960s that unemployment among black men was causing a breakdown of the black family. Moynihan's graphs for male unemployment rates and single motherhood rates showed a close relationship throughout the 1950s and early 1960s. During the late 1960s, however, the trends diverged. Extending Moynihan's time series into the 1970s, we find that both unemployment and single motherhood continue to rise, but overall the relationship is not as close as during the 1950s. In a time-series analysis (using lagged variables) for the the post-World War II period, South (1985) found a statistically significant relationship between unemployment rates and divorce rates. He also found a positive and statistically significant effect of women's employment on divorce.

Additional evidence for an effect of male unemployment on single motherhood comes from microlevel analyses of longitudinal and cross-sectional surveys. Using data from the PSID, several researchers found that the probability of marital disruption is greater for families in which the husband has been unemployed (Hoffman and Holmes, 1976; Ross and Sawhill, 1975). Cherlin (1976) and Moore and Waite (1976), in separate studies based on the NLS, found that the husband's working less than full-time as well as earning low wages increased the probability of marital disruption.

A problem with these studies is that a third factor such as alcoholism may be leading to both unemployment (or low wages) and divorce. Presumably, however, there is less chance of such an omitted variable being correlated with aggregate variations in unemployment rates across cities. Again, numerous aggregate-level studies have found a relationship between high unemployment rates and low wages on the one hand and high single motherhood and divorce rates on the other hand (Honig, 1973; Minarik and Goldfarb, 1976; Ross and Sawhill, 1975).

The most recent version of the male employment argument has

been proposed by William Julius Wilson and his colleagues (Aponte et al., 1985; Darity and Myers, 1983; Wilson, 1985b; Wilson and Aponte, 1985; Wilson and Neckerman, 1986). Like Moynihan, these researchers focus on black families and attribute the recent growth of mother-only families to increases in joblessness among black men. Their indicator, the "male marriageable pool index," is the ratio of employed men per 100 women of similar age in the population. It is somewhat broader than indicators used by previous researchers because it takes into account not only unemployment but also participation in the labor force and sex differences in mortality and incarceration rates (Wilson and Neckerman, 1986).

Wilson points out that declines in the pool of marriageable black men between 1960 and 1980 were greatest in the North Central and Northeast regions of the country. These regions also showed the greatest growth in mother-only families. Wilson and his colleagues note that declines in employment among blacks were due initially to a shift in unskilled jobs from the South to the North and later to a loss of jobs in central cities in the North where blacks are highly concentrated.[2] For example, during the 1970s, the number of unskilled jobs declined by more than 30 percent in some cities (e.g., New York, Philadelphia, and Baltimore). Although the loss of low-skilled jobs in these areas was offset somewhat by an increase in higher-paying jobs, this shift worked to the disadvantage of black males, who are less likely to have a high-school degree (Kasarda, 1985). Given that the increase in single motherhood has been especially pronounced among black women who have low levels of education— women whom we would have expected to marry men in low-skilled jobs—the researchers conclude that the loss of jobs in the central cities is a major factor in the growth of mother-only families.

THE FEMINIZATION OF POVERTY

One of the most serious problems facing mother-only families is

---

[2]The West, which accounts for only 9 percent of the total black population, did not fit the pattern. The marriageable pool of men in the West remained fairly constant while the number of female-headed families increased substantially. Wilson and Neckerman (1986) attribute this anomaly to the fact that black female heads of families in the West are more likely than are blacks in other parts of the country to be middle class and to behave more like whites. Thus, they should be expected to be more like whites in that they will respond to increases in opportunities for women rather than to declines in opportunities for men.

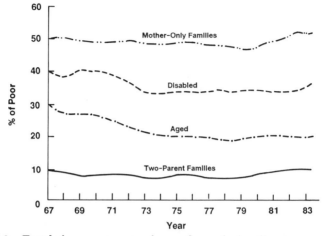

FIGURE 2   Trends in poverty rates for mother-only families, two-parent families, persons over 65, and disabled persons, 1967–1983. SOURCE: Ross (1984).

poverty. Although not all of these families are poor, they face a much
higher risk of poverty than other demographic groups. Roughly one
out of two single mothers is poor, according to the official government
definition of poverty. Figure 2 shows trends in the prevalence of
poverty for mother-only families, two-parent families, aged persons,
and disabled persons for 1967–1983. The figures include income
from cash transfer programs such as Aid to Families with Dependent
Children (AFDC), Social Security, and Disability Insurance (Ross,
1984). Women and children in mother-only families are the poorest
of all these groups, and the gap has been widening. In relation to
the elderly and the disabled, their economic position has declined
steadily during the past two decades. This does not mean that their
absolute income has deteriorated, however. In fact, the poverty rate
of those living in mother-only families actually declined until the late
1970s, only to rise again after 1978.

If the economic status of mother-only families has not declined,
why do we observe what some have called the "feminization of
poverty"? The concept was introduced in 1978 by Diana Pearce
(1978) and refers to the period between 1967 and 1978 when the proportion of the poor living in mother-only households was increasing.
In 1967, 21.4 percent of the non-aged poor were living in households
headed by single mothers, compared with 41.4 percent in two-parent
households. By 1978, the pattern was reversed: 35 percent of the

poor were living in mother-only families, compared with 29.8 percent in two-parent families.

A trend such as the one described by Pearce can occur for three reasons: (1) the standard of living of mother-only families has declined, (2) the standard of living of other poor groups has improved, or (3) the proportion of persons living in mother-only families has increased. The feminization of poverty that occurred between 1967 and 1978 was due entirely to the second and third factors (Garfinkel and McLanahan, 1985). The number of mother-only families grew dramatically during this period, as outlined above, and that growth increased the proportion of poor mother-only families relative to other poor subgroups.

In addition, while the economic status of single mothers and their children more or less stood still during this period, the situation of other groups improved substantially. Poverty among the elderly dropped by about half between 1967 and 1974 in response to major increases in Social Security benefits. Poverty among the disabled declined temporarily between 1967 and 1975. Poverty among two-parent families also declined during the early part of the 1970s. About half of the feminization of poverty was due to increases in the number of single mothers, and half was due to the improvement in the living standards of other groups (Garfinkel and McLanahan, 1985).

Apart from poverty, mother-only families also face economic instability and loss of income as a result of marital disruption. Duncan and Hoffman (1985) found that the income of mothers and their children a year after divorce is only 67 percent of their predivorce income, but the income of divorced fathers stays about the same. Job change, change of residence, and unemployment are all more common in mother-only families than they are in married-couple families (McLanahan, 1983).

A comparison of the sources of income available to different family types suggests three reasons why mother-only families are more likely to be poor: (1) lower earnings of the head of the family, (2) no child support from the second parent, and (3) meager public transfers.

Low Earnings of Single Mothers

The major source of income for all family types apart from those headed by widows is the earnings of the household head. Approxi-

TABLE 1 Average Income Receipts (in dollars) of Two-Parent and Mother-Only
Families, by Race, 1982

	Whites		Blacks	
Income Source	Two-Parent Families	Mother-Only Families	Two-Parent Families	Mother-Only Families
Total cash income	30,814	12,628	23,913	9,128
Earned income of family head	21,932	7,666	13,508	5,363
Earnings of other family members	6,377	928	8,096	837
Alimony and child support	227	1,246	253	322
Social Security, pensions, and other unearned income	2,171	1,782	1,720	907
Public assistance and food stamps	174	1,399	1,838	2,573

SOURCE: Garfinkel and McLanahan (1986).

mately 60 to 70 percent of a family's total income is accounted for by
the household head's earnings, which suggests that the earning ability
of single mothers is a critical determinant of their economic status.
Table 1 shows the average income from different sources received by
two-parent and mother-only families. Female breadwinners bring in
only about a third as much as married fathers, partly because they
work fewer hours and partly because they have lower hourly earnings.

Much of the difference in poverty rates among different family
types is due to the fact that single mothers work fewer hours than
married fathers. The significance of not working is profound. David
Ellwood (1985) has shown that only about 6 percent of single mothers
who worked full-time, year round, during the previous decade were
poor in any given year as compared with more than 70 percent
of nonworking women. These findings should not be interpreted
to mean, however, that if all single mothers worked full-time, only
6 percent of them would be poor. To some extent, the apparent
advantage of working mothers reflects the selection process that
channels women with higher earnings capacity into the labor force
and women with lower earnings capacity into homemaker status. On
this point, Sawhill (1976) found that most of the women on welfare
in the early 1970s had a very low earnings capacity and that even if
they worked full-time, more than half would still earn less than their
welfare grant.

Although the Sawhill study has not been replicated with more recent data, there is good reason to believe that a large proportion of women on welfare would be unable to earn their way out of poverty or significantly improve their economic position even if they worked full-time, year round. For example, a woman working 2,000 hours a year at the minimum wage of $3.35 an hour would earn only $6,700 a year, which is less than the $7,050 poverty level for a family of two. To earn more than $8,850, the poverty level for a family of three, a woman working 2,000 hours a year would have to earn more than $4.40 an hour. The lower wages of women, then, may be just as important as their labor force participation rates in explaining the high incidence of poverty in mother-only families.

The wage gap between women and men has not narrowed, and occupational segregation is still widespread despite increased participation by women in the labor force in recent decades. The median earnings of women who work full-time, year round, as a percentage of men's fell from 63.6 in 1955 to 60.2 in 1981 (Blau, 1984). Using an index of segregation that represents the minimum proportion of one group that would have to be shifted in order for its occupational distribution to be identical with that of the other, Reskin and Hartmann (1986) cite the index as .41 for segregation by sex for whites and .39 for sex segregation of nonwhites in 1981. A study by Bielby and Baron (1984) of nearly 400 California establishments suggests that the extent of segregation by institution may be even greater than the occupational segregation figures would suggest.

There are two major competing hypotheses that seek to explain occupational segregation and earnings inequality: (1) human capital (i.e., education, training, job experience) and (2) discrimination by employers. The human capital hypothesis is that (a) for various reasons (specialization within households, differences in lifetime labor force participation, time preferences, labor force attachment, etc.), women and men differ in their decisions to invest in human capital; (b) this leads to sex differences in human capital stock and, hence, productivity; and (c) rational employers paying workers according to their marginal productivities will pay women less than men. In short, women earn less than men because they are less productive. The discrimination hypothesis is that women earn less than men because employers discriminate against them.[3]

---

[3]Becker's (1957) discrimination hypothesis was postulated to deal with race discrimination, but it can be adapted to deal with discrimination against

Studies that use human capital variables such as education, training, and work experience typically explain between 10 percent and 44 percent of the wage gap between women and men (Treiman and Hartmann, 1981). Work history variables (e.g., years of full-time labor force experience and years of on-the-job training) are the most important factors in accounting for the portion of the wage gap that is explained (Corcoran and Duncan, 1979). Differences in human capital are clearly important in accounting for earnings differences between women and men.[4] It is also significant, however, that they account for less than half of the wage gap.

What seems to be missing in recent research on the earnings gap between women and men is a comprehensive model that takes

---

women. His hypothesis is based on the idea that employers, coworkers, or customers have an externally acquired "taste" for discrimination, so that employers will employ workers against whom there are discriminatory tastes only at a discount. In the discrimination model, occupational segregation is accounted for by variations in tastes for discrimination.

In the case of occupational segregation by gender, as Blau (1984) notes, an extreme distribution of tastes would have to be assumed to account for the observed extent of segregation. Blau suggests that rather than employers, coworkers, or customers having a preference for male employees in all jobs, it may be the case that certain jobs are viewed as "socially appropriate" for women. Employers would be willing to employ women in these jobs but would only employ women in "inappropriate" jobs at a discount.

England (1982) points out that the greater the proportion of women in an occupation, the lower the wage rate—contrary to what the discrimination model would predict. If certain jobs were seen as inappropriate for women, one would expect them to be employed in such jobs only at a discount; thus, women in male-dominated jobs would be paid less than women in the (presumably more appropriate) female-dominated jobs. Bergmann's (1974) "overcrowding" hypothesis gives a possible explanation for this discrepancy. She argues that occupational segregation will not automatically lead to pay differentials but will do so if supply exceeds demand in the female sector. The low wages will encourage the use of more labor-intensive technologies, which would result in female workers being less productive because they have less capital to work with.

[4]Human capital theories have been less successful in explaining the existence of widespread occupational segregation. For example, some research suggests that different occupations have different atrophy rates—that is, they differ in the extent to which market skills are lost while workers are out of the labor force—and that women who expect their labor force participation to be intermittent will tend to choose occupations with low atrophy rates (Mincer and Polachek, 1974; Polachek, 1977). The empirical evidence, however, shows no difference in atrophy rates between the earnings of women who are in male-dominated jobs and those in female-dominated jobs (England, 1982).

account of the insights from both the human capital and discrimination approaches. Choices made by women and the recruitment preferences of firms are important, but the interaction between the two may well be the most important factor: the choices women make given their expectations of the behavior of firms, and the employment practices of firms given their expectations of how women will behave.

Inadequate Child Support

The second reason for the greater poverty of mother-only families is that in most cases only one parent contributes to the family income. In two-parent households, according to Table 1, the earnings of white wives account for about one-third of family income. In mother-only families, child support payments from noncustodial fathers account for only one-tenth of family income for whites and less than one-twentieth for blacks. Income from child support is low partly because a large proportion of single mothers receive no child-support. The average amount received by single mothers who do receive child support payments is $3,129 for whites and $1,145 for blacks. These payments are much lower than the contribution of fathers in two-parent families and are also lower than the contribution of the other adults in two-parent families. Thus, even though a woman's earnings capacity is lower than a man's, and even though the contribution of the second parent is needed more in mother-only families than in two-parent families, absent fathers contribute a smaller proportion to child support in the former than women do in the latter.

When a family splits, it loses the economies of scale that result from living together in one household. Two homes must be bought or rented and furnished, heated, and maintained. Even if all noncustodial fathers paid a reasonable amount of child support, such payments would not compensate fully for the economic contribution of the father who is present. Yet most noncustodial fathers do not pay reasonable amounts of child support. National data on child support awards indicate that only about 60 percent of the children potentially eligible for child support even have an award from the courts. Nearly 30 percent of those with awards receive nothing (Bureau of the Census, 1981a).

To get an idea of what the poverty status of mother-only families (excluding widows) would be if noncustodial fathers paid a bigger share, Oellerich and Garfinkel (1985) simulated the effect of collecting 100 percent of the child-support obligation that the state of Wisconsin has set as a standard: 17 percent of the noncustodial parent's gross income for one child, 25 percent of income for two children, 29 percent for three children, 31 percent for four children, and 34 percent for five or more children. Their estimate indicated that the poverty gap—the difference between the incomes of poor families headed by women and the amount of money they would need to move above the poverty level—would be reduced by more than a quarter.

Low Welfare Payments

A final cause of poverty in mother-only families is the relatively meager public transfers these families receive. This effect can be seen in the contrast between the poverty status of widows and other single mothers. Fifty-one percent of all mother-only families are poor, compared with 34 percent of families headed by widows. This difference is largely due to the differences in benefits between Survivors Insurance, for which only widows are eligible, and Aid to Families with Dependent Children, for which all single mothers are eligible. White widows are far better off than any other group of single mothers, not because they earn more but because they receive a large proportion of their income through Social Security.

Welfare plays a much smaller role in the family income of the nonwidowed single mother than Survivors Insurance plays for the widowed mother. First, the proportion of all widows who receive Survivors Insurance is much higher than the proportion of other single mothers receiving welfare. Among widows, nearly 90 percent of whites and 70 percent of blacks receive Survivors Insurance. Only 22 percent and 33 percent, respectively, of white and black divorced women report receipt of welfare, and the proportion of separated and never-married women who do so ranges from 38 percent to 58 percent. Second, the average level of benefits in Survivors Insurance is much higher than the average level of welfare benefits: for whites, it is more than double; for blacks, the difference is smaller but is still a sizable 20 percent more. Third, benefits for the child from Survivors Insurance are not reduced when the custodial parent works.

By drastically reducing benefits as earnings increase, welfare programs replace rather than supplement earnings. Even when the AFDC program contained work incentives, as it did between 1967 and 1982, the gains from working were slight. The choice faced by poor single mothers is not an attractive one: become dependent on welfare, or work full-time and achieve, at best, a marginally better economic position. In addition, work is discouraged because it increases the risk of losing valuable in-kind benefits such as health care and public housing.

In summary, although single motherhood is not synonymous with poverty, the risk of long-term poverty is substantially greater for mother-only families. Their growth between 1960 and 1978 accounted for only one-half of the observed feminization of poverty, the remainder being accounted for by the lack of improvement in the living standards of families headed by single women at a time when other groups experienced increasing incomes. Finally, the principal reasons for poverty in families headed by women are the low earnings capacity of the single mother, lack of adequate (or any) support from the noncustodial father, and relatively low public transfers.

THE UNDERCLASS

Poverty and income insecurity are serious problems in their own right. Some analysts, however, go even farther in arguing that the mother-only family is responsible for the growth of an "underclass" in American cities (Auletta, 1982). To demonstrate such a relationship, one would have to show that mother-only families are more likely to be in the underclass than two-parent families, or that children who grow up in the former are more likely to be in the underclass than children who grow up in the latter.

Defining the Underclass

The term *underclass* has been used in a variety of contexts and defined in a variety of ways.[5] Based on his review of the literature and discussions with poverty researchers, Auletta (1982) identifies

---

[5]Many of the usages of the term *underclass* bear little relation to the concept of class in either the Weberian or the Marxist senses. Sociologists in the Weberian tradition see classes as groups of people with common economic "life-chances" based on their relative control over goods and skills in the marketplace (Giddens, 1973; Parkin, 1971; Weber, 1922). The Marxist concept of class is defined in terms of common structural positions within the social organization of production based on ownership or nonownership of factors of production (Bukharin, 1921; Lenin, 1914; Wright, 1985). (See Wright [1979] for an overview of the different concepts of social class.) The Weberian concept of class tends to be gradational, emphasizing the relative positions of the classes

the underclass as those who suffer from "behavioral as well as income deficiencies" and who "operate outside the mainstream of commonly accepted values." For him, this includes four distinct groups: hostile street criminals, hustlers, welfare mothers, and the chronically ill.[6]

Wilson and his colleagues speak of the underclass in the context of urban ghettos (Aponte et al., 1985; Wilson, 1985b; Wilson and Aponte, 1985; Wilson and Neckerman, 1986). They point to changes that have taken place in ghetto communities, including deindustrialization and the exodus of middle-class blacks, and contend that the groups left behind are collectively different from those who lived in the communities in the 1940s and 1950s. Wilson argues that poverty rates in ghetto neighborhoods were high throughout the first half of the century but that rates of joblessness, teenage pregnancies, out-of-wedlock births, female-headed families, welfare dependence, and serious crime did not reach alarmingly high levels until the mid-1970s. Although long-term welfare families and street criminals are distinct groups, the fact that they live and interact in the same community and are increasingly isolated from the mainstream patterns of norms and behaviors is a cause for concern (Wilson, 1985b).

In his analysis of urban problems, Wilson relies heavily on the work of Kasarda (1985), who shows that poor inner-city minorities have been especially vulnerable to the economic transformation occurring in central cities that is changing them from centers of production and distribution of physical goods to centers of administration, information exchange, trade, finance, and government services. Since

---

(e.g., lower class, middle class). The Marxist concept of class tends to emphasize the relationships of classes to each other and the possibility of conflict between them.

The definition of the underclass outlined in this paper is closer to the Marxist than to the Weberian concept of class because it emphasizes the nonownership of salable labor power by members of the underclass. A fuller analysis of the relationship of the underclass to the working class and to the capitalist class goes beyond the scope of this paper but would, at a minimum, involve a discussion of their role as a "reserve army" of labor.

[6] Auletta's data come from case studies of participants in supported work programs run by the Manpower Demonstration Research Corporation in New York City and Appalachia. The eligibility requirements for the New York program included being a recently released ex-offender, a recent ex-addict, a long-term welfare-dependent mother, or an unemployed high-school dropout—categories markedly similar to Auletta's four main divisions of the underclass. Auletta's arguments and methods are very close to those of the earlier culture-of-poverty approach (Lewis, 1966) in his emphasis on the behavioral deficiencies of the poor and in his reliance on case studies.

1948, vast numbers of unskilled jobs in wholesale, retail, and manufacturing in the nation's central cities have been lost, and this process has accelerated since the late 1960s. The new jobs in the growing service sector usually require levels of education and training that poor inner-city residents do not possess. The cumulative impact, according to Wilson, has been increasing ghettoization characterized by poverty, institutional problems (services and schools of poor quality), and an increase in social dislocations (joblessness, crime, mother-only families, teenage pregnancies, and welfare dependence).

Weak Attachment to the Labor Force

What these seemingly diverse groups have in common is a weak attachment to the legitimate labor force.[7] The underclass can be seen as made up of family units with no readily salable labor power or other factors of production. Labor power may be difficult to sell for a variety of reasons: disability, lack of human capital or salable skills, discrimination, or low demand. To the extent that members of the underclass do participate in the labor force, they tend to be in "secondary" jobs that offer little stability of employment.[8] Attachment to the labor force can be direct or indirect, and both kinds of attachment carry a "right" to income. Direct attachment involves the sale of one's own labor power with the corresponding right to a wage or salary income. Indirect attachment includes links to the labor force through former employment—in which the income is in the form of pensions or Social Security benefits—and through

---

[7] Perhaps a more precise definition would see the underclass as comprising families and individuals with a relatively weak attachment to the production process, because one would not wish to include owners of capital in the underclass. Given that few people have enough capital or wealth to make the sale of labor power unnecessary, however, the definition in terms of attachment to the labor force is adequate for most purposes.

[8] Dual labor market theory suggests that a dichotomization of the American labor market has occurred over time, forging two separate labor markets—a "primary" market and a "secondary" market in which workers and employers operate by fundamentally different behavioral rules (Gordon, 1977). The primary labor market is characterized by high wages, good working conditions, employment stability and job security, equity and due process in the administration of work rules, and chances for advancement. The secondary labor market has low wages, poor working conditions, unstable employment, harsh and often arbitrary discipline, and little opportunity for advancement (Piore, 1977).

family status—in which a spouse or dependent shares in the income of another family member who is attached to the labor force.[9]

Given their lack of access to the usual means of gaining a livelihood, members of the underclass must find another source of income such as public transfers or the underground economy (e.g., crime). It is their common need to find an alternative to wage or salary income, and the social stigma that accompanies their position, that allows such diverse groups as poor female-headed families, criminals, the unemployed, and the mentally ill to be grouped together.

Persistence and Social Isolation

In addition to weak attachment to the labor force, the notion of an underclass implies a persistence or permanence in status. Thus, individuals who are temporarily unemployed, ill, or dependent on welfare are not viewed as part of the underclass, whereas long-term welfare recipients and those with unstable work histories are prime candidates. Persistence may also occur across generations, and much of the concern over female-headed families arises from the belief that children who grow up in such families are more likely to become single parents and welfare recipients when they grow up.

The final characteristic of the underclass is the isolation of its members from a community activity. Isolation and persistence of nonemployment, be they in urban ghettos or rural areas of the South, are of concern because they are believed to encourage the development of a hostile or alienated subculture. We know, for example, that the longer an individual remains outside the labor force, the less likely he or she is to become employed. Many believe that this relationship is due to a change in values and a loss of motivation that goes along with being marginal to the labor force. In particular, there is concern over whether the children of welfare mothers are developing the motivation and the practical knowledge required to find and hold a steady job.

Not all analysts agree about whether the underclass has a unique culture. In fact, since the mid-1960s, liberal scholars have tended to avoid describing any behavior on the part of the poor or minorities that might be construed as unflattering or stigmatizing. Wilson

---

[9]Indirect links to the labor force typically bring a lower return than do direct links and tend to be seen as less legitimate. The indirect links that have traditionally received the blessing of social approval are those of the child through the parent and the wife through the husband.

(1985a) notes that the debate over the underclass was dominated by the conservatives until the recent resurgence of interest in the "underclass" and welfare dependency, partly in response to the failure of equal opportunity legislation to eradicate poverty and partly because of the increasing concentration of the poor in central cities.

In addition to the revival of research and scholarship oriented toward an understanding of the urban underclass, liberals recently have begun to discuss the consequences (rather than just the causes) of the distinct cultures that emerge in ghetto areas. Emphasizing the social structural constraints and opportunities that give rise to subcultures that are distinct from the mainstream, Wilson (1985a) nevertheless argues that the liberals of the 1960s did not give sufficient attention to the role that culture plays in influencing behavior. Culture, once it has emerged in response to structural conditions, can itself become a constraining or a liberating factor. Unlike the earlier culture-of-poverty theorists, Wilson places more stress on the lack of contact between ghetto residents and people with good jobs (leading to a lack of information about job openings and few role models for the young) than on the role played by distinct values in reproducing the ghetto underclass.

Being poor and being in the underclass are not the same, however, although the two statuses overlap a good deal. A family may be poor even though the parents (or parent) work full-time. Or, as noted earlier, a family may be poor because the parent is temporarily disabled or unemployed. In neither case would such a family be classified as being in the underclass. Similarly, not all members of the underclass are poor. In particular, some "hustlers" and street criminals may have incomes well above the poverty line. What distinguishes the underclass from the poor is the persistence of their nonemployment and their isolation from the values and behavior of the broader community.

Are Female-Headed Families Part of the Underclass?

We now turn to the question of whether families headed by single mothers are part of the underclass by virtue of their own position or that of their offspring. To what extent do single mothers have a persistent, weak attachment to the labor force? To what extent is this status passed on to their children? And to what extent are these women and their families socially isolated?

Persistent, Weak Attachment to the Labor Force

Single mothers can be linked to the labor force in three ways: directly, indirectly, or tenuously. First, mothers who have relatively stable employment are directly linked to the labor force. Second, widows who receive Survivors Insurance and divorced or separated women who receive child support are indirectly linked to the labor force through the past or present participation of their former husbands, whether or not they themselves work. (This link to past employment, albeit indirect, may account for the generally higher benefits received by widows as compared with welfare benefits, and for the widespread perception that such income is theirs by right.) Third, women who neither work consistently nor have indirect links to the labor force through a spouse have the most tenuous right to income and are most likely to be viewed as part of the underclass.

Because data on work history are less readily available than data on long-term welfare dependency, the latter can be used as an index of weak attachment to the labor force and persistent dependency. Cross-sectional data on welfare participation indicate that within the last decade, half of single mothers received some welfare in any year (Garfinkel and McLanahan, 1986). Most of these mothers have a very high degree of dependence while they are on welfare. Eighty-five percent of those receiving benefits do not work, and most have no sources of income other than food stamps, Medicaid, and, in some cases, public housing. Furthermore, Ellwood (1985) found that 65 percent of AFDC recipients at any point in time are in the midst of a welfare spell of 8 or more years. In short, about 30 percent of mother-only families can be classified as long-term dependents, which eliminates at least 70 percent of single mothers and their children from the underclass.

Intergenerational Dependence

To what extent are the children who grow up in families headed by single women likely to be part of the underclass? The literature on the consequences of family structure for children is quite large, and we do not attempt to cover all of it here. Rather, we have limited our discussion to outcomes that are directly related to labor force attachment: education and occupational attainment, family formation behavior, employment status, and welfare status. Low levels of education and low-status occupations are both associated with a higher risk of unemployment, and they help explain, as we have seen, the weak ties to the labor force of female-headed families. To the extent that the offspring from mother-only families are more likely to leave school sooner, to get low-status jobs, or to have out-of-wedlock births, their risk of being in the underclass is increased.[10]

Studies of educational attainment based on cross-sectional data have consistently found that offspring from single-parent families complete fewer years of schooling. Otis Dudley Duncan and his colleagues (1972) found that growing up in a married-couple family added between 0.6 and 1.2 years of schooling to the educational attainment of white males and about 0.4 to 0.8 years to that of blacks. Similar results were reported by Featherman and Hauser (1978) in their analysis of the more recent data from the Occupational Change in a Generation (OCG) study. Recent analyses based on the PSID and the NLS data are consistent with earlier findings. McLanahan (1985) found that living in a female-headed family increased the probability of dropping out of high school by 42 percent for whites and 70 percent for blacks, and Shaw (1979) and Krein and Beller (1986) reported similar results using the NLS data.

Children from single-parent families are also disadvantaged with respect to occupational status. Duncan et al. (1972) found that offspring from one-parent families had lower occupational status scores than those from married-couple families. The average score for white men from two-parent families was 45.12 compared with 40.28 for those from single-parent families. Among blacks, the scores were 21.8 and 17.93, respectively. Featherman and Hauser (1978) reported similar results and noted that differences in status were due both to differences in educational attainment and to differences in the returns to education.

Perhaps the strongest evidence for intergenerational effects comes from research on family formation behavior and intergenerational use of welfare. Several researchers have shown that daughters who grow up in single-parent families are more likely to marry early and to have children early (including both marital and premarital births), both of which are positively related to becoming a single mother. These daughters are also more likely to divorce than children from two-parent families (Bumpass and Sweet, 1972; Hogan and Kitagawa, 1985; McLanahan and Bumpass, 1986). McLanahan (1987)

---

[10]For major reviews of the literature on intergenerational consequences, see Herzog and Sudia (1973); Hetherington et al. (1983); Ross and Sawhill (1975); and Shinn (1978).

also found that daughters of single mothers were more likely than daughters from two-parent families to become single heads of families themselves and to receive welfare.

Part of the reason for the disadvantages suffered by children from mother-only families is low family income. Differences in income account for much of the difference in educational attainment among children from one- and two-parent families (Hetherington et al., 1983; Krein and Beller, 1986; McLanahan, 1985; Shaw, 1979). Yet income explains very little of the reproduction of single motherhood and welfare dependence (McLanahan, 1987). The residual influence probably comes from the absence of a second parent, which is likely to increase the perceived legitimacy of single parenthood and to reduce the amount of supervision of dating during adolescence, an important factor in accounting for teenage pregnancies (Hogan and Kitagawa, 1985; McLanahan and Bumpass, 1986). This hypothesis is consistent with the finding that children who grow up in father-only families also appear to fare less well than children from two-parent families (Hetherington et al., 1983; McLanahan, 1987; McLanahan and Bumpass, 1986).

A final explanation that must be considered is the possibility that differences between one- and two-parent families are due to selectivity, that is, to preexisting differences between families that break up and those that do not. Because research on single parenthood is necessarily nonexperimental, we cannot rule out the possibility that children in these families would have had more problems even if their parents had not divorced. Selectivity effects could stem from predivorce differences in family socioeconomic status or the nature of intrafamily relationships (parent conflict or abuse, parent–child conflict or abuse), or both. Support for the selection hypothesis comes from studies showing that children in unhappy, two-parent families are similar to children in single-parent families with respect to psychological adjustment and behavior (Emery, 1982; Peterson and Zill, 1986). Conflicting evidence comes from studies showing that widowhood also has negative consequences for offspring (Levy-Shiff, 1982). Widowhood is a more random event with respect to preexisting family interaction patterns even though it is more likely among poorer segments of the population.

Ghettoization

If families headed by mothers are to be classified as part of an emerging underclass, they would not only have to have a persistent weak attachment to the labor force but would also have to be socially isolated. Although social isolation may be present in a rural area, recent discussions of the underclass have focused on urban areas, and the data we use to crudely measure isolation pertain only to urban areas.

Our proxy for social isolation is living in an urban neighborhood that is predominantly poor. The census reports from which we derive these numbers give three classifications of poverty neighborhoods: those in which at least 20 percent, 30 percent, and 40 percent of their populations are poor. Although it seems reasonable to assume that the higher the percentage of poor people in a neighborhood, the greater the degree of cultural isolation, it is difficult to know exactly where to draw the line. Hence, when possible, we use all three classifications.

The top two rows in Table 2 present data on the proportion of families with children that are headed by single mothers and by others living in poverty areas of the 100 largest cities in the United States in 1979. The data are presented both as a proportion of families living in the central city and as a proportion of all families in the United States The bottom panel presents separate figures for black and white families headed by a single mother.

Several aspects of the table are worth noting. First, a comparison of the first and second rows clearly indicates that families headed by single mothers are much more likely than other families to live in poverty areas. The greater the proportion of the neighborhood that is poor, the bigger the difference in the proportion of mother-only and other families that live there. For neighborhoods that are at least 20 percent poor, the proportion of mother-only families is a bit more than twice as much as the proportion of other families. For neighborhoods that are at least 40 percent poor, the proportion of mother-only families is nearly five times as high. In view of the fact that families headed by single mothers are more likely to be poor, this is not surprising.

Second, the proportion of all mother-only families that live in poverty areas in central cities is very sensitive to the definition of a poverty area. If a poor population of 20 percent is the cutoff, we find that 56 percent of all mother-only families in central cities reside in poverty areas. If 40 percent is the cutoff, the figure drops to only 19 percent.

Third, if the denominator is the proportion of all U.S. families headed by single mothers rather than the proportion of such families

TABLE 2 Proportion of Families Living in Poverty Areas in the 100 Largest Central Cities, 1980

Family Type	In Census Tracts 20 Percent Poor		In Census Tracts 30 Percent Poor		In Census Tracts 40 Percent Poor	
	Central-City Families of Same Type	U.S. Families of Same Type	Central-City Families of Same Type	U.S. Families of Same Type	Central-City Families of Same Type	U.S. Families of Same Type
Mother-only families with children	56	19	36	12	9	7
Other families with children	25	5	12	2	4	1
White mother-only families with children	26	5	N.A.	N.A.	N.A.	N.A.
Black mother-only families with children	75	41	N.A.	N.A.	N.A.	N.A.

NOTE: Census tracts with 20 percent poor include tracts with 30 and 40 percent poor, and tracts with 30 percent poor also include those with 40 percent poor. N.A. = not available.

SOURCE: Bureau of the Census (1985a, 1985b).

living in central cities, the proportions are much smaller—ranging from 19 percent to 7 percent. The proportions are smaller because a large percentage of mother-only families do not live in central cities. Thus, even if one accepts the premise that social isolation is serious in neighorhoods that are 20 percent poor, only 19 percent of all families headed by single mothers would fit the classification of belonging to an emerging urban underclass.

The last two rows of Table 2 indicate that the proportions differ dramatically by race. The breakdown by race was available only for poverty areas in which 20 percent or more of the families were poor. For whites, only 26 percent of mother-only families in central cities live in poverty neighborhoods; for blacks, the figure is 75 percent. Black families headed by single mothers thus tend to be disproportionately concentrated in poverty areas.

On the other hand, black mother-only families who live in these neighborhoods constitute only about 41 percent of all black female-headed families. Furthermore, what the table does not show is that the children in these families represent only 17 percent of all black children. Finally, if the most stringent measure of social isolation is employed—that is, 40 percent of the population is poor—a crude estimate suggests that only about 15 percent of black children in mother-only families and about 7 percent of all black children are socially isolated in urban ghettos.[11]

To what extent did black mother-only families become more socially isolated during the 1970s? The data in Table 3 suggest that black mother-only families who reside in poor neighborhoods have become more socially isolated; in addition, the proportion of such families living in all poor neighborhoods has declined somewhat, but the proportion living in the poorest neighborhoods has increased. The two indicators of social isolation are the proportion of families dependent on public assistance in the neighborhood and the proportion of men employed. In both the 20 percent and 40 percent poverty areas, the proportion of families dependent on public assistance grew by 40 percent between 1970 and 1980. The percentage of men employed declined by 13 percent and 22 percent, respectively, in the 20 percent and 40 percent neighborhoods. By 1980, less than half of all

---

[11]This estimate is derived by multiplying the 41 percent and 17 percent figures for the 20 percent or more neighborhoods by 7/19—the ratio of the proportion of female-headed families living in 40 percent or more poverty neighborhoods to the proportion living in 20 percent or more poverty neighborhoods.

TABLE 3 Trends in Social Conditions and Proportion of Black Persons and Families Living in Poverty Areas in Large Central Cities, 1970-1980[a]

	Census Tracts with 20 Percent Poor			Census Tracts with 40 Percent Poor		
	Percentage		Percentage Change	Percentage		Percentage Change
	1970	1980		1970	1980	
Poverty Area Characteristics						
Employment rate,						
men aged 16+	63.3	56.0	-13	56.5	46.0	-22
AFDC recipiency, all						
families	19.8	28.0	40	30.2	42.0	40
Families and Persons in						
U.S. Living in Poverty Areas						
Black families	27.2	25.2	-8			
Poor black families	28.6	30.4	6			
Black mother-only families	30.5	29.7	-3			
Poor black mother-only						
families	30.7	31.4	2			
Black persons	27.2	26.5	-3	6.3	8.3	32
Poor black persons	28.3	30.5	8	9.4	13.1	40

NOTE: Census tracts with 20 percent poor include tracts with 30 and 40 percent poor, and tracts with 30 percent poor also include all those tracts with 40 percent poor. AFDC = Aid to Families with Dependent Children.

[a]The data are from the cities which were among the 50 largest cities in the United States in 1970.

SOURCE: Bureau of the Census (1973, 1985a, and 1985b).

men in 40 percent neighborhoods were employed, and nearly half of all families were dependent on welfare.

The proportion of both mother-only and all families in the 20 percent poverty neighborhoods (the only areas for which data on black families with children are available) declined somewhat between 1970 and 1980, whereas the proportion of poor black families and poor black mothers-only families increased.

Finally, to see if the picture changes when the 40 percent rather than the 20 percent cutoff is used, we present data for all black persons for both cutoffs. Whereas the proportion of all black persons in neighborhoods that are 20 percent or more poor decreased by 3 percent between 1970 and 1980, the proportion in neighborhoods that are 40 percent or more poor increased by 32 percent. This increase suggests that the proportion of mother-only families living in 40 percent areas also increased. Such findings appear to be consistent with

Wilson's hypothesis that a number of relatively poor neighborhoods have deteriorated as the nonpoor move out; these areas have now become very poor neighborhoods (Wilson and Aponte, 1985). Thus, both the number of very poor neighborhoods and the proportion of blacks living in such neighborhoods have increased, even though the proportion of blacks in all poor neighborhoods has declined slightly.

RECENT PUBLIC POLICIES REGARDING FAMILIES HEADED BY SINGLE WOMEN

Children who grow up in families headed by single women are clearly disadvantaged. As adults, they have lower socioeconomic status; they are more likely to become single parents themselves, either through out-of-wedlock births or divorce; and they are more likely to be dependent on government. Many of these problems arise from the economic insecurity and poverty of the families in which they grew up. Government can reduce these problems by increasing the incomes of mother-only families. But doing so may increase both the numbers of such families and their dependence on government.

Apart from a brief flirtation with social Darwinism toward the end of the nineteenth century, there has always been a general acceptance in this country of government responsibility for aiding the poor. Accompanying this historical constant has been a concern to avoid encouraging dependence on welfare and growth in the number of the poor. Policy makers today must decide which should receive greater priority: reducing the economic insecurity and poverty of families headed by women or not encouraging the growth of such families and their dependence on government.

This dilemma has led to the development of distinctions among groups of the poor, on the basis of which differential aid has been provided. The most important distinction has been between those who are and those who are not expected to work. This distinction has implications for policy toward mother-only families in that expectations about whether single mothers should work have recently changed.

Widows—especially war widows—have always received better treatment than other single mothers. In the eighteenth century, most single mothers were widows. Divorce, separation, and out-of-wedlock births were strongly discouraged by law and custom and were uncommon by today's standards. Widows were treated more favorably for two reasons: first, widowhood was an involuntary state and aiding widows was unlikely to increase their numbers; second, widows were commonly seen as more "deserving" because of their husband's service to the community, as was the case with war widows, for example.

The three most important recent trends in policies that affect families headed by women are (1) the large reduction in public benefits, (2) the increasingly strong legislation either to induce or require single mothers without preschool-age children to work, and (3) the strengthening of public enforcement of private child-support obligations. Each of these policies is designed to strengthen the links between mother-only families and the labor force—either directly, by encouraging or requiring the single mother to work, or indirectly, by increasing support from the noncustodial parent. The nature of each of these trends and their effects on the poverty, welfare dependence, and prevalence of families headed by single women is discussed in turn.

Reduction in Benefits

Throughout the 1970s, the real value of AFDC benefits declined because state legislatures failed to increase benefit levels to keep pace with inflation. Between 1975 and 1980, inflation cut the benefits received by mother-only families by about 13 percent. Apart from these passive benefit cuts, the Reagan administration actively sought to cut benefits. Reagan proposed a series of specific budget cuts that, when taken together, would have added up to large reductions in benefits to families headed by single women. Congress eventually adopted more modest cuts that amounted to about 12 percent of total federal benefits to mother-only families (Garfinkel and McLanahan, 1986).

The reductions in benefits to families headed by single women between 1975 and 1985 were substantial, wiping out more than one-third of the increases that had occurred during the previous two decades. Single mothers who both worked and received welfare absorbed two-thirds of the cuts. The administration abandoned the strategy of extending welfare eligibility to those not previously covered to reward behaviors such as working and marrying, in the hope that such incentives would reduce dependency in the long run.

In retrospect, perhaps the reductions in the real value of benefits are not surprising. Over the long run in the United States, the real wage level has been the principal determinant of the average level of living and of benefits to the poor (Garfinkel and McLanahan, 1986). Real wages in the United States fell during most of the 1970s and early 1980s. Although short-run changes in general living standards do not always lead to corresponding changes in benefit levels, that is what happened in 1975–1985. The decline in the real value of public benefits reflected but also exceeded the decline in real wages.

By the end of the Reagan administration's first term, Congress was no longer enacting legislation that even modestly reduced benefits; indeed, some of the earlier cuts to mother-only families were restored. Moreover, early in Reagan's second term, further cuts in the major programs that aided single mothers were specifically excluded from the stringent Gramm-Rudman-Hollings budget-cutting measures designed to reduce the large federal deficit. In view of both the recent growth in real wages and the recent resistance of Congress to enact further budget cuts, families headed by women will probably not be subjected to additional decreases in benefits in the near future.

The evidence suggests that the budget cuts increased the poverty of mother-only families by nontrivial amounts in return for small-to-trivial reductions in dependence and prevalence. Almost by definition, the elimination by the Reagan administration of eligibility for AFDC for many working mothers decreased their dependence on welfare. Some analysts have argued that these cuts may increase welfare dependence in the long run by encouraging those whose benefits were cut to leave work and return to AFDC and by discouraging nonworking mothers from working their way off the welfare rolls. Studies of the behavior of working mothers after the budget cuts, however, indicate that only a minority of recipients who were taken off the rolls returned to AFDC (Cole et al., 1983; Joe et al., 1984; Usher and Griffith, 1983). The decrease in benefits during 1975–1985 was accompanied by a noticeable decrease—more than one-sixth—in the dependence of mother-only families on welfare. This decline reversed the increase in welfare dependence that had accompanied the expansion of government benefits during the previous two decades.

Conversely, just as the large benefit increases between 1955 and 1975 caused, at most, a modest increase in the proportion of mother-only families during that period, the smaller reductions in benefits during 1975–1985 had little if any effect on the prevalence of these families. If one can assume that a cut in average benefit levels has the same effect as an equal-sized cut that is targeted primarily at those who work, estimates derived from the two most careful and comprehensive studies suggest that the 12 percent cut in welfare benefits would have reduced prevalence by between 0.9 percent and 1.6 percent. Further extreme cuts in benefits would have at most a modest effect on the proportion of families headed by single women.

Work Requirements

Although able-bodied men have always been expected to work, expectations regarding poor women who head families have changed considerably. Until the early twentieth century, single mothers were expected to work. For the next half-century, the stated objective of government policy was to provide enough aid to enable them to imitate what was then the current middle-class ideal of the mother who refrains from market work and stays at home to look after her children. Not until the late 1960s, however, was sufficient aid provided to make the objective achievable, and by that time, both the middle-class ideal and beliefs about whether poor women who head families should work had changed. There was increasing emphasis on the idea that single mothers should work.

At first, the federal government tried to induce AFDC mothers to work by creating work incentives within AFDC. When this failed to have much impact on either work or caseloads, Congress began legislating requirements for mothers with no children under age 6 to work. The Carter administration proposed a combination of a guaranteed jobs program and assistance that would have, in effect, required mothers without preschool-age children to work. The Reagan administration rejected the approach of creating work incentives within the AFDC program in favor of the pure work requirement. The administration sought to reinforce working by limiting benefits to women with no income from work and by requiring those who received benefits to work for them. Congress agreed to much but not all of this strategy.[12]

---

[12]The work incentive provision under AFDC that ignored the first $30 of earnings plus $1 out of every $3 in excess of this amount each month was limited to 4 months. Families with incomes of more than 150 percent of the state's need standard (the level of income for determining initial eligibility) were made ineligible for benefits. Individually determined work-related expense deductions with no upper limits were replaced by a flat rate of $50 per month for part-time work and $75 per month for full-time work. These restrictions were liberalized somewhat in 1984, and some of the benefit cuts were restored. The $30 set-aside was extended from 4 to 12 months, the $75 per month deduction for expenses

Since 1972, AFDC mothers without children under age 6 have been required to register for work and training, but only a minority of those who registered ever received services to help them find jobs. The Reagan administration proposed that states require AFDC mothers to work for their relief checks in community work experience programs (CWEPs). Congress passed legislation that permitted but did not require states to substitute work relief for cash relief. Under workfare, as it is called, participants work off their relief checks. They are paid at the minimum wage, and the hours they must work are limited to the check amount divided by the minimum wage. One anomaly of this procedure for calculating benefits, however, is that mothers with a greater number of children receive higher welfare benefits and thus will be required to work more hours.

Congress also passed several other provisions designed to encourage work. States may now require AFDC recipients to participate in a program of job searches for up to 8 weeks upon application and for an additional 8 weeks for each year benefits are received. States are also permitted to operate work supplementation, or grant diversion, programs in which federal funds that would ordinarily finance AFDC cash benefits may be used to subsidize a job for an AFDC recipient. With this program, unlike workfare, a participant's total income exceeds what would have been received on welfare alone. As of September 1985, 37 states had implemented one or more of these options, with workfare programs being the most common. Most programs are being run on a demonstration basis, however, and in the few states that have statewide programs, only a small proportion of the caseload is being served.

To enforce work requirements, the government must create or locate jobs. Some analysts have argued that it is not possible to find or create enough jobs to enforce work requirements when the unemployment rate is over 7 percent (General Accounting Office, 1985). Yet a number of states have already demonstrated their ability to create and find jobs. Furthermore, if it was possible to create 3.5 million WPA jobs during the Great Depression, it must be technically possible to find or create a similar number now with a lower unemployment rate and an expanded economy. Finally, scholars who have explored this issue have estimated that the supply of jobs is

---

was extended to part-time as well as full-time work, and the eligibility level for those already on welfare was raised to 185 percent of the state's need standard.

more than sufficient to warrant enforcement of work requirements (Fechter, 1975).

Apart from the issue of technical feasibility is the question of whether the benefits of enforcing work offset the costs. Studies of work and training programs for women who head families generally report sufficiently large gains in earnings to make the programs profitable within 3 or 4 years, although they do cost more initially in comparison to the payment of cash benefits only (Bassi and Ashenfelter, 1986; Hollister et al., 1984). The most carefully evaluated job creation program—the National Supported Work Demonstration—indicated that the net social benefit per participant was $8,000. Initial costs are higher than welfare costs, however, because the cost of finding or creating jobs must be paid as well as the cash benefit.

The effects of enforcing work requirements on the incomes of single mothers depend on the nature of the work programs created, the magnitude of the increased earnings of participants, and the rules of the AFDC program. Single mothers in work and training programs gain an average of $600 to $1,200 in earnings per year (Bassi and Ashenfelter, 1986)—an amount equaling one-quarter of the average poverty gap for mother-only families and representing a substantial proportion of the total earnings of poor single mothers. In the National Supported Work Demonstration, the average annual increase in earnings of $900 represented an increase of nearly 50 percent over the earnings of the control group (Hollister et al., 1984; Manpower Demonstration Research Corporation, 1980).

Although the potential gains in earnings can be relatively large, the increase in the incomes of single mothers will be smaller than the increase in earnings because they will lose some AFDC and other transfer benefits. Whether AFDC families realize gains or losses from the enforcement of work requirements will depend on the nature of the key programs that aid poor single mothers and on the attractiveness and availability of jobs in the regular labor market. Even if income increases, however, economic well-being may decrease because, in the absence of work requirements, many mothers may have chosen the combination of lower income from welfare and more time for childrearing, housework, and leisure.

The effects of enforced work will almost certainly reduce dependence on welfare. Even if the increased earnings of AFDC mothers lead to no decrease in AFDC receipts, the share of total income from welfare must decrease. Work programs, however, will probably decrease the total amount of welfare received because there will always be some recipients who are at the margin between choosing welfare and another alternative. Some research also suggests that if the labor market is strong, a nontrivial proportion of single mothers on AFDC need little more than good professional help in locating jobs. For example, preliminary evidence from San Diego, where unemployment rates are well below average, indicates that job search assistance has been the most profitable service provided there (Gueron, 1986, 1987).

The effect of enforced work requirements on the prevalence of mother-only households depends on the extent to which the economic well-being of single mothers is improved and on the extent to which the relative earnings opportunities of men and women are altered. If enforcing work requirements increases the earnings of single mothers relative to those of men, single mothers will probably become less dependent both on men and on welfare.

There are three reasons for caution in interpreting the above evidence in favor of compulsory work programs. First, whereas participation to date in most of the work and training programs evaluated has been voluntary, much of the current public discussion involves making work compulsory. Programs that involve significant elements of compulsion may be less profitable both to the beneficiaries and to society as a whole. Early experience with the workfare programs, however, suggests that to date, at least, enforcing work requirements also seems to be profitable (Gueron, 1986, 1987).

Second, and even more important, few single mothers of families in the work and training evaluations have had preschool-age children. The child-care costs for such children could easily be so high as to offset the earnings gains of the program. Long-run earnings gains could more than make up for child-care costs, but the opposite is equally possible. This issue warrants more experimentation and study.

Finally, it may be unrealistic to expect single mothers to work full-time, year round. As Ellwood (1985) points out, the only way that most single mothers can be self-supporting is by working full-time, full-year. Such complete participation in the labor force is the exception rather than the rule among all mothers, contrary to popular belief. Single mothers already work more hours than wives in married-couple households: 35 percent of single mothers with children under 6 work at least 1,500 hours per year, compared with 23 percent for comparable wives. Similarly, 50 percent of single mothers with older children are fully employed, compared with 37 percent of wives. Working 1,500 hours or more remains the exception, not the rule, for all mothers. Ellwood argues that, because the norm is for mothers to spend considerable time with their children, it may be unrealistic to expect behavior from single mothers that deviates markedly from this norm (Ellwood, 1985). This is especially true because work requirements impose a dual role on single mothers: because only one parent is present, that parent must undertake the roles of both caretaker and breadwinner. Requiring single mothers to work for their welfare checks places a heavy burden on them.

Child Support

Congressional interest in enforcing child support grew as the proportion of AFDC children with absent fathers grew. The biggest burst of federal legislation on child support followed hard on the heels of the 1965–1975 growth in the welfare rolls. In addition, a consensus had developed that the existing child-support system condoned parental irresponsibility. A special study conducted by the Census Bureau in 1979 found that only 59 percent of women with children potentially eligible for support were awarded payments. Of those awarded payments, only 49 percent received the full amount due them and 28 percent received nothing. In addition, award levels and enforcement efforts were arbitrary and inequitable (Bureau of the Census, 1981a).

The milestone 1976 act created federal and state offices of child support enforcement—the public bureaucratic machinery to enforce the private obligation to support one's children. During the 7 years that followed, several new acts strengthened this machinery. Then, in 1984, Congress unanimously enacted by far the strongest federal child-support legislation, requiring all states to enact laws that withhold from wages all future child-support payments once the obligor is delinquent in payments for one month. The legislation also requires states to appoint commissions to design statewide guidelines for child-support standards.

The 1984 act requires state child-support offices to provide assistance to nonwelfare as well as welfare cases. Although states may charge for these services and thereby target subsidies toward the poor, the service itself is provided universally to rich and poor custodial parents. The contrast between the restrictions for AFDC eligibility and the universalization of eligibility for child-support enforcement services could not be more stark.

Because the 1984 child-support legislation is so recent, an assessment of its effects relies heavily on theoretical expectations and rough empirical estimates. The incomes of mother-only families can increase as a result of the withholding of wages of the delinquent supporting parent; they can also increase depending on the state guidelines for determining child-support obligations, the incentives of states to increase non-AFDC collections, and the incentives for interstate collection of child support. The size of the increase will depend on how the 1984 legislation is implemented on both the federal and state levels. There will be few positive effects if the states enact weak standards and neither the number nor the amount of child-support awards increases much; if the states fail to effectively enforce the new law for withholding wages; and if federal, state, and local resources to enforce child support are cut. On the other hand, further strengthening of child-support enforcement could greatly increase the incomes of mother-only families.

To estimate the potential effect of child-support enforcement, we explored what would happen if all children potentially eligible for support obtained a child-support award based on some agreed-upon standard, and what the outcome would be if all such children received the full amount due them. According to a simple percentage-of-income standard used in Wisconsin, the child-support obligation is equal to 17 percent of the gross income of the noncustodial parent for one child, 25 percent for two, 29 percent for three, 31 percent for four, and 34 percent for five or more children. (In our calculation, we tax only the first $50,000 of income for child support.) Using this standard, we estimate that the incomes of families headed by women would increase by more than $10 billion (Garfinkel and McLanahan, 1986). The poverty gap would be reduced by nearly $2 billion. These estimates should be considered an upper bound, however, because even the most efficient collection system would fall short of 100 percent collection.

Increased enforcement of child support will raise the incomes of some single mothers who receive AFDC high enough to enable them to leave welfare. The precise effect of the child-support legislation on welfare dependence will vary according to the extent that collections will increase as a result of wage withholding and the new state standards, on the one hand, and the effect of the increased collections on caseloads, on the other. Some crude estimates are that (a) if existing awards are used as a standard, caseloads could be reduced by less than 5 percent; (b) if the Wisconsin standard described above is used, caseloads would decrease by 25 percent. Again, this estimate is an upper bound because it assumes a 100 percent collection rate.

Still, even 100 percent collection of child-support obligations derived from any reasonable standard would leave the overwhelming majority of AFDC recipients no better off than they were in the absence of the program. This situation prevails because most noncustodial parents of AFDC children do not earn enough to pay as much child support as their children are already receiving in AFDC benefits. Programs to increase the employment and earnings of poor noncustodial fathers would help. But even the best program imaginable would still leave a large proportion of the AFDC caseload poor and dependent on government benefits.

Most of the increases in collections of child support for families on welfare will accrue to the government in the form of AFDC savings. Low-income families on AFDC can share in some of the increased collections of child support in two ways. One approach is to ignore some of the child support payment in calculating AFDC grants. Congress has required all states to ignore the first $50 per month. That requirement modestly increases the incomes of mother-only families on AFDC in which there is a living, noncustodial father who makes child-support payments. It also increases by a small amount the number of mother-only families who will continue to receive AFDC.

An alternative approach is to use the increased child-support collections to help fund a nonwelfare benefit that encourages work. This approach is being pursued on a demonstration basis in Wisconsin. Under the Wisconsin child-support assurance system, child-support obligations are determined by a simple legislated formula that was described above. The obligation is withheld from wages and other sources of income in all cases, just as income and payroll taxes are. The child is entitled to receive either the money paid by the noncustodial parent or an assured child-support benefit, whichever is greater. Thus, the savings in AFDC that result from increased child-support collections are funneled back into the system, in the form of assured benefits and wage subsidies, to increase the economic well-being of families with children eligible for child support.[13]

---

[13]The state of Wisconsin is also considering a work expenses subsidy of $1.50 an hour to the custodial parent. Child-support legislation could address two dimensions of the disadvantage suffered by families headed by single women: the low earnings of mothers relative to fathers and the lack of support from the absent parent. Child-support legislation in general attempts to tackle the latter

We estimate that such a program could reduce the poverty gap among American families potentially eligible for child support by more than a third and AFDC caseloads by more than a half, and even reduce total public expenditures. The effects on poverty and welfare do not depend on how much collection improves, but the costs do. If 100 percent of the Wisconsin standard were collected, the program would save $2.4 billion. If only 70 percent were collected, the net cost would be about $60 million.

One criticism of the child-support assurance program is that it will benefit only those mothers who work. For those who are unable to work or who cannot find jobs or who simply prefer to take care of their children full-time, the program provides nothing. By contrast, the $50 per month set-aside that Congress enacted in 1984 provides more for this group than the child-support assurance program. Thus, the success of this latter approach will hinge largely on the extent to which both poor custodial mothers and poor noncustodial fathers work.

Enhanced enforcement of child support is, on balance, likely to reduce the prevalence of families headed by single women. It is also likely to reduce out-of-wedlock births by giving men an incentive to take responsibility for birth control. In order for enforcement of child support to have an appreciable effect on out-of-wedlock births, however, there would have to be a sizable increase in the number of cases in which paternity is established. Enforcement of child support may also reduce divorce by making it financially more difficult for the noncustodial parent. The impact of stronger enforcement on the behavior of the prospective custodial parent is likely to be smaller because welfare already exists as an alternative means of support.

---

issue by enforcing parental responsibility; in contrast, the Wisconsin assured benefit program represents an attempt to tackle the issue of the mother's earnings as well, both by providing an assured benefit and by providing a wage subsidy.

REFERENCES

Aponte, R., K. M. Neckerman, and W. J. Wilson
  1985   Race, family structure and social policy. Ch. 2 of *Working Paper 7: Race and Policy*. Project on the Social Role. Washington, D.C.: National Conference on Social Welfare.
Auletta, K.
  1982   *The Underclass*. New York: Random House.
Bassi, L. J., and O. Ashenfelter
  1986   The effect of direct job creation and training programs on low-skilled workers. Pp. 133–151 in S. H. Danziger and D. H. Weinberg, eds., *Fighting Poverty: What Works and What Doesn't*. Cambridge, Mass.: Harvard University Press.
Becker, G.
  1957   *The Economics of Discrimination*. Chicago: University of Chicago Press.
Bergmann, B. R.
  1974   Occupational segregation, wages and profits when employers discriminate by race or sex. *Eastern Economic Journal* 1(Apr.–July):103–110.
Bielby, W. T., and J. N. Baron
  1984   A woman's place is with other women: Sex segregation within organizations. Pp. 27–55 in B. F. Reskin, ed., *Sex Segregation in the Workplace: Trends, Explanations, Remedies*. Washington, D.C.: National Academy Press.
Blau, F. D.
  1984   Occupational segregation and labor market discrimination. Pp. 117–143 in B. F. Reskin, ed., *Sex Segregation in the Workplace: Trends, Explanations, Remedies*. Washington, D.C.: National Academy Press.
Bukharin, N.
  1921   *Historical Materialism*. (Authorized English Translation.) Ann Arbor, Mich.: Ann Arbor Paperbacks, 1969.
Bumpass, L. L.
  1984   Children and marital disruption: A replication and update. *Demography* 21:71–82.
Bumpass, L. L., and J. A. Sweet
  1972   Differentials in marital instability: 1970. *American Sociological Review* 37(Dec.):754–766.
Bureau of the Census
  1973   *Low Income Areas in Large Cities*. 1970 Census of Population. Subject Report PC(2)-9B. Washington, D.C.: U.S. Department of Commerce.
  1981a *Child Support and Alimony, 1978*. Current Population Reports Special Studies, Series P-23, No. 112. Washington, D.C.: U.S. Department of Commerce.
  1981b *Household and Family Characteristics: March 1980*. Current Population Reports, Series P-20, No. 366. Washington, D.C.: U.S. Department of Commerce.
  1984   *Household and Family Characteristics: March 1983*. Current Population Reports, Series P-20, No. 388. Washington, D.C.: U.S. Department of Commerce.
  1985a *Money Income and Poverty Status of Families and Persons in the United States: 1984*. Current Population Reports, Series P-60, No. 149. Washington, D.C.: U.S. Department of Commerce.

1985b *Poverty Areas in Large Cities (And Addendum)*. 1980 Census of Population. Subject Report PC-80-2-8D. Washington, D.C.: Department of Commerce.

Cherlin, A.
1976 Social and Economic Determinants of Marital Separation. Unpublished Ph.D. dissertation, Department of Sociology, University of Los Angeles.

Cole, S., S. Danziger, and I. Piliavin
1983 Poverty and Welfare Recipiency After OBRA: Some Preliminary Evidence from Wisconsin. Institute for Research on Poverty, University of Wisconsin. October.

Corcoran, M., and G. J. Duncan
1979 Work history, labor force attachment and earnings differences between the races and the sexes. *Journal of Human Resources* 14(Winter):3–20.

Cutwright, P., and P. Madras
1976 AFDC and the marital and family status of ever married women age 15–44: United States, 1950–1970. *Sociology and Social Research* 60:314–327.

Danziger, S. H., G. Jakubson, S. Schwartz, and E. Smolensky
1982 Work and welfare as determinants of female poverty and household headship. *Quarterly Journal of Economics* 97:519–534.

Darity, W., and S. M. Myers
1983 Changes in black family structure: Implications for welfare dependency. *American Economic Review Proceedings* 73(May):59–64.

Duncan, O. D., D. Featherman, and B. Duncan
1972 *Socioeconomic Background and Achievement*. New York: Seminar Press.

Duncan, G. J., and S. Hoffman
1985 Welfare Dynamics and Welfare Policy: Past Evidence and Future Research Directions. Paper presented at the Association for Public Policy Analysis and Management meetings, October, Washington, D.C.

Ellwood, D. T.
1985 Targeting the Would-be Long-term Recipients of AFDC: Who Should Be Served? Unpublished Preliminary Report. John F. Kennedy School of Government, Harvard University.

Ellwood, D. T., and M. J. Bane
1984 The Impact of AFDC on Family Structure and Living Arrangements. Report prepared for the U.S. Department of Health and Human Services (Grant No. 92A-82). John F. Kennedy School of Government, Harvard University.

Emery, R. E.
1982 Interparental conflict and the children of discord and divorce. *Psychological Bulletin* 92:310–330.

England, P.
1982 The failure of human capital theory to explain sex segregation. *Journal of Human Resources* 17(Summer):358–370.

Featherman, D., and R. Hauser
1978 *Opportunity and Change*. New York: Academic Press.

Fechter, A. E.
1975 *Public Employment Programs*. Washington, D.C.: American Enterprise Institute for Public Policy Research.

Garfinkel, I., and S. S. McLanahan
  1985   The Feminization of Poverty: Nature, Causes and a Partial Cure. Discussion Paper No. 776. Institute for Research on Poverty, University of Wisconsin.
  1986   *Single Mothers and Their Children: A New American Dilemma.* Washington, D.C.: Urban Institute Press.
General Accounting Office
  1985   *Evidence Is Insufficient to Support the Administration's Proposed Changes to AFDC Work Programs.* Report to the Chairman, Subcommittee on Intergovernmental Relations and Human Resources, House Committee on Government Operations. Washington, D.C.: General Accounting Office. August 27.
Giddens, A.
  1973   *The Class Structure of Advanced Societies.* New York: Harper and Row.
Gordon, D. M., ed.
  1977   *Problems in Political Economy: An Urban Perspective.* Lexington, Mass.: D.C. Heath and Company.
Groeneveld, L. P., M. T. Hanna, and N. B. Tuma
  1983   *Final Report of the Seattle-Denver Income Maintenance Experiments,* vol. 1, part 5. Menlo Park, Calif.: Stanford Research Institute International. May.
Gueron, J. M.
  1986   *Work Initiatives for Welfare Recipients.* March. New York: Manpower Demonstration Research Corporation.
  1987   Reforming Welfare with Work. February. Manpower Demonstration Research Corporation.
Herzog, E., and C. Sudia
  1973   Children in fatherless families. Pp. 141–231 in B. Caldwell and H. Ricciuti, eds., *Review of Child Development Research,* vol. 3. Chicago: University of Chicago Press.
Hetherington, E. M., K. A. Camara, and D. L. Featherman,
  1983   Achievement and intellectual functioning of children in one-parent households. Pp. 205–284 in J. Spence, ed., *Achievement and Achievement Motives.* San Francisco, Calif.: W. H. Freeman.
Hofferth, S.
  1985   Updating children's life course. *Journal of Marriage and the Family* 47:93–116.
Hoffman, S., and J. Holmes
  1976   Husbands, wives, and divorce. Pp. 23–75 in G. J. Duncan and J. Morgan, eds., *Five Thousand American Families,* vol. 4. Ann Arbor, Mich.: Institute for Social Research.
Hogan, D. P., and E. M. Kitagawa
  1985   The impact of social status, family structure, and neighborhood on the fertility of black adolescents. *American Journal of Sociology* 90(Jan.):825–856.
Hollister, R. G., Jr., P. Kemper, and R. A. Maynard, eds.
  1984   *The National Supported Work Demonstration.* Madison: The University of Wisconsin Press.
Honig, M.
  1973   The Impact of AFDC income, recipient rates, and family dissolution. *Journal of Human Resources* 9:303–322.

Hutchens, R. M.
    1969   Welfare, remarriage, and marital search. *American Economic Review* 69:369–379.

Joe, T., R. Sari, and M. Ginsberg
    1984   *Working Female Headed Families in Poverty: Three Studies of Income Families Affected by the AFDC Policy Changes of 1981.* Washington, D.C.: Center for the Study of Social Policy.

Kasarda, J. D.
    1985   Urban change and minority opportunities. Pp. 33–37 in Paul E. Peterson, ed., *The New Urban Reality.* Washington, D.C.: Brookings Institution.

Krein, S. F., and A. H. Beller
    1986   Family Structure and Educational Attainment of Children: Differences by Duration, Age, and Gender. Paper presented at the annual meeting of the Population Association of America, San Francisco.

Lenin, V. I.
    1914   A great beginning. Pp. 482–502 in *The Essentials of Lenin.* London: Lawrence and Wishart, 1947.

Levy-Shiff, R.
    1982   Coping with the loss of father: Family reaction to death or divorce. *Journal of Family Issues* 3:41–60.

Lewis, O.
    1966   *La Vida: A Puerto Rican Family in the Culture of Poverty—San Juan and New York.* New York: Random House.

Manpower Demonstration Research Corporation
    1980   *Summary and Findings of the National Supported Work Demonstration.* Cambridge, Mass.: Ballinger.

McLanahan, S. S.
    1983   Family structure and stress: Longitudinal comparison of male- and female-headed families. *Journal of Marriage and Family* 45:347–357.
    1985   Family structure and the reproduction of poverty. *American Journal of Sociology* 90:873–901.
    1988   Family structure and dependency: Early transitions to female household headship. *Demography,* forthcoming.

McLanahan, S. S., and L. L. Bumpass
    1986   Intergenerational Consequences of Family Disruption. Paper presented at the annual meeting of the Population Association of America, April 3–6, San Francisco, Calif.

Minarik, J., and R. Goldfarb
    1976   AFDC income, recipient rates, and family dissolution: A comment. *Journal of Human Resources* 9(Spring):243–257.

Mincer, J., and S. W. Polachek
    1974   Family investment in human capital: Earnings of women. *Journal of Political Economy* 82(March/April, Part 2):S76–S108.

Moore, K. A., and L. J. Waite
    1976   Marital dissolution, early motherhood and early marriage. *Social Forces* 60(September):20–40.

Moynihan, D. P.
    1965   *The Negro Family: The Case for National Action.* Office of Policy Planning and Research. Washington, D.C.: U.S. Department of Labor.

Oellerich, D., and I. Garfinkel
  1985   Distributional impacts of existing and alternative child support sys-
         tems. *Policy Studies Journal* 12:119–130.
Parkin, F.
  1971   *Class Inequality and Political Order*. New York: Praeger.
Pearce, D.
  1978   The feminization of poverty: Women, work, and welfare. *Urban and
         Social Change Review* 11:28–36.
Peterson, J. L., and N. Zill
  1986   Marital disruption, parent–child relationships, and behavior problems
         in children. *Journal of Marriage and the Family* 48:295–307.
Piore, M.
  1977   The dual labor market: Theory and implications. Pp. 93–97 in D.
         M. Gordon, ed., *Problems in Political Economy: An Urban Perspective*.
         Lexington, Mass.: D.C. Heath and Company.
Polachek, S. W.
  1977   Differences in expected post-school investment as a determinant of
         market wage differentials. Pp. 127–148 in P. A. Wallace and A.
         M. Lamond, eds., *Women, Minorities and Employment Discrimination*.
         Lexington, Mass.: Lexington Books.
Preston, S. H., and A. T. Richards
  1975   The influence of women's work opportunities on marriage rates. *De-
         mography* 12:209–222.
Reskin, B. F., and H. I. Hartmann, eds.
  1984   *Women's Work, Men's Work: Sex Segregation on the Job*. Committee
         on Women's Employment and Related Social Issues, Commission on
         Behavioral and Social Sciences and Education. Washington, D.C.:
         National Academy Press.
Ross, C.
  1984   Trends in poverty, 1965–1983. December. Paper prepared for the
         conference, "Poverty and Policy: Retrospect and Prospects." Insti-
         tute for Research on Poverty, University of Wisconsin, and the U.S.
         Department of Health and Human Services.
Ross, H., and I. Sawhill
  1975   *Time of Transition: The Growth of Families Headed by Women*. Washing-
         ton, D.C.: Urban Institute Press.
Sawhill, I.
  1976   Discrimination and poverty among women who head families. *Signs*
         2:201–211.
Shaw, L.
  1979   *Does Living in a Single-Parent Family Affect High School Completion for
         Young Women?* Columbus, Ohio: State University Center for Human
         Research.
Shinn, M.
  1978   Father absence and children's cognitive development, *Psychological
         Bulletin* 85:295–324.
South, S.
  1985   Economic conditions and the divorce rate: A time-series analy-
         sis of post-war United States. *Journal of Marriage and the Family*
         47(February):31–41.

Treiman, D. J., and H. I. Hartmann, eds.
  1981 *Women, Work, and Wages: Equal Pay for Jobs of Equal Value.* Committee
        on Occupational Classification and Analysis, Commission on Behav-
        ioral and Social Sciences and Education. Washington, D.C.: National
        Academy Press.
Usher, C. L., and J. D. Griffith
  1983 The 1981 AFDC Amendments and Caseload Dynamics. Research
        Triangle Park, N.C.: Research Triangle Institute.
Weber, M.
  1922 *Economy and Society,* edited by Gunther Roth. New York: Bedminster
        Press, 1968.
White, L.
  1981 A note on racial differences in the effect of female economic opportu-
        nity on marriage rates. *Demography* 18(August):349–354.
Wilson, W. J.
  1985a Cycles of deprivation and the underclass debate. *Social Science Review*
        59(December):541–559.
  1985b The urban underclass in advanced industrial society. Pp. 129–160
        in *The New Urban Reality,* Paul E. Peterson, ed. Washington, D.C.:
        Brookings Institution.
Wilson, W. J., and R. Aponte
  1985 Urban poverty. *Annual Review of Sociology* 11:231–258.
Wilson, W. J., and K. M. Neckerman
  1986 Poverty and family structure: The widening gap between evidence and
        public policy issues. Pp. 232–259 in S. H. Danziger and D. H. Wein-
        berg, eds., *Fighting Poverty: What Works and What Doesn't.* Cambridge,
        Mass.: Harvard University Press.
Wright, E. O.
  1979 *Class Structure and Income Determination.* New York: Academic Press.
  1985 *Classes.* London: Verso.

Jobs, Migration, and
Emerging Urban Mismatches

JOHN D. KASARDA

Spatial disparities in economic growth and corresponding migration adjustments have been constant features of our nation's development. As more efficient transportation and communication technologies evolve, modes of production organization and services are transformed; labor and natural resource requirements of industry change; and locational advantages shift, with new areas of opportunity rising while others decline. America's people, in turn, have tended to follow opportunity. In particular, this tendency has been the case for our nation's disadvantaged who historically have fled areas experiencing economic distress (often characterized by a substantial labor surplus relative to jobs) for areas of better opportunity. Indeed, it is not mere chance the three great symbols of opportunity for the disadvantaged in America all represent migration—the Statue of Liberty, the underground railway, and the covered wagon.

One consequence of the constant search of Americans for economic opportunity and a better life is that cities, suburbs, nonmetropolitan areas, and entire regions have frequently experienced uneven demographic growth. Before World War II the metropolitan areas of the Northeast and Midwest contained the majority of the nation's industrial locational advantages (excellent deep-water ports, extensive railroad and inland waterway systems, well-developed inter- and intrametropolitan highways, proximity to rich coal deposits, ubiquitous public utilities, a diverse and relatively better-educated labor force, and strong local markets). Such externalities provided firms locating in metropolitan areas of the North with competitive cost and market advantages that allowed them to expand much faster than their counterparts in more isolated, less-developed regions of the South and West. In fact, as late as 1950, more than 70 percent of all manufacturing jobs were in the Northeast and Midwest, mostly concentrated in and around the largest cities.

Since World War II a number of economic, political, and technological forces have combined to accelerate industrial restructuring and shift the nation's employment growth pole—first to the West and then to the South. The rapid postwar growth of aerospace, defense, solid-state electronics, and other advanced technology industries, together with expanding construction and services, fueled the economies of the Far West, especially California. Growth of these industries was instrumental in attracting over 3 million migrants to California alone between 1945–1960 (Bureau of the Census, 1975b).

With diversified economic expansion continuing in the West, the region's total employment doubled during 1960–1985. Nevertheless, the South emerged in the 1960s as the nation's leader in absolute employment gains. Between 1960–1985, the South added 17 million jobs to its economy, compared with a growth of just over 11 million in the West. During the same period, the Midwest added 7.3 million and the Northeast just over 5 million jobs (Bureau of the Census, 1960, 1985).

The South's economic surge has been attributed to its improved accessibility to national and international markets through newer interstate highway systems and expanded airports; shifting energy sources; upgraded public schools and universities; more modern physical plants; a sunny, benign climate; and relatively lower taxes and wage rates (Cobb, 1984; Goldfield, 1982). To these technological and financial considerations were added healthy doses of progrowth attitudes and industrial solicitation on the part of southern states and communities (Cobb, 1982; Kasarda, 1980). Thus, while manufacturing employment in the Frostbelt (Northeast and Midwest regions) declined by over a million jobs between 1960–1985, manufacturing employment in the South grew by over 2 million. Moreover, employment growth in southern manufacturing was far overshadowed by substantial increases in construction, trade, and services, which added more than 15 million jobs to the South's economy between 1960–1985 (Bureau of the Census, 1960, 1985).

The expanding post-World War II economies of the West and

South sequentially attracted major streams of migrants. The net interregional migration exchanges for the past three decades presented in Table 1 reflect the nation's shifting demographic growth poles from the West to the South. Before 1970 the West was the net beneficiary of migration streams from all census regions. These streams were especially large during the 1950s. During the 1970s the Current Population Survey indicates that more persons from the West began moving to the South than vice versa, while net flows from the Northeast and Midwest to the South rose dramatically. Between 1975–1980, overall net migration to the South was double that to the West. Spurred by a marked increase in net flows from the Midwest, net migration to the South was nearly triple that to the West between 1980–1985 (1.9 million versus 649,000). During the past 15 years the Northeast and Midwest have experienced combined net migration losses of 8 million people, most of whom moved to the South. Since 1980 the Midwest has experienced a net migration loss of 1.5 million, of which 1.1 million may be attributed to this region's negative exchange with the South.

The research literature points to a complex of interacting factors that have transformed the South from a net exporter of people until the early 1950s to a demographic magnet in the 1970s and 1980s. These factors include: (1) a sun-seeking retirement population whose private pensions, Social Security payments, and other sources of income free them from their previous work locations; (2) the introduction and spread of central air-conditioning systems that permit far more comfortable summertime living and working conditions; (3) life-style changes oriented to more recreation and year-round outdoor activities; (4) changing racial attitudes permitting blacks and Hispanics new opportunities to participate in mainstream southern institutions; (5) more progressive political orientations; (6) generally lower costs for land, living, and amenities; (7) a major improvement in the quantity and quality of consumer services brought about by rising personal incomes; and (8) the emergence of the South as an economic growth pole for the reasons mentioned earlier in this paper (for additional discussion, see Kasarda, 1980).

What about the demographic composition of the migrants? Table 2 shows the net interregional migration exchanges between 1975–1980, and between 1980–1985, by race and ethnicity. These exchanges, which were computed from the machine-readable files of the Bureau of the Census' Current Population Survey, show that

TABLE 1 Net Interregional Migration Flows (in thousands), 1955-1985

Regional Migration Exchanges	Net Migration (in thousands)				
	1955-1960[a]	1965-1970[b]	1970-1975[c]	1975-1980[d]	1980-1985[e]
South with					
Northeast	314	438	964	945	737
Midwest	122	275	790	813	1,100
West	-380	-56	75	176	60
Total other regions	56	657	1,829	1,935	1,897
West with					
Northeast	285	224	311	518	234
Midwest	760	415	472	634	475
South	380	56	-75	-176	-60
Total other regions	1,425	695	708	976	649
Midwest with					
Northeast	40	53	67	146	50
South	-122	-275	-790	-813	-1,100
West	-760	-415	-472	-634	-475
Total other regions	-842	-637	-1,195	-1,302	-1,525
Northeast with					
Midwest	-40	-53	-67	-146	-50
South	-314	-438	-964	-945	-737
West	-285	-224	-311	-518	-234
Total other regions	-639	-715	-1,342	-1,609	-1,022

NOTE: Some columns do not sum precisely because of rounding.

[a]From Bureau of the Census (1963:Table 237).
[b]From Bureau of the Census (1973:Table 274).
[c]From Bureau of the Census (1975c).
[d]From Bureau of the Census (1980b).
[e]From Bureau of the Census (1985).

non-Hispanic whites accounted for nearly 90 percent of the net southern migration gains from other regions. Indeed, both the absolute number and the percentage of net migrants to the South who were non-Hispanic whites rose from the 1975–1980 period to the 1980–1985 period. In the West, on the other hand, there has been a substantial decline in the number and percentage of net inmigration accounted for by non-Hispanic whites. Much of this decrease is due to a dramatic decline in the migration of non-Hispanic whites from the Northeast from the 1975–1980 period to the 1980–1985 period.

Of related interest, the net return of non-Hispanic blacks to the South from other regions declined from 194,000 between 1975–1980 to 87,000 between 1980–1985, with most of this slowdown due to a drop in the number of black migrants (59,000) from the Northeast. Furthermore, the migration of non-Hispanic blacks from the South to the Northeast increased by 50,000 between the 1975–1980 and 1980–1985 periods.

Table 2 also reveals the accelerating loss of non-Hispanic whites from the Midwest. Between 1980–1985, the Midwest experienced a negative net migration exchange of nearly 1.4 million non-Hispanic whites with other regions of the country, compared with a net loss of 1.2 million between 1975 and 1980. The accelerated out-migration of non-Hispanic whites from the Midwest was due largely to an increase in this region's negative net exchange with the South.

Another migration stream of growing importance is movers from abroad. Table 3 shows these movers, by region, for a series of 5-year periods between 1955–1960 and 1980–1985. Two trends are immediately apparent. First, there has been a substantial increase in the total number of movers to the United States during the past three decades. Second, since 1965 virtually all of the increase has been captured by the West and the South, with the West pulling ahead of the South as the primary destination. Between 1975–1985, over 2.8 million persons from abroad moved to the West, 2.3 million moved to the South, 1.7 million moved to the Northeast, and slightly over 1 million moved to the Midwest. In fact, since 1980 the West has gained more than twice as many movers from abroad as from the other regions of the nation.

A more detailed analysis of these data by race and ethnicity shows that during the last 10 years the West has received approximately 1 million Asian immigrants, more than all other regions combined. The vast majority of Asian immigrants have settled in California. The West has also been the largest receiver of Hispanic immigrants, gaining over 900,000 between 1975–1985. The South has exhibited major increases in Hispanic immigrants during the 1980s, falling closely behind the West. The South also registered increases in Asian immigrants but still trails the West substantially as the regional destination of this group. Between the 1975–1980 and 1980–1985 periods, Hispanic immigrants to the Northeast and

TABLE 2 Interregional Net Migration Flows (in thousands), 1975-1980 and 1980-1985

Regional Migration Exchanges	Non-Hispanic White		Non-Hispanic Black		Hispanic		Asian and Others	
	1975-1980	1980-1985	1975-1980	1980-1985	1975-1980	1980-1985	1975-1980	1980-1985
South with								
Northeast	731	630	139	30	64	51	12	28
Midwest	762	981	30	67	21	51	2	0
West	145	84	26	-10	20	6	-15	-20
Total other regions	1,637	1,695	194	87	105	108	-1	8
West with								
Northeast	432	166	32	13	26	34	26	21
Midwest	596	416	28	8	-3	12	13	39
South	-145	-84	-26	10	-20	-6	15	20
Total other regions	884	498	34	31	3	40	54	80
Midwest with								
Northeast	141	38	3	6	-1	-11	3	16
South	-762	-981	-30	-67	-21	-51	-2	0
West	-596	-416	-26	-8	-3	-12	-13	-39
Total other regions	-1,217	-1,359	-52	-69	-25	-74	-12	-23
Northeast with								
Midwest	-141	-38	-3	-6	-1	11	-3	-16
South	-731	-630	-139	-30	-64	-51	-12	-28
West	-432	-166	-32	-13	-26	-34	-26	-21
Total other regions	-1,304	-834	-174	-49	-92	-74	-42	-65

NOTE: Some columns do not sum precisely because of rounding.

SOURCE: Bureau of the Census (1975a, 1980b, and 1985b).

TABLE 3 Movers from Abroad (in thousands) by Region, 1955-1985

Region	1955-1960[a]	1965-1970[b]	1970-1975[c]	1975-1980[d]	1980-1985[e]
Northeast	592	821	903	834	832
Midwest	361	440	638	590	457
South	505	740	1,082	1,164	1,180
West	545	697	980	1,475	1,387

[a] From Bureau of the Census (1963:Table 237).
[b] From Bureau of the Census (1977:Table 274).
[c] From Bureau of the Census (1975c).
[d] From Bureau of the Census (1980b).
[e] From Bureau of the Census (1985b).

Midwest increased modestly, while Asian immigrants to these regions declined slightly.

The shift in regional residence of movers from abroad during the past three decades reflects a major change in the principal countries of origin of such movers. Until the late 1950s the origin of most U.S. immigrants was in Europe, geographically to the east and north of the United States. The majority of immigrants therefore found their closest ports of entry in New York and other northern states. During the past two decades the territorial locus of origin nations has increasingly shifted to the west and south of the United States (principally Mexico, Latin America, and Asia). As a result, Los Angeles, San Francisco, Miami, and Houston have become primary ports of immigrant entry. Between 1970–1983, more than a million Hispanics, Asians, and other foreign-born persons settled in Los Angeles County (Muller and Espenshade, 1986), lending empirical credence to anecdotal reports that Los Angeles has replaced New York City as the exemplary "melting pot" of the nation.

With increased immigration supplementing substantial internal net migration flows to the South and West, population growth in these regions has dwarfed that of the Northeast and Midwest. Table 4 describes population change in each region between 1975–1980, and between 1980–1985, by race and ethnicity. Over the past 10 years, the South has added 12.3 million residents, the West has added 8.8 million, the Midwest 2.2 million, and the Northeast 1.2 million. Further examination of Table 4 shows that, between both 1975–1980 and 1980–1985, the South and West have accounted for more than 85 percent of the nation's population growth.

Table 4 also illustrates significant racial/ethnic differences in

TABLE 4 Absolute (in thousands) and Percentage Change in U.S. Population by Region and Race/Ethnicity, 1975-1985

Population Changes	1975-1980				1980-1985			
	Northeast	Midwest	South	West	Northeast	Midwest	South	West
Total population								
Absolute change	435	1,363	7,109	4,806	784	835	5,212	4,076
Percentage change	0.9	2.4	10.6	12.6	1.6	1.6	7.0	9.6
White, non-Hispanic								
Absolute change	-160	288	4,904	2,590	-554	55	2,376	1,770
Percentage change	-0.4	0.6	9.7	8.9	-1.4	0.1	4.3	5.6
Black, non-Hispanic								
Absolute change	316	537	1,109	133	475	241	1,353	64
Percentage change	7.3	11.2	8.9	6.4	10.3	4.5	10.0	2.9
Asian and others								
Absolute change	238	404	316	985	90	195	296	976
Percentage change	49.7	184.5	61.2	51.2	12.6	31.3	35.6	33.6
Hispanic								
Absolute change	41	134	780	1,098	773	344	1,187	1,266
Percentage change	1.8	14.2	23.0	23.6	32.6	31.9	28.5	22.0

SOURCE: Bureau of the Census (1975a, 1980b, and 1985b).

regional population growth. The Northeast is the only region to experience an absolute and percentage increase in population during the 1980s compared with the latter half of the 1970s, yet its non-Hispanic white population losses accelerated. Between 1980–1985, the non-Hispanic white population of the Northeast declined by 554,000, while the region's Hispanic population expanded by 773,000, its black population increased by 475,000, and its Asian population expanded by 90,000.

The population increase that occurred in the Midwest during the first half of the 1980s also was predominantly through increases in that region's minority populations. On the other hand, the South and the West experienced major growth of their non-Hispanic white populations between 1975–1985. An aggregate comparison of the Frostbelt (Northeast and Midwest) with the Sunbelt (South and West) reveals that, between 1975–1985, the Sunbelt added 11.64 million non-Hispanic whites, whereas the Frostbelt lost 371,000 non-Hispanic whites. The Sunbelt also added more minorities than did the Frostbelt, although absolute differences in minority population growth were not nearly as striking as they were for non-Hispanic whites.

Along with racial/ethnic changes of migration flows among regions, there have been changes in the racial/ethnic composition of metropolitan central cities, suburbs, and nonmetropolitan areas of each region. Table 5 presents these composition changes from 1975–1985. With modest growth in the black, Asian, and Hispanic populations, and absolute declines in non-Hispanic whites, the minority proportion of central cities in the Northeast grew from 33 percent to 42 percent during this period. In the Midwest, central-city minority proportions increased from 28 percent to 36 percent. Concurrently, central cities in the South exhibited monotonic rises in their overall minority proportions, primarily through growth in the number of Hispanics. Substantial growth in the Hispanic and Asian populations occurred in western central cities. Indeed, increases in the number of Hispanics and Asians in these cities were so substantial between 1975–1985 that, despite an absolute increase in the number of blacks there during the period, the black proportion of central-city total population fell by nearly 3 percent.

The racial/ethnic compositions and compositional changes that occurred between 1975–1985 in the metropolitan suburban rings and nonmetropolitan areas reveal some striking interregional contrasts. In the Northeast and Midwest, non-Hispanic whites constitute more

TABLE 5 Percentage Distribution of Population in Metropolitan Central Cities, Suburban Rings, and Nonmetropolitan Areas by Region and Race: 1975, 1980, and 1985

Regional Minority Population	Central Cities			Suburban Rings			Nonmetropolitan Areas		
	1975	1980	1985	1975	1980	1985	1975	1980	1985
Northeast									
White, non-Hispanic	67.0	63.7	57.7	92.8	92.0	91.1	97.3	96.3	95.9
Black, non-Hispanic	20.1	22.4	23.7	4.1	4.5	5.2	1.9	1.8	2.0
Asian and others	1.6	2.7	3.0	0.9	1.0	1.0	0.3	0.8	1.2
Hispanic	11.2	11.2	15.6	2.2	2.4	2.7	0.6	1.2	0.9
Total minority	33.0	36.3	42.3	7.2	8.0	8.9	2.7	3.7	4.1
Midwest									
White, non-Hispanic	71.7	67.1	64.5	95.4	94.0	93.5	97.3	96.7	96.3
Black, non-Hispanic	23.7	26.8	28.6	3.4	4.0	3.3	1.7	1.6	1.6
Asian and others	0.8	1.7	1.5	0.2	0.9	1.5	0.3	0.8	1.2
Hispanic	3.7	4.5	5.3	1.0	1.0	1.7	0.7	0.9	0.9
Total minority	28.3	32.9	35.5	4.6	6.0	6.5	2.7	3.3	3.7
South									
White, non-Hispanic	60.3	58.7	55.2	84.9	80.6	78.7	78.5	80.2	78.7
Black, non-Hispanic	30.4	29.6	29.7	8.9	11.6	12.3	18.0	16.6	17.7
Asian and others	0.8	0.8	1.7	0.8	1.7	1.8	0.8	1.0	1.0
Hispanic	8.5	11.0	13.5	5.4	6.1	7.1	2.7	2.3	2.6
Total minority	39.7	41.3	44.8	15.1	19.4	21.3	21.5	19.8	21.3
West									
White, non-Hispanic	67.2	66.3	61.3	79.9	77.2	73.7	84.7	80.0	82.0
Black, non-Hispanic	11.7	9.9	9.0	3.2	4.0	4.0	1.8	1.2	1.1
Asian and others	7.6	8.2	11.2	4.9	6.3	7.2	1.9	6.1	6.8
Hispanic	13.5	15.6	18.5	11.9	12.5	15.2	11.6	12.8	10.1
Total minority	32.8	33.7	38.7	20.1	22.8	26.3	15.3	20.0	18.0

SOURCE: Special tabulations of data from Bureau of the Census (1975a, 1980b, 1985b) from unsuppressed machine-readable files using constant area (1970) boundaries.

than 90 percent of the suburban populations of these regions and
more than 95 percent of their nonmetropolitan populations. These
percentages changed very little between 1975–1985. In the South and
West, the minority percentages of the population in the suburban
rings and nonmetropolitan areas were much higher. The growth
of black, Asian, and Hispanic populations in the suburban rings of
southern metropolitan areas increased the minority percentage in
these areas from 15 percent to 21 percent between 1975–1985. The
minority percentage in western metropolitan suburbs concurrently
rose from 20 percent to 26 percent.

Led by a steady growth in the Asian population, minority percentages of nonmetropolitan areas in the West increased from 15
percent to 18 percent during 1975–1985. In the South, minority percentages of nonmetropolitan areas remained constant at slightly over
21 percent.

It is important to emphasize that, although the overall minority
proportions of central cities in the four regions are similar, there
are significant differences between the Frostbelt and Sunbelt regions
in their suburban and nonmetropolitan minority proportions. In
1985, the *highest* overall minority percentage in the metropolitan
suburbs or nonmetropolitan areas of the Frostbelt was 8.9 percent
in Northeast suburbs. Conversely, the *lowest* overall suburban or
nonmetropolitan minority proportion in the Sunbelt was 18 percent,
which was registered in nonmetropolitan areas of the West. Clearly,
then, minorities are less confined to central cities in the South and
West than in the Northeast or Midwest.

Recent minority immigrant locational trends reinforced these
relative differences in minority confinement. Between 1975–1985,
most minority immigrants to the Northeast and Midwest settled in
the central cities of metropolitan areas, whereas in the South and
West, most have settled in the suburban rings and nonmetropolitan
areas. As we will see later, such settlement patterns have important
implications for entry-level job opportunities for minorities.

COMPETITIVE EFFECTS AND REGIONAL GROWTH

A fundamental reason for the substantial growth of the South and
West during the past decade has been the ability of their economies
to weather recessions better than those of the Northeast and Midwest. In accounting for differential local and regional economic performance during economic downturns, industry mix has received a

good deal of attention. It is argued that areas whose economic bases are dominated by firms whose products are disproportionately concentrated in cyclically sensitive industries (e.g., as consumer durable goods manufacturing) will experience more severe declines in their local employment during recessions than those places whose employment mix is less sensitive to recessions, such as places where higher order producer service industries predominate (Bergman and Goldstein, 1983; Bluestone and Harrison, 1982; Noyelle and Stanback, 1983).

Conversely, localities with especially advantageous industrial mixes often experience employment gains in the face of recessions and expand much faster than national growth rates during periods of economic prosperity (Noyelle and Stanback, 1983). These localities have high proportions of younger, more vibrant industries that are adapted to macrostructural transformations in the broader economy (Bell, 1973; Castells, 1985).

Yet the industrial structure of localities and regions is not always predictive of how their employment bases will respond to business cycles. The South, for example, added substantial employment during the most recent recession (1980–1982), despite having an overall industrial mix that was not nearly as favorable as that of the Northeast. The analysis of employment change among all 3,200 U.S. counties further revealed numerous counties with unfavorable industrial mixes that exhibited marked employment gains during recent national recessions; yet other counties with favorable industrial mixes experienced considerable employment decline, even during periods of national economic prosperity (Kasarda and Irwin, 1986). Such localities appear to possess competitive advantages or disadvantages that overcome both the effects on employment growth of local industrial structure and national business cycles.

To measure these competitive effects and assess their role in regional job growth and decline, shift/share techniques were applied to analyze employment changes in all counties within each region during the last two recessions (1974–1976 and 1980–1982) and the business cycle upswings that followed them. Very briefly, shift/share analysis decomposes an area's employment change between any two points in time into three parts: (1) that portion accounted for by national employment change, (2) that due to the area's industrial mix, and (3) that due to unique local features (see Dunn, 1960, 1980; Perloff et al., 1960). The third term, known as the shift or competitive component, is the amount of an area's employment

Structure industry vs. locale # jobs

change that cannot be explained by national economic conditions or local industry mix. It is an outcome of such factors as transportation access, land availability and cost, wage rates, taxes, union strength, federal investment, business regulations, physical climate, and local attitudes toward growth. As these locally unique competitive factors come into play, some localities and regions fall behind, while others surge ahead.

Table 6 presents aggregate summaries of the competitive effects of metropolitan core, metropolitan ring, and nonmetropolitan counties in each region during different phases of the business cycle.[1] These summary statistics were obtained by aggregating the competitive components of all counties in each spatial category at each cycle phase. The algorithm for computing the competitive components standardizes the effects in a zero-sum manner such that industry-specific employment gains in one county come at the expense of another county's loss (hence, the "shift" terminology). Thus, each column of competitive effects sums to zero.

Competitive effects were computed for 10 categories of counties within each region along an urban/rural continuum (from counties containing large metropolitan central cities to nonmetropolitan counties containing no place larger than 2,500 residents); corresponding local industrial mix ("share") effects were computed for the same 10 categories. Space constraints preclude tabular presentation of these finer grain results; comments are made about them where pertinent, however. For example, prior to 1978 the employment growth of the Northeast was hampered by exceptionally weak competitive effects

---

[1] The shift/share analysis presented in this paper was based on industry-specific employment obtained for 3,101 U.S. counties from the *County Business Patterns* (CBP) machine-readable files of the Bureau of the Census (1974, 1976, 1978, 1980a, 1982a, 1984). Since 1977 CBP employment has been the count of employees during the pay period including March 12 for each year, as reported on Treasury Form 941, Schedule A. The form is used to indicate all employment covered by Social Security or other retirement systems. Prior to 1977 coverage included only employment covered by Social Security. This change affected employment coverage in industries in which private retirement systems are prevalent, such as health and educational services. CBP covers approximately 88 percent of total civilian, nongovernment employment. For a discussion of the industrial categories used in the shift/share analysis and related methodological issues, see Kasarda and Irwin (1986). In Table 6, "metropolitan core counties" refers to counties in which the metropolitan central city is located. "Metropolitan ring counties" refers to those counties not containing the central city in multiple-county metropolitan areas.

TABLE 6 County Competitive Effects (in thousands of employees) During National Business Cycle Stages, Aggregated by Region and Metropolitan Status, 1974-1984

Region and County Type	N	Recession 1974-1976	Expansion 1976-1978	Expansion 1978-1980	Recession 1980-1982	Expansion 1982-1984	Span 1974-1984
Northeast							
Metropolitan core	45	-541	-620	-192	-86	-112	-1,770
Metropolitan ring	42	-35	-10	-12	90	131	165
Nonmetropolitan	130	-9	-26	26	15	-5	-3
Total	217	-585	-655	-178	19	14	-1,608
Midwest							
Metropolitan core	67	-135	-273	-457	-685	-198	-1,852
Metropolitan ring	101	34	141	-70	-55	77	151
Nonmetropolitan	885	121	-39	-202	-211	-71	-380
Total	1,053	20	-171	-729	-951	-192	-2,081
South							
Metropolitan core	88	-2	-63	131	445	-160	361
Metropolitan ring	169	132	158	156	258	191	960
Nonmetropolitan	1,162	112	79	15	130	-14	360
Total	1,419	242	174	302	833	17	1,681
West							
Metropolitan core	42	132	452	541	17	184	1,405
Metropolitan ring	21	43	95	69	77	28	329
Nonmetropolitan	349	148	103	-5	5	-51	273
Total	412	323	650	605	99	161	2,007

SOURCE: See note, Table 10. Shift-share analysis of data on county employment from Bureau of the Census, County Business Patterns, 1974-1984.

of the region's large and medium-sized metropolitan core counties. After 1978, however, the competitive position of these larger urban counties and the region improved. By the 1980–1982 recession, the Northeast's overall competitive effect was positive (see Table 6). This regional improvement in the competitive effect is indicative of important changes in defense expenditures, new industry demands for better educated and more highly skilled labor, and reduced business regulations, taxation rates, and ecological structure as the decentralization of population and industry acted to decrease problems of congestion in certain core cities at the same time it boosted economic growth in the suburban ring counties. Led by a remarkable transformation of the Northeast's largest cities to white-collar services, industrial mix effects in the Northeast became much more favorable to growth during the 1980s.

Trends in competitive effects in the Midwest ran counter to those of the Northeast, with the midwestern situation steadily deteriorating between 1974–1982. This deterioration occurred in most types of counties but was especially severe in metropolitan core counties. Such factors as high wage rates, union restrictions, aging infrastructure, and a negative balance of tax payments with Washington have apparently compounded problems of the Midwest's disadvantaged industrial mix during economic downturns and substantially weakened the region's ability to compete for jobs (Checkoway and Patton, 1985). Even during the post-1982 recovery, the positive competitive effects of midwestern metropolitan ring counties did not compensate for the competitive disadvantages of midwestern metropolitan core counties and nonmetropolitan counties. Thus, the regional totals in Table 6 show that all other regions grew since 1982 at the competitive expense of the Midwest.

The South's competitive edge increased sharply between 1978 and 1982, then atrophied. During the 1980–1982 recession, all types of counties—from the most rural to the most urbanized—gained far more jobs than can be accounted for by either national growth trends or the southern counties' industrial structures. Smaller metropolitan central-city counties showed particularly strong competitive effects during the 1980–1982 recession, as did the central-city and suburban counties in the region's largest metropolitan areas. The highly unfavorable industry mix of the South's nonmetropolitan counties was not entirely offset by these counties' positive competitive effects, and consequently southern nonmetropolitan counties had modest employment declines during each of the last two recessions.

With agricultural problems, falling oil prices, and foreign competition striking particularly hard at the South's rural manufacturing industries, negative competitive multipliers rippled through the region's nonmetropolitan areas while previous overbuilding and problems related to the energy industry severely dampened a number of large metropolitan core counties, such as Harris County (Houston) in Texas. During the 1982–1984 period, the combined competitive effects of metropolitan core counties in the South were less than those in the Northeast and almost as weak as in the Midwest's metropolitan core counties—a dramatic reversal from the strong competitive position of the South's metropolitan core counties during the 1980–1982 recession.

The competitive components of growth in the West were strongest during the 1976–1980 economic upswing. Although the region maintained a consistently positive advantage throughout the business cycle, its competitive edge weakened during the 1980–1982 recession. The West's industrial mix, however, remained highly conducive to employment growth during both national economic booms and busts. Thus, the western regional economy, led by its spatially expansive metropolitan core counties (e.g., Los Angeles, Maricopa [Phoenix], San Diego), was particularly vibrant during periods of national economic growth and only mildly affected by economic downturns.

Overall, the shift/share analysis of county-level employment change showed that the competitive effects of nonmetropolitan counties have weakened: the counties exhibited negative effects in all regions during the 1982–1984 interval. The analysis also indicated that the marked expansion of jobs in the South during the past decade occurred largely because of the region's strong competitive features. These features (which did deteriorate after 1982) more than offset the poor industrial mixes of the South's nonmetropolitan counties. The large employment declines in the Midwest resulted from a disadvantaged industrial mix that was highly sensitive to economic downturns, coupled with weak competitive effects relative to other regions. (The industrial mix of the Midwest, however, was conducive to employment growth during business cycle upswings.) The Northeast has improved its competitive features and its industrial mix in recent years, increasing its ability to hold and attract jobs. Finally, the West has been blessed with a favorable industrial mix and with competitive features that have resulted in its steady employment growth through all phases of the business cycle.

If the shift/share results are predictive of what should be happening during the current postrecession period, we would expect the South and West to still lead the nation in employment growth, with the Northeast closing the gap and the Midwest still lagging behind. Table 7 shows the changes in the number of nonagricultural employees across the four regions by major industry groupings for 2-year intervals between March 1980–March 1986. The industry groupings are production (mining, construction, and manufacturing), trade (retail and wholesale), and services (finance, insurance, real estate, civilian government employees, and other service industries).

Comparing total nonagricultural employment changes during the 1980s (column 1 of each panel in the table) reveals interesting cross-regional dynamics. Whereas the South added the most employment both in absolute and proportional terms between 1980–1986, it lost its lead in percentage growth rate to the West following the 1982 recession. The Northeast exhibited a strong turnaround (from employment loser to employment gainer) from 1982–1984, as did the Midwest. The economies of both regions further strengthened between March 1984–March 1986 with the Midwest actually surpassing the Northeast in absolute (although not proportional) job growth. The recent improvement of the Midwest was due primarily to the significant economic recoveries of Ohio, Michigan, and Indiana, whose cyclically sensitive industrial bases responded to the business cycle upswing. Between 1983–1986, these states added more than 620,000 nonagricultural jobs to the Midwest's employment base.

Facilitated by its improved competitive situation and industrial mix, the Northeast's employment growth rates during the 1984–1986 interval were nearly as high as those of the South and West. In fact, between March 1985–March 1986, total employment growth in the Northeast equaled that of the South, whose economy slowed for reasons that will be noted shortly.

Employment changes within the three industry groups illustrate the major economic restructuring that is taking place in the regions. Nowhere is this more apparent than in the Northeast. This region added 1.73 million jobs to its employment base between 1980–1986; yet it lost 495,000 production jobs.[2] Service industries alone added

---

[2]Manufacturing employment in the Northeast actually declined by 686,000 jobs, and mining employment declined by 14,400 jobs; construction, on the other hand, expanded by 205,700 jobs.

TABLE 7 Changes in Number (in thousands) and Percentage (in parentheses) of Nonagricultural Employees by Region and Major Industry Groups, March 1980-March 1986

Year	Northeast				Midwest			
	Total	Production	Trade	Service	Total	Production	Trade	Service
1980-1982	-136.7	-394.6	-25.9	283.3	-1,266.2	-1,002.9	-245.6	-17.7
	(-0.7)	(-6.7)	(-0.6)	(2.8)	(-5.3)	(-13.7)	(-4.5)	(-0.2)
1982-1984	745.2	-102.2	343.0	504.8	407.8	-29.7	198.3	239.0
	(3.7)	(-1.9)	(8.2)	(4.8)	(1.8)	(-0.5)	(3.8)	(2.2)
1984-1986	1,116.7	2.1	378.1	736.5	1,136.3	96.6	380.7	658.9
	(5.3)	(0.0)	(8.3)	(6.7)	(5.0)	(1.5)	(7.1)	(5.9)
1980-1986	1,725.2	-494.7	695.2	1,524.6	277.9	-936.0	333.4	880.2
	(8.5)	(-8.4)	(16.5)	(14.8)	(1.2)	(-12.8)	(6.2)	(8.0)

Year	South				West			
	Total	Production	Trade	Service	Total	Production	Trade	Service
1980-1982	689.2	-147.8	245.5	592.1	2.5	-226.0	27.2	201.4
	(2.4)	(-1.8)	(3.8)	(4.2)	(0.0)	(-5.3)	(0.7)	(2.2)
1982-1984	1,238.6	-45.1	479.5	803.3	909.7	145.1	295.6	468.8
	(4.2)	(0.5)	(7.2)	(5.5)	(5.2)	(3.6)	(7.2)	(5.0)
1984-1986	1,914.5	108.6	670.4	1,135.6	1,257.5	131.8	362.6	762.9
	(6.2)	(1.3)	(9.4)	(7.3)	(6.8)	(3.2)	(8.3)	(7.7)
1980-1986	3,042.3	-84.3	1,395.4	2,531.0	2,169.7	50.9	685.4	1,433.1
	(13.3)	(-1.0)	(21.7)	(18.0)	(12.4)	(1.2)	(16.9)	(15.5)

SOURCE: Bureau of Labor Statistics (1986b).

1.52 million employees during the first 6 years of the decade.[3] By March 1986 over half of all employment in the Northeast was in the services sector.

Also remarkable was the Midwest's loss of more than 1 million production jobs (in mining, construction, and manufacturing) during the 1980–1982 recession. Despite the modest recovery of this sector following the recession, overall employment gains in the Midwest since 1982 have been largely through the expansion of services and trade—industries whose average wages are generally lower than the production jobs they replace.

Employment is only one side of the regional job outlook, however. The other is unemployment, which reflects growth in the labor force as well as numbers of jobs. Table 8 presents labor force sizes, the number of persons employed, the number unemployed, and unemployment rates for the four regions from March 1976–March 1986, with biennial data during the 1980s.

Once again, we can see the uneven regional effects of the most recent recession: marked declines in the number of people employed in the Northeast and Midwest between March 1980–March 1982 in contrast to growth in the South and West. After the recession, however, the number of *unemployed* persons in the Northeast and Midwest fell more sharply than in the West and South. Indeed, between March 1984–March 1986, the number of people unemployed in the South actually increased by 162,000, making it the only census region to experience a rise in its unemployment rate.

The more recent rise in the number of the unemployed in the South not only reflects such factors as agricultural distress, falling oil prices, and foreign competition for southern textiles and other products but also the substantial in-migration of labor to the region during the 1980s (see Tables 1 and 3). Although the South has added more jobs than any other region of the country since 1982, it has also added the largest number of individuals to its labor force.

The Northeast and Midwest, on the other hand, have continued to experience net out-migration, bringing the sizes of their labor forces into better balance with employment opportunities. This pattern is most pronounced in the New England census division in

---

[3]Civilian government employment increased by 16,300; employment in the areas of finance, insurance, and real estate increased by 276,900; and employment in other services rose by 1,236,800.

TABLE 8 Labor Force Size, Employment, and Unemployment (in thousands) by Region, March 1976–March 1986

Region	Year	Labor Force	Employed	Unemployed	Percentage Unemployed
Northeast	1976	21,561	19,438	2,122	9.84
	1980	22,943	21,351	1,592	6.94
	1982	23,277	21,193	2,084	8.95
	1984	23,593	21,818	1,775	7.52
	1986	24,383	22,852	1,531	6.28
Midwest	1976	25,742	23,784	1,958	7.61
	1980	27,856	25,811	2,045	7.34
	1982	28,159	24,991	3,167	11.25
	1984	28,272	25,559	2,713	9.60
	1986	29,032	26,686	2,345	8.08
South	1976	29,804	27,705	2,101	7.05
	1980	33,946	31,931	2,015	5.94
	1982	35,865	32,805	3,060	8.53
	1984	37,379	34,559	2,820	7.54
	1986	38,963	35,982	2,982	7.65
West	1976	16,078	14,571	1,506	9.37
	1980	19,155	17,901	1,254	6.55
	1982	20,083	18,108	1,974	9.83
	1984	20,661	18,904	1,757	8.50
	1986	21,934	20,285	1,651	7.52

SOURCE: Bureau of Labor Statistics (1986b).

which substantial job growth, along with slowing yet continued out-migration, depressed that division's unemployment rate to just 4.43 percent in March 1986, nearly half of what it was in March 1983. Much of New England today is experiencing a labor force squeeze, in dramatic contrast to 1976 when the division had a huge surplus of labor.[4]

The numerical balance between labor availability and jobs (as manifested in unemployment rates) is central to understanding the numerous problems facing regions and cities. Beyond the raw numbers, however, are the matches between the composition of jobs and the mix of skills held by the resident work force in transforming local economies. If these matches are disjointed, the unemployment

---

[4]This prior labor surplus is reflected in the 10.3 percent unemployment rate of the New England census division in March 1976. This division then had a total of 575,000 people unemployed, compared to 294,000 in March 1986.

rates of mismatched labor may well rise simultaneously with substantial job growth in their localities. Nowhere are the problems of demographic–employment opportunity mismatches and corresponding structural unemployment more acute than in the older, larger cities of the North. The remainder of this chapter describes how the redistribution of people and jobs in urban America has resulted in widening demographic–employment opportunity mismatches in these cities and the consequences of such mismatches for their disadvantaged residents.

TRANSFORMING URBAN ECONOMIES

America's older, larger cities have always been leaders in the development and transition of the nation's employment base. They spawned the nation's industrial revolution, which generated massive numbers of blue-collar jobs that served to attract and economically upgrade millions of migrants. More recently, these same cities were instrumental in transforming the U.S. economy from one primarily of manufacturing to one of basic services (during the 1950s and 1960s) and from a basic service economy to one of information and administrative control (during the 1970s and 1980s).

The transformation of major cities from centers of goods processing to centers of information processing was accompanied by corresponding changes in the size and composition of their employment bases. Manufacturing dispersed to the suburbs, exurbs, non-metropolitan areas, and abroad. Warehousing activities relocated to more regionally accessible beltways and interstate highways. Retail establishments followed their suburbanizing clientele and relocated in peripheral shopping centers and malls. The urban exodus of the middle class further diminished the number of blue-collar service jobs such as domestic workers, gas station attendants, and delivery personnel. Many secondary commercial areas of cities withered as the income levels of the residential groups that replaced a suburbanizing middle class could not economically sustain them.

Although most parts of the central city continued to experience an erosion of their employment base, pockets of economic vitality emerged offering entertainment, cultural, and leisure services to younger white-collar workers residing in the cities and to growing numbers of tourists and conventioneers (Kasarda, 1985). The central business districts also experienced a resurgence in investment, particularly in high-rise office structures. In contrast to the expansive space per worker typically consumed in processing, storing, and selling material goods, the worker space required for processing, storing, and transmitting information is small. Moreover, unlike material goods, information can be transferred vertically as efficiently as it can be transferred horizontally. Those who process information, therefore, can be stacked, layer upon layer, in downtown office towers, and the resulting proximity actually increases the productivity of those who require extensive, nonroutine, face-to-face interaction.

[handwritten margin notes: space eff. communic. over manu.]

The intensive use of prime space by information-processing functions has driven up central business district rents to such a high level that other functions often have difficulty competing. Thus, during the past two decades, we have witnessed the closing of many traditional downtown department stores and of other large, space-consuming retail and wholesale facilities, concurrent with the boom in central business district office construction.

Table 9, which is derived from *County Business Patterns* data for five major northern cities whose boundaries match or approximate county boundaries, illustrates the nature and scope of urban industrial transformation. Between 1953–1985, New York City lost over 600,000 jobs in manufacturing. During this same period, white-collar service industries (defined as those in which executives, managers, professionals, and clerical employees constitute more than 50 percent of the industry work force) grew by nearly 800,000 jobs.[5] Retail and wholesale employment since 1970, corresponding to the industrial redistributional patterns discussed above, declined by 168,000, with blue-collar service employment dropping by 58,000.

Philadelphia, Baltimore, Boston, and St. Louis likewise experienced substantial employment declines in manufacturing and in retail and wholesale trade, as well as in blue-collar services. Between 1953–1985, Philadelphia lost more than two-thirds of its manufacturing jobs (which dropped from 359,000 to 109,000), decreasing employment in this industry from more than 45 percent of the city's

---

[5] White-collar and blue-collar service industries were determined by categorizing industries using occupation data from the Bureau of Labor Statistics (1981) industry-by-occupation matrix for 1970. Those service industries with fewer than 50 percent of their employees classified in executive, managerial, professional, or clerical occupations were designated blue-collar service industries; those with more than half of their employees classified in these same occupations were designated white-collar service industries.

TABLE 9 Central-City Employment (in thousands) by Sector: 1953, 1970, and 1985

Central City and Sector	1953 Number	Percentage	1970 Number	Percentage	1985 Number	Percentage
New York						
Total employment[a]	2,976	100.0	3,351	100.0	2,990	100.0
Manufacturing	1,070	35.9	864	25.8	464	15.5
Retail/wholesale	805	27.1	779	23.3	611	20.4
White-collar services[b]	646	21.7	1,172	35.0	1,427	47.7
Blue-collar services[c]	344	11.6	424	12.6	366	12.2
Other	111	3.7	112	3.3	122	4.1
Philadelphia						
Total employment[a]	788	100.0	773	100.0	604	100.0
Manufacturing	359	45.5	257	33.3	109	18.0
Retail/wholesale	206	26.1	180	23.3	134	22.2
White-collar services[b]	98	12.5	220	28.5	277	45.9
Blue-collar Services[c]	85	10.8	81	10.5	62	10.3
Other	40	5.1	35	4.5	22	3.6
Boston						
Total employment[a]	402	100.0	465	100.0	483	100.0
Manufacturing	114	28.4	84	18.1	49	10.1
Retail/wholesale	132	32.8	111	23.9	84	17.4
White-collar services[b]	87	21.7	194	41.6	278	57.6
Blue-collar services[c]	51	12.6	55	11.7	59	12.2
Other	18	4.4	21	4.6	13	2.7

Baltimore						
Total employment[a]	342	100.0	367	100.0	323	100.0
Manufacturing	130	38.1	105	28.6	55	17.0
Retail/wholesale	89	26.1	94	25.5	71	22.0
White-collar services[b]	44	12.8	108	29.5	139	43.0
Blue-collar services[c]	51	14.9	44	12.1	40	12.4
Other	28	8.1	16	4.2	18	5.6
St. Louis						
Total employment[a]	432	100.0	376	100.0	262	100.0
Manufacturing	194	44.9	133	35.3	66	25.2
Retail/wholesale	103	23.9	89	23.6	54	20.6
White-collar services[b]	50	11.5	96	25.5	97	37.0
Blue-collar services[c]	46	10.6	44	11.8	34	13.0
Other	39	9.1	14	3.8	11	4.2

[a] Total classified employment and industry subcategories excluding government employees and sole proprietors.
[b] Service industries (excluding government, retail, and wholesale) in which more than one-half of the employees hold executive, managerial, professional, or clerical positions.
[c] Service industries (excluding government, retail, and wholesale) in which fewer than one-half of the employees hold executive, managerial, professional, or clerical positions.

SOURCE: Bureau of the Census (1953, 1970, 1985a); Bureau of Labor Statistics (1981).

total employment in 1953 to just 18 percent in 1985. During the same period, manufacturing employment in Boston declined from 114,000 to 49,000; in Baltimore, it went from 130,000 to 55,000; and in St. Louis, it dropped from 194,000 to 66,000. Employment declines in retail and wholesale trade and in blue-collar services followed suit, although the absolute and proportional losses were not as steep as those for manufacturing employment.

As in New York City, white-collar service employment expanded substantially in the four cities between 1953–1985. Boston's white-collar service employment increased from 87,000 to 278,000; Philadelphia's rose from 98,000 to 277,000; Baltimore's went from 44,000 to 139,000; and St. Louis's increased from 50,000 to 97,000. St. Louis is the only northern city in which white-collar service employment did not exceed 40 percent of the city total in 1985. By the same token, 58 percent of all Boston's jobs were in white-collar service industries in 1985, compared with 22 percent in 1953. Such increases in white-collar service employment across these northern cities clearly manifest their emerging information-processing roles in the computer age.

Table 10 further highlights the overriding significance of predominantly information-processing industries for contemporary urban employment growth. This table divides total employment change between 1970–1985 for each city into that accounted for by (1) its service sector industries in which more than 60 percent of the employees in 1978 were classified in executive, managerial, professional, and clerical occupations and (2) all other industries combined (Bureau of Labor Statistics, 1981). In addition to the five northern cities discussed above, four southern and western cities with closely corresponding city–county boundaries (Atlanta, Houston, Denver, and San Francisco) are presented for comparative purposes.

Observe that all five northern cities experienced substantial employment growth in their predominantly information-processing industries and marked employment declines in their other combined industries. For example, New York City added 385,000 jobs between 1970–1985 in its predominantly information-processing industries (a 41 percent increase) while losing more than 700,000 jobs in other industries (a 30 percent decrease). By 1985, 44 percent of all jobs in New York City were in service industries in which executives, managers, professionals, and clerical workers constituted more than 60 percent of the industry's total employment.

Boston's information-processing industries expanded by 42.3

percent between 1970–1985 while its other industries declined by 21.4 percent. Boston, in fact, is the only major northern city that added more jobs during this period to its predominantly information-processing industries than it lost in other industries. For the other three northern cities—Philadelphia, Baltimore, and St. Louis—job increases in their predominantly information-processing industries were overwhelmed by job losses in their more traditional industries. This is especially the case for St. Louis, which lost more than half of its manufacturing jobs between 1970–1985.

In contrast to larger, older cities in the North, Atlanta, Houston, Denver, and San Francisco experienced employment gains in both their predominantly information-processing industries and in all other industries combined. Like larger cities in the North, however, the older, major cities in the South and West (Atlanta, San Francisco, and Denver) exhibited substantially greater absolute and proportional gains in their information-processing industries than they exhibited in their other combined industries. Indeed, all three cities lost manufacturing employment between 1970–1985. Houston, on the other hand, added substantial employment across all industries between 1970–1985, no doubt reflecting the city's economic surge during much of this period.

A major difference, then, between large cities in the Frostbelt and large cities in the Sunbelt is that since 1970 Sunbelt cities have added jobs in many other industries besides information-processing, jobs that have contributed to these cities' overall employment growth. Conversely, many Frostbelt cities have experienced overall employment decline since 1970 because growth in their predominantly information-processing industries did not compensate for substantial losses in their more traditional industrial sectors, especially manufacturing. In this regard, we find a strong negative correlation between the percentage of the city's employment in manufacturing in prior decades and total job change since 1970. Those cities in which manufacturing constituted at least 35 percent of their employment bases in 1953 (Philadelphia, Baltimore, St. Louis, and New York) all experienced significant overall job declines between 1970–1985; in contrast, the others (Boston, Atlanta, Houston, Denver, and San Francisco) all added jobs during this period.

The functional transformation of major northern cities from centers of goods processing to centers of information processing during the past three decades corresponds to an important change in the education required for employment in these cities. Job losses have been

TABLE 10 Central-City Industrial Employment (in thousands) by Percentage of Jobs in Industry Classified as Information Processors, 1970-1985

City and Industry Type[a]	1970		1985		Change, 1970-1985	
	Number	Percentage	Number	Percentage	Number	Percentage
New York						
Over 60% information processors	946	28.2	1,331	44.1	385	40.7
All other industries	2,404	71.8	1,687	55.9	-717	-29.8
Philadelphia						
Over 60% information processors	208	26.9	263	43.2	55	26.4
All other industries	564	73.1	346	56.8	-218	-38.7
Boston						
Over 60% information processors	189	40.7	269	55.3	80	42.3
All other industries	276	59.3	217	44.7	-59	-21.4
Baltimore						
Over 60% information processors	95	25.5	129	39.7	34	35.8
All other industries	272	74.5	196	60.3	-76	-27.9
St. Louis						
Over 60% information processors	92	24.5	100	37.9	8	8.7
All other industries	284	75.5	164	62.1	-120	-42.3

Atlanta						
Over 60% information processors	92	24.7	151	32.9	59	64.1
All other industries	280	75.3	308	67.1	28	10.0
Houston						
Over 60% information processors	130	20.6	327	26.9	197	151.5
All other industries	500	79.4	888	73.1	388	77.6
Denver						
Over 60% information processors	70	27.6	125	35.4	55	78.6
All other industries	183	72.0	228	64.6	45	24.6
San Francisco						
Over 60% information processors	149	37.1	220	42.3	71	47.7
All other industries	253	62.9	300	57.7	47	18.6

[a]Information processors include executive, managerial, professional, and clerical occupations.

SOURCE: Bureau of the Census (1970, 1985a), and Bureau of Labor Statistics (1981).

greatest in those northern urban industries in which educational requirements for employment tend to be low (e.g., a high-school degree typically is not required). Job growth has been primarily concentrated in urban industries in which education beyond a high-school degree is the norm.

effed
ed.

To illustrate this phenomenon, Table 11 presents the employment changes from 1959–1985 in industries classified by the mean years of schooling completed by their jobholders. Two categories of industries were selected: (1) industries whose jobholder educational levels in 1982 averaged less than 12 years (i.e., employees did not complete high school), and (2) industries whose jobholders averaged more than 13 years of schooling (i.e., employees, on average, acquired some higher education).[6]

The figures reveal that all major northern cities had consistent employment losses in industries with lower educational requisites. The heaviest job losses occurred in these industries after 1970. New York City, for instance, lost more than half a million jobs between 1970–1985 in those industries in which mean jobholder educational levels in 1982 were less than high school completion; the city added 268,000 jobs in those industries in which mean employee educational levels exceeded 13 years of schooling. Philadelphia, Baltimore, and St. Louis have also lost substantial numbers of jobs with low educational requisites since 1970, with St. Louis experiencing a small loss of jobs in those of its industries with high mean jobholder educational levels as well.

Boston, on the other hand, added more jobs in industries with high educational requisites than it lost in industries with low educational requisites, a tendency that has contributed to overall city

---

[6]Industry employment changes in cities by average educational level of jobholders were estimated by synthesizing individual-level data on the schooling completed by jobholders in detailed classified industries with data on the aggregate job changes that have occurred within each industry in each city. To measure the average educational level of employees in detailed urban industries, the March 1982 *Current Population Survey* (Bureau of the Census, 1982b) was used to compute the mean years of schooling completed by all central-city residents who were employed in two-, three-, and four-digit Standard Industrial Classification (SIC)-coded industries. Mean educational levels were then computed for each detailed industry classified in *County Business Patterns*. Aggregate job changes within each educationally classified industry were then traced between 1959 and 1985 for the nine major cities (see Table 11) whose boundaries are either identical to or closely approximate those for which place-specific industrial employment data are available in *County Business Patterns*.

TABLE 11 Central-City Jobs in Industries (in thousands) by Mean
Education of Employees: 1959, 1970, and 1985

City and Educational Mean of Industry	Number of Jobs			Change	
	1959	1970	1985	1959-1970	1970-1985
New York					
Less than high school	1,561	1,525	1,048	-9	-504
Some higher education	682	1,002	1,270	320	268
Philadelphia					
Less than high school	466	430	243	-36	-187
Some higher education	135	205	256	70	51
Boston					
Less than high school	180	189	137	-1	-52
Some higher education	117	185	261	68	76
Baltimore					
Less than high school	236	207	132	-29	-75
Some higher education	59	90	124	31	34
St. Louis					
Less than high school	221	210	117	-11	-93
Some higher education	61	98	97	37	-1
Atlanta					
Less than high school	130	179	182	49	3
Some higher education	42	92	143	50	51
Houston					
Less than high school	192	348	567	156	219
Some higher education	59	144	368	85	224
Denver					
Less than high school	92	120	130	28	10
Some higher education	42	72	132	30	60
San Francisco					
Less than high school	143	155	174	12	19
Some higher education	82	138	218	56	80

SOURCE: Bureau of the Census (1959, 1970, 1982b, 1985a).

job growth since 1970. By 1985 Boston had nearly twice as many
jobs in industries with high mean employee educational levels than it
had in industries with low mean levels of employee education. This
fact would appear to indicate that Boston's economy has adapted
especially well to the emerging postindustrial order, an adaptation
that should sustain that city's employment growth into the 1990s.

New York City likewise has a much higher percentage of its labor employed in knowledge-intensive service industries, implying that this city, too, should fare well in employment growth during the remainder of the 1980s.

Employment growth in industries whose jobholders' educations averaged more than 13 years in 1982 was also marked in major cities in the South and West. Yet in contrast to major cities in the North, each of the four cities in the South and West gained jobs in industries with low educational requisites between 1959–1985. Even after 1970 these cities added jobs in their industries with low educational requisites, although Houston (Harris County) is the only city to experience a boom in jobs with low educational requisites during the 1970s and early 1980s.

The oil price decline of the mid-1980s has cooled Houston's economy considerably and has also depressed recent employment growth in Denver. At the same time the transformed service economies of Boston, New York City, and a number of other northeastern cities have led to a recent resurgence in their employment growth. Although job losses are continuing in manufacturing and other blue-collar sectors of these cities, their vigorous information-processing sectors are more than compensating for blue-collar job losses, reversing decades of net employment decline.

WIDENING DEMOGRAPHIC–EMPLOYMENT OPPORTUNITY MISMATCHES IN CITIES

We have seen how jobs in industries with lower educational requisites have increasingly disappeared from northern cities to be partially replaced by information-processing jobs requiring substantial education or skills. Unfortunately, the northern cities that have lost the greatest numbers of jobs with lower educational requisites during the past three decades have simultaneously experienced large increases in the number of their minority residents, many of whom are workers whose limited educations preclude their employment in the new urban growth industries.

In this section, we examine urban demographic changes and assess the role played by educational distributions of residents in urban structural unemployment. We begin with an overview of the changing size and racial/ethnic compositions of selected cities. Table 12 presents these demographic changes between 1970–1980 within the four largest northern cities (New York, Chicago, Philadelphia, and

TABLE 12 Decomposition of Total Population and Population Changes in the Four Largest Northern Cities by Race and Ethnicity, 1970-1980

Central City	Total Population	Non-Hispanic Whites	Non-Hispanic Blacks	Non-Hispanic Others	Hispanics	Percentage Minority
New York						
1980	7,071,639	3,668,945	1,694,127	302,543	1,406,024	48
1970	7,894,851	5,061,663	1,517,967	112,940	1,202,281	36
Change, 1970-1980	-823,212	-1,392,718	176,160	189,603	203,743	
Chicago						
1980	3,005,072	1,299,557	1,187,905	95,547	422,063	57
1970	3,362,825	1,998,914	1,076,483	39,571	247,857	41
Change, 1970-1980	-357,753	-699,357	111,422	55,976	174,206	
Philadelphia						
1980	1,688,210	963,469	633,485	27,686	63,570	43
1970	1,948,609	1,246,940	646,015	10,975	44,679	36
Change, 1970-1980	-260,399	-283,471	-12,530	16,711	18,891	
Detroit						
1980	1,203,339	402,077	754,274	18,018	28,970	67
1970	1,511,336	820,181	651,847	9,254	30,054	46
Change, 1970-1980	-307,997	-418,104	102,427	8,764	-1,084	
Total change for all cities, 1970-1980	-1,749,361	-2,793,650	377,479	271,054	395,756	

SOURCE: Bureau of the Census, Census of Population machine-readable files, 1970 and 1980.

Detroit). New York City, which experienced an overall population decline of more than 823,000 people during the decade, actually lost 1.39 million non-Hispanic whites. Approximately 40 percent of the loss of non-Hispanic whites in New York City was replaced by an infusion of more than 570,000 Hispanics, blacks, and "others" (mostly Asian minorities) during the 1970s.

Chicago's demographic experience during the 1970s was similar to that of New York City. More than 50 percent of Chicago's minority population increase during the decade consisted of Hispanics. It is important to point out, however, that Chicago also experienced the third largest absolute increase of non-Hispanic blacks (111,422) of any U.S. city. By 1980, 57 percent of Chicago's resident population was composed of minorities.

Philadelphia had the smallest aggregate population decline of the four cities. The number of non-Hispanic whites and non-Hispanic blacks in Philadelphia declined between 1970–1980; the number of Hispanic and Asian minorities increased. Philadelphia's substantial decline in the number of non-Hispanic whites, together with its net increase of 23,000 minority residents during the 1970s, raised its minority population percentage to 43 percent in 1980.

Detroit experienced the highest rate of non-Hispanic white residential decline of any major city in the country. Between 1970–1980, Detroit lost more than half of its non-Hispanic white residents. Concurrently, Detroit had the fourth-largest absolute increase of non-Hispanic blacks (102,427) of any city in the country, falling just behind Chicago in its rate of increase in black residents. Detroit's large increase in numbers of black residents and its sharp drop in non-Hispanic white residents, combined with modest increases in the number of "non-Hispanic others," transformed the city's residential base from 46 percent minority in 1970 to 67 percent minority in 1980.

The Bureau of the Census's Current Population Survey (1985) is not designed to provide population size estimates by race and ethnicity for individual cities, so estimates for 1985 from this survey must be interpreted with extreme caution. Bearing this caveat in mind, aggregated summary statistics were computed for these four large cities and their suburban rings to obtain rough estimates of total and minority population shifts during the first half of the 1980s. The 1985 estimates suggest that New York City added more than 200,000 residents during the first half of the 1980s, that Chicago's population essentially stabilized, and that Philadelphia's and Detroit's losses slowed substantially. These results are consistent with independent local and Bureau of the Census mid-decade estimates. For all four cities, however, the Current Population Survey aggregates indicate that their non-Hispanic white populations continued to decline while the minority populations of all but Philadelphia grew. By 1985 the Current Population Survey estimates suggest that minorities had become a demographic majority in New York City (54 percent) and had grown to 46 percent of Philadelphia's resident population, 61 percent of Chicago's, and 72 percent of Detroit's. The corresponding 1985 sample estimates of minority percentages in the suburban rings of these four cities were 13 percent for Chicago, 6 percent for Detroit, 9 percent for Philadelphia, and 20 percent for New York.

The point at issue, however, is that all four central cities experienced increasing minority dominance of their residential bases at the same time they were losing massive numbers of traditional blue-collar jobs. This is particularly the case in the cities' manufacturing sectors. Between 1972–1982, the U.S. Censuses of Manufacturing show that Chicago lost 47 percent of its manufacturing jobs, Detroit lost 41 percent, Philadelphia 38 percent, and New York City 30 percent. Bureau of Labor Statistics data further reveal that manufacturing job losses continued in these cities into the mid-1980s. For example, although New York City added 239,000 jobs in the period from 1980–1986 (a 7 percent overall increase), it lost 108,000 jobs in manufacturing—a 22 percent drop in this sector (Bureau of Labor Statistics, 1986b).

Manufacturing job decline is by no means the only pertinent measure of urban blue-collar job loss, but it is a good general indicator of the continuing ability of a city to sustain large numbers of residents with limited educational attainment. Such figures, combined with the industrial employment data cross-classified by occupation and mean education of jobholders (Tables 10 and 11), imply that urban racial/ethnic differences in the years of education completed will have significant effects on the employment prospects of each group. Table 13 presents these differences, by race and sex, for the central cities of the four census regions.

Bearing in mind the selective employment and demographic changes in large northern cities during the past 15 years, compare the 1985 distribution of education completed by white male residents of central cities in the Northeast and Midwest with that of black male residents in the same central cities. Note that the modal category of education completed by white men in northern cities is "completed 1+ years of higher education." The smallest representative category

TABLE 13 Number of Central-City Residents Aged 16-64 by Race, Sex, and Years of School Completed, 1985

	Region			
Race, Sex, and Schooling	Northeast	Midwest	South	West
White men				
Did not complete high school	944,964	743,105	950,060	825,810
Completed high school only	1,096,986	1,136,702	1,283,903	984,280
Completed 1+ years of				
higher education	1,205,944	1,291,168	1,869,914	1,694,782
Black men				
Did not complete high school	445,349	479,141	636,271	102,811
Completed high school only	366,932	404,121	574,247	151,870
Completed 1+ years of				
higher education	234,723	352,993	315,924	186,187
White women				
Did not complete high school	1,073,245	750,902	984,791	736,821
Completed high school only	1,486,641	1,435,176	1,486,740	1,085,916
Completed 1+ years				
higher education	1,128,071	1,150,689	1,720,628	1,469,271
Black women				
Did not complete high school	501,588	523,110	595,935	95,995
Completed high school only	555,176	543,309	704,946	154,321
Completed 1+ years				
higher education	351,755	393,324	575,190	169,732

SOURCE: Computed from Bureau of the Census (1985b).

for white men residing in northern central cities is "did not complete high school." The education-completed distribution of white men is therefore consistent with the distribution of job changes classified by education.

The opposite educational distributions hold for black men residing in central cities of the Northeast and Midwest. Despite substantial gains in educational attainment during the past two decades, black men (16 years of age and older) in northern cities are still mainly concentrated in the education-completed category in which employment opportunities declined the fastest; they are least represented in that category in which northern central-city employment has expanded the most since 1970 (see Table 11). The consequence, to reiterate, is a serious mismatch between the current educational distribution of minority residents in large northern cities and the changing educational requirements of their rapidly transforming industrial bases. This mismatch is one major reason why unemployment rates and labor force dropout rates among central-city blacks are much higher than those of central-city white residents, and why black unemployment rates have not responded well to economic recovery in many northern cities. Let us now assess these concrete manifestations of mismatch.

Table 14 presents the changing unemployment rates of whites and minorities, by sex, within the four large northern cities whose transforming demographic compositions were described in Table 12. It is immediately apparent that white unemployment rates in all four cities in 1985 were substantially below those of blacks and others. The gap is particularly large in those cities that lost the greatest percentages of their manufacturing bases during the 1970s and early 1980s (Chicago and Detroit). Note that in these two cities minority unemployment rates actually rose during the 1980s while their white

TABLE 14 Unemployment Rates (percentage) in Selected Major Northern Central Cities by Race and Sex: 1976, 1980, and 1985

City and Sex	Whites			Blacks and Others		
	1976	1980	1985	1976	1980	1985
New York						
Total	10.7	7.7	7.2	12.8	10.8	10.1
Men	10.9	7.5	7.4	14.4	12.6	11.2
Women	10.3	7.9	6.9	11.0	8.9	8.8
Philadelphia						
Total	7.9	7.7	6.5	19.2	20.4	12.0
Men	8.5	7.8	6.1	24.9	21.8	13.4
Women	7.0	7.6	7.0	11.7	18.9	11.4
Chicago						
Total	5.9	9.0	8.0	14.6	15.4	24.6
Men	6.6	9.8	8.8	16.7	17.7	25.8
Women	5.0	7.8	7.0	12.3	12.8	23.0
Detroit						
Total	11.3	16.2	13.3	15.0	26.2	30.3
Men	11.3	18.9	15.9	12.5	31.6	29.7
Women	11.3	12.4	9.5	18.2	22.2	30.9

SOURCE: Computed from Bureau of Labor Statistics, Geographic Profiles of Employment and Unemployment, 1976-1980; 1985 figures provided by the Bureau of Labor Statistics.

resident unemployment rates fell. In point of fact the unemployment rates of whites in all four northern cities declined between 1980–1985, along with the size of their white populations.

One interesting figure in Table 14 is the rather sharp recent decline in the minority unemployment rate in Philadelphia. Philadelphia was the only major northern city listed in Table 12 that also experienced a decline in its black population between 1970–1980. The Census Bureau's Current Population Survey estimates suggest that this city's black population declined further between 1980–1985, in contrast to New York, Chicago, and Detroit. Yet the minority unemployment drop is greater than might have been predicted by demographics alone. Even with this decline, however, Philadelphia's male minority unemployment rate was still more than twice that of its white resident rate in 1985 (Bureau of the Census, 1985).

The Current Population Survey does not contain a sufficiently large sample to provide reliable estimates of unemployment rates by both race and education level for individual cities. Such detailed decomposition might explain the Philadelphia case. It is possible, however, to aggregate central-city samples by region and calculate central-city unemployment rates, by race and education completed, for each region. These computations, which are presented in Table 15, illustrate the increasingly important role education has played in urban employment prospects. Consistent with the mismatch thesis, one finds a precipitous rise in unemployment rates between 1969–1982 for those who have not completed high school. Within central cities in the Northeast and Midwest, the unemployment rates of black men without a high-school degree exceeded 30 percent in 1985. Indeed, for blacks in northeastern cities who lack a high-school degree, the economic recovery had no effect—their unemployment rates actually increased from 26.2 percent in 1982 to 30.4 percent in 1985.

Another statistic revealing the growing importance of education for urban employment prospects is the substantial increase in the absolute gap in unemployment rates between the poorly educated and the better educated in 1969 versus 1985, regardless of race. For central-city white residents in all regions combined, the education-level gap in unemployment rates in 1969 was 2.7 (4.3 − 1.6) percent. By 1985 it was 11.9 (15.5 − 3.6) percent. For central-city blacks, the gap was 2.9 (6.6 − 3.7) percent in 1969 and 14.2 (27.3 − 13.1) percent in 1985. This widening gap over time between the unemployment rates of lesser educated labor and those of more highly educated labor appears within all four regions.

TABLE 15 Unemployment Rates (percentage) of Central-City Men Aged 16-64 by Race, Region, and Years of School Completed: 1969, 1977, 1982, and 1985

Region and Schooling	White				Black			
	1969	1977	1982	1985	1969	1977	1982	1985
All regions								
Did not complete high school	4.3	12.2	17.7	15.5	6.6	19.8	29.7	27.3
Completed high school only	1.7	8.0	11.0	8.3	4.1	16.2	23.5	18.4
Completed 1+ years of higher education	1.6	4.7	4.4	3.6	3.7	10.7	16.1	13.1
Northeast								
Did not complete high school	3.7	13.9	17.2	16.0	7.6	20.9	26.2	30.4
Completed high school only	1.7	9.4	10.3	9.7	3.4	18.2	21.9	13.6
Completed 1+ years of higher education	1.4	6.0	4.8	3.9	7.1	13.9	18.6	11.7
Midwest								
Did not complete high school	4.9	12.8	24.3	23.2	8.3	26.2	34.8	32.8
Completed high school only	1.1	8.0	14.5	10.8	3.3	18.0	35.8	24.9
Completed 1+ years of higher education	1.3	3.5	3.8	3.7	1.4	12.3	22.2	18.4
South								
Did not complete high school	3.4	9.9	13.2	10.8	3.8	14.5	28.2	21.5
Completed high school only	0.8	5.9	6.8	5.2	3.6	13.5	16.6	16.9
Completed 1+ years of higher education	1.7	3.1	2.9	3.2	3.6	6.2	13.6	10.7
West								
Did not complete high school	6.4	12.0	17.3	13.5	11.6	22.2	32.9	29.8
Completed high school only	4.2	8.6	13.4	7.8	9.6	17.7	15.9	20.1
Completed 1+ years of higher education	1.9	6.4	6.0	3.7	2.9	13.2	9.9	9.1

SOURCE: Computed from Bureau of the Census (1969, 1977, 1982b, 1985b).

In examining central-city unemployment rate changes across regions since 1982, note that although white male unemployment rate declines were generally consistent for all education categories, declines in black male unemployment were consistent only for those who had completed further years of education beyond high school. The relatively large 1985 unemployment rates among better-educated black urban men (particularly in the Midwest) is troublesome and difficult to interpret. The quality of education may play a role here, as could racial ceilings in the hiring practices of firms in major midwestern cities with exceptionally large minority percentages (e.g., Chicago and Detroit).

Unemployment rates reveal only part of the picture of demographic-economic opportunity mismatch and the corresponding displacement of many minorities from the urban economic mainstream. These rates do not include persons who have given up looking for work because they believe no jobs are available (discouraged workers) and those who want work but cannot hold employment for a variety of physical or personal reasons. Such individuals are not considered to be in the labor force and therefore are not counted among the unemployed.

To measure the proportions of discouraged workers and other urban labor force nonparticipants, we can compute a statistic that taps the percentage of each city's men (aged 16–64) who are neither in school nor in the labor force. The numerator of this statistic is men aged 16–64 who are *not* classified as in school, employed, or unemployed. The denominator is the total number of males (aged 16–64) classified as employed, unemployed, and (excluding those in school) not in the labor force. Thus, the "in school" population has been removed from the "not in labor force" numerator *and* from the "labor force" plus the "not in labor force" denominator.

Table 16 presents age-specific unemployment rates along with corresponding labor force nonparticipation rates, by race, between 1969–1985 for central-city male residents (aged 16–64) across the four census regions. This table reaffirms the sharp increase since 1969 in unemployment rates among young (aged 16–24) black men residing in central cities of the Northeast and Midwest. It also shows the large percentages of male working-age blacks in northeastern and midwestern metropolitan cities who are both out of school and out of the labor force. If one combines black unemployment rates with black labor force nonparticipation rates, the dire straits of black

TABLE 16 Unemployment Rates (percentage) and Proportion of Male Central-City Residents (Aged 16-64) Who Are Not in School and Not in the Labor Force, by Region, Race, and Age: 1969, 1980, and 1985

Region, Race, and Age	Unemployment Rates			Percentage Not in School and Not in the Labor Force		
	1969	1980	1985	1969	1980	1985
All regions						
White						
Aged 16-24	7.3	12.1	13.5	4.5	5.2	6.1
Aged 25-64	1.6	5.2	6.2	5.8	9.8	10.4
Black						
Aged 16-24	13.0	29.0	37.1	8.2	13.7	14.1
Aged 25-64	3.4	10.9	14.6	10.3	18.6	20.4
Northeast						
White						
Aged 16-24	7.4	16.5	16.7	6.9	5.5	9.4
Aged 25-64	1.6	6.2	7.1	6.9	11.9	12.7
Black						
Aged 16-24	12.0	33.8	43.5	12.2	19.2	24.5
Aged 25-64	4.8	12.5	13.1	10.7	17.7	19.0
Midwest						
White						
Aged 16-24	7.0	14.7	19.1	3.2	2.6	7.1
Aged 25-64	1.4	6.8	8.1	5.1	9.6	10.5
Black						
Aged 16-24	16.3	40.5	44.5	7.2	19.4	N.A.
Aged 25-64	3.0	15.2	18.6	9.9	19.9	27.0
South						
White						
Aged 16-24	6.0	8.4	8.9	4.0	8.7	3.7
Aged 25-64	1.0	3.6	4.5	5.0	9.0	9.6
Black						
Aged 16-24	8.5	19.4	29.2	6.9	9.5	14.3
Aged 25-64	2.4	7.1	13.9	10.6	19.3	17.1
West						
White						
Aged 16-24	9.5	9.3	11.3	4.5	3.8	5.5
Aged 25-64	2.8	4.9	5.8	6.0	8.8	9.1
Black						
Aged 16-24	19.7	30.0	29.6	6.0	N.A.	9.3
Aged 25-64	4.8	9.1	11.7	9.3	15.0	17.4

NOTE: N.A. = not available.

SOURCE: Bureau of the Census (1969, 1980b, 1985b).

men residing in central cities in the Northeast and Midwest may be quickly seen.

Corresponding black male unemployment and labor force non-participation rates tend not to be as high in the central cities of the South and West. For one reason, recall that these cities have experienced relatively fewer blue-collar job losses during the past two decades, and some cities have added large numbers of jobs in industries that do not require substantial education in their work forces. Moreover, the West, which has the lowest combined unemployment and labor force nonparticipation rates for black men, is also the only region in which the educational distribution of black men is skewed toward the upper end (see Table 13). It is not fortuitous, then, that black males residing in central cities of the West also showed the smallest increases in rates of unemployment and rates of labor force nonparticipation between 1969–1985.

CONCLUSIONS AND POLICY ISSUES

A key policy construct developed in the preceding sections is "mismatch," which is defined as a discordant distribution of labor qualifications vis-à-vis the qualifications required for available jobs at a particular point in time. Mismatch has both nonspatial (nationwide) and spatially specific (community) aspects. The nonspatial aspect results from transformations in the overall economy from an industrial to a postindustrial base and the corresponding shrinking demands for traditional blue-collar labor (Bell, 1973; Singlemann, 1978). A tacit assumption in much of the literature on postindustrial society is that, through the interplay of market forces, displaced labor will adapt to the transforming economy by "shifting" from one sector to another (e.g., from manufacturing to services). Appropriate skills will eventually be acquired or sufficient numbers of service-sector jobs (both low-skill and high-skill) will be created, absorbing the displaced and relieving the mismatch. This, of course, has been slow to happen in the United States, giving credence to those who argue that some structural unemployment will remain a permanent feature of the national economy.

Spatially specific mismatches emerge in those areas in which transformations in local employment bases occur faster than their local labor can adapt, either through retraining or relocation. These mismatches are most apparent in larger, older cities in the North in which declines in traditional blue-collar industries and the growth of information-processing industries have been rapid and substantial. So different are the skills used and the education required in these growing as opposed to declining urban industrial sectors that adaptation by the displaced is exceedingly difficult. This difficulty is concretely represented in the exceptionally high unemployment rates of those central-city residents who have not completed high school, regardless of race, and the widening gap over time between the central-city unemployment rates of the poorly and the better educated.

It follows from the above that unemployment rates and labor force dropout rates will be higher for resident groups whose educational distributions are inconsistent with the changing job opportunity structures of their localities. Such circumstances are particularly the case for black men (aged 16 or older) in major cities in the North who are most concentrated in the education-completed category in which matching local jobs are contracting (less than high-school degree) and least represented in the education-completed category in which local jobs are expanding (some higher education typically required).

Exacerbating resident labor force–job opportunity mismatches have been recent demographic trends in these cities. During the past two decades, northern cities that lost the largest numbers of blue-collar and other jobs with low educational requisites simultaneously added large numbers of poorly educated minorities to their working age population. This demographic phenomenon, which contrasts sharply with that anticipated on the basis of market equilibrium models, leads to an important policy question: What is continuing to attract and/or hold large numbers of less skilled minorities in urban centers while employment opportunities appropriate to their skills are disappearing? To be sure, such factors as racial discrimination, a lack of sufficient low-income housing in outlying areas, and the dependence of low-income minorities on public transportation account for a significant part of the explanation. There is also the vast urban underground economy that enables many of those displaced from the mainstream economy to survive. Indeed, for many who lack the educational, technical, or interpersonal skills for employment in mainstream institutions, the inner city may provide the only environment in which they can stay afloat economically.

It has been suggested elsewhere (Kasarda, 1983, 1985) that certain public policies may also be anchoring disadvantaged persons in areas of rapid blue-collar job decline. These policies are based on the seemingly reasonable principle of spatially targeting public assistance: areas of the greatest economic distress (measured by such factors as poverty rates and persistent unemployment) receive the largest allocations of funds for public housing, community nutritional and health care, and other locationally focused government aid (U.S. Department of Housing and Urban Development, 1978, 1980). Formula-based community assistance programs have also been introduced such that the greater a locality's employment loss or other indicator of economic distress, the more federal aid it could receive (U.S. Department of Housing and Urban Development, 1980, 1984; Swanson and Vogel, 1986). Thus, as the blue-collar employment bases of cities have withered, additional public assistance has been provided, serving as a partial subsistence surrogate for many of those displaced from the economic mainstream (for data, see Kasarda, 1985).

Although these policies helped relieve certain problems associated with declining blue-collar job bases (e.g., the inability of the unemployed to afford private sector housing or adequate nutrition and health care), they did nothing to reduce the growing skills mismatch between the resident labor force and available jobs. In fact, such spatially targeted assistance may have inadvertently increased the mismatch and the plight of the poor by bonding distressed people to distressed places.

For those with some resources and for the fortunate portion of that population whose efforts break the bonds of dependency, spatially concentrated public assistance may not impede mobility. But for many inner-city poor without skills, local concentrations of public assistance and community services can be sticking forces. With a low perceived marginal utility of migration relative to the opportunity costs of giving up their in-place assistance, they see themselves as better off staying where they are.

Yet such immobility is detrimental to the longer term economic prospects of both the unemployed and the places in which they reside. Imagine, for instance, what might have happened in the first half of this century if the millions of structurally displaced southerners who migrated to economically expanding northern cities in search of jobs and a better life had been sustained in their distressed communities by public assistance. It is possible that many would never have moved, and the significant advances in income levels and living standards that the South and its out-migrants eventually attained would not have occurred.

Circumstances in today's distressed inner-city areas are roughly analogous. These areas are characterized by excesses of structurally displaced labor as their blue-collar job bases wither. Large concentrations of the unemployed who are increasingly dependent on welfare or the underground economy, or both, pose negative externalities (crime, alcoholism, drug abuse, loitering, vandalism) that further dissuade new businesses from locating nearby. Eventually, neighborhood deterioration and residential abandonment will probably thin out the population to the extent that spatially extensive private sector reinvestment becomes feasible. This process often takes a generation or more, however, and in the meantime it imposes heavy social and economic costs on the city and on those remaining.

To alleviate the problems engendered by excesses of structurally displaced labor in inner-city areas of decline, some have suggested a national development bank, a new Reconstruction Finance Corporation, enterprise zones, or government-business-labor partnerships that might "reindustrialize" these areas or otherwise rebuild their blue-collar employment bases (see Butler, 1981; Hanson, 1983; Rohatyn, 1979, 1981; U.S. Department of Housing and Urban Development, 1978, 1980, 1984). Such jobs-to-people strategies may be as unrealistic in terms of their objective as they are nostalgic. The government subsidies, tax incentives, and regulatory relief contained in existing and proposed urban policies are not nearly sufficient to overcome technological and market forces that are redistributing urban blue-collar jobs and shaping the economies of our major cities. Economic advancement of cities and maximum job creation can best be accomplished through private and public initiatives that promote information-processing and other advanced service sector industries whose functions are consistent with the roles computer-age cities most effectively perform.

Cities that are proactive in capitalizing on their emerging service sector roles should experience renewed overall employment growth, as, it has been noted, is already occurring in Boston and New York City. But if large portions of their residents lack the appropriate education to be hired by information processing and other white-collar service industries beginning to dominate urban employment bases, the plight of the poorly educated could further deteriorate. For this reason, and because demographic forces portend potential shortages of educationally qualified resident labor for the knowledge-intensive industries that are already expanding in the cities, there have been cogent calls from both the public and private sectors to upgrade city schools and increase the proportion of urban residents who receive some higher education.

Policies geared to improving the education of urban residents are essential to longer term solutions of mismatch and the social and economic health of cities. Such policies, however, are unlikely to alleviate the persistent unemployment problems currently facing a large number of displaced older workers and yet-to-be-placed younger workers with serious educational deficiencies—those caught in the web of urban change. Such unemployment persists because the educational qualifications demanded by most urban information-processing industries are difficult to impart through short-term, nontraditional programs. Qualifications for employment in these industries typically accrue through prolonged formal schooling during which marketable benefits accumulate as one passes through certifying educational thresholds (e.g., high school, baccalaureate, M.B.A., law degrees). It seems overly optimistic to think that sizable numbers of those displaced because of their educational deficiencies (especially older persons) will desire or be capable of reentering prolonged schooling programs to obtain the appropriate qualifications.

The implausibility of rebuilding urban blue-collar job bases or of providing sufficient education to large numbers of displaced urban laborers so they may be reemployed in expanding white-collar industries necessitates a renewed look at the traditional means by which Americans have adapted to economic displacement—that is, migration. Despite the mass loss of lower skill jobs in many cities during the past decade, there have been substantial increases in these jobs nationwide. For example, between 1975–1985, more than 2.1 million nonadministrative jobs were *added* in eating and drinking establishments, which is more than the total number of production jobs that currently exist in America's automobile, primary metals, and textile industries combined (1.86 million in 1985) (Bureau of Labor Statistics, 1975, 1986). Unfortunately, essentially all of the national growth in entry-level and other jobs with low educational requisites has occurred in the suburbs, exurbs, and nonmetropolitan areas, all of which are far removed from growing concentrations of poorly educated minorities. It is both an irony and a tragedy that we have such huge surpluses of entry-level labor in the inner cities at the same time suburban businesses are facing serious entry-level labor shortages.

The inability of disadvantaged urban minorities to follow decentralizing entry-level jobs (either because of racial discrimination, inadequate knowledge or resources, or government-subsidized anchoring) has increasingly isolated these minorities from shifting loci of employment opportunity and has contributed to their high rates of unemployment, labor force nonparticipation, and welfare dependency. Such isolation, blocked mobility, and dependency breed hopelessness, despair, and alienation that, in turn, foster drug abuse, family dissolution, and other social problems that disproportionately afflict the urban disadvantaged. For many young men, confined as they are in commercially abandoned ghettos in which stable husband–wife families are few, pimps, pushers, and toughs replace working fathers as role models. The cultural isolation of these young men and their socialization-by-the-street prevent them from developing the positive work values and interpersonal skills that are as important as technical skills in obtaining and holding a job. The result is a powerful spatial interaction of social and economic malaise.

To sum up the working thesis of this paper, America's jobs and people have moved about continuously. Now it appears that at least one segment of our population has become increasingly immobilized in culturally and economically isolated inner-city areas of decline. Without jobs and without much hope for jobs, the "new immobiles" are caught in a downward socioeconomic spiral that is unprecedented for urban dwellers in this country.

To improve the mobility options of the urban disadvantaged and reduce their spatial isolation from job opportunities that are better matched with their skills, a number of strategies should be considered. These might include: (1) a computerized job opportunity network providing up-to-date information on available jobs throughout the particular metropolitan area, the region, and the nation; (2) partial underwriting of more distant job searches by the unemployed; (3) need-based temporary relocation assistance, once a job has been secured; (4) housing vouchers for those whose income levels require such assistance, as opposed to additional spatially fixed public housing complexes; (5) stricter enforcement of existing fair-housing and fair-hiring laws; (6) public–private cooperative efforts to van pool unemployed inner-city residents to suburban businesses facing labor shortages; and (7) a thorough review of all public assistance programs to ensure that they are not inadvertently anchoring those with limited resources to distressed areas in which there are few prospects for permanent or meaningful employment.

The strategies enumerated above are not suggested as replacements for efforts to make cities more attractive to blue-collar industries or imperative programs to improve the educational qualifications of inner-city residents but rather as complements to them. All three general strategies (jobs-to-people, people-to-jobs, and educational upgrading) must be further complemented by national economic development policies that foster sustained private sector employment growth. The economic health of cities is inexorably interwoven with the health of the national economy. Moreover, programs assisting the retraining or relocation of the structurally unemployed will prove fruitless unless there are new and enduring jobs at the end of the training programs or moves.

Thus, rather than subsidizing the relocation of industries to urban areas of greater cost or lower productivity (thus lowering the net national return on investment), cities should be encouraged to introduce economic development strategies aimed at creating productive, cost-competitive environments that would attract such industries. The prior appraisal of regional employment shifts suggests that there are a number of important competitive factors that city officials can influence such as local taxes and business regulations. They can also influence local policies regarding public schools, safety, and municipal service delivery, all of which might make the margin of difference for middle-income families and businesses that are considering locating in (or leaving) the city.

In other words, local officials are not helpless in determining the fate of their cities. They must think strategically about their own city's future, however, and candidly assess its competitive strengths and weaknesses in a changing national and international economic arena. They must implement policies that will be oriented more toward the future, building on their city's emerging strengths in this transforming arena.

Let us take public infrastructure development policy as one brief example. Just as canals, railway terminals, paved streets, running water, and electric power lines once provided cities with comparative advantages for processing and transporting goods, successful cities of the future will develop computer-age infrastructures that will provide them with comparative advantages for processing and transmitting information. As a start, concerted efforts must be made to "wire" cities with fiber optics and broad-band cables so that businesses locating in them can quickly and efficiently receive, process, store, and transmit immense amounts of data and information. Cities, likewise, should take advantage of their economies of scale and provide municipally owned supercomputer facilities and teleports to service their growing information-processing industries on a cost-sharing basis. They should also nurture national and international accessibility through their unrivaled airports (a unique comparative strength of major cities) by further improving these facilities and expanding airline connections for business people and tourists.

To repeat, the destinies of cities are not entirely shaped by external forces beyond their control. All have enormous latent strengths that can be built upon in constructing brighter urban futures. Even those of our older industrial cities that have experienced the greatest population and job losses over the past two decades have a rich architectural heritage, diverse ethnic character, and urban ambience that cannot be replicated in most newer Sunbelt cities. Recognizing and exploiting such strengths will require foresight and action on the part of local leaders. In the end, the economic and demographic future of cities will be determined less by national urban policies than by how effectively local leadership fosters new urban roles and meets the needs and aspirations of various population groups and firms.

ACKNOWLEDGMENT

Research reported herein was supported, in part, by a grant from the National Science Foundation. Tabular assistance was provided by Andrea M. Bohlig, Holly L. Hughes, and Michael D. Irwin. This paper was originally titled "The Regional and Urban Redistribution of People and Jobs."

REFERENCES

Bell, Daniel
    1973   *The Coming of Post-Industrial Society.* New York: Basic Books.
Bergman, Edward M., and Harvey A. Goldstein
    1983   Dynamics and structural change in the structure of metropolitan economies. *Journal of the American Planning Association* 49(3):263–279.
Bluestone, Barry, and Bennett Harrison
    1982   *The Deindustrialization of America.* New York: Basic Books.
Bureau of the Census
    1953   *County Business Patterns.* Machine-Readable Files. Washington, D.C.: U.S. Department of Commerce.
    1959   *County Business Patterns.* Machine-Readable Files. Washington, D.C.: U.S. Department of Commerce.

1960   *Census of Population and Housing.* Washington, D.C.: U.S. Department of Commerce.

1963   *Census of Population: 1960.* Vol. 1, Characteristics of the Population, Part 1, United States Summary. Washington, D.C.: U.S. Department of Commerce.

1969   *Current Population Survey.* Machine-Readable Files, March Surveys. Washington, D.C.: U.S. Department of Commerce.

1970   *County Business Patterns.* Machine-Readable Files. Washington, D.C.: U.S. Department of Commerce.

1973   *Census of Population: 1970.* Vol. 1, Characteristics of the Population, Part 1, United States Summary—Section 2. Washington, D.C.: U.S. Department of Commerce.

1974   *County Business Patterns.* Machine-Readable Files. Washington, D.C.: U.S. Department of Commerce.

1975a   *Current Population Survey.* Machine-Readable Files, March Surveys. Washington, D.C.: U.S. Department of Commerce.

1975b   *Historical Statistics of the United States.* Washington, D.C.: U.S. Department of Commerce.

1975c   *Mobility of the Population of the United States, March 1970–March 1975.* Current Population Reports, Series P-20, No. 285. Washington, D.C.: U.S. Department of Commerce.

1976   *County Business Patterns.* Machine-Readable Files. Washington, D.C.: U.S. Department of Commerce.

1977   *Current Population Survey.* Machine-Readable Files. Washington, D.C.: U.S. Department of Commerce.

1978   *County Business Patterns.* Machine-Readable Files. Washington, D.C.: U.S. Department of Commerce.

1980a   *County Business Patterns.* Machine-Readable Files. Washington, D.C.: U.S. Department of Commerce.

1980b   *Current Population Survey.* Machine-Readable Files, March Surveys. Washington, D.C.: U.S. Department of Commerce.

1982a   *County Business Patterns.* Machine-Readable Files. Washington, D.C.: U.S. Department of Commerce.

1982b   *Current Population Survey.* Machine-Readable Files, March Survey. Washington, D.C.: U.S. Department of Commerce.

1985a   *County Business Patterns.* Machine-Readable Files. Washington, D.C.: U.S. Department of Commerce.

1985b   *Current Population Survey.* Machine-Readable Files, March Survey. Washington, D.C.: U.S. Department of Commerce.

Bureau of Labor Statistics

1975   *Employment and Earnings* 22 (September). Washington, D.C.: U.S. Department of Labor.

1976,   *Geographic Profiles of Employment and Unemployment.* Washington, D.C.:
1980   U.S. Department of Labor.

1981   *The National Industry-Occupation Employment Matrix, 1970, 1978, and Projected 1990.* Washington, D.C.: U.S. Department of Labor.

1986a   *Employment and Earnings* 33 (August). Washington, D.C.: U.S. Department of Labor.

1986b   *Establishment Data and Labor Force Data, 1939–1986.* Machine-Readable Files. Washington, D.C.: U.S. Department of Labor.

Butler, Stuart M.
1981　*Enterprise Zones: Green Lining the Inner Cities.* New York: Universe Books.
Castells, Manuel
1985　High technology, economics restructuring and the urban-regional process in the United States. Pp. 11–40 in Manuel Castells, ed., *High Technology, Space and Society.* Beverly Hills, Calif.: Sage.
Checkoway, Barry, and Carl V. Patton, eds.
1985　*The Metropolitan Midwest: Policy Problems and Prospects.* Urbana, Ill.: University of Illinois Press.
Cobb, James C.
1982　*The Selling of the South: The Southern Crusade for Industrial Development, 1936–1980.* Baton Rouge, La.: Louisiana State University Press.
1984　*Industrialization and Southern Society, 1877–1984.* Lexington, Ky.: University of Kentucky Press.
Dunn, Edgar S.
1960　A statistical and analytical technique for regional analysis. *Papers and Proceedings for the Regional Science Association* 6:97–112.
1980　*The Development of the U.S. Urban System.* Baltimore, Md.: Johns Hopkins University Press.
Goldfield, David M.
1982　*Cotton Fields and Skyscrapers: Southern City and Region, 1607–1980.* Baton Rouge, La.: Louisiana State University Press.
Hanson, Royce, ed.
1983　*Rethinking Urban Policy: Urban Development in an Advanced Economy.* Committee on National Urban Policy, Commission on Behavioral and Social Sciences and Education. Washington, D.C.: National Academy Press.
Kasarda, John D.
1980　The implications of contemporary redistribution trends for national urban policy. *Social Science Quarterly* 61:373–400.
1983　Entry-level jobs, mobility and urban minority unemployment. *Urban Affairs Quarterly* 19(Sept.):21–40.
1985　Urban change and minority opportunities. Pp. 33–67 in Paul E. Peterson, ed., *The New Urban Reality.* Washington, D.C.: Brookings Institution.
Kasarda, John D., and Michael D. Irwin
1986　National Business Cycles and Community Competition for Jobs. Unpublished manuscript. Department of Sociology, University of North Carolina at Chapel Hill.
Muller, Thomas, and Thomas Espenshade
1986　*The Fourth Wave: California's Newest Immigrants.* Washington, D.C.: Urban Institute Press.
Noyelle, Thierry J., and Thomas M. Stanback, Jr.
1983　*The Economic Transformation of American Cities.* Landmark Studies. Totowa, N.J.: Rowman & Allanheld.
Perloff, Harvey S., Edgar S. Dunn, E. E. Lampard, and Richard F. Muth
1960　*Regions, Resources, and Economic Growth.* Baltimore, Md.: Johns Hopkins University Press.

Rohatyn, Felix
  1979   Public-private partnerships to stave off disaster. *Harvard Business Review* 57(6):6–9.
  1981   The older America: Can it survive? *New York Review of Books* 27(21):13–16.
Singlemann, Joachim
  1978   *From Agriculture to Services—The Transformation of Industrial Employment.* Beverly Hills, Calif.: Sage.
Swanson, Bert E., and Ronald K. Vogel
  1986   Rating American cities—credit risk, urban distress and the quality of life. Journal of Urban Affairs 8(2):67–84.
U.S. Department of Housing and Urban Development
  1978   *The President's National Urban Policy Report, 1978.* Washington, D.C.: U.S. Department of Housing and Urban Development.
  1980   *The President's National Urban Policy Report, 1980.* Office of Community Planning and Development. Washington, D.C.: U.S. Department of Housing and Urban Development.
  1984   *The President's National Urban Policy Report, 1984.* Office of Policy Development and Research. Washington, D.C.: U.S. Department of Housing and Urban Development.

Local Area Economic Growth Patterns: A Comparison of the 1980s and Previous Decades

DANIEL H. GARNICK

Looking back from the vantage point of the 1980s, it is clear that the much publicized reversal of growth that occurred in the 1970s—from metropolitan to nonmetropolitan areas—was temporary. In three earlier articles documenting the resumption of higher growth in metropolitan areas in the 1980s, the author showed that (1) the perceived growth reversal was not uniform among all regions, (2) there are underlying industrial and regional continuities, apparently of a structural nature, as well as cyclical or shorter term elements, that may from time to time result in or exaggerate perceived shifts and reversals, (3) tests of hypotheses associated with polarization/polar reversal (counterurbanization) theory failed to support the theories of polar growth and reversal, and (4) the wage rate as the equilibrating mechanism in area growth only weakly supported neoclassical theory (Garnick, 1983, 1984, 1985). The import of these results is that, although there appear to be many long-term industrial and regional structural elements at work underlying the shifting balances in metropolitan and nonmetropolitan area growth, no single or overarching theory appears to be able to describe adequately the

The views expressed in this paper are not necessarily those of the U.S. Department of Commerce or of the Bureau of Economic Analysis where the author is associate director for regional economics.

dynamics of area growth and decline. Thus, no overarching policy
or single instrument is likely to resolve the problems associated with
the uneven development and differential growth patterns of regions
and areas.

This paper is developed in four sections. The first section briefly
updates the review of metropolitan–nonmetropolitan area patterns
in the 1980s thus far, contrasting them with the patterns in the
1960s and 1970s; the section focuses on the same metropolitan and
nonmetropolitan designations and the same economic and population aggregates dealt with in the earlier articles. The second section
follows the fortunes of the 50 largest metropolitan statistical areas
(MSAs) over the same time spans, adding employment to the list
of economic aggregates reviewed and placing particular emphasis on
the relationship between employment change and population change.
The third section disaggregates the geography further into four categories of county groups within each of the MSA and non-MSA
designations. Additional economic aggregates are introduced into
the analysis of the patterns in these geographic configurations. The
final section interweaves the findings from the first three sections
with a longer term review of national production and employment
patterns and with an outlook for policy.

MSA/NON-MSA GROWTH PATTERNS

Tables 1, 2, and 3 show the average annual rates of growth in
total personal income, population, total earnings, and in earnings
excluding farm and manufacturing. (Earnings are the sum of wages
and salaries, other labor income, and proprietors' income.) Growth
rates are shown for the United States and its regions by non-MSA
and MSA areas, and by size class of the latter, for three time spans:
1959–1969, 1969–1979, and 1979–1984. The choice of years for the
first two tables is based on national business cycle peaks, with the
aim of separating trend from cyclical changes. The last year is the
most recent for which data are available.

Thus far in the 1980s, MSA growth has continued to exceed
non-MSA growth in total personal income, population, and earnings
in the nation as a whole and in all but three highly urbanized regions: the New England, Mideast, and Great Lakes regions, in which
population growth in non-MSAs continued to exceed that in MSAs.[1]

---

[1] The Bureau of Economic Analysis' regional classification differs somewhat
from that of the Bureau of the Census (see Appendix A, p. 59).

TABLE 1 Average Annual Growth Rates (percentage) of Total Personal Income, Population, and Earnings by Region, County Type (MSA or non-MSA), and MSA Population Size Class, 1959-1969

Regions, County Type, and MSA Size Classes	Personal Income	Total Population	Earnings			
			Total	Excluding Farm	Excluding Manufacturing	Excluding Manufacturing and Farm
United States	6.93	1.29	6.72	6.86	6.93	7.14
Total, non-MSA counties	6.71	0.35	6.16	6.56	5.78	6.26
Total, MSA counties	6.98	1.60	6.83	6.91	7.18	7.30
Less than 0.5 million	6.96	1.49	6.78	6.92	6.92	7.13
0.5 to 1 million	7.20	1.66	6.93	7.03	7.23	7.40
1 to 2 million	7.40	2.14	7.26	7.34	7.51	7.62
More than 2 million	6.64	1.31	6.59	6.61	7.12	7.17
New England	6.77	1.18	6.49	6.54	7.15	7.26
Total, non-MSA counties	6.92	0.97	6.20	6.42	6.44	6.79
Total, MSA counties	6.75	1.21	6.52	6.56	7.25	7.32
Less than 0.5 million	7.01	1.41	6.74	6.79	7.06	7.15
0.5 to 1 million	6.65	1.16	6.12	6.15	6.98	7.03
1 to 2 million	7.34	1.93	7.46	7.56	7.78	7.95
More than 2 million	6.58	0.99	6.53	6.55	7.39	7.42
Mideast	6.41	0.98	6.16	6.20	6.74	6.80
Total, non-MSA counties	6.28	0.42	5.65	5.78	5.66	5.86
Total, MSA counties	6.41	1.03	6.19	6.23	6.80	6.86
Less than 0.5 million	6.26	0.79	6.03	6.10	6.34	6.48
0.5 to 1 million	6.79	1.44	6.25	6.32	6.55	6.69
1 to 2 million	6.53	1.01	6.33	6.36	6.94	6.98
More than 2 million	6.32	0.97	6.18	6.20	6.89	6.92

TABLE 1 (Continued)

Regions, County Type, and MSA Size Classes	Personal Income	Total Population	Earnings			
			Total	Excluding Farm	Excluding Manufacturing	Excluding Manufacturing and Farm
Great Lakes	6.53	1.06	6.38	6.44	6.64	6.76
Total, non-MSA counties	6.82	0.55	6.16	6.34	5.87	6.10
Total, MSA counties	6.47	1.20	6.42	6.46	6.80	6.88
Less than 0.5 million	6.82	1.42	6.65	6.75	6.94	7.13
0.5 to 1 million	6.52	1.14	6.54	6.58	6.86	6.94
1 to 2 million	6.10	1.11	6.14	6.17	6.77	6.82
More than 2 million	6.42	1.09	6.37	6.39	6.71	6.74
Plains	6.53	0.64	6.38	6.48	6.27	6.38
Total, non-MSA counties	6.55	-0.12	6.05	6.16	5.75	5.78
Total, MSA counties	6.52	1.35	6.57	6.62	6.63	6.70
Less than 0.5 million	5.89	1.02	5.39	5.91	6.03	6.08
0.5 to 1 million	6.77	1.64	6.52	6.48	6.92	6.88
1 to 2 million	6.66	1.32	6.60	6.69	6.65	6.78
More than 2 million	6.89	1.61	7.06	7.10	7.03	7.10
Southeast	7.85	1.32	7.61	7.96	7.36	7.80
Total, non-MSA counties	7.42	0.32	6.89	7.66	6.03	6.97
Total, MSA counties	8.04	1.99	7.92	8.07	7.88	8.08
Less than 0.5 million	7.84	1.62	7.58	7.74	7.44	7.65
0.5 to 1 million	7.87	1.88	7.76	7.93	7.81	8.04
1 to 2 million	8.02	2.35	8.11	8.23	7.99	8.12
More than 2 million	9.23	3.40	9.35	9.44	9.40	9.52

Southwest	7.31	1.64	7.05	7.41	6.71	7.13
Total, non-MSA counties	5.84	0.21	5.00	5.75	4.69	5.50
Total, MSA counties	7.79	2.27	7.66	7.82	7.37	7.57
Less than 0.5 million	6.36	1.17	6.16	6.35	6.00	6.23
0.5 to 1 million	7.92	2.27	7.79	7.94	7.39	7.58
1 to 2 million	8.87	3.06	8.84	8.99	8.30	8.48
More than 2 million	8.30	3.42	8.12	8.21	8.24	8.37
Rocky Mountain	6.55	1.58	6.43	6.56	6.42	6.58
Total, non-MSA counties	5.56	0.39	5.27	5.40	5.16	5.28
Total, MSA counties	7.15	2.50	7.12	7.15	7.22	7.25
Less than 0.5 million	7.27	2.54	7.16	7.19	7.20	7.24
0.5 to 1 million	6.46	2.19	6.48	6.51	6.66	6.70
1 to 2 million	7.41	2.65	7.42	7.44	7.53	7.55
Far West	7.44	2.34	7.26	7.43	7.48	7.73
Total, non-MSA counties	5.99	0.91	5.86	6.15	6.23	6.72
Total, MSA counties	7.56	2.49	7.37	7.52	7.58	7.79
Less than 0.5 million	7.25	2.40	7.15	7.56	7.39	7.91
0.5 to 1 million	8.15	3.42	7.07	7.91	6.95	7.91
1 to 2 million	8.14	3.03	7.79	7.91	7.80	7.95
More than 2 million	6.84	1.64	6.93	6.98	7.41	7.49

NOTE: MSA = metropolitan statistical area.

TABLE 2 Average Annual Growth Rates (percentage) of Total Personal Income, Population, and Earnings by Region, County Type (MSA or non-MSA), and MSA Population Size Class, 1969–1979

Regions, County Type, and MSA Size Classes	Personal Income	Total Population	Earnings			
			Total	Excluding Farm	Excluding Manufacturing	Excluding Manufacturing and Farm
United States						
Total, non-MSA counties	10.02	1.10	9.35	9.39	9.73	9.81
Total, MSA counties	10.98	1.29	10.01	10.31	10.04	10.47
Less than 0.5 million	9.81	1.04	9.21	9.22	9.67	9.69
0.5 to 1 million	10.83	1.59	10.09	10.13	10.38	10.46
1 to 2 million	10.23	1.32	9.54	9.56	10.15	10.20
More than 2 million	10.27	1.35	9.77	9.78	10.22	10.24
	8.66	0.25	8.19	8.19	8.69	8.70
New England						
Total, non-MSA counties	8.82	0.51	8.22	8.25	8.55	8.59
Total, MSA counties	10.07	1.53	8.73	8.85	8.84	9.03
Less than 0.5 million	8.64	0.33	8.15	8.17	8.50	8.53
0.5 to 1 million	9.83	1.24	9.14	9.19	9.58	9.68
1 to 2 million	8.46	0.24	7.83	7.84	8.32	8.34
More than 2 million	8.49	0.26	8.17	8.21	9.10	9.17
	8.36	-0.03	8.04	8.04	8.13	8.13
Mideast						
Total, non-MSA counties	8.21	0.06	7.46	7.48	7.92	7.95
Total, MSA counties	9.37	0.82	8.11	8.25	8.26	8.49
Less than 0.5 million	8.12	-0.02	7.42	7.43	7.90	7.92
0.5 to 1 million	9.18	0.59	8.33	8.40	8.86	8.99
1 to 2 million	9.03	0.61	8.42	8.47	9.06	9.14
More than 2 million	7.73	-0.36	7.52	7.53	8.06	8.07
	7.77	-0.27	6.99	6.99	7.52	7.52

Great Lakes	9.16	0.42	8.52	8.53	8.90	8.92
Total, non-MSA counties	10.13	0.96	9.11	9.18	9.22	9.36
Total, MSA counties	8.94	0.27	8.41	8.42	8.83	8.85
Less than 0.5 million	9.85	0.76	9.18	9.21	9.49	9.54
0.5 to 1 million	8.93	0.19	8.19	8.20	8.80	8.83
1 to 2 million	8.66	0.09	8.28	8.28	8.69	8.70
More than 2 million	8.40	-0.02	8.01	8.01	8.50	8.50
Plains	9.95	0.54	9.52	9.72	9.59	9.86
Total, non-MSA counties	10.16	0.42	9.44	9.96	9.15	9.72
Total, MSA counties	9.80	0.64	9.56	9.61	9.87	9.93
Less than 0.5 million	10.53	0.96	10.43	10.56	10.47	10.64
0.5 to 1 million	9.47	0.74	9.32	9.50	9.83	10.07
1 to 2 million	9.76	0.53	9.36	9.33	9.81	9.78
More than 2 million	9.33	0.39	9.04	9.05	9.44	9.45
Southeast	11.44	1.81	10.61	10.73	10.85	11.02
Total, non-MSA counties	11.56	1.42	10.55	10.88	10.61	11.11
Total, MSA counties	11.39	2.05	10.63	10.67	10.93	10.99
Less than 0.5 million	11.33	1.97	10.47	10.51	10.65	10.71
0.5 to 1 million	11.53	2.04	10.69	10.74	11.13	11.20
1 to 2 million	11.16	2.13	10.54	10.56	10.69	10.72
More than 2 million	11.52	2.22	11.15	11.17	11.67	11.69
Southwest	12.51	2.44	12.06	12.13	12.18	12.27
Total, non-MSA counties	12.34	1.75	11.43	11.60	11.19	11.36
Total, MSA counties	12.56	2.70	12.22	12.24	12.45	12.48
Less than 0.5 million	11.95	2.12	11.34	11.40	11.19	11.26
0.5 to 1 million	12.28	2.68	11.70	11.69	11.99	11.99
1 to 2 million	12.12	2.86	11.73	11.74	12.20	12.22
More than 2 million	14.50	3.57	14.73	14.72	15.06	15.05

TABLE 2 (Continued)

Regions, County Type, and MSA Size Classes	Personal Income	Total Population	Earnings			
			Total	Excluding Farm	Excluding Manufacturing	Excluding Manufacturing and Farm
Rocky Mountain	12.54	2.68	12.17	12.62	12.10	12.63
Total, non-MSA counties	12.43	2.38	11.74	12.90	11.72	13.05
Total, MSA counties	12.61	2.88	12.40	12.49	12.31	12.42
Less than 0.5 million	13.01	3.22	12.54	12.73	12.03	12.24
0.5 to 1 million	12.08	2.69	11.81	11.86	11.69	11.75
1 to 2 million	12.51	2.63	12.56	12.60	12.85	12.90
Far West	10.83	1.81	10.10	10.10	10.42	10.43
Total, non-MSA counties	12.27	2.58	10.91	11.14	10.83	11.13
Total, MSA counties	10.72	1.73	10.04	10.03	10.39	10.38
Less than 0.5 million	12.24	2.74	11.17	11.19	11.13	11.15
0.5 to 1 million	13.02	2.73	11.83	11.80	11.91	11.89
1 to 2 million	11.21	1.92	10.49	10.51	10.67	10.69
More than 2 million	8.76	0.57	8.66	8.65	9.33	9.32

NOTE: MSA = metropolitan statistical area.

TABLE 3 Average Annual Growth Rates (percentage) of Total Personal Income, Population, and Earnings by Region, County Type (MSA or non-MSA), and MSA Population Size Class, 1979-1984

Regions, County Type, and MSA Size Classes	Personal Income	Total Population	Earnings			
			Total	Excluding Farm	Excluding Manufacturing	Excluding Manufacturing and Farm
United States	9.20	1.01	7.89	8.07	8.58	8.85
Total, non-MSA counties	8.46	0.84	6.08	6.74	6.16	7.09
Total, MSA counties	9.37	1.07	8.26	8.32	9.07	9.16
Less than 0.5 million	8.93	1.21	7.20	7.32	7.96	8.15
0.5 to 1 million	9.82	1.20	8.54	8.61	9.40	9.50
1 to 2 million	9.92	1.41	9.02	9.06	9.65	9.71
More than 2 million	9.06	0.62	8.30	8.32	9.22	9.24
New England	10.41	0.37	9.77	9.80	10.36	10.41
Total, non-MSA counties	10.22	0.80	8.80	8.97	9.21	9.47
Total, MSA counties	10.44	0.29	9.90	9.91	10.52	10.53
Less than 0.5 million	10.86	0.72	10.15	10.18	10.66	10.70
0.5 to 1 million	9.80	0.18	8.75	8.75	9.76	9.76
1 to 2 million	10.35	0.39	9.53	9.55	11.23	11.28
More than 2 million	10.90	0.14	10.87	10.87	10.81	10.81
Mideast	9.13	0.18	8.13	8.17	9.26	9.33
Total, non-MSA counties	8.26	0.21	6.11	6.31	6.93	7.27
Total, MSA counties	9.20	0.17	8.26	8.29	9.40	9.44
Less than 0.5 million	8.43	0.18	6.69	6.75	8.40	8.54
0.5 to 1 million	9.51	0.44	8.07	8.11	9.29	9.36
1 to 2 million	9.23	-0.30	8.29	8.92	9.79	9.80
More than 2 million	9.23	0.18	8.58	8.60	9.49	9.51

TABLE 3 (Continued)

Regions, County Type, and MSA Size Classes	Personal Income	Total Population	Earnings			
			Total	Excluding Farm	Excluding Manufacturing	Excluding Manufacturing and Farm
Great Lakes	7.00	-0.01	5.18	5.29	6.36	6.58
Total, non-MSA counties	7.29	0.13	4.94	5.43	5.06	5.86
Total, MSA counties	6.93	-0.05	5.23	5.27	6.62	6.70
Less than 0.5 million	7.03	0.08	5.07	5.15	6.23	6.40
0.5 to 1 million	6.72	-0.08	4.48	4.51	5.84	5.92
1 to 2 million	7.54	0.06	6.01	6.05	7.39	7.46
More than 2 million	6.57	-0.21	5.13	5.14	6.64	6.67
Plains	8.40	0.48	6.57	7.13	6.91	7.54
Total, non-MSA counties	7.92	0.22	5.03	5.95	5.01	6.19
Total, MSA counties	8.73	0.71	7.55	7.66	8.03	8.17
Less than 0.5 million	8.04	0.68	6.31	6.43	7.04	7.23
0.5 to 1 million	8.67	0.63	7.72	7.79	8.02	8.11
1 to 2 million	8.39	0.68	7.08	7.28	7.46	7.73
More than 2 million	9.37	0.75	8.60	8.64	8.99	9.05
Southeast	10.10	1.40	8.80	9.00	9.21	9.49
Total, non-MSA counties	8.94	0.85	6.82	7.33	6.69	7.43
Total, MSA counties	10.58	1.70	9.55	9.60	10.04	10.11
Less than 0.5 million	9.99	1.56	8.33	8.38	8.82	8.90
0.5 to 1 million	10.54	1.58	9.62	9.67	10.22	10.30
1 to 2 million	10.80	1.81	9.87	9.89	10.19	10.21
More than 2 million	12.14	2.47	12.52	12.53	12.61	12.61

Southwest	11.03	2.72	9.92	10.29	10.30	10.77
Total, non-MSA counties	9.49	2.04	6.41	7.90	6.38	8.17
Total, MSA counties	11.46	2.96	10.70	10.77	11.21	11.31
Less than 0.5 million	10.29	2.35	8.71	8.80	9.16	9.27
0.5 to 1 million	12.15	3.27	11.18	11.28	11.33	11.45
1 to 2 million	12.49	2.95	12.52	12.61	12.81	12.92
More than 2 million	10.63	3.68	9.95	9.95	11.20	11.21
Rocky Mountain	9.87	2.16	8.57	8.80	8.60	8.88
Total, non-MSA counties	8.46	1.92	6.24	6.68	6.32	6.83
Total, MSA counties	10.62	2.32	9.67	9.75	9.75	9.84
Less than 0.5 million	9.73	1.94	8.39	8.57	8.22	8.43
0.5 to 1 million	10.00	3.02	8.97	9.01	8.59	8.64
1 to 2 million	11.69	2.31	10.99	10.99	11.40	11.39
Far West	9.42	1.85	8.18	8.36	8.22	8.45
Total, non-MSA counties	7.55	1.83	4.47	5.11	4.76	5.65
Total, MSA counties	9.57	1.86	8.45	8.57	8.48	8.64
Less than 0.5 million	8.88	2.23	6.86	7.25	6.98	7.24
0.5 to 1 million	9.81	2.45	7.66	8.61	7.44	8.52
1 to 2 million	10.05	1.94	9.18	9.21	9.15	9.19
More than 2 million	9.12	1.32	8.22	8.23	8.52	8.52

NOTE: MSA = metropolitan statistical area.

In addition, in the Great Lakes region, non-MSA growth rates of personal income and earnings exceeded MSA rates. This tendency is due to continued weakness in durable goods manufacturing industries (other than motor vehicle production), which tend to be heavily concentrated in the region's MSAs. This pattern contrasts with that of the 1970s, when non-MSA growth exceeded MSA growth in the three measures in the nation as a whole and in the four highly urbanized regions, also including the Far West. The pattern of the 1980s resembles that of the 1960s when MSA growth exceeded non-MSA growth in the three measures in the nation as a whole and in all but two regions. In the New England and Great Lakes regions, personal income growth (but not earnings) was higher in non-MSAs, owing to the somewhat relatively higher rates of property and retirement income growth in the non-MSA portions of these two regions.

Industrial Bases of Area Growth

The last four columns in Tables 1, 2, and 3 show growth rates in total earnings and in earnings when farm, manufacturing, and farm and manufacturing earnings are excluded from total earnings. A comparison of the growth rates in total earnings and in earnings that exclude a particular industry shows the combined effect of that industry's growth rate and its relative importance (weight) on the total. When farm earnings are excluded, the differential impact of the farm and the nonfarm industries on non-MSAs is readily shown. Likewise, when manufacturing earnings are excluded, the different effects of manufacturing industries on MSA and non-MSA growth patterns become evident. Other industries, for the most part, are consumer services industries, which respond to, rather than shape, area growth; or they are industries that tend to be concentrated geographically. Mining and some recreation- and retirement-related industries in non-MSAs and selected service industries in MSAs are examples of geographically concentrated industries.

Using the earnings columns of the three tables, the following discussion of non-MSA and MSA growth patterns since the 1960s focuses on how such patterns have been affected by farm employment decline, the geographic dispersion of industry, and the internationalization of the U.S. economy. In many respects, the internationalization of the national economy may be looked at as an extension of the geographic dispersion of industry.

Non-MSA Areas

In the 1960s, as had been the case since before World War II when the agricultural revolution led to large increases in farm productivity growth, non-MSAs in all regions were characterized by continued declines in farm employment and large-scale population out-migration. With continued improvements in their access to national markets, however, owing to the large increase in federal outlays for highway construction, non-MSAs began to benefit increasingly from manufacturing industries that were dispersing in search of lower cost locations and diversification insurance against strikes and other potential impedances to access to supplies and markets. Technological change also contributed significantly to the regional dispersion of industry and to the deconcentration of firms from the urban core (Garnick, 1978).

In Table 1 these developments are seen in the earnings columns: farm earnings subtract almost one-half of a percentage point from the growth rate of total earnings in non-MSAs nationally, and manufacturing earnings add almost one-half of a percentage point. With the pool of redundant farm workers diminishing as the 1960s progressed and employment in growing nonfarm industries increasing in these areas, the net population out-migration from non-MSAs slowed toward the end of the decade.

By the 1970s non-MSAs were characterized by net in-migration of population, which reflected growing nonfarm job opportunities and slowing farm employment decline (a result, in part, of a worldwide shortfall in grain production early in the decade and of rising farm prices). During this period, manufacturing earnings and employment grew faster in non-MSAs than in MSAs. One explanation of this growth may be that the effect on international trade of the declining value of the dollar mitigated the effects of increased imports, which threatened the labor-intensive manufacturing jobs that had been increasing in non-MSAs. Other nonfarm, nonmanufacturing industries grew even faster, however, spurred, in part, by increased population migration to recreation and retirement communities and by boom conditions in fuel and other natural resource industries. These industrial developments induced growth in the construction and consumer services industries in non-MSAs at rates exceeding those of MSAs. (In the less urbanized regions of the Southeast, Southwest, Plains, and Rocky Mountains, however, MSAs continued to grow faster than non-MSAs. The economic linkages between the non-MSAs and MSAs in these regions reinforced the continuing trend of growth that was faster than the national average in the MSAs there.)

In the 1980s all the major factors that had contributed to the growth of non-MSAs had reversed. Although farm income in 1984 rose from its very low levels in 1983, the decline in farm population reaccelerated. This decline reflected the longer term farm financial crisis associated with world agricultural surplus stocks and the disinflation of the 1980s. Mining and related industrial activities similarly slumped. Although the oil industry had not yet been hit by the 1985–1986 sharp decline in prices, prices began sliding downward following the second sharp rise in petroleum prices in 1980–1981. In addition, the number of labor-intensive manufacturing jobs declined faster in the face of increased competition from foreign producers, who gained an advantage from the sharp strengthening of the trade-weighted value of the dollar in the first half of the decade.

MSA Areas

Although a number of cities, especially in the Mideast region, experienced declines in population in the 1960s, their suburbs generally continued to grow, more than offsetting city-core decline; the exception was the Pittsburgh MSA, which experienced a small overall population decline. By the 1970s, however, suburban growth in the more urbanized regions of New England, the Mideast, and the Great Lakes was insufficient to offset an acceleration in the decline of cities in the long-established industrial areas. (A falloff in civilian and military aircraft production contributed to the slowdown in MSA growth in the Far West region.)

An industrial shakeout was in progress. Beginning in New England with the southern migration of the textiles industry, the shift continued through the 1950s and 1960s. But even as the employment decline and the associated out-migration of the redundant work force were hitting very hard, the region was incubating new technology and producer-services industries that would subsequently govern its growth. Although its employment growth fell behind the national rate in the 1970s also, it did so to a significantly lesser extent than was the case with the other regions in the old manufacturing belt.

The southern migration of textiles and other industries manufacturing nondurable goods also affected the Mideast region in the 1950s. To this was added the decline of the region's steel and other durable goods manufacturing industries in the 1960s and 1970s, the period of the heaviest industrial shakeout in the Mideast region. The Great Lakes region and, to a lesser extent, the Plains region were the last of the regions in the old manufacturing belt to experience industrial shakeout. Except for steel in the Ohio River Valley, which borders on the western reaches of the Mideast region, the Great Lakes region was able to preserve some of its durable goods manufacturing advantage up through the early 1970s.

Manufacturing employment in the nation grew fitfully in the 1970s. The faster growing regions in the South and West benefited most from the industrial dispersion in which non-MSAs in those regions participated along with MSAs.

Manufacturing employment overall fell during the 1979–1984 time span at an average annual rate of 1.58 percent. The old smokestack industries in the Great Lakes region's MSAs were especially hard hit. Nationally, primary metals manufacturing employment fell at an annual average rate of 3.0 percent, motor vehicles fell at a rate of 3.1 percent, rubber at 5.2 percent, and nonelectrical machinery at 2.5 percent. In all, 1 million manufacturing jobs were lost in the Great Lakes region, more than half the total national loss of 1.75 million manufacturing jobs. Whereas the nation was able to generate 10 million jobs in nonmanufacturing for a net gain of 8 million jobs, the Great Lakes region was only able to offset 60 percent of its loss of manufacturing jobs with new nonmanufacturing jobs.

The Great Lakes was the only region to experience a net job loss. Most of it occurred in the MSAs, which also experienced a net decrease in population. Elsewhere, with the exception of those medium-sized MSAs in the Mideast with industrial compositions similar to those of MSAs in the Great Lakes region, MSAs experienced employment and population growth more favorable than that of non-MSAs (Table 4).

In New England the employment situation was much improved, rising from 6.3 million in 1979 to over 7 million in 1984, a 2.06 percent annual average increase in the number of jobs, compared with 1.38 percent for the nation. Even the number of manufacturing jobs remained relatively stable over the period. Technology and defense jobs held manufacturing employment steady in the face of continued declines in textiles, apparel, and shoes, all industries that had once been very important to the fortunes of New England.

In the 1980s the Mideast experienced an increase of 1 million jobs over its total in 1979, a 1.08 percent average annual increase. This growth was a substantial improvement over the 1970s when the

TABLE 1 Average Annual Growth Rates (percentage) of
Employment by Region, 1969-1984

Regions	Period	
	1969-1979	1979-1984
Total United States	2.16	1.38
New England	1.62	2.06
Mideast	0.68	1.08
Great Lakes	1.36	-0.38
Plains	2.10	0.61
Southeast	2.70	1.86
Southwest	3.71	3.04
Rocky Mountain	4.44	2.16
Far West	3.36	1.97

Mideast's average growth rate was 0.68 percent, compared with a 2.16 percent average annual growth rate for the nation. Still, the number of manufacturing jobs in the region continued to fall from over 4 million in 1979 to slightly more than 3.5 million in 1984. Thus, the shakeout in manufacturing jobs continued, particularly in those MSAs in which the earlier established industries were concentrated. The growth of technology and service jobs in the region more than offset the losses, however.

In the South and West, there was much less in the way of earlier established manufacturing industries. In the Southeast, where textile manufactures continued to be important and where the loss in jobs by 1984 had left the industry 15 percent below its employment level in 1979, the increase in jobs in printing and publishing, machinery, and motor vehicles almost offset other manufacturing job losses. Overall, the Southeast experienced a 1.86 percent average annual employment growth rate, with MSA growth outstripping that in non-MSAs severalfold.

Manufacturing jobs also remained at about the same or higher levels in the Southwest, Rocky Mountain, and Far West regions. Total employment in the three regions from 1979–1984 increased at average annual rates of 3.04, 2.16, and 1.97 percent, respectively. Whereas employment growth was widely distributed in those fast-growing regions, the MSA rate tended to be more than double that of the non-MSAs.

The growth story of the 1980s thus far has continued to be centered in services. Many of the differences in earnings growth rates among areas can be seen when looking at total earnings versus earnings that exclude the farming and manufacturing industries in Tables 1, 2, and 3. Invariably, in all regions and all areas for MSAs and non-MSAs alike, the growth rates were considerably larger in the latter category, mainly owing to the large increase in the number of service jobs. Wholesale and retail trade added almost 2.5 million jobs during the period. The finance, insurance, and real estate group added more than a million jobs—and the service industries more than 5 million—to the national total between 1979–1984. But it was producer services—those high-earnings business, financial, and professional services that tend to concentrate in major metropolitan areas—that thus far have accounted for much of the shift in favor of MSAs in the 1980s.

MAJOR METROPOLITAN AREA PATTERNS

In this section the growth patterns of the 50 largest primary MSAs are reviewed. The MSAs are ranked by the size of their populations in 1984, the most recent year for which all the data are available for this study. Tables 5, 6, and 7 show the average annual growth rates for the same variables that appeared in Tables 1, 2, and 3, with the addition of employment in Tables 6 and 7. (In the late 1960s, the Bureau of Economic Analysis [BEA] began preparing area employment estimates on a comparable basis with their area earnings estimates.)

In the 1960s the 50 major MSAs had an average annual population growth rate of 1.66 percent, compared with 1.29 percent for the nation as a whole; only Pittsburgh showed a small population decline. Other MSAs in the slower growing northern and central regions grew at rates below the group average, with the exception of Washington, D.C.; Nassau-Suffolk; Hartford; and Rochester. These MSAs benefited by rapidly growing industries and sectors—government, aircraft and engineering, insurance, and photographic products and business machines, respectively.

In the 1970s the average annual population growth rate in the 50 major MSAs fell well below that for the nation: 0.76 percent compared with 1.1 percent. Of these MSAs, 11 experienced declining population totals—all were in the old manufacturing belt. Only one, New York, had an employment decline, more than half of which was accounted for by manufacturing job losses.

During the most recent time span, the average annual population

TABLE 5 Average Annual Growth Rates (percentage) of Total Personal Income, Population, and Earnings for the 50 Largest MSAs, 1959–1969

MSA	Personal Income	Total Population	Earnings			
			Total	Excluding Farm	Excluding Manufacturing	Excluding Manufacturing and Farm
Total United States	6.93	1.29	6.72	6.86	6.93	7.14
Total MSAs	6.97	1.66	6.87	6.92	7.27	7.34
New York	5.70	0.36	5.72	5.72	6.45	6.46
Los Angeles	6.84	1.64	6.93	6.98	7.41	7.49
Chicago	6.01	1.01	5.90	5.90	6.40	6.41
Philadelphia	6.14	1.02	5.88	5.93	6.52	6.59
Detroit	7.06	1.20	7.25	7.28	7.42	7.46
Boston	6.58	0.99	6.53	6.55	7.39	7.42
Washington, D.C.	8.56	2.97	8.70	8.75	8.87	8.93
Houston	8.30	3.42	8.12	8.21	8.24	8.37
Nassau–Suffolk	7.78	2.55	6.86	6.88	7.37	7.40
St. Louis	6.16	1.12	6.02	6.05	6.37	6.43
Atlanta	9.03	3.13	9.14	9.25	9.18	9.32
Baltimore	7.21	1.42	7.32	7.35	8.20	8.26
Minneapolis–St. Paul	7.63	2.06	7.82	7.90	7.48	7.59
Dallas	8.72	3.20	8.90	9.07	8.38	8.59
Pittsburgh	5.33	-0.01	5.36	5.38	5.99	6.03
Anaheim–Santa Ana	11.84	7.11	10.56	10.82	9.52	9.87
San Diego	8.45	2.81	8.03	8.07	8.51	8.57
Newark	6.63	1.06	6.47	6.49	7.10	7.13
Oakland	7.52	2.17	6.85	6.89	7.24	7.29
Cleveland	6.13	0.75	6.16	6.17	6.79	6.82
Tampa–St. Petersburg	8.60	3.12	8.22	8.57	7.95	8.36

Riverside-San Bernardino	8.68	3.48	7.09	7.41	6.93	7.33
Phoenix	9.95	3.94	9.54	9.78	8.55	8.81
Miami-Hialeah	9.26	3.25	9.47	9.60	9.28	9.43
Seattle	7.82	2.53	7.95	7.99	7.62	7.67
Denver	7.41	2.65	7.42	7.44	7.52	7.55
San Francisco	6.30	1.24	6.99	7.00	7.41	7.42
Kansas City	6.66	1.32	6.60	6.69	6.65	6.78
Cincinnati	5.80	0.88	5.87	5.91	6.49	6.55
Milwaukee	5.66	1.03	5.64	5.70	6.43	6.53
San Jose	10.35	5.04	10.12	10.47	9.01	9.50
New Orleans	6.90	1.57	7.16	7.18	7.08	7.10
Bergen-Passaic	7.05	1.42	6.66	6.69	7.22	7.27
Columbus	6.58	1.68	6.51	6.54	7.15	7.20
Norfolk-Va. Beach	7.62	1.80	7.53	7.56	7.44	7.47
Sacramento	6.82	2.53	6.23	6.50	7.69	8.10
Indianapolis	6.53	1.58	6.86	6.89	7.14	7.19
San Antonio	7.96	1.98	7.90	7.95	7.89	7.95
Fort Worth-Arlington	8.70	2.66	8.35	8.54	7.41	7.70
Portland, Oreg.	7.10	1.93	7.38	7.45	7.23	7.32
Fort Lauderdale	12.39	6.27	11.20	11.37	10.76	10.94
Hartford	7.34	1.93	7.46	7.56	7.78	7.95
Charlotte-Gastonia	8.14	1.77	8.39	8.49	8.30	8.45
Salt Lake City	6.46	2.19	6.48	6.51	6.66	6.70
Rochester	7.07	1.76	7.10	7.23	7.04	7.30
Buffalo	5.55	0.47	5.66	5.69	6.26	6.32
Louisville	6.97	1.36	7.23	7.30	6.98	7.08
Oklahoma City	7.55	1.86	7.43	7.52	7.19	7.29
Memphis	7.42	1.41	7.50	7.84	7.20	7.63
Dayton-Springfield	6.85	1.59	6.94	6.94	6.80	6.81

NOTE: MSA = metropolitan statistical area.

TABLE 6 Average Annual Growth Rates (percentage) of Total Personal Income, Population, Earnings, and Employment for the 50 Largest MSAs, 1969-1979

MSA	Personal Income	Total Population	Earnings Total	Earnings Excluding Farm	Earnings Excluding Manufacturing	Employment Total	Employment Excluding Farm	Employment Excluding Manufacturing
Total United States	10.03	1.10	9.35	9.40	9.74	2.16	2.29	2.62
Total MSAs	9.38	0.76	8.86	8.86	9.35	1.94	1.96	2.51
New York	6.43	-0.83	5.66	5.66	6.24	-1.06	-1.06	-0.47
Los Angeles	8.76	0.57	8.66	8.65	9.32	2.16	2.17	2.71
Chicago	8.15	0.02	7.87	7.87	8.51	0.68	0.68	1.44
Philadelphia	8.16	-0.10	7.17	7.18	7.96	0.26	0.26	1.11
Detroit	8.81	-0.09	8.21	8.22	8.46	0.96	0.97	1.73
Boston	8.36	-0.03	8.04	8.04	8.13	1.37	1.38	1.71
Washington, D.C.	10.22	0.84	9.72	9.72	9.71	2.48	2.49	2.50
Houston	14.50	3.57	14.73	14.72	15.06	5.74	5.81	5.99
Nassau-Suffolk	8.49	0.33	8.18	8.20	8.70	2.27	2.27	2.74
St. Louis	8.77	-0.03	8.21	8.19	8.70	1.25	1.27	1.93
Atlanta	11.34	2.35	10.92	10.94	11.81	3.46	3.52	4.20
Baltimore	9.30	0.64	8.44	8.44	9.14	1.56	1.57	2.35
Minneapolis-St. Paul	9.83	0.79	9.70	9.72	10.00	2.86	2.92	3.40
Dallas	11.56	2.36	11.43	11.41	12.18	3.66	3.74	4.14
Pittsburgh	8.66	-0.52	8.13	8.13	8.31	0.73	0.74	1.38
Anaheim-Santa Ana	13.37	3.23	13.33	13.34	14.28	6.91	6.96	7.42
San Diego	12.00	3.14	10.82	10.83	10.93	4.26	4.27	4.30
Newark	7.72	-0.14	7.39	7.40	7.87	0.49	0.50	1.21
Oakland	10.04	0.81	8.98	9.00	9.23	2.34	2.39	2.75
Cleveland	7.55	-0.70	7.22	7.23	7.55	0.41	0.41	1.19
Tampa-St. Petersburg	13.26	3.81	12.46	12.49	12.78	4.89	4.98	5.16

Riverside–San Bernardino	13.07	2.92	10.49	10.50	10.68	3.91	4.05	4.14
Phoenix	13.92	4.41	13.51	13.62	14.18	6.29	6.44	6.88
Miami–Hialeah	10.73	2.40	10.37	10.40	10.49	3.16	3.17	3.24
Seattle	10.18	1.04	10.12	10.12	11.10	3.02	3.03	3.77
Denver	12.51	2.63	12.56	12.60	12.85	4.74	4.79	5.01
San Francisco	8.78	0.02	8.43	8.43	8.69	1.66	1.66	1.92
Kansas City	9.76	0.53	9.36	9.33	9.81	1.97	2.06	2.47
Cincinnati	8.78	0.17	8.59	8.61	8.86	1.56	1.59	2.16
Milwaukee	9.10	0.00	8.67	8.68	8.99	1.77	1.80	2.44
San Jose	11.83	2.09	12.21	12.25	11.56	5.39	5.46	5.15
New Orleans	10.79	1.29	10.35	10.36	10.65	2.53	2.55	2.88
Bergen–Passaic	7.88	-0.40	8.32	8.33	9.24	1.64	1.63	2.66
Columbus	9.86	1.02	9.33	9.33	9.94	2.40	2.47	3.09
Norfolk–Va. Beach	10.20	1.05	9.27	9.31	9.26	2.19	2.23	2.31
Sacramento	11.95	2.62	10.91	10.97	11.21	4.23	4.30	4.40
Indianapolis	9.11	0.62	8.72	8.74	9.09	1.75	1.81	2.43
San Antonio	10.90	1.87	10.01	10.02	9.85	2.21	2.25	2.13
Fort Worth–Arlington	11.62	2.17	10.64	10.60	11.95	3.26	3.34	4.11
Portland, Oreg.	11.29	1.77	11.02	11.05	10.98	3.55	3.63	3.76
Fort Lauderdale	15.10	5.17	13.52	13.54	13.43	6.43	6.47	6.44
Hartford	8.49	0.26	8.17	8.21	9.10	1.74	1.78	2.82
Charlotte–Gastonia	10.53	1.50	10.00	9.96	10.88	2.44	2.55	3.51
Salt Lake City	12.08	2.69	11.81	11.86	11.69	4.34	4.42	4.25
Rochester	7.97	0.29	7.45	7.55	6.87	1.12	1.14	1.59
Buffalo	7.50	-0.70	6.73	6.75	6.91	0.29	0.28	1.12
Louisville	9.35	0.70	8.77	8.81	9.31	1.53	1.59	2.50
Oklahoma City	11.84	1.98	11.44	11.46	11.27	3.59	3.70	3.59
Memphis	10.55	0.92	10.15	10.13	10.57	2.30	2.40	2.75
Dayton–Springfield	7.95	-0.23	7.08	7.06	8.35	0.70	0.72	1.99

NOTE: MSA = metropolitan statistical area.

TABLE 7 Average Annual Growth Rates (percentage) of Total Personal Income, Population, Earnings, and Employment for the 50 Largest MSAs, 1979-1984

MSA	Personal Income	Total Population	Earnings			Employment		
			Total	Excluding Farm	Excluding Manufacturing	Total	Excluding Farm	Excluding Manufacturing
United States	9.20	1.01	7.89	8.07	8.58	1.38	1.48	2.04
50 Largest MSAs	9.46	1.00	8.61	8.63	9.40	1.73	1.75	2.44
New York	9.50	0.17	9.41	9.41	10.24	1.20	1.20	1.90
Los Angeles	9.12	1.32	8.22	8.22	8.52	1.39	1.49	2.00
Chicago	7.33	0.20	6.28	6.28	7.66	-0.02	-0.01	1.14
Philadelphia	8.73	0.20	7.76	7.78	8.87	1.08	1.08	2.00
Detroit	5.37	-0.79	3.45	3.45	4.75	-1.41	-1.41	-0.07
Boston	10.89	0.14	10.87	10.87	10.81	2.63	2.64	2.89
Washington, D.C.	10.72	1.11	10.17	10.20	10.04	2.61	2.62	2.54
Houston	10.63	3.67	9.95	9.95	11.20	2.89	2.91	3.83
Nassau-Suffolk	10.63	0.40	11.05	11.05	11.25	3.18	3.20	3.48
St. Louis	8.76	0.17	7.64	7.73	8.61	0.78	0.82	1.71
Atlanta	12.10	2.55	12.07	12.07	12.34	4.24	4.29	4.61
Baltimore	9.22	0.32	7.83	7.87	8.78	1.04	1.05	1.72
Minneapolis-St. Paul	9.60	1.14	8.84	8.89	8.88	1.74	1.78	2.04
Dallas	12.95	3.00	13.64	13.68	14.25	5.08	5.12	5.78
Pittsburgh	6.43	-0.51	4.23	4.25	6.78	-1.18	-1.18	0.42
Anaheim-Santa Ana	10.35	1.87	11.02	11.05	11.23	3.79	3.82	4.40
San Diego	10.84	2.46	10.02	10.05	9.69	2.75	2.83	2.72
Newark	9.79	-0.14	9.25	9.26	10.41	1.72	1.72	2.80
Oakland	10.50	1.44	8.68	8.72	9.52	2.40	2.42	3.10
Cleveland	6.74	-0.47	4.83	4.83	6.60	-1.03	-1.02	0.27
Tampa-St. Petersburg	13.18	2.85	12.45	11.54	12.67	5.52	5.61	5.80

Riverside-San Bernardino	11.31	3.88	8.53	8.42	9.28	2.91	3.06	3.47
Phoenix	12.14	3.31	11.17	11.38	11.07	4.50	4.54	4.71
Miami-Hialeah	9.99	1.49	9.18	9.16	9.46	2.48	2.51	2.89
Seattle	8.40	1.65	6.70	6.70	7.01	1.76	1.78	2.54
Denver	11.68	2.31	10.99	10.99	11.39	3.45	3.46	3.89
San Francisco	10.04	0.76	9.07	9.05	9.33	1.93	1.94	2.17
Kansas City	8.39	0.68	7.08	7.28	7.46	0.76	0.78	1.31
Cincinnati	7.87	0.12	6.42	6.44	7.36	0.23	0.24	1.34
Milwaukee	7.14	-0.02	5.53	5.55	7.33	-0.26	-0.26	1.25
San Jose	11.24	1.53	13.10	13.17	11.66	4.30	4.35	3.96
New Orleans	9.05	1.27	7.87	7.87	8.48	1.15	1.16	1.67
Bergen-Passaic	9.83	-0.03	9.09	9.09	10.42	1.88	1.88	2.96
Columbus	8.90	0.48	7.78	7.91	8.39	1.16	1.21	1.90
Norfolk-Va. Beach	11.21	1.70	10.75	10.79	10.82	2.69	2.70	2.79
Sacramento	9.47	2.62	7.87	8.16	7.71	3.02	3.14	3.05
Indianapolis	7.80	0.55	6.58	6.66	7.79	0.53	0.55	1.51
San Antonio	11.95	2.35	11.46	11.45	11.61	3.87	3.92	4.09
Fort Worth-Arlington	13.13	3.95	11.04	11.05	11.75	3.87	3.92	4.59
Portland, Oreg.	7.11	0.97	5.40	5.40	5.82	0.22	0.20	0.85
Fort Lauderdale	11.76	2.08	11.96	11.97	12.10	4.62	4.64	4.87
Hartford	10.35	0.39	9.53	9.55	11.23	1.80	1.83	2.96
Charlotte-Gastonia	10.71	1.64	10.14	10.10	10.24	2.09	2.19	2.75
Salt Lake City	10.00	3.02	8.97	9.01	8.59	2.41	2.42	2.44
Rochester	9.11	0.29	7.83	7.90	9.01	1.18	1.22	2.26
Buffalo	6.93	-0.94	4.68	4.68	7.20	-0.75	-0.75	0.64
Louisville	7.93	0.05	6.21	6.21	7.65	-0.27	-0.27	0.90
Oklahoma City	11.05	2.73	10.53	10.65	10.53	3.29	3.34	3.63
Memphis	8.55	0.67	7.66	7.81	8.50	0.64	0.66	1.29
Dayton-Springfield	7.28	-0.25	5.48	5.57	6.13	-0.44	-0.42	0.45

NOTE: MSA = metropolitan statistical area.

growth rate in the 50 major MSAs (1.0 percent) approximated that of the nation as a whole (1.1 percent). Eight of these MSAs showed declining population, and of the eight, all but Newark and Bergen-Passaic had declining employment rates as well. In all of these MSAs except Detroit, the loss of manufacturing jobs more than accounted for the total job loss. The industrial compositions of each of these MSAs were heavily weighted toward smokestack industries suffering declining employment.

Four of the major MSAs with declining populations in the 1970s shifted to a position of increasing population in the first half of the 1980s; these MSAs included New York, Philadelphia, and Boston in the Northeast, and St. Louis in the Plains region. New York has also shifted to increasing employment. The Boston MSA has experienced rapid employment growth during the most recent period (1979–1984) and is said to be experiencing a labor shortage.

The short-term relationship between employment change and population change is loose, for two main reasons: (1) population change is in part dependent on births and deaths, which vary with the population age profiles of the area rather than with employment change, and (2) increasing employment may also reflect extended journeys to work from neighboring areas or the increased employment of otherwise unemployed residents, rather than population growth due to increased in-migration of transferred employees or other new residents.

Population growth in an area may be constrained by the availability and relative cost of housing over the short term. Over the longer term, job growth may be constrained by these very same housing factors, as well as by other social and economic externalities, such as traffic congestion and crime. That is, in the absence of affordable housing and infrastructure, employment costs may rise prohibitively, to the subsequent competitive disadvantage of the area with respect to plant location and expansion.

FURTHER AREA DISAGGREGATION

It has been argued that MSA designations may not adequately reflect the dynamics of the urban growth process because of possible distortions that may otherwise result from discontinuities in the process of redefining MSAs, both over time and geographically. Redefinitions of MSAs do not occur with regular periodicity; in large part the timing of changes is based on the timing of data collection, the most important being the decennial population censuses. Moreover, MSAs are aggregations of counties, and, when the redefinitions occur, entire counties are being added or deleted. Thus, MSA redefinition reflects more than the incremental suburban expansion around city core areas; it also includes preexisting populations at some distance from the urban expansion. (To preclude the latter discontinuity, BEA retrospectively reclassifies an MSA according to the most current definition of its boundaries.)

In this section the geographic configuration is broken down into four classes of MSA counties and four classes of non-MSA counties. County boundaries have been retrospectively reclassified, and the counties are sorted by population size and by geographic adjacency to core MSA counties (a core county is one with a population of 1 million or more, including residents and nonresidents who daily commute to work there). Non-MSA counties are sorted by adjacency to MSAs. Each of these county classes is then reviewed: first in Tables 8, 9, and 10, for its growth characteristics with respect to the aggregates reviewed earlier, and then in Tables 11–14, for a profile of the sources of total personal income over each of the years bracketing the time spans.

Summary Growth Patterns

Tables 8, 9, and 10 are similar to Tables 1, 2, and 3, except for the inclusion of employment variables in the 1969–1979 and 1979–1984 time spans and for the row stub that breaks down MSAs and non-MSAs into four county groupings each, by size and geographic proximity characteristics. With the change in geographic configuration, more information is available on the county categories composing MSA and non-MSA areas.

It may be noted that for any county category, earnings and employment growth rates in any time span are not well correlated with population growth rates. It was mentioned in the preceding section that the short-term relationship between employment change and population change was loose with respect to individual MSA configurations. Broken down by individual county classes, the relationship is even looser if not altogether nonexistent. This is because, in addition to the two reasons cited for the loose relationship that may obtain with respect to individual MSAs, county portions of MSAs, even more than MSAs as a whole, reflect different places of

TABLE 8 Average Annual Growth Rates (percentage) of Total Personal Income, Population, and Earnings by Region and County Type, 1959-1969

Region and County Type[a]	Personal Income	Total Population	Earnings			
			Total	Excluding Farm	Excluding Manufacturing	Excluding Manufacturing and Farm
Total United States	6.93	1.29	6.72	6.86	6.93	7.14
County Type 0	6.23	1.03	6.51	6.53	7.00	7.04
County Type 1	7.71	2.17	7.04	7.14	7.18	7.32
County Type 2	7.21	1.85	7.08	7.18	7.47	7.63
County Type 3	7.68	1.88	7.34	7.52	7.41	7.68
County Type 4	6.44	0.32	5.86	6.18	5.57	6.01
County Type 5	6.71	0.57	6.37	6.72	6.05	6.48
County Type 6	7.06	0.23	6.19	6.92	5.62	6.34
County Type 7	6.57	-0.20	5.88	6.34	5.42	5.78
New England	6.77	1.18	6.49	6.54	7.15	7.26
County Type 0	6.82	1.36	7.29	7.34	7.91	7.99
County Type 1	6.47	0.87	6.16	6.20	6.97	7.04
County Type 2	6.78	1.24	6.21	6.24	7.15	7.20
County Type 3	7.11	1.59	6.94	6.99	6.93	7.01
County Type 4	7.20	1.45	6.36	6.50	6.57	6.78
County Type 5	6.46	0.38	5.95	6.29	6.25	6.78
County Type 7	6.77	0.29	6.09	6.56	6.36	7.03
Mideast	6.40	0.98	6.16	6.20	6.74	6.80
County Type 0	5.10	-0.11	5.67	5.68	6.47	6.48
County Type 1	7.91	2.45	7.27	7.33	7.86	7.96
County Type 2	6.67	1.41	6.34	6.39	6.69	6.78
County Type 3	6.54	0.82	5.81	5.95	6.02	6.26
County Type 4	6.19	0.45	5.61	5.78	5.53	5.80
County Type 5	6.43	0.31	5.70	5.68	6.05	6.04
County Type 6	6.87	0.43	6.20	6.31	5.85	5.94
County Type 7	7.64	0.45	6.43	6.57	5.93	6.06

Great Lakes	6.53	1.06	6.38	6.44	6.64	6.76
County Type 0	5.83	0.63	6.02	6.03	6.54	6.55
County Type 1	7.83	2.49	7.61	7.73	7.61	7.82
County Type 2	6.37	1.21	6.53	6.57	7.19	7.29
County Type 3	6.94	1.30	6.54	6.64	6.55	6.74
County Type 4	6.86	0.69	6.30	6.45	6.00	6.19
County Type 5	6.70	0.65	6.16	6.38	6.15	6.46
County Type 6	7.01	0.21	5.72	5.82	5.45	5.48
County Type 7	6.57	0.05	5.62	5.92	5.26	5.56
Plains	6.53	0.64	6.38	6.48	6.27	6.38
County Type 0	5.39	0.36	6.10	6.12	6.49	6.51
County Type 1	8.19	2.80	8.35	8.51	7.67	7.88
County Type 2	5.65	0.79	5.67	5.71	6.30	6.36
County Type 3	6.12	1.07	6.06	6.07	6.07	6.07
County Type 4	6.55	0.56	6.30	6.67	5.97	6.39
County Type 5	6.45	0.35	6.30	6.55	5.80	6.03
County Type 6	6.69	-0.15	5.59	5.62	5.49	5.46
County Type 7	6.55	-0.59	5.92	5.75	5.74	5.43
Southeast	7.85	1.32	7.61	7.95	7.36	7.80
County Type 0	6.63	1.16	7.87	7.99	7.96	8.11
County Type 1	6.30	0.22	4.56	4.63	4.32	4.40
County Type 2	8.05	2.25	8.20	8.30	8.22	8.36
County Type 3	9.95	3.14	9.64	9.93	9.70	10.13
County Type 4	5.98	-0.61	5.36	5.85	4.85	5.50
County Type 5	7.54	0.63	7.23	7.81	6.47	7.18
County Type 6	8.28	0.67	7.60	9.02	6.32	7.98
County Type 7	7.72	0.11	7.01	8.31	5.67	7.03
Southwest	7.31	1.64	7.05	7.41	6.71	7.13
County Type 0	8.41	3.34	8.60	8.64	8.46	8.51
County Type 1	8.26	2.69	6.14	7.02	5.61	6.67
County Type 2	7.80	2.21	7.74	7.83	7.47	7.58
County Type 3	6.74	1.22	6.28	6.59	5.89	6.24
County Type 4	6.19	0.69	5.30	6.03	4.89	5.71
County Type 5	5.75	0.60	5.30	5.69	5.03	5.47
County Type 6	5.76	-0.43	4.51	5.20	4.28	4.98
County Type 7	5.44	-0.47	4.53	5.72	4.34	5.55

TABLE 8 (Continued)

Region and County Type[a]	Personal Income	Total Population	Earnings			
			Total	Excluding Farm	Excluding Manufacturing	Excluding Manufacturing and Farm
Rocky Mountain	6.55	1.58	6.43	6.56	6.42	6.58
County Type 0	5.24	0.60	7.13	7.14	7.13	7.14
County Type 1	9.80	0.60	8.82	8.95	8.64	8.79
County Type 2	7.09	2.89	7.26	7.27	7.50	7.51
County Type 3	6.18	1.49	5.89	5.90	6.20	6.23
County Type 4	6.77	1.09	6.50	6.66	6.33	6.49
County Type 5	5.36	1.02	5.09	5.37	5.09	5.42
County Type 6	5.43	-0.14	4.96	5.25	4.81	5.09
County Type 7	5.46	-0.20	5.17	5.09	5.03	4.88
Far West	7.44	2.34	7.26	7.43	7.48	7.72
County Type 0	7.48	2.32	7.41	7.47	7.62	7.72
County Type 1	8.35	3.18	7.96	8.08	7.77	7.91
County Type 2	7.49	2.74	7.03	7.47	7.37	7.94
County Type 3	7.32	2.21	7.11	7.59	7.51	8.13
County Type 4	6.34	1.50	6.21	6.70	6.38	7.08
County Type 5	5.71	0.49	5.47	5.46	5.97	6.06
County Type 6	6.11	0.89	7.28	7.90	7.69	8.57
County Type 7	5.44	0.00	4.75	5.14	5.27	5.97

[a]County types: 0 = metropolitan statistical area (MSA) core counties that contain at least 1 million people; 1 = all MSA core-contiguous counties; 2 = all MSA counties that are not core contiguous and that have populations between 250,000 and 1 million; 3 = all MSA counties that are not core contiguous and that have populations of less than 250,000; 4 = all non-MSA, MSA-adjacent counties that have populations of at least 20,000; 5 = all non-MSA, not MSA-adjacent counties that have populations of at least 20,000; 6 = all non-MSA, MSA-adjacent counties that have populations of less than 20,000; and 7 = all non-MSA, not MSA-adjacent counties that have populations of less than 20,000.

TABLE 9 Average Annual Growth Rates (percentage) of Total Personal Income, Population, Earnings, and Employment by Region and County Type, 1969-1979

Region and County Type[a]	Personal Income	Total Population	Earnings			Employment		
			Total	Excluding Farm	Excluding Manufacturing	Total	Excluding Farm	Excluding Manufacturing
Total United States	10.03	1.10	9.35	9.40	9.74	2.16	2.29	2.62
County Type 0	8.47	0.12	8.24	8.24	8.70	1.26	1.26	1.79
County Type 1	10.46	1.51	10.06	10.08	10.62	3.12	3.21	3.77
County Type 2	10.36	1.43	9.76	9.76	10.27	2.65	2.68	3.25
County Type 3	10.97	1.61	10.02	10.10	10.32	2.48	2.65	2.95
County Type 4	10.77	1.42	9.68	9.84	9.75	2.07	2.40	2.31
County Type 5	11.24	1.48	10.40	10.62	10.55	2.45	2.85	2.65
County Type 6	11.21	1.13	10.25	10.87	10.11	1.84	2.60	1.78
County Type 7	10.98	0.82	10.14	10.83	9.95	1.84	2.68	1.73
New England	8.82	0.51	8.22	8.25	8.54	1.62	1.65	2.22
County Type 0	8.28	-0.09	8.40	8.42	8.64	1.88	1.90	2.44
County Type 1	8.54	0.09	7.93	7.94	8.15	1.19	1.20	1.59
County Type 2	8.64	0.49	7.99	8.01	8.57	1.41	1.43	2.30
County Type 3	9.62	0.94	8.70	8.75	8.99	2.13	2.15	2.73
County Type 4	10.06	1.62	8.64	8.74	8.76	2.05	2.10	2.55
County Type 5	10.06	1.37	8.84	9.03	8.97	2.14	2.37	2.43
County Type 7	10.39	2.08	9.05	9.14	8.69	2.79	2.94	2.80
Mideast	8.21	0.06	7.46	7.48	7.92	0.68	0.69	1.35
County Type 0	6.45	-1.10	6.01	6.01	6.59	-0.96	-0.96	-0.32
County Type 1	9.04	0.57	8.98	9.00	9.56	2.32	2.34	3.06
County Type 2	8.86	0.51	8.23	8.26	8.81	1.37	1.39	2.29
County Type 3	9.65	0.94	8.40	8.50	9.03	1.45	1.50	2.33
County Type 4	9.26	0.75	7.96	8.06	8.13	1.13	1.18	1.68
County Type 5	9.68	1.06	8.62	8.87	8.61	1.60	1.73	1.99
County Type 6	9.51	0.75	8.05	8.38	8.79	1.28	1.44	2.09
County Type 7	10.60	1.39	8.37	8.68	9.00	1.11	1.28	2.23

TABLE 9 (Continued)

Region and County Type [a]	Personal Income	Total Population	Earnings			Employment		
			Total	Excluding Farm	Excluding Manufacturing	Total	Excluding Farm	Excluding Manufacturing
Great Lakes	9.16	0.42	8.52	8.53	8.89	1.36	1.43	2.04
County Type 0	7.48	-0.60	7.49	7.49	7.89	0.37	0.37	1.08
County Type 1	11.06	1.61	10.26	10.31	11.01	3.17	3.29	4.05
County Type 2	9.09	0.20	8.61	8.62	9.06	1.51	1.53	2.52
County Type 3	9.87	0.78	9.18	9.22	9.49	1.80	1.92	2.51
County Type 4	9.85	0.86	8.83	8.90	8.96	1.47	1.71	1.83
County Type 5	10.61	1.17	9.78	9.82	9.86	2.04	2.30	2.27
County Type 6	10.43	0.92	9.30	9.58	9.29	1.23	1.65	1.32
County Type 7	10.85	1.22	9.38	9.34	9.31	1.50	1.88	1.55
Plains	9.95	0.54	9.52	9.72	9.59	2.10	2.43	2.28
County Type 0	8.02	-1.13	8.06	8.06	8.35	1.04	1.05	1.52
County Type 1	10.62	1.74	10.66	10.68	11.31	3.65	3.79	4.33
County Type 2	9.76	0.44	10.05	10.07	10.29	2.65	2.67	2.99
County Type 3	10.40	0.90	10.16	10.34	10.22	2.56	2.74	2.86
County Type 4	10.49	0.87	9.89	10.23	9.61	2.34	2.75	2.32
County Type 5	10.11	0.65	9.48	9.64	9.46	1.92	2.28	2.00
County Type 6	10.40	0.58	9.26	10.17	8.82	1.58	2.48	1.31
County Type 7	9.96	0.06	9.27	10.03	8.88	1.42	2.26	1.20
Southeast	11.44	1.81	10.61	10.73	10.85	2.70	3.01	3.00
County Type 0	10.25	1.83	10.43	10.45	10.68	2.93	2.95	3.18
County Type 1	12.37	2.88	11.89	11.96	12.36	4.26	4.45	4.69
County Type 2	11.13	1.83	10.54	10.57	10.86	3.11	3.15	3.48
County Type 3	11.56	2.01	10.35	10.41	10.54	2.52	2.74	2.89
County Type 4	11.58	1.67	10.50	10.80	10.38	2.23	2.77	2.25
County Type 5	11.58	1.43	10.67	10.91	10.87	2.28	2.78	2.43
County Type 6	11.56	1.24	10.88	11.40	11.22	1.98	2.74	2.10
County Type 7	11.40	1.06	10.09	10.52	10.01	1.52	2.42	1.35

Southwest	12.51	2.44	12.06	12.13	12.18	3.71	4.00	3.79
County Type 0	12.47	2.58	13.13	13.12	13.74	4.68	4.69	5.12
County Type 1	17.10	4.81	14.43	14.40	14.01	5.35	5.92	5.15
County Type 2	12.00	2.61	11.68	11.70	11.88	4.06	4.13	4.26
County Type 3	12.52	2.38	11.26	11.32	11.07	3.11	3.31	3.06
County Type 4	12.98	2.33	11.81	11.88	11.75	3.05	3.62	2.96
County Type 5	12.00	1.98	11.21	11.24	11.03	2.78	3.14	2.69
County Type 6	12.41	1.35	11.78	12.28	11.20	2.07	3.05	1.69
County Type 7	11.53	0.70	10.73	10.99	10.52	1.43	2.31	1.27
Rocky Mountain	12.54	2.68	12.17	12.62	12.10	4.41	4.79	4.43
County Type 0	8.97	-0.32	10.35	10.35	10.76	2.36	2.36	2.66
County Type 1	15.09	4.58	16.18	16.49	15.93	8.21	8.63	8.11
County Type 2	12.02	2.89	11.91	11.93	11.65	4.40	4.45	4.22
County Type 3	12.31	2.67	11.75	11.95	11.68	4.17	4.35	4.25
County Type 4	12.53	3.10	11.46	12.17	10.71	3.87	4.60	3.64
County Type 5	13.25	2.80	12.77	13.27	12.85	4.74	5.19	4.85
County Type 6	12.01	2.08	9.72	11.38	9.51	2.59	3.55	2.62
County Type 7	11.71	1.85	11.19	12.95	11.26	3.41	4.36	3.51
Far West	10.83	1.81	10.10	10.10	10.42	3.36	3.42	3.67
County Type 0	9.95	1.22	9.57	9.56	9.94	2.95	2.96	3.29
County Type 1	11.72	2.25	11.12	11.13	11.68	4.36	4.48	4.94
County Type 2	12.12	2.55	10.84	10.79	10.88	3.77	3.88	3.85
County Type 3	13.15	3.26	12.32	12.58	12.24	5.03	5.40	5.10
County Type 4	12.70	2.84	11.43	11.60	11.23	4.02	4.32	4.15
County Type 5	11.84	2.33	10.77	10.96	11.04	3.51	3.75	4.02
County Type 6	11.70	2.46	9.19	9.86	8.71	2.87	3.34	2.78
County Type 7	12.15	2.37	10.62	10.79	10.54	3.32	3.53	3.53

[a]County types: 0 = metropolitan statistical area (MSA) core counties that contain at least 1 million people; 1 = all MSA core-contiguous counties; 2 = all MSA counties that are not core contiguous and that have populations between 250,000 and 1 million; 3 = all MSA counties that are not core contiguous and that have populations of less than 250,000; 4 = all non-MSA, MSA-adjacent counties that have populations of at least 20,000; 5 = all non-MSA, not MSA-adjacent counties that have populations of at least 20,000; 6 = all non-MSA, MSA-adjacent counties that have populations of less than 20,000; and 7 = all non-MSA, not MSA-adjacent counties that have populations of less than 20,000.

TABLE 10 Average Annual Growth Rates (percentage) of Total Personal Income, Population, Earnings, and Employment by Region and County Type, 1979–1984

Region and County Type[a]	Personal Income	Total Population	Earnings			Employment		
			Total	Excluding Farm	Excluding Manufacturing	Total	Excluding Farm	Excluding Manufacturing
Total United States	9.20	1.01	7.89	8.07	8.58	1.38	1.48	2.04
County Type 0	8.82	0.66	8.02	8.02	8.93	1.08	1.09	1.85
County Type 1	9.91	1.14	9.36	9.44	10.21	2.58	2.64	3.31
County Type 2	9.76	1.39	8.40	8.48	9.13	1.84	1.89	2.52
County Type 3	9.12	1.18	7.32	7.45	7.96	1.19	1.28	1.85
County Type 4	8.61	0.92	6.31	6.74	6.58	0.61	0.81	1.22
County Type 5	8.54	0.93	6.46	6.84	6.57	0.71	0.90	1.13
County Type 6	8.16	0.76	5.32	6.69	5.17	0.45	0.83	0.73
County Type 7	8.19	0.58	5.35	6.54	5.28	0.37	0.75	0.61
New England	10.41	0.37	9.77	9.80	10.36	2.06	2.09	2.79
County Type 0	10.83	0.09	10.90	10.98	11.18	2.71	2.73	3.19
County Type 1	10.75	0.36	10.27	10.28	10.69	2.23	2.24	2.73
County Type 2	10.07	0.27	9.02	9.02	9.90	1.49	1.50	2.50
County Type 3	10.35	0.53	9.77	9.79	10.51	2.02	2.07	2.78
County Type 4	10.67	1.01	9.36	9.40	9.73	2.46	2.53	3.18
County Type 5	9.38	0.48	7.85	8.21	8.33	1.90	2.02	2.57
County Type 7	10.80	1.08	9.40	9.70	10.64	3.08	3.21	4.12
Mideast	9.13	0.18	8.13	8.17	9.26	1.08	1.10	1.95
County Type 0	8.32	-0.34	7.83	7.83	8.93	0.25	0.25	1.05
County Type 1	9.88	0.49	9.27	9.30	10.51	2.23	2.24	3.11
County Type 2	9.40	0.46	8.02	8.05	9.06	1.26	1.27	2.24
County Type 3	9.00	0.28	7.26	7.40	8.62	0.97	1.02	2.03
County Type 4	8.06	0.17	5.85	6.17	6.71	0.11	0.13	1.07
County Type 5	8.86	0.29	6.97	6.75	7.63	1.01	1.09	1.76
County Type 6	8.53	0.12	6.66	7.21	7.04	0.85	1.02	1.33
County Type 7	9.01	1.02	4.64	4.12	6.25	-0.14	-0.12	1.08

Great Lakes	7.00	-0.01	5.18	5.29	6.36	-0.38	-0.33	0.70
County Type 0	6.63	-0.40	5.09	5.09	6.74	-0.87	-0.87	0.43
County Type 1	7.68	0.60	6.74	6.85	7.64	1.19	1.27	2.13
County Type 2	6.69	-0.14	4.62	4.64	6.12	-0.82	-0.81	0.52
County Type 3	6.84	0.01	4.69	4.81	5.59	-0.53	-0.49	0.46
County Type 4	7.20	0.07	4.89	5.23	5.17	-0.45	-0.32	0.35
County Type 5	7.66	0.28	5.57	6.01	5.42	0.21	0.38	0.63
County Type 6	7.00	0.15	4.32	5.32	4.46	-0.22	0.16	0.30
County Type 7	7.64	0.26	4.57	5.66	4.40	0.01	0.35	0.41
Plains	8.40	0.48	6.67	7.13	6.91	0.61	0.80	1.02
County Type 0	8.51	0.11	6.76	6.77	7.43	-0.13	-0.13	0.52
County Type 1	9.64	1.15	9.93	10.09	10.01	2.82	2.90	3.23
County Type 2	8.46	0.68	7.37	7.40	7.97	0.85	0.87	1.59
County Type 3	7.79	0.65	5.85	6.03	6.59	0.30	0.38	0.90
County Type 4	7.95	0.44	5.30	5.82	5.79	0.26	0.45	0.88
County Type 5	8.21	0.41	5.83	6.39	5.72	0.35	0.53	0.52
County Type 6	7.48	0.28	3.84	5.82	3.56	0.03	0.54	0.14
County Type 7	7.85	-0.05	4.65	5.60	4.66	-0.20	0.22	0.00
Southeast	10.10	1.39	8.80	9.00	9.21	1.86	2.04	2.36
County Type 0	10.57	1.60	9.83	9.82	10.21	2.78	2.80	3.19
County Type 1	11.60	2.38	11.93	12.02	12.52	4.35	4.46	4.86
County Type 2	10.53	1.60	9.44	9.46	9.97	2.34	2.39	2.83
County Type 3	10.16	1.57	8.58	8.64	8.84	1.76	1.88	2.26
County Type 4	9.45	1.23	7.31	7.78	7.39	0.99	1.28	1.41
County Type 5	8.64	0.75	6.73	7.03	6.62	0.42	0.63	0.77
County Type 6	8.67	0.68	6.45	7.13	6.29	0.31	0.58	0.56
County Type 7	8.71	0.44	6.25	7.22	5.67	0.41	0.78	0.53
Southwest	11.03	2.72	9.92	10.29	10.30	3.04	3.20	3.49
County Type 0	10.82	2.98	11.29	11.29	12.25	3.62	3.63	4.42
County Type 1	14.14	4.39	11.32	11.62	11.73	4.41	4.68	4.83
County Type 2	11.59	2.80	10.70	10.75	10.87	3.61	3.64	3.90
County Type 3	11.03	2.78	9.20	9.39	9.66	2.65	2.77	3.17
County Type 4	10.10	2.27	6.99	7.63	6.86	1.43	1.64	1.72
County Type 5	9.75	2.09	7.66	8.24	7.99	1.80	1.99	2.33
County Type 6	8.94	1.76	5.14	7.86	5.01	1.48	2.03	1.77
County Type 7	8.46	1.75	4.67	8.01	4.59	1.38	2.00	1.58

TABLE 10 (Continued)

Region and County Type [a]	Personal Income	Total Population	Earnings			Employment		
			Total	Excluding Farm	Excluding Manufacturing	Total	Excluding Farm	Excluding Manufacturing
Rocky Mountains	9.87	2.16	8.57	8.80	8.60	2.16	2.25	2.34
County Type 0	9.12	0.38	9.16	9.16	10.30	1.44	1.44	2.20
County Type 1	12.49	2.95	12.50	12.72	12.03	5.01	5.08	5.14
County Type 2	10.90	2.85	10.38	10.40	9.72	3.25	3.26	3.13
County Type 3	8.26	1.93	6.02	6.12	6.57	0.79	0.80	1.08
County Type 4	9.25	1.99	7.73	8.11	6.58	1.58	1.65	1.35
County Type 5	8.71	2.35	6.84	7.09	7.13	1.36	1.44	1.64
County Type 6	8.84	1.88	5.13	5.92	5.43	1.40	1.61	1.71
County Type 7	7.89	1.49	5.38	5.92	5.56	0.66	0.78	0.87
Far West	9.42	1.85	8.18	8.36	8.22	1.97	2.07	2.32
County Type 0	9.68	1.61	8.91	8.93	9.02	2.04	2.07	2.47
County Type 1	9.53	1.60	7.93	8.00	8.13	2.50	2.58	2.98
County Type 2	9.62	2.58	7.62	8.05	7.59	2.24	2.50	2.40
County Type 3	8.34	1.98	5.92	6.26	5.62	1.28	1.46	1.34
County Type 4	8.34	2.18	5.54	6.10	5.61	1.20	1.45	1.53
County Type 5	6.34	1.32	2.79	3.38	3.25	-0.26	-0.17	0.32
County Type 6	7.83	1.81	5.47	6.49	5.81	1.11	1.40	1.32
County Type 7	7.48	1.79	4.23	5.10	4.91	1.08	1.34	1.64

[a]County types: 0 = metropolitan statistical area (MSA) core counties that contain at least 1 million people; 1 = all MSA core-contiguous counties; 2 = all MSA counties that are not core contiguous and that have populations between 250,000 and 1 million; 3 = all MSA counties that are not core contiguous and that have populations of less than 250,000; 4 = all non-MSA, MSA-adjacent counties that have populations of at least 20,000; 5 = all non-MSA, not MSA-adjacent counties that have populations of at least 20,000; 6 = all non-MSA, MSA-adjacent counties that have populations of less than 20,000; and 7 = all non-MSA, not MSA-adjacent counties that have populations of less than 20,000.

employment and of residence. That is, employment (and earnings) is measured in the county in which the person is employed; population, on the other hand, is measured in the county of residence. The two need not be, and often are not, the same.

Despite the looser relationships that may obtain for the county categories within any time span, Tables 8, 9, and 10 show different patterns over the time spans for the core MSA counties, the three noncore MSA county classes as a group, and the non-MSA county classes as a group.

Core MSA counties tend to exhibit consistently below-average growth rates over all time spans except for the somewhat above-average growth rates in earnings during 1979–1984. If manufacturing is excluded from total earnings, the residual earnings aggregate shows an even greater difference above the average, suggesting that there was a greater rise in earnings per worker in core MSAs than elsewhere in service industries. This pattern, in turn, reflects the propensity for high-income financial, business, and professional services to locate in core MSA counties. These counties also tend to exhibit slower population growth than noncore MSA counties and, often, slower growth than non-MSA counties as well. Whereas core MSA counties tend to grow more slowly than noncore MSA counties in terms of all of the aggregates, the relative difference in the population growth rates is larger than the relative differences in earnings and employment growth rates, suggesting that core MSA counties are increasingly becoming places of work rather than places of residence.

As a group, the three noncore MSA county classes exhibit above-average growth rates for all aggregates over all the time spans. This grouping is the only one that appears to exhibit a consistent or structural growth pattern. The functional relationship of these county classes with the core MSA counties through work commutation fields and interindustry flows, however, does not allow the inference that the structural growth patterns are internally generated within the noncore MSA counties as an independent class.

The non-MSA counties do not exhibit any consistent growth patterns. Before and after the 1970s, all of the county classes in this category exhibited below-average growth rates. The non-MSAs appear to be more prone to boom-and-bust conditions than to growth regularities. That is, given the price volatility of the commodities that tend to be produced in non-MSAs, and the related industry effects, growth in these areas appears to be less structured on an internal developmental dynamic than on such exogenous forces as international price movements. Because of the BEA practice of retrospective reclassification, holding MSA geography fixed over the entire time series, it is possible that internally generated growth in non-MSA counties might be masked. Analyses by the author of non-MSA county growth patterns using other classification schemes, however, does not indicate this to be the case.

Sources of Total Personal Income

Tables 11–14 retain the same row stubs as Tables 8, 9, and 10, but instead of presenting growth rates of related economic and demographic aggregates, they present shares of the major components of total personal income (TPI) as a percentage of TPI for each of the initial and terminal years in the time spans under study. That is, for the four years 1959, 1969, 1979, and 1984, a cross-sectional profile of the major sources of TPI is presented to permit a comparison, for each year, of the relative importance of each major source of TPI for each of the county types, and, over the course of the four time points, of the changes in the relative importance of the income sources.

Among all TPI components, wages and salaries are by far the most important over all county classes and over all the years in the tables. The weight or relative importance of wages and salaries tend to diminish as the population size of county classes diminishes. Because this component (and the related benefits of other labor income) is measured by place of employment, its rank correlation with the population size of county classes provides further evidence to support the observation that core (and, to some extent, other large) MSA counties tend to be more places of work than of residence. Wages and salaries declined as a share of TPI over the years under study, and their geographic distribution has become less disparate, reflecting both the regional and MSA/non-MSA dispersion of industry in the nation.

Proprietors' (and partners') income includes profits as well as self-employment wage income. This component has also declined as a share of TPI over time, although in the forthcoming comprehensive state and local area personal income revisions, adjustments for underreporting this source of TPI will substantially raise its component share (Regional Economic Measurement Division, 1986). Geographic disparity has not narrowed; the continued importance of this component in rural counties reflects the continued relative importance of farm income as well as nonfarm proprietors' income.

Nonfarm proprietors' income also continues to remain relatively more important in suburban fringe, core-adjacent counties than in other MSA county classes. This pattern may reflect a reporting bias, however. The data source for this income component is Internal Revenue Service tax records; individual proprietors and partners may be reporting their incomes at their residence address (adjacent to core MSA counties) rather than at a work address (possibly in the core MSA counties).

The continued relative importance of property income—personal interest, dividend, and rental income (including imputed rents for home ownership)—in non-MSA and suburban fringe MSA counties reflects the higher degree of home ownership in these counties as well as the higher incidence of retirees for whom personal interest, dividend, and rental income constitutes a relatively important share of their TPI. This last observation is reinforced by reference to the last column of Tables 11–14.

The last two columns in the tables list government and business transfers to persons, split into two categories. Income maintenance transfers consist mainly of assistance payments, and all other transfers consist mainly of unemployment insurance and Social Security, government, and railroad retirement benefits. It will be noted that the geographic disparity of income maintenance transfers shows a substantial narrowing over time. Although the geographic distribution of all other transfers initially was not as disparate as that for income maintenance, it has become somewhat more disparate over time, reflecting both the geographic distribution of unemployment rates and retirees' residential patterns.

The growing relative importance of transfer payments in the most populated and least populated counties tends to reflect both relatively rising unemployment rates and the aging of the populations in those counties that have fallen below the average in employment growth. County populations tend to age where there is high unemployment or slow employment growth (except those in which retirees decide to relocate to preferred retirement communities), because the younger members of the population move to locations with more favorable employment opportunities.

SUMMARY REVIEW AND POLICY OUTLOOK

The U.S. economy is experiencing a reallocation of employment, both industrially and geographically. To a large extent, this reallo-

TABLE 11 Total Personal Income (as percentages) of Major Components by Region and County Type, 1959

Region and County Type[a]	Total Personal Income					
	Wages and Salaries	Other Labor Income	Proprietors' Income	Property Income	Income Maintenance Transfers[b]	All Other Transfers
Total United States	65.85	2.71	12.10	12.40	0.84	6.09
County Type 0	71.21	2.99	8.20	11.82	0.70	5.08
County Type 1	62.93	2.63	12.44	15.70	0.50	5.81
County Type 2	67.66	2.88	10.18	12.82	0.68	5.78
County Type 3	65.32	2.65	12.80	11.53	0.85	6.84
County Type 4	59.85	2.38	17.64	10.81	1.27	8.06
County Type 5	59.78	2.29	18.11	10.58	1.39	7.86
County Type 6	45.67	1.58	29.94	11.63	2.21	8.96
County Type 7	44.93	1.42	30.66	12.17	2.10	8.72
New England	67.21	2.81	9.03	13.60	0.78	6.56
County Type 0	67.06	3.01	8.84	14.82	0.58	5.68
County Type 1	70.83	2.76	7.40	11.91	0.87	6.23
County Type 2	66.77	3.09	8.74	13.99	0.79	6.62
County Type 3	66.44	2.38	9.59	13.60	0.69	7.30
County Type 4	63.27	2.06	11.30	15.07	0.75	7.55
County Type 5	60.97	2.08	15.69	11.55	1.27	8.45
County Type 7	55.69	1.60	17.24	13.78	1.41	10.28
Mideast	68.40	2.93	9.03	12.73	0.57	6.33
County Type 0	72.43	2.92	6.59	11.85	0.69	5.53
County Type 1	61.71	2.79	12.19	17.11	0.28	5.93
County Type 2	69.84	3.32	8.64	11.24	0.45	6.51
County Type 3	64.55	2.79	11.89	10.52	0.74	9.51
County Type 4	63.26	2.82	13.25	9.69	0.89	10.10
County Type 5	63.38	2.81	14.45	9.66	0.77	8.92
County Type 6	56.95	2.02	18.75	9.45	1.06	11.77
County Type 7	53.73	1.94	20.75	10.28	0.99	12.31

Great Lakes						
County Type 0	68.19	3.24	10.82	11.46	0.63	5.65
County Type 1	72.58	3.37	7.41	11.34	0.64	4.66
County Type 2	61.77	3.09	13.68	15.69	0.43	5.34
County Type 3	71.90	3.78	8.19	10.54	0.49	5.10
County Type 4	67.16	3.23	12.20	10.72	0.55	6.15
County Type 5	60.11	2.66	18.04	10.44	0.75	8.01
County Type 6	59.03	2.41	18.21	9.98	1.17	9.19
County Type 7	48.56	2.19	28.03	10.33	1.04	9.85
	49.93	1.86	25.17	10.07	1.65	11.31
Plains	58.82	2.26	17.94	13.72	1.01	6.25
County Type 0	74.65	3.20	7.32	9.35	0.74	4.75
County Type 1	59.24	2.33	14.39	18.58	0.41	5.05
County Type 2	69.70	2.87	10.57	11.89	0.51	4.45
County Type 3	63.83	2.59	12.89	13.60	0.81	6.27
County Type 4	52.93	1.98	21.92	14.69	1.07	7.41
County Type 5	55.18	1.73	20.89	13.61	1.38	7.20
County Type 6	36.69	1.07	35.84	15.79	1.81	8.80
County Type 7	39.00	1.19	34.41	15.38	1.73	8.29
Southeast	64.00	2.35	14.85	10.92	1.15	6.73
County Type 0	67.25	2.47	11.07	13.71	0.47	5.03
County Type 1	69.68	1.97	10.88	11.05	0.56	5.85
County Type 2	66.41	2.53	10.96	13.72	0.65	5.72
County Type 3	66.58	2.51	13.31	9.92	1.06	6.62
County Type 4	60.97	2.19	19.13	8.52	1.65	7.54
County Type 5	60.36	2.68	18.92	8.16	1.60	8.29
County Type 6	49.32	1.64	28.42	7.90	3.01	9.71
County Type 7	47.27	1.55	29.85	7.55	3.29	10.49
Southwest	62.91	2.66	14.96	12.97	1.19	5.31
County Type 0	69.69	3.56	10.75	12.34	0.38	3.28
County Type 1	61.43	2.41	18.02	11.00	1.41	5.73
County Type 2	67.15	2.70	10.77	13.51	0.69	5.17
County Type 3	62.25	2.28	14.58	14.10	1.14	5.65
County Type 4	55.52	2.47	19.35	12.35	2.87	7.43
County Type 5	61.84	2.40	16.36	11.27	1.89	6.23
County Type 6	44.58	1.73	29.79	13.60	2.82	7.48
County Type 7	42.68	1.39	32.24	12.69	2.48	6.52

TABLE 11 (Continued)

Region and County Type [a]	Total Personal Income					
	Wages and Salaries	Other Labor Income	Proprietors' Income	Property Income	Income Maintenance Transfers [b]	All Other Transfers
Rocky Mountain	61.78	2.05	15.59	13.17	1.23	6.18
County Type 0	72.14	2.46	9.22	10.47	1.19	4.52
County Type 1	52.12	1.52	18.39	20.69	1.42	5.85
County Type 2	67.68	2.24	10.44	13.46	0.89	5.30
County Type 3	66.96	2.44	11.35	12.35	0.82	6.07
County Type 4	57.61	1.57	19.10	11.72	1.79	8.22
County Type 5	59.71	2.04	16.75	13.26	1.15	7.10
County Type 6	49.26	1.24	25.96	11.67	2.93	8.94
County Type 7	52.32	1.65	25.15	12.22	1.50	7.16
Far West	64.94	2.28	12.68	13.36	1.02	5.72
County Type 0	68.78	2.60	10.43	12.05	0.88	5.25
County Type 1	56.28	2.17	16.18	17.93	1.01	6.43
County Type 2	60.21	1.68	15.10	15.64	1.29	6.08
County Type 3	56.42	1.56	17.04	15.94	1.43	7.61
County Type 4	54.68	1.45	19.84	15.24	1.53	7.25
County Type 5	59.61	1.47	17.96	12.58	1.22	7.16
County Type 6	53.22	1.20	25.76	12.98	1.01	5.83
County Type 7	55.15	1.28	23.50	11.55	1.20	7.31

[a] County types: 0 = metropolitan statistical area (MSA) core counties that contain at least 1 million people; 1 = all MSA core-contiguous counties; 2 = all MSA counties that are not core contiguous and that have populations between 250,000 and 1 million; 3 = all MSA counties that are not core contiguous and that have populations of less than 250,000; 4 = all non-MSA, MSA-adjacent counties that have populations of at least 20,000; 5 = all non-MSA, not MSA-adjacent counties that have populations of less than 20,000; 6 = all non-MSA, MSA-adjacent counties that have populations of at least 20,000; and 7 = all non-MSA, not MSA-adjacent counties that have populations of less than 20,000.

[b] Includes Supplemental Security Income (SSI), Aid to Families with Dependent Children (AFDC), general assistance payments, food stamps, energy assistance payments, refugee assistance, foster home care payments, earned income tax credits, and energy assistance.

TABLE 12 Total Personal Income (as percentages) of Major Components by Region and County Type, 1969

Regions and County Type[a]	Total Personal Income				Income Maintenance Transfers[b]	All Other Transfers
	Wages and Salaries	Other Labor Income	Proprietors' Income	Property Income		
Total United States	65.76	3.67	8.63	13.33	0.92	7.69
County Type 0	70.50	3.87	5.77	12.52	1.09	6.25
County Type 1	63.17	3.57	8.66	16.39	0.66	7.55
County Type 2	67.61	3.82	7.20	13.06	0.78	7.53
County Type 3	65.62	3.69	8.98	12.48	0.71	8.51
County Type 4	59.78	3.46	12.71	13.05	0.96	10.03
County Type 5	60.29	3.41	13.06	12.24	1.06	9.93
County Type 6	47.38	2.65	22.35	14.57	1.40	11.66
County Type 7	45.41	2.40	24.52	15.02	1.36	11.30
New England	65.62	3.82	6.83	14.91	0.92	7.90
County Type 0	67.30	4.06	6.40	14.85	0.72	6.66
County Type 1	68.28	3.73	5.57	13.63	1.22	7.57
County Type 2	64.56	4.00	6.87	15.63	0.94	7.99
County Type 3	65.47	3.55	7.24	14.28	0.66	8.80
County Type 4	61.43	3.13	8.31	16.95	0.63	9.56
County Type 5	59.70	3.24	11.74	13.95	1.00	10.37
County Type 7	56.32	2.65	11.29	17.21	0.95	11.58
Mideast	67.00	3.64	6.70	13.99	1.08	7.58
County Type 0	71.04	3.53	4.74	12.62	1.54	6.53
County Type 1	61.64	3.48	8.68	17.90	0.63	7.66
County Type 2	68.40	4.14	6.43	12.62	0.75	7.65
County Type 3	62.73	3.75	9.03	12.79	0.78	10.91
County Type 4	61.32	3.73	10.32	12.55	0.81	11.28
County Type 5	59.35	3.65	12.32	13.40	0.87	10.40
County Type 6	53.85	3.11	15.50	14.04	0.82	12.68
County Type 7	52.97	2.94	15.39	14.35	0.73	13.62

TABLE 12 (Continued)

Regions and County Type[a]	Total Personal Income					
	Wages and Salaries	Other Labor Income	Proprietors' Income	Property Income	Income Maintenance Transfers[b]	All Other Transfers
Great Lakes	67.79	4.32	7.90	12.60	0.58	6.81
County Type 0	72.06	4.35	5.28	11.94	0.74	5.61
County Type 1	64.15	4.24	9.14	15.43	0.38	6.67
County Type 2	71.69	4.93	5.99	10.79	0.48	6.12
County Type 3	66.25	4.40	8.83	12.68	0.45	7.40
County Type 4	59.01	3.84	13.80	13.67	0.43	9.25
County Type 5	58.81	3.50	13.10	13.05	0.67	10.87
County Type 6	46.18	3.21	22.68	15.84	0.50	11.59
County Type 7	50.05	2.81	18.04	14.35	0.98	13.77
Plains	59.22	3.26	14.20	14.69	0.74	7.89
County Type 0	74.30	4.12	5.20	10.20	0.68	5.50
County Type 1	63.65	3.72	8.70	16.93	0.47	6.53
County Type 2	68.57	3.96	7.72	12.90	0.71	6.14
County Type 3	63.98	3.49	10.26	13.48	0.72	8.07
County Type 4	55.08	2.98	16.20	15.66	0.70	9.38
County Type 5	56.37	2.90	16.10	14.66	0.90	9.07
County Type 6	35.64	1.76	31.08	19.01	1.03	11.49
County Type 7	37.35	1.92	30.84	18.46	0.95	10.47
Southeast	65.43	3.52	9.45	12.05	0.92	8.63
County Type 0	68.97	3.65	6.67	13.65	0.54	6.51
County Type 1	67.23	3.08	8.20	12.83	0.49	8.18
County Type 2	67.47	3.57	7.13	13.55	0.59	7.69
County Type 3	67.86	3.61	8.25	11.28	0.76	8.23
County Type 4	62.16	3.39	12.63	10.65	1.38	9.79
County Type 5	62.53	3.93	12.14	10.00	1.31	10.09
County Type 6	55.08	3.13	16.88	10.85	2.04	12.04
County Type 7	52.26	3.00	18.92	10.41	2.40	13.01

Southwest	64.25	3.60	9.93	13.59	0.80	7.82
County Type 0	70.64	4.31	7.21	13.16	0.29	4.39
County Type 1	61.82	3.39	9.50	15.20	0.87	9.23
County Type 2	67.23	3.63	7.49	13.42	0.62	7.60
County Type 3	63.78	3.34	10.06	13.37	0.80	8.64
County Type 4	56.61	3.43	12.18	13.95	1.88	11.94
County Type 5	61.25	3.30	11.55	12.49	1.32	10.09
County Type 6	44.05	2.50	23.44	15.81	1.83	12.38
County Type 7	43.99	2.26	25.94	15.50	1.57	10.74
Rocky Mountain	62.49	2.93	12.01	13.68	0.76	8.12
County Type 0	73.43	3.49	6.17	10.58	0.77	5.56
County Type 1	56.48	2.55	12.48	18.91	0.72	8.86
County Type 2	69.01	3.05	7.06	12.78	0.67	7.42
County Type 3	66.12	3.12	9.26	12.56	0.75	8.19
County Type 4	57.25	2.74	15.32	13.50	0.91	10.28
County Type 5	59.86	2.92	12.77	14.43	0.71	9.32
County Type 6	49.33	2.17	21.84	14.12	1.40	11.14
County Type 7	50.38	2.45	23.10	14.22	0.81	9.04
Far West	65.55	3.31	8.66	13.32	1.35	7.82
County Type 0	68.29	3.69	6.98	12.81	1.27	6.96
County Type 1	58.73	3.10	10.85	17.53	1.18	8.62
County Type 2	62.85	2.54	10.40	13.21	1.81	9.18
County Type 3	59.36	2.28	11.99	14.51	1.23	10.63
County Type 4	57.39	2.34	14.72	13.46	1.58	10.52
County Type 5	58.21	2.39	15.65	12.30	1.30	10.15
County Type 6	57.81	2.05	19.35	12.52	0.60	7.68
County Type 7	54.62	2.19	18.32	13.47	0.95	10.45

aCounty types: 0 = metropolitan statistical area (MSA) core counties that contain at least 1 million people; 1 = all MSA core-contiguous counties; 2 = all MSA counties that are not core contiguous and that have populations between 250,000 and 1 million; 3 = all MSA counties that are not core contiguous and that have populations of less than 250,000; 4 = all non-MSA, MSA-adjacent counties that have populations of at least 20,000; 5 = all non-MSA, not MSA-adjacent counties that have populations of at least 20,000; 6 = all non-MSA, MSA-adjacent counties that have populations of less than 20,000; and 7 = all non-MSA, not MSA-adjacent counties that have populations of less than 20,000.

bIncludes Supplemental Security Income (SSI), Aid to Families with Dependent Children (AFDC), general assistance payments, food stamps, energy assistance payments, refugee assistance, foster home care payments, earned income tax credits, and energy assistance.

TABLE 13 Total Personal Income (as percentages) of Major Components by Region and County Type, 1969

Regions and County Type [a]	Total Personal Income				Income Maintenance Transfers [b]	All Other Transfers
	Wages and Salaries	Other Labor Income	Proprietors' Income	Property Income		
Total United States	60.94	5.67	6.32	14.69	1.33	11.04
County Type 0	65.80	6.01	4.14	13.47	1.62	8.95
County Type 1	59.35	5.50	6.32	17.13	0.90	10.79
County Type 2	62.33	5.78	5.14	14.52	1.20	11.02
County Type 3	60.65	5.75	6.41	13.98	1.10	12.11
County Type 4	54.89	5.44	8.94	15.23	1.43	14.07
County Type 5	56.32	5.38	9.15	14.16	1.48	13.50
County Type 6	46.32	4.49	15.80	16.94	1.63	14.83
County Type 7	44.92	4.14	17.64	17.29	1.61	14.40
New England	60.71	5.86	4.96	15.59	1.48	11.40
County Type 0	64.14	6.20	4.50	14.83	1.00	9.33
County Type 1	63.62	5.72	4.12	14.09	1.73	10.73
County Type 2	59.68	6.05	4.86	16.12	1.70	11.60
County Type 3	59.76	5.79	5.06	15.28	1.26	12.85
County Type 4	53.96	5.13	6.22	19.04	1.27	14.38
County Type 5	52.87	5.25	8.90	16.78	1.73	14.47
County Type 7	48.20	4.28	9.49	20.68	1.74	15.61
Mideast	61.47	5.64	4.53	14.96	1.63	11.78
County Type 0	65.31	5.52	2.99	13.31	2.49	10.38
County Type 1	58.11	5.41	5.88	18.26	0.88	11.46
County Type 2	62.97	6.21	4.15	13.74	1.19	11.75
County Type 3	57.09	5.62	5.77	14.18	1.28	16.07
County Type 4	54.99	5.77	6.97	14.02	1.44	16.81
County Type 5	54.76	5.88	7.69	14.90	1.44	15.32
County Type 6	49.05	5.16	9.87	16.40	1.39	18.12
County Type 7	45.17	4.72	11.05	17.34	1.68	20.05

Great Lakes	62.96	6.48	5.65	13.62	1.22	10.06
County Type 0	67.27	6.65	3.54	12.22	1.59	8.73
County Type 1	60.42	6.25	6.46	16.55	0.76	9.57
County Type 2	67.19	7.28	3.95	11.36	1.04	9.18
County Type 3	62.12	6.59	6.03	13.72	1.05	10.49
County Type 4	54.63	5.80	9.86	15.84	1.01	12.86
County Type 5	54.77	5.51	9.13	15.04	1.23	14.32
County Type 6	43.70	4.91	16.67	19.18	0.96	14.59
County Type 7	44.56	4.45	13.67	17.84	1.70	17.77
Plains	57.23	5.31	10.69	15.46	0.80	10.51
County Type 0	69.91	6.50	4.12	10.88	0.92	7.67
County Type 1	61.11	5.80	6.92	16.35	0.57	9.25
County Type 2	66.84	6.37	5.79	12.19	0.77	8.04
County Type 3	62.36	5.75	7.12	13.49	0.83	10.46
County Type 4	54.27	5.11	11.05	16.61	0.71	12.25
County Type 5	53.77	4.81	12.33	16.09	0.91	12.09
County Type 6	37.70	3.35	22.13	21.31	0.86	14.65
County Type 7	38.81	3.53	23.21	20.38	0.84	13.23
Southeast	59.91	5.53	6.68	13.92	1.39	12.57
County Type 0	64.68	5.76	4.95	14.17	1.19	9.26
County Type 1	61.68	5.07	6.11	14.42	0.79	11.94
County Type 2	61.65	5.46	5.03	15.42	1.01	11.43
County Type 3	61.16	5.78	6.13	13.24	1.19	12.49
County Type 4	57.02	5.41	8.27	13.19	1.95	14.16
County Type 5	57.80	5.92	8.15	11.97	1.93	14.24
County Type 6	52.54	5.20	11.33	12.67	2.59	15.66
County Type 7	47.84	4.80	13.62	13.07	3.16	17.51
Southwest	61.02	5.68	7.59	14.81	0.86	10.04
County Type 0	69.97	6.58	5.27	12.50	0.38	5.30
County Type 1	58.23	5.52	7.30	17.62	0.78	10.55
County Type 2	62.58	5.72	5.49	14.77	0.85	10.58
County Type 3	58.79	5.33	7.91	15.63	0.93	11.40
County Type 4	52.12	5.26	9.63	16.37	1.57	15.05
County Type 5	56.25	5.26	9.31	14.57	1.35	13.26
County Type 6	42.99	4.23	19.07	18.28	1.42	14.02
County Type 7	41.49	3.71	22.11	18.41	1.40	12.89

TABLE 13 (Continued)

Regions and County Type [a]	Total Personal Income					
	Wages and Salaries	Other Labor Income	Proprietors' Income	Property Income	Income Maintenance Transfers [b]	All Other Transfers
Rocky Mountain	61.56	4.94	7.91	14.86	0.72	10.01
County Type 0	71.24	5.71	4.78	10.78	0.78	6.70
County Type 1	59.26	4.59	8.94	17.23	0.55	9.44
County Type 2	65.13	5.07	5.70	13.53	0.66	9.91
County Type 3	62.98	5.09	6.76	13.58	0.76	10.82
County Type 4	54.57	4.98	9.91	15.90	1.08	13.56
County Type 5	59.92	4.84	7.90	15.75	0.62	10.97
County Type 6	49.87	3.84	11.41	18.52	1.18	15.18
County Type 7	54.39	4.49	12.30	17.23	0.78	10.81
Far West	60.42	5.20	6.52	15.96	1.56	10.34
County Type 0	63.59	5.75	5.09	15.03	1.52	9.03
County Type 1	53.68	4.73	8.46	20.69	1.22	11.22
County Type 2	57.26	4.25	7.84	16.29	1.94	12.42
County Type 3	56.63	4.10	8.07	17.14	1.32	12.74
County Type 4	52.55	4.44	10.84	17.03	1.70	13.45
County Type 5	53.64	4.19	11.37	15.64	1.57	13.58
County Type 6	53.05	3.83	13.26	17.65	0.88	11.32
County Type 7	48.33	3.99	14.57	17.98	1.21	13.92

[a] County types: 0 = metropolitan statistical area (MSA) core counties that contain at least 1 million people; 1 = all MSA core-contiguous counties; 2 = all MSA counties that are not core contiguous and that have populations between 250,000 and 1 million; 3 = all MSA counties that are not core contiguous and that have populations of less than 250,000; 4 = all non-MSA, MSA-adjacent counties that have populations of at least 20,000; 5 = all non-MSA, not MSA-adjacent counties that have populations of at least 20,000; 6 = all non-MSA, MSA-adjacent counties that have populations of less than 20,000; and 7 = all non-MSA, not MSA-adjacent counties that have populations of less than 20,000.

[b] Includes Supplemental Security Income (SSI), Aid to Families with Dependent Children (AFDC), general assistance payments, food stamps, energy assistance payments, refugee assistance, foster home care payments, earned income tax credits, and energy assistance.

TABLE 14 Total Personal Income (as percentages) of Major Components by Region and County Type, 1984

Region and County Type[a]	Total Personal Income					
	Wages and Salaries	Other Labor Income	Proprietors' Income	Property Income	Income Maintenance Transfers[b]	All Other Transfers
Total United States	54.47	6.21	4.86	18.23	1.28	11.96
County Type 0	63.16	6.53	3.33	15.84	1.54	9.59
County Type 1	56.49	6.03	5.18	20.19	0.79	11.32
County Type 2	58.74	6.32	4.06	17.90	1.12	11.86
County Type 3	55.83	6.27	5.11	18.29	1.14	13.36
County Type 4	49.96	5.93	6.36	20.44	1.55	15.76
County Type 5	51.64	6.00	6.81	19.00	1.55	15.00
County Type 6	42.80	5.11	10.15	23.51	1.68	16.74
County Type 7	41.16	4.74	12.42	23.77	1.66	16.26
New England	58.10	6.68	4.42	18.21	1.08	11.50
County Type 0	62.20	7.03	4.12	16.84	0.72	9.09
County Type 1	61.61	6.67	3.91	16.17	1.07	10.58
County Type 2	56.48	6.74	4.38	19.14	1.28	11.99
County Type 3	56.91	6.71	4.48	17.99	1.00	12.92
County Type 4	50.23	5.96	5.34	22.60	1.02	14.86
County Type 5	49.86	6.05	6.79	20.43	1.62	15.25
County Type 7	45.35	5.03	7.48	24.85	1.44	15.85
Mideast	58.17	6.08	4.08	17.83	1.41	12.43
County Type 0	62.96	5.98	2.98	15.00	2.15	10.93
County Type 1	55.09	5.84	5.27	21.14	0.72	11.94
County Type 2	58.83	6.76	3.65	17.25	1.04	12.47
County Type 3	52.59	5.90	4.55	18.75	1.24	16.97
County Type 4	49.84	6.09	5.12	18.87	1.65	18.43
County Type 5	49.33	6.36	6.86	19.43	1.40	16.62
County Type 6	44.46	5.79	6.79	22.11	1.43	19.43
County Type 7	37.86	4.70	8.81	24.32	1.76	22.56

TABLE 14 (Continued)

Regions and County Type [a]	Total Personal Income					
	Wages and Salaries	Other Labor Income	Proprietors' Income	Property Income	Income Maintenance Transfers [b]	All Other Transfers
Great Lakes	57.57	6.66	4.59	17.68	1.52	11.98
County Type 0	62.24	6.79	3.24	15.43	1.87	10.43
County Type 1	55.99	6.42	5.23	20.28	0.94	11.15
County Type 2	61.21	7.35	3.39	15.29	1.39	11.37
County Type 3	55.97	6.78	4.77	18.37	1.43	12.69
County Type 4	48.97	6.15	7.40	21.08	1.41	14.99
County Type 5	50.08	6.02	6.34	19.93	1.57	16.06
County Type 6	39.00	5.27	11.68	25.86	1.33	16.85
County Type 7	40.13	4.84	8.72	24.13	2.17	20.02
Plains	52.97	5.85	8.61	20.11	0.86	11.59
County Type 0	65.89	6.97	3.96	13.83	0.92	8.43
County Type 1	58.74	6.43	5.85	19.08	0.54	9.37
County Type 2	62.39	7.17	5.46	15.15	0.84	9.00
County Type 3	56.39	6.22	6.25	18.24	0.99	11.91
County Type 4	48.47	5.48	8.48	22.64	0.86	14.06
County Type 5	48.55	5.41	9.68	21.78	1.03	13.55
County Type 6	33.87	3.85	15.20	29.27	0.98	16.82
County Type 7	34.01	3.95	18.44	27.75	0.90	14.94
Southeast	56.35	6.14	5.30	17.71	1.25	13.24
County Type 0	63.07	6.32	4.28	15.93	1.09	9.31
County Type 1	59.45	5.74	5.01	17.52	0.67	11.61
County Type 2	58.37	6.00	4.26	18.63	0.83	11.90
County Type 3	56.54	6.46	5.25	17.27	1.09	13.40
County Type 4	52.48	6.05	5.86	18.17	1.83	15.61
County Type 5	53.04	6.59	6.42	16.55	1.91	15.48
County Type 6	48.24	5.86	8.11	17.94	2.51	17.35
County Type 7	44.06	5.53	9.59	18.64	3.02	19.16
Southwest	59.11	6.35	4.99	18.41	0.80	10.34
County Type 0	68.63	7.21	4.22	14.11	0.40	5.44
County Type 1	55.17	6.19	4.95	22.31	0.63	10.75
County Type 2	60.66	6.41	4.01	17.55	0.75	10.63

County type[a]						
County Type 3	55.52	5.94	5.58	20.24	0.89	11.83
County Type 4	47.35	5.70	5.95	23.07	1.52	16.41
County Type 5	52.63	5.81	5.86	20.17	1.38	14.15
County Type 6	42.01	5.04	9.14	26.81	1.33	15.67
County Type 7	41.12	4.64	10.74	27.16	1.32	15.03
Rocky Mountain						
County Type 0	58.58	5.85	5.55	18.38	0.75	10.89
County Type 1	69.05	6.67	4.01	12.67	0.72	6.87
County Type 2	58.55	5.86	6.18	19.63	0.47	9.31
County Type 3	63.76	6.29	3.42	15.86	0.68	9.99
County Type 4	57.63	5.71	4.80	18.11	0.91	12.83
County Type 5	50.72	5.90	6.55	20.85	1.06	14.92
County Type 6	55.13	5.53	5.87	19.96	0.76	12.76
County Type 7	44.93	4.16	7.10	25.32	1.30	17.20
	49.62	5.12	8.74	22.72	0.92	12.88
Far West						
County Type 0	58.23	5.95	3.83	19.16	1.57	11.25
County Type 1	61.97	6.52	3.05	17.51	1.48	9.48
County Type 2	51.03	5.50	5.14	24.81	1.16	12.36
County Type 3	54.34	5.02	4.59	20.11	2.05	13.89
County Type 4	52.27	4.86	4.64	22.01	1.36	14.86
County Type 5	48.17	4.97	6.41	22.68	1.87	15.90
County Type 6	47.51	4.52	6.67	21.82	1.82	17.66
County Type 7	50.83	4.53	7.02	23.03	0.95	13.64
	44.52	4.57	7.99	24.08	1.43	17.41

[a]County types: 0 = metropolitan statistical area (MSA) core counties that contain at least 1 million people; 1 = all MSA core-contiguous counties; 2 = all MSA counties that are not core contiguous and that have populations between 250,000 and 1 million; 3 = all MSA counties that are not core contiguous and that have populations of less than 250,000; 4 = all non-MSA, MSA-adjacent counties and that have populations of at least 20,000; 5 = all non-MSA, not MSA-adjacent counties that have populations of at least 20,000; 6 = all non-MSA, MSA-adjacent counties that have populations of less than 20,000; and 7 = all non-MSA, not MSA-adjacent counties that have populations of less than 20,000.

[b]Includes Supplemental Security Income (SSI), Aid to Families with Dependent Children (AFDC), general assistance payments, food stamps, energy assistance payments, refugee assistance, foster home care payments, earned income tax credits, and energy assistance.

cation is a continuation of long-term trends. Regions and areas have, in the past, experienced the loss of one industrial source of employment and income and gained another source. With the increasing internationalization of the U.S. economy, however, the requirements for adjustment seem to be becoming more difficult, more diverse, and more widespread. Should policy be directed toward areas, industries, trade, or persons?

The shifting patterns and longer term trends shown in the 25-year time span included in this study are part and parcel of an even longer history of labor reallocation. Ehrenhalt (1986) calls attention to the milestone reached in the first decade of this century when the number of blue-collar workers first exceeded the number of farmers; now, in the ninth decade of the century, the number of professional, technical, and managerial workers is fast approaching the point at which it will exceed the number of blue-collar workers.

In 1929, the first year for which BEA prepared estimates, the number of persons engaged (full time-equivalent employment and self-employment) in goods-producing industries and the number engaged in service-producing industries were approximately equal. By 1985, the most recent year for which estimates have been prepared, goods-producing industries accounted for only 28 percent of persons engaged in production; service-producing industries accounted for the other 72 percent. Over this more than 50-year time span, the number of persons engaged in production more than doubled, from 45.66 million to 102.96 million, and both population settlement and industrial location patterns across America underwent vast changes.

From 1929 through 1936 the number of persons (excluding unpaid family members) engaged in farming held steady at about 8.3 million. By 1947 the number had fallen to 6.4 million, and it fell further during the next two decades to 2.8 million by 1969. Throughout the 1970s the number of persons engaged in farming declined at a much reduced rate, falling to 2.5 million by 1979; the rate of decline reaccelerated in the 1980s, however, and by 1985 there were only 2.1 million persons engaged in farming. Further decreases appear to be in the offing owing to rising world production. The agricultural revolution has spread to densely populated countries that formerly were net importers of farm products. Continued subsidies to farmers in industrially advanced countries are increasingly less effective in maintaining farm population and increasingly more burdensome on national government budgets. Areas experiencing falling employment in agriculture would like to see policies that would protect farmers against competing imports and that would promote exports. Yet the net effect of such policies is that they raise prices and invoke trade wars that disadvantage trade in the products of other industries.

Mining, another major goods-producing industry located mainly in rural areas, has had a somewhat more checkered pattern in terms of persons engaged in production. In 1929 more than 1 million persons were engaged in mining production. The number fluctuated somewhat during the Depression and post-World War II years but then began a steep decline in the 1950s, falling to 625,000 by 1972. With the fossil fuel price explosion, mining employment began to rise, and with the second oil price "shock," it reached 1.6 million in 1981. But it then fell slowly to 926,000 in 1985 and since then has fallen much further, with the steep slide in world oil prices and the sympathetic movement of competing fuel prices.

Mining employment exhibits a somewhat different pattern than farm employment, which has continued to fall over the last 50 years, albeit at a different rate. The different pattern of employment can be explained in part by the different patterns of productivity change in the two industries, which are so important to the fortunes of non-MSAs. Table 15 shows real gross national product (GNP) by industry for selected years from 1947–1985, the first and most recent years for which BEA has prepared these estimates; Table 16 shows persons engaged in production by industry. In these tables, the industry detail is given at the major division level. Farming is included in agriculture, and in 1985 farm employment accounted for 71 percent of agricultural employment, which also includes agricultural services, forestry, and fisheries—all industries that tend to concentrate in non-MSAs. In 1947 farm employment accounted for 96 percent of agricultural employment.

Table 17 shows the ratio of real GNP by industry to the number of persons engaged in production in each industry—a measure of labor productivity. As can be seen in the table, productivity in agriculture rose over the entire period, but mining productivity fell sharply in the 1970s. Mining output growth was not commensurate with employment growth, but internationally determined rising product prices were more than enough to offset the rising wage bill. Falling prices will have the opposite effect. Areas experiencing falling employment in mining would like to see mining product prices kept

TABLE 15 Gross National Product (GNP) (in millions of 1982 dollars) by Industry,
for Selected Years

Industry	1947	1959	1969	1979	1985
Total GNP	1,066.8	1,629.1	2,423.3	3,192.3	3,585.3
Goods-producing sector	426.0	658.3	914.5	1,076.7	1162.8
Agriculture	55.6	65.8	65.3	76.1	92.2
Mining	67.6	94.1	128.9	130.0	130.6
Construction	76.7	160.4	183.6	173.5	163.1
Manufacturing	226.1	338.0	536.7	697.1	776.9
Service-producing sector	641.7	976.4	1,504.0	2,070.3	2,389.4
Transportation	100.0	123.5	200.3	293.4	323.3
Wholesale trade	54.6	89.2	149.0	217.3	264.5
Retail trade	103.2	151.5	212.7	294.4	339.8
Finance, insurance, and real estate	103.0	195.9	314.0	459.2	523.9
Services	124.7	183.5	287.8	429.8	538.5
Government	156.2	232.8	340.2	376.2	399.4
	1947	1959	1969	1979	1985
Total GNP	100.0	100.0	100.0	100.0	100.0
Goods-producing sector	39.9	40.4	37.7	33.7	32.4
Agriculture	5.2	4.0	2.7	2.4	2.6
Mining	6.3	5.8	5.3	4.1	3.6
Construction	7.2	9.8	7.6	5.4	4.5
Manufacturing	21.2	20.7	22.1	21.8	21.7
Service-producing sector	60.1	59.6	62.3	66.3	65.6
Transportation	9.4	7.6	8.3	9.2	9.0
Wholesale trade	5.1	5.5	6.1	6.8	7.4
Retail trade	9.7	9.3	8.8	9.2	9.5
Finance, insurance, and real estate	9.7	12.0	13.0	14.4	14.6
Services	11.7	11.3	11.9	13.5	15.0
Government	14.6	14.3	14.0	11.8	11.1

high through the use of tariffs imposed on competing imports, a
policy that could invoke countermoves from countries that export
mining products.

Manufacturing employment rose relatively continuously over the
period, although at declining rates of increase in the late 1960s and
1970s. The same is true of manufacturing productivity. In the 1980s,

employment has fallen but productivity growth has begun to rise from \$33,000 in real GNP per worker to \$40,000 per worker. The increase in productivity growth, all other things being equal, would be expected to enhance U.S. competitiveness in world markets. Areas experiencing falling employment in manufacturing industries, how-

TABLE 16 Persons Engaged in Production (in thousands) by Industry[a] and as a Percentage of the Total Number of Persons Engaged in Production, for Selected Years

Industry	1947	1959	1969	1979	1985
Total persons engaged in production	57,320	63,965	78,853	95,502	102,957
Goods-producing sector	26,028	25,350	28,132	30,674	28,922
Agriculture	6,657	4,704	3,193	3,161	2,960
Mining	968	742	626	957	926
Construction	3,007	3,533	4,256	5,607	5,823
Manufacturing	15,396	16,371	20,057	20,949	19,213
Service-producing sector	31,292	38,615	50,721	64,828	74,035
Transportation	4,231	4,083	4,488	5,166	5,301
Wholesale trade	2,620	3,351	4,041	5,339	5,814
Retail trade	8,376	8,911	10,596	14,086	15,930
Finance, insurance, and real estate	1,864	2,668	3,653	5,305	6,370
Services	7,444	9,430	13,313	18,849	23,879
Government	6,762	10,306	14,652	16,106	16,765
Rest of world	-5	-134	-22	-23	-24
	1947	1959	1969	1979	1985
Persons engaged in production (%)	100.0	100.0	100.0	100.0	100.0
Goods-producing sector	45.4	39.6	35.7	32.1	28.1
Agriculture	11.6	7.4	4.0	3.3	2.9
Mining	1.7	1.2	0.8	1.0	0.9
Construction	5.2	5.5	5.4	5.9	5.7
Manufacturing	26.9	25.6	25.4	21.9	18.7
Service-producing sector	54.6	60.4	64.3	67.9	71.9
Transportation	7.4	6.4	5.7	5.4	5.1
Wholesale trade	4.6	5.2	5.1	5.6	5.6
Retail trade	14.6	13.9	13.4	14.7	15.5
Finance, insurance, and real estate	3.3	4.2	4.6	5.6	6.2
Services	13.0	14.7	16.9	19.7	23.2
Government	11.8	16.1	18.6	16.9	16.3
Rest of world	-0.0	-0.2	-0.0	-0.0	-0.0

[a]Persons engaged in production equals the number of full time-equivalent employees plus the number of self-employed persons. Unpaid family workers are not included.

TABLE 17 Ratio of Gross National Product (GNP) to Persons Engaged in Production[a] (in thousands of 1982 dollars), by Industry, for Selected Years

Industry	1947	1959	1969	1979	1985
Total GNP	18,610	25,469	30,732	33,428	34,822
Goods-producing sector	16,367	25,968	32,508	35,101	40,205
Agriculture	8,352	13,968	20,451	24,075	31,149
Mining	69,835	126,819	205,911	135,841	141,037
Construction	25,507	45,401	43,139	30,943	28,010
Manufacturing	14,686	20,646	26,759	33,276	40,436
Service-producing sector	20,478	25,140	29,747	32,634	32,720
Transportation	23,635	30,247	44,630	56,794	60,988
Wholesale trade	20,840	26,619	36,872	40,701	45,494
Retail trade	12,321	17,001	20,074	20,900	21,331
Finance, insurance, and real estate	55,258	73,426	85,957	86,560	82,245
Services	16,752	19,459	21,618	22,802	22,551
Government	23,100	22,589	23,219	23,358	23,823

[a]Persons engaged in production equals the number of full-time equivalent employees plus the number of self-employed persons. Unpaid family workers are not included.

ever, would like to see these industries protected. Removing competition could result in higher product prices and in countermoves by other countries that are adversely affected.

The fortunes of these goods-producing industries in world markets directly affect the fortunes of the areas in which the industries are located. Therefore, the question has been raised: Should there be an overall U.S. regional or urban policy, or a national industrial policy? Because regional and area growth patterns are influenced by a wide variety of economic policies, as suggested in the preceding paragraphs, it does not make sense to establish regional policies in isolation from other major areas of policy concern. Moreover, the complexity of the public and private forces affecting regional growth patterns is sufficiently great to cast doubt on the efficacy of fine-tuning regional policy.

If policy is to be made, its objectives must be distinguished more clearly. In particular, is the objective in most cases to slow down the pace of change because of the high externality costs of rapid regional transformation? Or is the objective in most cases to facilitate change because of the high social costs associated with the failure to adjust rapidly to forces for change?

There is also a need to match policy tools to policy objectives more effectively. For example, if the objective is primarily to facilitate change, general investments in human capital that increase individual mobility would seem appropriate. If the objective is primarily to mitigate the costs of "excessively rapid" change, direct payments to the persons affected may be more effective than policies directed specifically at particular government or industrial entities.

The growth in services industries, particularly those producer services that tend to locate in major metropolitan areas, has increasingly taken up the slack in falling employment in the goods-producing industries in MSAs and non-MSAs alike. Advances in telecommunications technology permit "backroom" operations in producer services to locate at distances remote from face-to-face operations; thus local jurisdictions will be subject to competitive pressures, but this is not a question of national urban policy. Ehrenhalt (1986) notes that half of all professional, technical, and managerial jobs are currently held in the service-producing industries. These jobs require high levels of human capital investment. Policies geared to improved and enhanced training of people may well prove to be the most effective approach to improving the national urban situation.

ACKNOWLEDGMENTS

I have relied on and benefited from the comments and statistical work of Daniel Zabronsky, who organized the data base for this study and constructed the detailed analytical tables, and Gary Kennedy's statistical work. As always, I have benefited from Vernon Renshaw's insightful comments in general and with particular respect to the discussion on policy issues.

REFERENCES

Ehrenhalt, S. M.
  1986 Work-force shifts in the 80's. *New York Times*, August 15, 1986, p. D2.
Garnick, D. H.
  1978 Reappraising the Outlook for Northern States and Cities in the Context of U.S. Economic History. Working Paper No. 51. Joint Center for Urban Studies of the Massachusetts Institute of Technology and Harvard University.
  1983 Shifting patterns in the growth of metropolitan and nonmetropolitan areas. *Survey of Current Business* 63(May):39–44.

    1984   Shifting balances in U.S. metropolitan and nonmetropolitan area growth. *International Regional Science Review* 9(3):257–273.

    1985   Patterns of growth in metropolitan and nonmetropolitan areas: An update. *Survey of Current Business* 65(May):33–38.

Regional Economic Measurement Division

    1986   State personal income, 1969–1985: Revised estimates. *Survey of Current Business* 66(August):21–35.

Fiscal Conditions in Large American Cities, 1971–1984

PHILIP M. DEARBORN

The period 1971–1984 was a difficult one for major U.S. cities. Many had to cope with a loss in population and tax base or with the need to provide services for a fast-growing population. Of 30 major American cities, two-thirds lost population, with decreases of more than 20 percent in 5 cities. At the other extreme, 4 cities grew more than 20 percent, and 1 grew by more than 40 percent. Overall, the population of these 30 cities shrank by 4.4 percent from 1970–1984 (Table 1).

Over this same period, some cities had fiscal crises; others experienced good times. In some years, policy makers and researchers were very concerned about urban problems; at other times they and the public lost interest in cities. In view of these shifting currents, which have affected cities from 1971–1984, it is therefore appropriate to ask some questions about major city finances in the context of this history.

Are fiscal conditions in major cities better or worse than they were a decade ago? Have changes in federal policy in the 1980s affected urban fiscal conditions? What are urban fiscal conditions today? These are seemingly simple questions; yet the answers to them are important as we evaluate past urban policies and consider the appropriate future role of cities in our federal system. Unfortunately, the answers are also not easy to discern, the reasons for

TABLE 1 Population Changes (in thousands) of Selected Major Cities, 1970-1984

City[a]	Population 1984	Population 1970	Difference, 1970-1984	Percentage Change
St. Louis	429.3	622.2	-192.9	-31.0
Detroit	1,089.0	1,511.3	-422.3	-27.9
Cleveland	546.5	751.0	-204.5	-27.2
Buffalo	339.0	462.8	-123.8	-26.8
Pittsburgh	402.6	520.2	-117.6	-22.6
Cincinnati	370.5	452.6	-82.1	-18.1
Minneapolis	358.3	434.4	-76.1	-17.5
Baltimore	763.6	905.8	-142.2	-15.7
Philadelphia	1,646.7	1,948.6	-301.9	-15.5
Atlanta	426.1	497.0	-70.9	-14.3
Milwaukee	620.8	717.1	-96.3	-13.4
Kansas City	443.1	507.2	-64.1	-12.6
Chicago	2,992.5	3,362.8	-370.3	-11.0
Boston	570.7	641.1	-70.4	-11.0
New York	7,164.7	7,894.9	-730.2	-9.2
Seattle	488.5	530.9	-42.4	-8.0
New Orleans	559.1	593.5	-34.4	-5.8
Indianapolis	710.3	744.6	-34.3	-4.6
Denver	504.6	514.7	-10.1	-2.0
San Francisco	712.8	715.7	-2.9	-0.4
Nashville	462.5	448.0	14.5	3.2
Memphis	648.4	623.8	24.6	3.9
Columbus	566.1	539.4	26.7	4.9
Jacksonville	578.0	528.9	49.1	9.3
Los Angeles	3,096.7	2,816.1	280.6	10.0
Dallas	974.2	844.2	130.0	15.4
San Antonio	842.8	654.3	188.5	28.8
San Diego	960.5	696.6	263.9	37.9
Houston	1,705.7	1,232.4	473.3	38.4
Phoenix	853.3	581.6	271.7	46.7
Total	31,826.9	33,293.7	-1,466.8	-4.4

[a]These were the 30 largest cities in 1970, excluding Honolulu, the District of Columbia, and San Jose.

SOURCE: Bureau of the Census.

which this paper will discuss. Taking these difficulties into account, the paper will then provide some answers based on an analysis of the 30 large cities listed in Table 1.

BACKGROUND

In 1972 it was said (Advisory Commission on Intergovernmental Relations, 1973:3):

> An incredible and seemingly insoluble array of financial difficulties confront urban governments in America today. . . . It is in cities that are found outdated capital facilities, demands for increased services for minorities and poor persons, worn-out equipment, the inability to increase the tax because of tax restrictions, the inability to exceed debt ceilings, citizen tax rebellions, competition with other governmental units for state and local revenue sources, and a general inability to make revenue resources stretch to fit the expenditures mandated by the state and demanded by the people.

With a few minor changes this statement might describe a general view of the urban financial situation in any year since 1972. There were, of course, years in which urban financial problems were more discussed than they were in others, such as when New York defaulted on its bonds in 1975, when Proposition 13 was approved in California in 1978, and when President Reagan announced his intention to make major reductions in federal aid to cities in 1981. But despite the continuing interest and concern about how urban areas are doing financially, there are few quantitative measures of urban fiscal conditions; even more scarce are measures that describe changes that have occurred over time.

There are several reasons for this lack: (a) problems in defining what we mean by "urban fiscal conditions"; (b) difficulties in getting good information; and (c) an inability to understand how urban finances are affected by local and national actions. Before discussing what we do know about urban fiscal conditions from 1971 to 1984, let us review these problems of measurement so that the reasons for the paucity of information and the difficulties involved in getting a clear picture of urban finances can be understood.

MEASURING URBAN FISCAL CONDITIONS

There are two distinctly different approaches to viewing urban fiscal conditions. The first might be characterized as the local, or "bottom up," view taken by officials within a local government and those directly involved with the policies of the government. The second is the "top down," or external, view typically taken by most academic researchers, federal policy makers, and others with a national concern as opposed to a local concern about urban finances. Each view will be described briefly.

The Local View

Local officials are generally concerned with fiscal conditions only in their own city, and they are concerned in a very real and pragmatic context. Their judgment of the city's fiscal condition often relates to the next bond sale or local election. Some of the criteria that are used to judge fiscal condition, and whether it is getting better or worse, are the following:

• What is the government's record on balancing revenues and expenditures? Overspending revenues, unless it is intentional to use up some excess revenues from a prior year, is usually considered a sign that the government has encountered fiscal problems.

• Are the government's fund balances in a surplus or deficit condition on its balance sheet? Fund balances give both a cumulative view of past budgetary performance and a measure of the reserves available to meet unexpected financial demands on the government. A fund deficit is a clear sign that the government has had serious problems balancing its budget and is in weakened financial condition to cope with future problems.

• Are tax rates stable or declining? Most local officials judge the need for increased tax rates as a symptom of problems in the government's finances. Achieving a stable tax rate depends on several factors: (a) government revenues keeping pace with inflation and local real economic growth; (b) the government work force increasing only enough to meet real growth in the community's needs; and (c) the cost for needed capital facilities, as measured by the percentage of operating expenditures needed for debt service, remaining about the same from year to year.

If the above three conditions are being met, revenues and expenditures will probably grow at about the same rate over time, and tax increases will not be necessary to balance budgets.

• Is the government able to meet its cash needs internally, or if it borrows for cash flow, can it repay the borrowings well before the end of the fiscal year?

• Does the government have a good bond rating? Although ratings are related to a variety of factors, they also depend on the same internal financial indicators looked at by city officials themselves and thus are perceived as an independent confirmation of fiscal condition.

The above criteria obviously do not describe all the ways in which local officials judge their fiscal condition,[1] but they constitute some of the most common ones.

Two well-publicized national surveys (Matz and Petersen, 1983; National League of Cities, 1986) have been conducted to determine local conditions as local officials view them. Both of these surveys were based on the declarations of local officials who estimated how their finances would fare in current or future years. Although the conclusions of the surveys were as valid as the views of local officials, they were not based on audited financial results. The 1983 study found that many cities raised taxes, reduced work forces, and ran operating deficits in 1982 and 1983. A later study by Petersen and Matz (1985) found that government finances had recovered in 1984 and 1985. The 1986 National League of Cities study found that cities were reducing fund balances to finance revenue–expenditure imbalances. All of these conclusions are consistent with the findings in this paper. Cities did have problems balancing their budgets in 1983, apparently as a result of the recession, but they had recovered by 1984. Cities routinely budget to reduce fund balances, as shown in the 1986 projections, but actual results often reverse the plans and add to balances.

The National View

At the national level, much of the work on urban fiscal conditions has been comparative. The following are some of the approaches used in making comparisons:

• Ranking of fiscal stress by combining a variety of economic, fiscal, and demographic measures into an index number for each city. This type of work became so extensive that in 1978 the U.S. Treasury listed the results of six separate rankings of fiscal strain, including its own, which was a composite of the other five rankings (U.S. Department of the Treasury, 1978).

• Comparative tax burdens, tax capacity, and tax effort. These studies have suggested that a key determinant of fiscal condition is the amount of resources available to meet the government's needs and the extent to which they must burden their residents to meet their needs (Advisory Commission on Intergovernmental Affairs, 1981).

---

[1] Some cities are now using the International City Management Association Financial Trend Monitoring System indicators to formally review their condition. See Poister (1986).

- Comparisons between groups of governments, such as central city/suburban or Sunbelt/Frostbelt. These studies usually focus on disparities between the economic situations of governments as a measure of fiscal condition.

Another general type of research related to fiscal condition has been directed at determinants of urban revenues and expenditures. This work has attempted to quantify the inherent spending needs of urban governments relative to their ability to obtain resources. Those cities that need to spend unusually large amounts because of their economic or demographic characteristics but have low ability to generate revenues are considered to be in a poor fiscal condition (Ladd et al., 1985).

Another important direction in evaluating urban fiscal conditions has been the analysis of national aggregate trends, as measured by such indicators as the surplus or deficit in the state–local sector of the national income accounts (U.S. Department of the Treasury, 1985).

Although there are other types and examples of national studies of urban fiscal conditions, this sampling shows that there are very different views of such conditions at the national level, compared with the local level.

The most controversial of these studies found that "the fiscal outlook for the states and localities is more favorable today than it has been at virtually any other time in recent history" (U.S. Department of the Treasury, 1985:420). State and local officials took strong exception to this conclusion on the basis that it was derived from national income accounts information and not from local financial information (see, for example, U.S. Department of the Treasury, 1985:442).

Developing Alternative Measures of Fiscal Condition

The wide variety of approaches to measuring urban fiscal conditions has enriched our perspective, but they are often controversial and inconclusive. There remains a major unmet need: an evaluation of urban fiscal conditions on a national basis in the context used by local officials. Such an evaluation should be based on actual financial information and be acceptable to officials at all levels of government. Developing a consensus about urban fiscal conditions is important as we move into a period of federal budget retrenchment and changes in the structure of federalism, both of which may result in increased financial burdens on local governments. It would be helpful to be

able to look at urban fiscal conditions nationally through the eyes of
local officials to see the extent to which our urban governments are
in good fiscal condition and to see whether conditions have been getting better or worse under the changing federal policies of the 1980s.
Unfortunately, there are some serious problems in evaluating fiscal
conditions nationally in a local context. A key to any research is
good data, and such data are hard to obtain on the internal financial
workings of local governments.

Sources of Information

The comprehensive information provided by the Bureau of the
Census about city governments does not contain most of the key
elements used by local officials to evaluate their financial condition.
Census information recasts each local government's data into a single
national format that ignores the fund structures of local governments,
treats capital spending and debt service in a manner different from
that required by local accounting practices, and makes it generally
impossible to determine whether operating revenues and expenditures are in balance. There is, of course, no information about how
results compared to what was budgeted, so that, for example, there
is no way to tell the difference between a decline in revenues caused
by a planned tax cut and a decline caused by worsening economic
conditions. Balance-sheet information at the end of the fiscal year
is not presented, and it is impossible to determine the relationship
between a local government's current assets and its current liabilities.
Information about debt and the costs of debt service is also confusing and not usable. The Bureau of the Census (1976:4) itself has
cautioned researchers that "development of a measure of the ability
of a city to deal with its problems is not possible through a purely
statistical approach" using its data.

The alternative to using census data is to collect financial information directly from local governments by using questionnaires or
the governments' own financial reports. Questionnaires are difficult
to use, however, because of the diversity of accounting terminologies
and definitions used by local governments and because of the complexity of government finances. Take, for example, the apparently
simple question of whether the city's budget balanced last year. This
question is not as simple as it appears once we begin to look at the
details. For example, the survey must specify whether the question
refers to the general fund or all governmental funds; whether the

balance was on a GAAP (generally accepted accounting principles) basis or the government's budgetary basis; whether the definition of "balanced" includes the use of prior years' surpluses as revenues; and whether transfers to and from other funds should be counted. Questionnaires are probably most feasible for collecting opinions of local officials about their finances or for gathering a very few clearly defined bits of financial information. The financial reports of the governments provide a wealth of financial information, but these, too, have problems in providing comparable time-series information. After New York's financial crisis, analysts, accountants, and city officials recognized the need for better accounting and reporting by local governments. Changes were made in generally accepted accounting principles, and by the early 1980s every major city except Los Angeles substantially conformed to the revised principles. This transition from old accounting, which was often on a cash basis, to new accounting creates comparability problems between the years before and after the change was made. Because not all cities made changes in the same year, it also creates problems of comparability among cities.

The general conformity to uniform accounting principles since 1980 has eased the problem of comparability; yet some changes in the principles have created new problems. A particular difficulty arises because many cities report operating results on two separate bases: to conform to GAAP, they report on one basis, but to conform to their non-GAAP budget, they also report on a budget basis. Some cities end up with revenues and expenditures that are balanced on one basis but out of balance on the other basis. In such situations, it is confusing to try to understand the government's budget intentions, to say nothing of trying to compare these intentions to actual results.

Nevertheless, short of conducting onsite financial case studies, the financial reports of the governments are the best source of financial information about them. The data used in this paper have been taken from these financial reports unless otherwise noted. In some cases, especially in the years prior to 1980, adjustments were made to make information comparable. In addition, New York City information has not been included in most totals because its general fund revenues and expenditures are larger than the other 29 large cities combined and would distort results. It has also been necessary to omit some cities from the analysis for some years because they changed fiscal year definitions, made major changes in accounting, or did not publish a financial report for that year.

Presentation of Financial Information

The financial reports of cities are organized by accounting funds. Funds exist because of the restrictions imposed on a government's use of its resources. For example, revenues from gasoline taxes often must be used only for highway purposes and thus must be segregated in a separate fund. Similarly, proceeds from bond sales usually must be used only for capital improvements and therefore must also be kept in a separate fund. Any analysis of a city's internal financial condition must cope with the problem of how to present information from different funds in an accurate, meaningful fashion.

Although maintaining separate funds is necessary for legal and accounting reasons, the funds can be grouped into three general categories for the purpose of reviewing government finances:

1. Governmental operating funds. These funds receive revenue from most taxes, federal and state operating grants, and other general revenue sources, and are used to pay for salaries, supplies, debt service, and other operating costs associated with providing basic government services. The most important fund in this category is the general fund, which receives all unrestricted revenues and which may be spent for any legal governmental purpose. All governments have a general fund, but they do not necessarily have other funds. The other funds, when used, are classified as either special-revenue funds or debt service funds.

2. Governmental capital-improvement funds. Major expenditures for property, plant, and equipment to support basic government services are recorded in these funds. Proceeds from bond sales and federal capital grants are the principal sources of receipts into capital funds.

3. Proprietary funds. These funds account for certain operations of the government that are similar to businesses, such as water supply, sewage treatment, or the municipal airport. Revenues come from service charges that are usually set at rates sufficient to recover full costs including depreciation.

Previous examinations of major-city financial health by the author were primarily concerned only with the general fund. These studies were published in 1973 by the Advisory Commission on Intergovernmental Relations, and later updated in 1977 and 1978 for The First Boston Corporation, in 1979 for the Urban Institute, and in 1985 for the Advisory Commission on Intergovernmental Relations again. For most local governments, the general fund is the largest fund and the most important. It customarily receives most tax revenues, and it contains discretionary funds that can be used to support inadequacies of resources in other funds.

Yet the general fund does not provide information about most capital expenditures or restricted federal and state operating grants. Accounting for these activities occurs in capital funds and special-revenue funds. Debt service expenditures are usually shown in a separate debt service fund and thus are also not included in general fund expenditures.

There is an additional problem of general fund comparability among cities because the amount of activity accounted for by the general fund varies from city to city. New York, for example, accounts for about 80 percent of its expenditures in the general fund, whereas Phoenix, at the other extreme, accounts for less than 20 percent of its revenues in the general fund.

New Approaches to Measuring Fiscal Condition

This paper, in addition to reviewing and analyzing the historical and current general fund financial results of 30 major cities, will consider more comprehensive measures of financial activity encompassing all governmental funds, both operating and capital. Proprietary funds, because they are self-supporting, will not be included. Because of data problems, this analysis of the combined funds will cover only four years—1981 to 1984. The broader scope of the analysis, however, makes it possible to look at changes in the funding of debt service and capital improvements, federal aid, and overall government liquidity.

This paper will also consider the extent to which government operating results occur because the governments purposely budget for an imbalance between their revenues and expenditures to use up accumulated surpluses. If financial condition is judged by government's annual balancing of revenues and expenditures, then such purposeful imbalances must be taken into consideration in judging performance.

One other feature in the analysis of fiscal condition that was considered but found not feasible for this paper is an evaluation of changes in property tax rates. Most governments provide information in their financial reports about property tax rates, both for the

current and past years. For several reasons, however, this information
is not readily usable. Comparability is a problem because some
governments include only the tax rate that supports general city
services, whereas others include rates for other independent agencies,
such as school districts, and for special purposes, such as retirement
funding. Another problem with comparing changes in tax rates arises
from differences in assessment policies. Governments that reassess
annually get the benefit of inflation growth and may not need to
change rates. But governments that reassess only periodically may
need to increase their tax rates to provide inflationary growth in
their revenues in those years when reassessment does not occur; they
can then reduce rates in the years when assessments are increased.
Further work will be necessary to develop a reasonable measure of
major-city tax rate changes, a key indicator of financial condition in
the eyes of most local officials.

RESULTS OF THE ANALYSIS

We now turn to the results of our analysis, bearing in mind
the difficulties described. The general fund operating results and
balance-sheet condition of the 30 large cities will be presented first
in the same general framework that has been used in previous reports dating from 1971. New data series on other funds—special
revenue, capital improvement, and debt service—in the period 1981–
1984 will then be reviewed. Most of the information in both parts
will be in summarized form. A discussion of individual cities is a
problem because presenting various types of information for 30 cities
requires large, complex tables and because it is not possible for this
paper to present what would amount to case studies of 30 cities. In
some instances in which reference to an individual city is necessary
to understand the point, the reference will be made. The conclud-
ing section of the report presents the author's views on a general
categorization of cities by financial condition.

General Fund Results of Operation

Every local government is concerned about balancing its operating revenues with its expenditures because experience has shown
that a persistent or unusually large amount of spending in excess of
revenues leads to a weakened financial condition and, in a few in-

stances, a financial emergency. In addition, most local governments are required by law to have a balanced budget.[2]

The experience of the 30 large cities surveyed over the period 1971–1984 shows that in the aggregate the governments (excluding New York) had an excess of revenues, as compared with expenditures, in 9 of those years and a deficiency of revenues in 5 of them (Table 2). By comparing the recessions during this period with the results, it is clear that the years in which the deficiencies occurred were those following national recessions (Figure 1). This pattern includes the deficiency in 1971 that followed the recession of 1970. It seems likely, therefore, that the experience of the major cities in balancing revenues and expenditures is cyclical and that it relates to national recession.

Because of the nation's strong economic recovery following the 1981–1982 recession, major cities in 1984 had the largest dollar excess in revenues of any year examined and the highest excess as a percentage of expenditures since 1977. Based on past experience, this favorable performance can be expected to continue until after the next national recession.

Why revenue–expenditure deficiencies occur following the recessions and not concurrent with them is not clear. The reason may simply be because of technical causes such as the alignment of fiscal years or budget cycles with the recession or the timing of tax payment dates. But changes in annual growth rates of revenues and expenditures as a result of the recession would also seem to be a likely cause.

When revenue growth in current dollars is compared with national recessions, however, there is little apparent pattern (Figure 2). Revenue growth went down during the recession of the mid-1970s, but it went up in the years following the recession. Although revenues also went down in the mild recession of 1980, they subsequently went up in each of the following years, including the more severe recession of 1981–1982.

Percentage changes in spending show a similarly inconsistent pattern (Figure 3). It is difficult to see how changes in the growth

---

[2]In most cases, this requirement does not mean that revenues and expenditures actually have to balance. The laws generally permit the government to treat an accumulated surplus from prior years (or nonrevenue sources of funds such as the sale of assets) as revenues for balancing purposes.

TABLE 2 Comparison of Total General Fund[a] Revenues to Expenditures for Selected Major Cities[b]

Year	Number of Cities in Which Expenditures Exceeded Revenues	Total Excess or Deficiency of Revenue for All Cities	Percentage of Total Expenditures
1971[c]	16	-23.1	-0.5
1972	12	16.1	0.3
1973	8	175.1	3.5
1974	9	156.1	2.9
1975	16	-28.4	-0.4
1976	13	-154.2	-2.2
1977	6	230.6	3.1
1978	12	73.6	1.0
1979	9	98.8	1.2
1980	19	-188.7	-2.2
1981	10	212.6	1.5
1982	12	168.9	1.2
1983	16	-164.4	-1.3
1984	6	309.9	2.4

[a]These figures do not include New York for any year; they also exclude some other cities for some years in which information was not available.

[b]The selected major cities in this and subsequent references refer to the 30 cities listed in Table 1.

[c]See Advisory Commission on Intergovernmental Relations (1973, p. 50). Their figures include some 1970 results in cases in which 1971 data were not available.

SOURCE: Data were derived from the published annual financial reports of the cities.

rates of expenditures and revenues, when taken together, could account for the consistent cyclical pattern of revenue–expenditure deficiencies.

Another possibility is that it is not what actually happens to revenues or expenditures that causes deficiencies but what happens relative to what the governments expected to happen at the time they made their budgets. Budget information is not available for all cities over the years, but it is possible to examine 21 of the 30 cities for 1982, 1983, and 1984 (Table 3). For cities that budget on either a fiscal- or calendar-year basis, most of 1982 was a recession year.

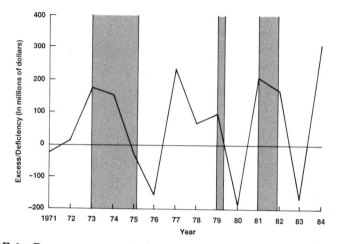

FIGURE 1   Revenues compared with expenditures for all major cities. Note:
The shaded areas represent recession periods.   Data were derived from the
published annual financial reports of the cities.

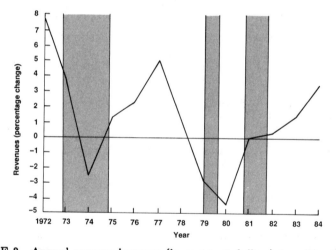

FIGURE 2   Annual revenue increase (in constant dollars) for all major cities.
Note: The shaded areas represent recession periods. Data were derived from
the published annual financial reports of the cities.

In contrast, 1983 and 1984 were strong recovery years. The 21 cities
included in the sample had an excess of revenues over expenditures
of $20.1 million in 1982 and $137.8 million in 1984; in 1983, however,
these cities had a deficiency of revenues to expenditures of $127.4
million. Thus, the sample reflects the same postrecession deficiency
that all 30 cities experienced.

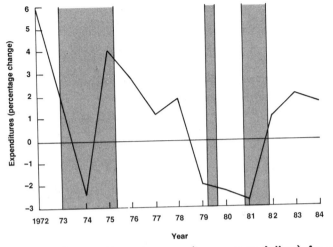

FIGURE 3 Annual expenditure increase (in constant dollars) for all major cities. Note: The shaded areas represent recession periods. Data were derived from the published annual financial reports of the cities.

The budgeting experience of the sample cities was similar in that most cities budgeted to spend more than their revenues.

In 1984 2 fewer cities than in the previous years budgeted a deficiency, and the total deficiency budgeted by the 21 cities was about $100 million less, perhaps in reaction to their unfavorable experiences in 1983. Yet even if part of the explanation for more favorable results in 1984 was more conservative budgeting, it would not explain why 1982, a recession year, had better results than 1983, a recovery year.

An examination of each year's actual revenues and expenditures, compared with what was budgeted, reveals a consistent pattern. In

TABLE 3 Comparison of Budgeting Experience for 21 Major Cities

Experience	1982	1983	1984
Cities budgeting a deficiency	20	20	18
Cities budgeting an excess	1	1	3
Total	21	21	21
Amount of aggregate deficiency budgeted (in millions)	$321.4	$312.3	$216.0

SOURCE: Data were derived from the published annual financial reports of the cities.

TABLE 4 General Fund Actual Revenues and Expenditures (in millions of dollars) Compared with City Budgets for 21 Major Cities: 1982, 1983, and 1984

Year and Fiscal Category	Budget	Actual (Unfavorable)	Difference (Favorable)
1982			
Revenues	7,761.0	7,763.2	2.2
Expenditures	8,082.4	7,743.1	339.3
Difference	(321.4)	20.1	
1983			
Revenues	8,408.1	8,201.5	(206.6)
Expenditures	8,720.4	8,328.9	391.5
Difference	(312.3)	(127.4)	
1984			
Revenues	8,822.1	8,815.3	(6.8)
Expenditures	9,038.1	8,677.5	360.6
Difference	(216.0)	137.8	

SOURCE: Data were derived from the published annual financial reports of the cities.

each year, actual expenditures were below budget. This is consistent with the conservative budget practices used by most local governments. Although the actual revenues in 1982 and 1984 were very close to the budget estimates, however, the actual revenues in 1983 fell well below the estimates. The shortfall was big enough to offset the favorable expenditure results of 1983 and cause a budget deficiency for this year (Table 4).

The aggregate deficiency of revenues that occurred in 1983 resulted when 11 of the cities had revenues below their estimates. These 11 were mostly the larger cities, including Chicago, Philadelphia, and Detroit, which together were $216.7 million below estimates (Table 5). Nine of these 11 cities were on a fiscal-year basis (year ending other than December 31), which may suggest that fiscal-year timing relative to the recession was a partial cause. However, any exact determination of why the revenue estimates were high in 1983, and not in the other 2 years, would require more research than was possible in this paper.

General Fund Balance-Sheet Condition

The cities' balancing of revenues and expenditures is directly tied to the condition of the governments' balance sheets as measured by unreserved surpluses. For example, there were relatively large surpluses in 1982; 15 cities had surpluses equal to more than 5 percent of their prior-year expenditures. As a result, most cities budgeted the use of varying amounts of surplus to fund their 1983 budgets. The resulting deficiencies, which were discussed earlier, caused a decrease of about one-quarter in the amount of surplus at the end of 1983 (Table 6). However, the surplus condition was still strong enough that most governments again planned to use surpluses to help balance their 1984 budgets. When stronger than expected revenues occurred in 1984, total surplus rose to an amount at the end of the year that exceeded the level at the end of 1982.

We would expect that those cities with balance-sheet deficits would want to end the year with an excess of revenues to eliminate the deficit and build reserves, and that those cities with a large surplus would want expenditures to exceed revenues and thereby

TABLE 5 Revenues (in millions of current dollars) Compared with City Budgets for 21 Selected Cities, 1983

City	Budget	Actual	Difference
Chicago	1,219.0	1,123.9	(95.1)
Philadelphia	1,323.3	1,287.1	(36.2)
Detroit	876.1	790.7	(85.4)
Baltimore	631.3	630.5	(0.8)
Dallas	375.6	370.8	(4.8)
San Francisco	802.7	840.6	37.9
San Diego	217.1	214.8	(2.3)
San Antonio	216.6	209.3	(7.3)
St. Louis	275.7	266.9	(8.8)
New Orleans	327.9	295.7	(32.2)
Phoenix	222.6	215.5	(7.1)
Columbus	164.1	164.2	0.1
Seattle	194.7	195.7	1.0
Jacksonville	193.4	195.7	2.3
Pittsburgh	207.6	211.8	4.2
Kansas City	204.6	201.1	(3.5)
Atlanta	165.8	182.9	17.1
Buffalo	331.9	334.7	2.8
Cincinnati	138.7	147.2	8.5
Nashville	207.6	208.4	0.8
Minneapolis	111.8	114.0	2.2
Total	8,408.1	8,201.5	(206.6)

SOURCE: Data were derived from the published annual financial reports of the cities.

TABLE 6 General Fund Unreserved Surpluses (in millions of current dollars) of Selected Major Cities: 1982, 1983, and 1984

Year	Surplus	As a Percentage of Revenues
1982	336.1	1.1
1983	247.1	0.9
1984	364.7	1.2

NOTE: These figures include New York but exclude Los Angeles.

SOURCE: Data were derived from the published annual financial reports of the cities.

reduce their surplus. Those expectations were not borne out by events from 1982–1984. Seven cities had a balance-sheet unreserved fund deficit at the end of at least 2 of the 3 years; yet five of them continued to experience a deficiency of revenues to expenditures in those years. On the other hand, 10 cities had unreserved surpluses greater than 5 percent at the end of each year, but 7 of those cities had a deficiency of revenues in only 1 or less of the 3 years. In short, it appears that the cities with problem balance sheets had a hard time improving their condition, whereas those with healthy fiscal conditions continued to improve.

As a result, by the end of 1984, when 25 of the 30 cities accounted for over $300 million in excess revenues, 5 cities (Chicago, Detroit, Cleveland, Boston, and Buffalo) still had deficits on their balance sheets. At the other extreme, 4 cities (San Francisco, Atlanta, Minneapolis, and Seattle) had unreserved surpluses in excess of 10 percent of their prior year's spending (Table 7). On closer examination, however, in 3 of the cities with deficits at the end of 1984, the picture is not entirely bleak. Chicago has a persistent deficit because it spends property taxes a year before they are collected, and Cleveland and Buffalo both had deficits amounting to less than 1 percent of spending. Thus, as judged by balance-sheet conditions, the major cities were in relatively good condition in 1984 compared with selected prior years.

A Broader View of the 1980s

The advent of improved accounting and financial reporting in the

TABLE 7 General Fiscal Condition (balance or deficit[a] as a percentage of total revenues) of Selected Major Cities for Selected Years

City	1971	1976	1981	1984
New York	(9.2)	(31.1)	(0.5)	0.1
Chicago	(47.5)	(24.8)	(10.5)	(8.5)
Los Angeles	N.A.	N.A.	3.1	N.A.
Philadelphia	(6.1)	(10.2)	4.4	1.8
Detroit	(3.7)	(5.6)	(16.2)	(3.1)
Houston	10.8	7.4	15.5	3.7
Baltimore	2.4	8.1	2.7	0.7
Dallas	4.3	6.7	6.9	5.9
Cleveland	(16.6)	0.2	(7.4)	(0.9)
Indianapolis	4.5	2.7	3.8	6.1
Milwaukee	12.3	21.8	18.6	6.8
San Francisco	15.8	9.5	23.5	21.8
San Diego	7.3	8.3	8.6	9.5
San Antonio	5.7	(3.9)	10.0	6.8
Boston	13.4	(10.7)	(7.5)	(6.0)
Memphis	6.7	2.7	5.0	9.3
St. Louis	(2.9)	1.2	(0.7)	0.8
New Orleans	(1.2)	4.5	8.4	2.3
Phoenix	4.4	3.0	0.1	4.4
Columbus	3.3	3.4	(0.2)	4.3
Seattle	22.9	1.3	6.3	12.3
Jacksonville	26.3	11.9	11.4	6.6
Pittsburgh	7.9	5.6	1.1	0.7
Denver	8.2	6.4	5.1	3.1
Kansas City	1.2	4.5	9.6	6.5
Atlanta	17.3	25.0	17.5	18.2
Buffalo	2.1	(15.0)	(0.3)	(0.03)
Cincinnati	0.9	2.7	10.6	5.9
Nashville	6.3	16.9	6.3	4.2
Minneapolis	12.9	6.6	15.7	14.4
Unweighted Average	3.8	2.0	5.0	4.7

NOTE: Values within parentheses are deficits. N.A. = not applicable.

[a]Because of deficiencies in financial reporting, especially in 1971 and 1976, many balances or deficits are not in accordance with generally accepted accounting principles. Pro forma adjustments were made to reported balances and deficits in some cases to make them more compatible with accepted accounting principles. For 1981 and 1982 balances, the undesignated fund balance was generally used, but in some cities it was referred to as unrestricted.

SOURCE: Data were derived from the published annual financial reports of the cities.

early 1980s has made possible a broader and more detailed examination of major-city finances. Instead of examining only the general funds, we can analyze all governmental operating funds and capital funds. Governmental operating funds include the general fund, debt service funds, and special-revenue funds. The review that follows covers the 30 cities discussed earlier, except for Los Angeles, for 1981, 1982, 1983, and 1984. For most purposes, New York is again omitted because its size dominates the totals. Information about several cities is not available for 1983.

The early 1980s was an unusual period that was marked by a high inflation rate in 1981, a recession in 1982, and relatively high municipal bond interest rates that peaked in January 1982 and declined somewhat in 1984. In addition, federal aid to states and cities was reduced in 1981 and 1982. In short, a great deal happened in those 4 years, and it is difficult to determine which factors accounted for various changes in urban finances. A review of several of the trends over the period, however, gives some insight into what may have influenced urban finances.

Operating Results

First, it is helpful to assess whether this broader measure of operating results reflects the same cyclical operating results as the general fund. For each of the 4 years, the aggregate operating revenues of the major cities exceeded their operating expenditures. The excess revenues expressed as a percentage of expenditures was as follows:

1981	1.9
1982	1.1
1983	0.2
1984	2.2

Thus, although there was not a deficiency in 1983, as occurred when only the general funds were used as a gauge, the considerably poorer operating results of the cities in 1983, compared with 1982 or 1984, were repeated by this broader measure.

Liquidity

Earlier reports in this series included a measurement of governments' liquidity as a test of the governments' financial condition—that is, whether they had cash available to meet obligations. For this purpose, liquidity is defined as the government's total cash and investments except for retirement fund investments, and its proprietary fund-restricted cash and investments, less any short-term loans. To be meaningful, liquidity needs to be compared with a measure of the cash demands on the government. In previous reports, we compared liquidity with general fund spending. With the broadening of the analysis to include all government operating funds, we can compare liquidity as a percentage of the more relevant measure of total government operating fund expenditures. On this basis, liquidity was relatively unchanged from 1981 to 1983 but surged in 1984 as shown below:

1981	33.0
1982	37.4
1983	35.8
1984	46.9

Confirming this improved liquidity is the fact that although 6 cities had liquidity below 15 percent in 1982, in 1984 only 1 had liquidity below that figure. From 1983 to 1984, 28 cities improved the total dollar amount of their liquidity, and 21 of those also increased their liquidity as a percentage of spending. The liquidity of major cities was clearly very good in 1984, especially as compared with the preceding 3 years. This improvement was obviously the result in part of the excess revenues received in 1984, but it may also have been due to governments issuing bonds at lower interest rates in 1984. Local governments typically stockpile capital funds, and thus increase liquidity, by issuing bonds in periods of low interest rates and "spending down" funds in periods of high interest rates.

Effects of Changes in Federal Aid

Federal grants, except for capital grants, are usually received by a city as a revenue that goes into special-revenue funds, but generally they are lumped together with state aid for reporting purposes and shown only as intergovernmental aid. Thus, it is impossible to ascertain from financial reports the exact extent to which changes in federal aid affected governments over the period in question.

If a decrease in federal aid had any substantial effect on a city's fiscal condition, it should show up as a decrease in the importance of restricted revenues, with a shifting of expenditures to the general fund. This did not occur. Special-revenue fund revenues were slightly higher in 1984 at 27.1 percent of total operating revenues, compared with 26.4 percent in 1981. If there were any effects from federal aid reduction, therefore, they must have been offset by faster growth in state aid or other restricted revenues. There was a dip to 23.3 percent for restricted revenues in 1982 that could have been attributable to the 1981 federal budget cuts, but the recovery to the higher percentage in 1984, despite the lack of a significant increase in federal aid, makes it likely that nonfederal funds were causing the fluctuation. The effects of federal aid reductions on capital spending will be discussed in the next section.

Despite the lack of evidence that changes in federal aid levels in the 1980s have had any adverse effects on major-city finances, cities are faced with the prospect that elimination of the general revenue-sharing program will have an effect in 1987. To evaluate the possible consequences of such a loss, we can examine the relationship of general revenue sharing to local finances in 1984. The 30 large cities, excluding Los Angeles, received $730 million in revenue sharing in 1984. This amount was equal to 2.2 percent of their total operating revenues, with a range from a low of 1.2 percent of Buffalo's revenues to a high of 5 percent of New Orlean's revenues (Table 8). Most of these governments consider revenue sharing a basic part of their financing of current operations. As a result, over the long term, they will have to increase their local operating revenues or decrease their operating expenditures by about the percentage loss of revenue sharing.

The ability of the cities to absorb the loss of revenue sharing in the first year, without straining their current financial condition, depends on their ability to adjust their budgets quickly and on the availability of general fund surpluses to cushion the loss. As was reported earlier (see Table 6), the cities had unreserved surpluses at the end of 1984 totaling $364.7 million. This amount represents about half of the $730 million general revenue-sharing receipts for that year. If all of the cities had had to finance the loss from their surpluses (which they would not have done), 15 cities instead of 5 would have ended the year with balance-sheet deficits (Table 9).

TABLE 8 General Revenue Sharing (in millions of dollars)
Compared with Total Operating Revenues for Selected
Cities, 1984

City	Total Operating Revenue	Revenue Sharing	Percentage of Total
New York	17,420.3	272.2	1.6
Chicago	1,652.5	68.2	4.1
Los Angeles	N.A.	N.A.	N.A.
Philadelphia	2,417.1	45.8	1.9
Detroit	1,054.9	32.3	3.1
Houston	710.5	23.5	3.3
Baltimore	994.5	23.7	2.4
Dallas	498.7	14.3	2.9
Cleveland	371.5	13.6	3.7
Indianapolis	260.7	12.1	4.6
Milwaukee	389.8	10.7	2.7
San Francisco	912.8	21.4	2.3
San Diego	278.8	11.3	4.1
San Antonio	337.5	9.2	2.7
Boston	827.9	18.8	2.3
Memphis	540.2	12.6	2.3
St. Louis	347.9	10.5	3.0
New Orleans	353.4	17.8	5.0
Phoenix	407.8	10.6	2.6
Columbus	273.0	9.2	3.4
Seattle	356.6	10.0	2.8
Jacksonville	292.1	9.9	3.4
Pittsburgh	269.7	11.5	4.3
Denver	430.9	12.2	2.8
Kansas City	301.5	10.4	3.4
Atlanta	229.4	7.5	3.3
Buffalo	413.7	4.9	1.2
Cincinnati	244.7	9.1	3.7
Nashville	401.6	10.5	2.6
Minneapolis	286.8	6.2	2.2
Total	33,276.8	730.0	2.2

NOTE: N.A. = not applicable.

SOURCE: Data were derived from the published annual financial
reports of the cities. Revenue Sharing Information was obtained
from the U.S. Department of the Treasury, Office of State and
Local Finance.

TABLE 9 General Revenue Sharing Compared with General
Fund Surplus/Deficit (in millions of dollars) for Selected
Cities, 1984

City	Revenue Sharing	Surplus/ (Deficit)	Surplus/ (Deficit) Less Revenue Sharing
New York	272.2	24.9	(247.3)
Chicago	68.2	(101.9)	(170.1)
Los Angeles	N.A.	N.A.	N.A.
Philadelphia	45.8	25.5	(20.3)
Detroit	32.3	(27.3)	(59.6)
Houston	23.5	23.8	0.3
Baltimore	23.7	4.6	(19.1)
Dallas	14.3	24.4	10.1
Cleveland	13.6	(2.2)	(15.8)
Indianapolis	12.1	12.2	0.1
Milwaukee	10.7	20.9	10.2
San Francisco	21.4	177.8	156.4
San Diego	11.3	23.3	12.0
San Antonio	9.2	14.7	5.5
Boston	18.8	(41.1)	(59.9)
Memphis	12.6	23.5	10.9
St. Louis	10.5	2.2	(8.3)
New Orleans	17.8	7.4	(10.4)
Phoenix	10.6	10.6	0.0
Columbus	9.2	7.5	(1.7)
Seattle	10.0	26.6	16.6
Jacksonville	9.9	15.0	5.1
Pittsburgh	11.5	1.6	(9.9)
Denver	12.2	9.5	(2.7)
Kansas City	10.4	14.1	3.7
Atlanta	7.5	32.1	24.6
Buffalo	4.9	(0.1)	(5.0)
Cincinnati	9.1	8.0	(1.1)
Nashville	10.5	9.3	(1.2)
Minneapolis	6.2	17.8	11.6
Total	730.0	364.7	(365.3)

NOTE: N.A. = not applicable.

SOURCE: Data were derived from the published annual
financial reports of the cities. Revenue Sharing
Information was obtained from the U.S. Treasury,
Office of State and Local Finance.

Although the effects of federal aid loss were not apparent through 1984, the likely loss of revenue sharing in 1987 can be expected to require a 2 or 3 percent adjustment in revenues or expenditures by most cities. This adjustment will create budgetary strains, especially for those cities that are already experiencing problems in keeping revenues and expenditures in balance.

Capital Spending

It has generally been observed that city governments have been decreasing capital spending in recent years. A comparison of capital expenditures as a percentage of government operating expenditures confirms this trend from 1981–1984 as shown below:

1981	11.6
1982	10.6
1983	8.8
1984	7.6

It should be noted that the governmental capital fund expenditures used in this analysis do not contain capital expenditures for proprietary fund purposes such as water, electric, and sewer utilities and airports. Nevertheless, the clear downward trend is apparent; the reasons for it are less clear. Capital spending could be going down because needs are decreasing, because federal grants are less, because interest rates were high for most of these years, or for other reasons. The exact causes cannot be determined with precision, but circumstantial evidence suggests that federal aid reductions and reduced bond sales (because of higher interest rates) may have been major causes.

Federal capital grants are received into capital funds as revenues, together with state capital grants, interest on invested capital funds, and a few other minor revenue sources. Bond proceeds are not treated as revenues. An examination of capital fund revenues shows a decline that parallels the capital spending decline over 1981–1984. Actual capital revenues as a percentage of operating revenues were as follows:

1981	7.6
1982	5.8
1983	5.1
1984	3.9

This decrease suggests that federal capital grants lost some of their significance as a source of capital spending over those years. Although it is possible that the decline resulted from other revenue losses, such a cause is unlikely because state grants and interest earnings are not generally major revenue sources for capital spending.

High interest rates in the early 1980s may have caused an increase in debt service costs as a percentage of total operating expenditures, as shown below:

1981	7.8
1982	7.7
1983	8.0
1984	8.8

As was discussed earlier, local officials prefer to keep debt service costs stable as a percentage of overall operating expenditures. When interest costs rise, officials must either divert money from current programs to finance the increase or raise taxes. Neither is a desirable alternative, and it is thus likely that reductions in bond sales and subsequent capital spending may have occurred from 1981–1984 as officials sought to keep debt service costs from escalating even further.

Regardless of the reason, it appears that the cities were not spending as much of their budgets on capital improvements in 1984 as they had been in prior years. Whether this change was caused by the unusual series of economic conditions in the early 1980s cannot be determined, but it does not seem to be the result of any overall weakness in the cities' financial condition. It is more likely to be the result of political decisions made in light of the city's needs, the availability of capital revenues, and interest rates.

Categorizing the Cities by Financial Condition

This paper has considered 30 major U.S. cities primarily as a unit over the period 1971–1984 for the purpose of looking at urban financial conditions. It is obvious, however, that the composite does not do justice to the varied experiences of individual cities. Despite the ups and downs of these cities when viewed in the aggregate, some cities have had consistently good financial conditions while others have faced problems in most years or for extended periods.

Not surprisingly, bond ratings and general impressions of the major cities closely align with the cities' financial experiences. The cities that have maintained a consistently good financial condition in virtually every year, as measured by their revenue–expenditure balance and balance-sheet condition, include San Francisco, Minneapolis, Indianapolis, Jacksonville, Milwaukee, Atlanta, and San Diego. In addition, Los Angeles would almost certainly fall into this category if its financial reporting permitted a clearer view of its financial results.

On the other hand, at one time or another for extended periods, New York, Chicago, Philadelphia, Detroit, Boston, Cleveland, St. Louis, and Buffalo have had fund deficits, low liquidity, and severe or persistent revenue–expenditure imbalances. The rest of the cities fit no clear pattern. They have generally had good but not exceptional financial experiences and only occasionally years with indications of potential problems.

This categorization, although based on financial facts, is still subjective because there are other facts that might be pointed to by local officials to justify a different categorization. Also, it may not give sufficient credit to such cities as New York, Cleveland, and Philadelphia and their belief that they have permanently reformed their finances. Such confidence may be justified, but it is also the case that for most years of the 1980s, except 1983, all of the major cities have shown good results and improving financial conditions. Thus, until the next period in which major cities generally experience financial troubles, it is hard to judge whether these cities have permanently recovered.

CONCLUSIONS

The record from 1971–1984 shows that national recessions have caused major-city finances to falter, with lower revenues than expected in the year following the end of the recession. This revenue deficiency then weakens the cities' balance sheets by reducing their balance-sheet operating surpluses or by increasing deficits. The major cities have weathered several such difficult years since 1971 and as of 1984 were in perhaps the best financial condition they had been in since 1971, as judged by their success in balancing budgets and maintaining balance-sheet surpluses and liquidity. This favorable condition can be expected to continue for most major cities, at least as long as the national economy remains healthy. Because of the city financial problems that are likely to occur following the next national recession, some preventive measures should be considered, either in the form of federal antirecession aid or improved methods for cities to predict recession-caused revenue problems and take action to avoid them.

The changes in federal aid in the 1980s do not appear to have had an effect on operating results, but the probable end of general revenue sharing can be expected to reduce overall city revenues by about 2.2 percent in the first year it occurs. The end of revenue sharing will create a problem for some cities with weak balance sheets and difficulties in balancing revenues and expenditures. As long as the economy is strong, however, one-time budget adjustments of this magnitude should be manageable.

The loss of federal capital grants probably contributed to a decline in capital spending by major cities. In addition, high interest rates caused debt service costs to increase and may also have contributed to the decrease in capital spending.

Measuring the financial condition of urban governments in a way that is meaningful from both local and national perspectives remains a difficult challenge, but improvements in accounting practices have made some advances possible. There are still many unanswered questions, but we are now able to observe at least a few key indicators of financial condition on an annual basis and to make judgments about the general financial performance of major cities, as well as about the condition of individual cities.

REFERENCES

Advisory Commission on Intergovernmental Relations
  1973   *City Financial Emergencies: The Intergovernmental Dimension.* Report A-42. Washington, D.C.: Advisory Commission on Intergovernmental Relations.
  1981   *Measuring the Fiscal Capacity and Effort of State and Local Areas.* Report M-58. Washington, D.C.: Advisory Commission on Intergovernmental Relations.
  1985   *Bankruptcies, Defaults, and Other Government Financial Emergencies.* Report A-99. Washington, D.C.: Advisory Commission on Intergovernmental Relations.
Bureau of the Census
  1976   *Financial Environment Indicators for City Governments.* Washington, D.C.: U.S. Department of Commerce.
Dearborn, Philip M.
  1978   *The Financial Health of Major U.S. Cities in Fiscal 1977.* New York: First Boston Corporation.
  1979   *The Financial Health of Major U.S. Cities in 1978.* Washington, D.C.: Urban Institute Press.

Ladd, Helen F., John Yinger, Katherine L. Bradbury, Ronald Ferguson, and Avis Vidal
    1985   The Changing Economic and Fiscal Conditions of Cities. Draft Final Report to the U.S. Department of Housing and Urban Development. State, Local, and Intergovernmental Center, Kennedy School of Government, Harvard University.

Matz, Deborah, and John E. Petersen
    1983   *Trends in the Fiscal Condition of Cities: 1981–1983.* A study prepared for the use of the Subcommittee on Economic Goals and Intergovernmental Policy, Joint Economic Committee, Congress of the United States. Senate Print 98-119. Washington, D.C.: U.S. Government Printing Office.

National League of Cities
    1986   *1986 Fiscal Survey.* Washington, D.C.: National League of Cities.

Petersen, John E., and Deborah Matz
    1985   Trends in the Fiscal Condition of Cities: 1983–1985. Unpublished study prepared for the Joint Economic Committee, Congress of the United States. Government Finance Officers Association, Washington, D.C.

Poister, Theodore H.
    1986   A HUD capacity sharing effort: The financial trend monitoring system. *Public Budgeting and Finance* 6(Spring):20–32.

U.S. Department of the Treasury
    1978   *Report on the Fiscal Impact of the Economic Stimulus Package on 48 Large Urban Governments.* Washington, D.C.: U.S. Department of the Treasury.
    1985   *Federal-State-Local Fiscal Relations: Report to the President and the Congress.* Office of State and Local Finance. Washington, D.C.: U.S. Department of the Treasury.

State Fiscal Conditions

STEVEN D. GOLD

The fiscal condition of state governments is a critical factor in determining how much aid states can provide to local governments. State fiscal conditions have been volatile over the past decade. The finances of most states were generally healthy in the late 1970s, but they deteriorated significantly in the early 1980s; they began to recover in 1983. Although most states are still considerably better off than they were in the depths of the recessions of the early 1980s, their fiscal conditions are generally not as strong as in the late 1970s, in part because of the legacy of the tax revolt, which in a number of states limits the reserves they are able to maintain.

This report consists of four parts: (1) a discussion of various measures of state fiscal conditions; (2) descriptions of state fiscal conditions in recent years and the fluctuations that have occurred in state tax levels; (3) an analysis of state aid to local governments; and (4) the conclusion of the report, a discussion of future prospects for state fiscal conditions and local aid policies.

The views expressed in this paper are solely those of the author and do not reflect the official position of the National Conference of State Legislatures, for which he serves as director of fiscal studies.

MEASURES OF STATE FISCAL CONDITIONS

The two most widely cited measures of state fiscal conditions are the surpluses (or deficits) of state and local governments as estimated by the U.S. Department of Commerce's national income and product accounts and the year-end general fund balances for state governments as reported annually by the National Conference of State Legislatures (see, e.g., Gold et al., 1985) and the National Governors' Association/National Association of State Budget Officers (1986). A third measure is the financial assets held by states.

The Commerce Department's national income and product accounts (NIPA) estimate the operating surplus or deficit of state and local governments, usually on a combined basis but intermittently on a separated basis. Because this report is concerned with state finances, we will consider only the surplus or deficit statistics for state governments alone. The NIPA estimates cover all state government activities, including those of independent or quasi-independent institutions established by states. The estimates aggregate all state balances into a single number; they represent flows during a specific period of time, and they do not consider funds raised by borrowing as revenue, although they count expenditures financed by the borrowing.

NIPA data are reported both to include and to exclude social insurance funds. Although these funds always have a large surplus because money is being accumulated to provide future pension benefits, they are not available to fund current services. Thus, while it is appropriate to include social insurance funds in macroeconomic analyses, they should not be considered when measuring short-run state fiscal conditions. This distinction is important because the surplus in the social insurance funds invariably dwarfs the remaining surplus. In 1985, for example, the total NIPA surplus for state and local governments was $59 billion, of which the social insurance funds surplus accounted for $52.9 billion (Levin and Peters, 1986).

The general fund is the account into which most state tax revenue is deposited and from which most current spending is financed. Each state defines its general fund in its own way, and accounting practices also differ substantially from state to state, so comparisons of general fund statistics among states must be made with care. As a general rule, the general fund does not include most revenue from charges and fees, nor do most states include federal aid in the general fund. Most states earmark certain taxes to go to special funds outside the general fund—for example, for highway construction and maintenance. Despite the complications arising from the diversity of state fund structures, the general fund is the best indicator of state fiscal activity—that is, if balances in budget stabilization funds are added to a state's general fund and if the spending, tax, and accounting practices that influence it are taken into account (National Governors' Association/National Association of State Budget Officers, 1978).

There are three important differences between state general fund balances and NIPA surplus/deficit estimates:

1. As explained earlier, the general fund is much less inclusive, excluding many autonomous state bodies, most if not all user charges, federal aid, and earmarked revenue.

2. Unlike NIPA estimates, state surveys of general fund balances make it possible to disaggregate national trends and to determine if a few large states are having a major impact on aggregate totals.

3. The balance in the state general fund is a stock of money, not a flow, and it includes any surpluses or deficits carried over from the previous fiscal period.

A recent study by the National Conference of State Legislatures concluded that the general fund balance is a better indicator of state fiscal conditions than the NIPA surplus figure (Gold, 1986b). One important advantage is the disaggregation by state, which shows whether a small number of states may be distorting the national situation. A second advantage of using the general fund balance is that it avoids NIPA's treatment of capital finance; the NIPA measure distorts the state fiscal position by giving a bias toward deficit when debt-financed capital projects are expanding and a bias toward surplus when the financing for such projects is being retired. Third, the general fund is a better measure of available funds than NIPA, which includes statutorily and constitutionally earmarked funds. Indeed, NIPA's all-inclusiveness is a disadvantage in periods such as the late 1970s and early 1980s, when oil prices rose sharply. During these periods, huge increases occurred in the permanent funds of a small number of energy states. These increases added significantly to the surpluses in these states, but they created a false picture of robust fiscal health because the revenue in such funds generally cannot be tapped without a constitutional change.

An important issue in assessing the value of the general fund surplus as an indicator of fiscal health is the extent to which states transfer money between it and other funds. If such transfers are large and are frequently made whenever the general fund is short of funds, it would be seriously misleading to ignore accounts outside the general fund. This is not the case, however. Some outside accounts were tapped during the period of state fiscal stress in 1982–1983, but such transfers are usually not significant from a national perspective. Overall, general fund balances fluctuate much more than balances in most other accounts. Although state special funds may have larger total balances than the general fund, they do not have to be considered if the balances are relatively stable (Gold, 1986b).

An important qualification to this statement, however, concerns budget stabilization or "rainy day" funds. More than half of the states have established such funds, most within the past 5 years. Their function is to receive revenues during periods of relative fiscal ease so that budget adjustments during fiscal crises will not have to be as large. Because these stabilization funds are expected to augment the general fund when revenue receipts lag, the division of balances between a state's general fund and its rainy day fund is largely arbitrary, and it is appropriate to consider rainy day funds along with general fund balances in assessing state resources.

Projections of general fund balances have often proved inaccurate: they tend to be too optimistic when the economy is in a recession and too pessimistic when economic trends are positive. A small error in forecasting revenues can lead to a large error in the projected year-end balance. Suppose, for example, that a state has projected a 4 percent year-end balance and $10 billion in revenues for the year. If revenues were just 5 percent below the level forecasted, which is not a particularly large forecasting error, the state would have a 1 percent budget deficit, which would probably be dealt with by reducing expenditures below the level originally appropriated. To avoid such a problem, it is prudent for states to maintain relatively large balances. A widely used benchmark is that the year-end balance of both the general fund and the rainy day fund should be at least 5 percent of general fund expenditures. This standard is cited frequently by Wall Street analysts who evaluate the creditworthiness of states. Some states traditionally have maintained smaller balances, but this method usually requires accounting practices that enable them to tap other resources when revenue shortfalls occur.

A third indicator of a state's fiscal condition is the financial assets held by the state, as reported by the Bureau of the Census in its series of annual reports on state governments. This measure is available for individual states, but for any particular state it suffers from the same problem as NIPA data—a high degree of aggregation. All state assets that are not in social insurance or bond funds are added together; consequently, a large proportion of this total may be the assets held by independent or quasi-independent organizations such as housing finance agencies and universities (Gold, 1986b).

Although many past analyses have concentrated on a single figure—the NIPA surplus or the general fund balance as a proportion of expenditures—as an indicator of fiscal conditions, this approach is incomplete. It is necessary to consider as well the spending, tax, and accounting practices that were in effect in a state. If a state has a relatively large surplus only because it reduced spending and raised taxes, for example, that is quite a different matter from a surplus that occurs in the face of higher spending and reduced taxes.

Most states adopt fiscal and accounting practices that understate the true degree of fluctuation in balances. In order to avoid a deficit, which is not permitted in most states by constitutional provision or statute, states may defer certain expenditures (e.g., aid to school districts) and accelerate revenues. This action was taken by many states during the 1982–1983 period of severe fiscal stress. Some of these actions were then reversed when fiscal conditions improved. Although changes in accounting practices affect how fiscal conditions appear from year to year, they have not biased trends systematically over time and consequently are not discussed in the next section of this report.

STATE FISCAL CONDITIONS IN RECENT YEARS

State fiscal conditions have been volatile over the last 10 years—very good in the late 1970s, very poor in the early 1980s, then improved in the mid-1980s—but not as good as they were in the 1970s. Economic trends and changing tax policies are of primary importance in explaining these trends. Spending policies have followed rather than led the deterioration and improvements in fiscal conditions. Cutbacks in federal aid have been a negative factor affecting the fiscal condition of the states.

Table 1 shows total general fund balances annually from fiscal years 1978–1985, as reported by the the National Governors' Association/National Association of State Budget Officers (NGA/NASBO). The balances peaked in fiscal year 1980 at $11.8 billion, representing 9 percent of expenditures. They then declined steadily until 1983, when they were only $2 billion or 1.3 percent of spending. In the next

TABLE 1 States' General Fund Year-End Balances
(in billions of dollars), Fiscal Years 1978-1985

Year	Year-End Balance	Percentage of Expenditures
1985	8.0	4.3
1984	5.6	3.3
1983	2.0	1.3
1982	4.5	2.9
1981	6.5	4.4
1980	11.8	9.0
1979	11.2	8.7
1978	8.9	8.6

NOTE: Fiscal years in 46 states conclude on June 30.

SOURCE: National Governors' Association/National
Association of State Budget Officers (1986:17).

2 fiscal years, general fund balances rebounded, reaching $8 billion in 1985.

National figures on budget stabilization funds are available only for 1984 and 1985 when the funds stood at $0.8 billion and $1.7 billion, respectively (National Governors' Association/National Association of State Budget Officers, 1986).[1] Adding the stabilization funds makes the total balances in 1984 and 1985 $6.4 billion and $9.7 billion, respectively, or 3.8 percent and 5.3 percent of general fund expenditures. The improvement in state fiscal conditions that had been occurring since their low point in 1983 ended in fiscal year 1986. According to NGA/NASBO's survey, states ended that year with balances of $6.5 billion, of which $1.5 billion was in stabilization funds. This figure represented about 3.2 percent of expenditures.

NIPA figures show a similar pattern during the 1980s, as Table 2 indicates. (Note that these figures are for calendar rather than

---

[1] The National Governors' Association/National Association of State Budget Officers reports smaller stabilization funds than the National Conference of State Legislatures because it does not include the balances in some states in which the entire year-end balance is included as part of the stabilization fund. This difference of treatment affects the division between the general fund and stabilization fund but not the total reported balance (Gold et al., 1985). In earlier years, balances in stabilization funds were considerably lower, especially at the end of 1983.

TABLE 2 State and Local Surplus or Deficit (in
billions of dollars) in National Income and Product
Accounts, Calendar Years 1970-1984

Calendar Year	States	Local Governments
1984	11.5	4.3
1983	-0.9	6.4
1982	-7.4	5.7
1981	1.2	3.0
1980	0.0	-0.2
1979	1.6	2.2
1978	4.5	4.1
1977	3.0	6.0
1976	-1.4	1.0
1975	-5.8	-2.9
1974	-3.9	0.2
1973	0.6	3.2
1972	3.4	1.4
1971	-4.3	-0.8
1970	-4.4	-0.7

SOURCE: Levin and Peters (1986).

fiscal years.) After a \$4.5 billion surplus in 1978, states' finances deteriorated significantly, plunging to a \$7.4 billion deficit in 1982. A small deficit also occurred the next year, but the surplus soared to \$11.5 billion in 1984. Separate surplus figures for state and local governments are not available yet for 1985, but the combined surplus fell from \$15.9 billion to \$6.1 billion, with the states presumably being responsible for most of this decrease (Levin and Peters, 1986). Table 2 also shows the local surplus for comparison purposes. It has not been as unstable as the state surplus, nor was it as low in the 1981–1983 period.

A major value of general fund data is that they are available for all states, thus permitting comparisons of state fiscal conditions. Table 3 shows balances (including rainy day funds) for fiscal years 1985, 1986, and 1987 (projected). The differences among the states were even greater in 1983, when 8 states ended the fiscal year with deficits and 15 others had balances equal to 1 percent or less of spending while 9 states had balances equal to 5 percent or more of spending (Gold and Benker, 1983). One of the ironies of the present situation is the reversal of fortunes that has taken place in state fiscal conditions. Currently, the most fiscally stressed states are those rich in natural resources and the farm states, which were among the leaststressed when oil and grain prices were high in the 1970s; some of the northeastern states that were depressed in the mid-1970s are now relatively well off.

Three major factors account for these fluctuations in fiscal conditions: (1) the economy, (2) changes in state tax policy, and (3) cutbacks in federal aid.

Economic Trends

The American economy, which is the most important determinant of state fiscal conditions, underwent two recessions in the early 1980s—in 1980 and 1981–1982. The first recession was intense but brief, and the second was the most severe in 40 years. Their impact is clearly visible in Tables 1 and 2: they caused massive revenue shortfalls that plunged many states close to deficit situations. The impact of the recessions on the states was particularly severe because many had based their fiscal year 1983 budgets on predictions that the recession would end by the summer of 1982 (Gold, 1983). The economic recovery that began in December 1982 did not become apparent to state budgeters until mid-1983 because of the lags that exist between economic developments and state tax collections. The nation's improved economy was one of the two main reasons for the enhanced fiscal condition of the states in the mid-1980s.

Tax Policies

Tax policy was another important influence on state fiscal conditions. Although California's Proposition 13 dealt with local rather than state taxes, the tax revolt it dramatized encouraged many states to cut their state taxes. Thirty-two states reduced their personal income or general sales taxes in 1978, 1979, or 1980. Some of these reductions were temporary, but many were permanent. They resulted in an immediate reduction in tax collections, which kept balances below the level they would have otherwise achieved and also in many cases reduced the productivity of the tax system in future years (Gold, 1983).

The tax revolt not only resulted in tax reductions; it also inhibited the enactment of tax rate increases for a number of years. Only two states raised income or sales taxes in the 1978–1980 period, and there were no personal income tax increases and only five sales tax

TABLE 3 Year-End Total Balances as a Percentage of General Fund Spending by Region and State, Fiscal Years 1985, 1986, and 1987

Region and State	1985	1986	1987	Region and State	1985	1986	1987
U.S. average	4.5	2.7	0.9	Southeast			
				Alabama	13.2	0.0	0.0
New England				Arkansas	3.2	0.0	-18.7
Connecticut[b]	16.2	4.7	5.0	Florida[b]	2.3	4.3	2.0
Maine	2.4	1.0	0.6	Georgia[b]	0.9	2.6	2.6
Massachusetts	2.0	2.5	2.6	Kentucky[b]	3.8	7.7	4.5
New Hampshire	11.5	5.4	0.6	Louisiana[b]	0.0	-1.5	0.0
Rhode Island[b]	5.6	4.9	1.6	Mississippi[b]	5.1	3.5	0.4
Vermont	-5.7	1.8	1.4	North Carolina	0.3	6.3	0.0
				South Carolina	3.6	3.8	3.7
Mid-Atlantic				Tennessee	7.2	3.6	1.7
Delaware[b]	20.1	14.7	9.6	Virginia[b]	3.8	5.2	1.0
Maryland[b]	0.3	1.1	1.6	West Virginia	3.0	2.1	0.2
New Jersey	10.6	5.7	3.5				
New York[b]	0.5	0.7	0.7	Southwest			
Pennsylvania[b]	3.6	2.6	0.6	Arizona	0.4	0.3	0.6
				New Mexico[b]	9.3	5.2	-3.5
				Oklahoma[b]	4.6	0.0	5.4

Great Lakes			
Illinois	4.6	2.7	4.7
Indiana b	5.1	7.6	7.3
Michigan b	8.9	7.7	6.1
Ohio b	5.6	6.3	1.9
Wisconsin	7.7	4.7	2.0
Plains			
Iowa b	0.0	0.0	0.5
Kansas	8.3	2.1	5.5
Minnesota b	9.3	5.6	1.4
Missouri b	6.6	4.3	0.1
Nebraska	1.6	2.1	-0.2
North Dakota	25.4	20.2	-4.9
South Dakota	9.2	5.5	1.3

Texas	1.7	-3.3	-17.4
Rocky Mountain			
Colorado b	2.5	0.4	7.8
Idaho b	2.1	0.0	0.9
Montana	2.8	3.7	0.5
Utah b	0.0	0.0	0.3
Wyoming	49.7	49.8	71.3
Far West			
Alaska b	8.2	-1.4	-23.9
California b	4.9	1.4	3.4
Hawaii	7.4	3.6	2.5
Nevada	8.9	17.4	14.4
Oregon	11.0	5.3	6.0
Washington	0.1	0.4	1.0

[a]Figures for 1987 are projections.
[b]Year-end total balances include rainy day funds in these states.

SOURCE: National Governor's Association/National Association of State Budget Officers (1986).

increases in 1981. This legacy of the tax revolt began to weaken in 1982, however. In John Shannon's colorful terminology, tax increases in the post-Proposition 13 environment were acts of fiscal desperation that occurred only when there was already "blood on the floor." Nine states raised their income or sales taxes in 1982, five of them in the last 2 months of the year. Looking back, this pattern was a precursor of the greatest explosion of state tax increases ever: in 1983, tax increases enacted by the states totaled $8.25 billion. (In a few earlier years—particularly 1967, 1969, and 1971—tax increases were a larger percentage of total state tax revenue, but in absolute terms tax increases were never as great.) Thirty-eight states raised at least 1 tax, and there were 16 personal income tax and 11 general sales tax raises. There were no significant tax cuts. These tax increases contributed substantially to the improvement in state fiscal conditions in fiscal years 1984 and 1985 (Gold, 1984).

By 1984, however, the tax increases were beginning to be reversed. Many of them had originally been temporary, and contrary to the cynical attitude that temporary taxes are seldom lifted, most of them did expire, especially the increases in personal income taxes. In addition, as general fund balances grew, many states rolled back "permanent" increases enacted in 1982 and 1983. The great majority of sales tax increases remained in effect, but three-quarters of the states that increased their personal income taxes in 1982 and 1983 either eliminated or partially rolled back those increases by the end of 1985. These reductions contributed to the decrease in the NIPA surplus in 1985 and the drop in general fund balances in fiscal year 1986. Although numerous, most of these tax cuts were moderate in size. As a result, the net first-year reduction in tax revenue resulting from tax cuts legislated in 1985 was considerably less than 1 percent of total state tax revenue. When fully phased in, the tax cuts will represent less than 2 percent of total tax revenue (Gold, 1986a).

Tables 4 and 5 summarize recent tax policy and provide some long-term perspective. Table 4 shows the magnitude of state tax increases and decreases legislated each year since 1963. The decrease in 1985 was only the third over this 23-year period. One reason for the preponderance of net increases is that at least a few states every year raise their excise taxes on such products as gasoline and cigarettes.

Yet these statistics about legislative actions tell only part of the story. Most of the increase in state tax revenue occurs as the result of economic growth and inflation, which together tend to push up

TABLE 4 Tax Increases (in billions of dollars)
Legislated by States, Calendar Years 1963-1985

Year	Increase[a]	Percentage of Tax Revenue[b]
1963	1.0	4.9
1964	0.125	0.5
1965	1.3	5.0
1966	0.5	1.7
1967	2.5	7.8
1968	1.3	3.6
1969	4.0	9.5
1970	0.8	1.7
1971	5.0	9.7
1972	0.875	1.5
1973	0.5	0.7
1974	0.35	0.5
1975	1.6	2.0
1976	0.975	0.9
1977	0.48	0.5
1978	-2.3	-2.0
1979	-2.0	-1.6
1980	0.42	0.3
1981	3.8	2.5
1982	2.9	1.8
1983	8.25	4.8
1984	0.9	0.5
1985	-1.3	0.6

[a]Except for 1984 and 1985, figures on tax increases
were obtained by the Tax Foundation from individuals in
each state. Some minor tax increases may not be
included. Tax increases are reported in annual rates.
[b]This column shows tax increases legislated
during a calendar year as a proportion of total tax
revenue during the fiscal year that ended during that
calendar year.

SOURCE: Tax increases: Information provided by Elsie
Watters, The Tax Foundation. Data for 1984 and 1985 were
collected from state legislative fiscal offices by the
National Conference of State Legislatures. Tax revenue:
Information provided by the U.S. Bureau of the Census.

revenue every year. Table 5 traces the path of state and local tax
revenue as a proportion of personal income annually from 1970–1985.
State tax revenue rose faster than personal income in the early 1970s,
fell sharply in reaction to the tax revolt, and then shot up again in
1984. In 1985, state tax revenue per $100 of personal income was
about 10 percent higher than in 1970. By contrast, local tax revenue

TABLE 5   State/Local Tax Revenue per $100 of Personal Income, Fiscal Years
1970-1985

Fiscal Year	Total[a]	Total State	Total Local	State Tax Revenues		
				Property[b]	General Sales	Personal Income
1985[c]	11.45	7.08	4.37	3.43	2.27	2.11
1984	11.71	7.22	4.49	3.53	2.30	2.16
1983	11.07	6.69	4.38	3.47	2.09	1.94
1982	11.07	6.79	4.28	3.41	2.10	1.91
1981	11.31	6.95	4.36	3.47	2.15	1.90
1980	11.57	7.13	4.45	3.55	2.24	1.93
1979	12.03	7.34	4.69	3.80	2.32	1.92
1978	12.75	7.49	5.26	4.37	2.33	1.93
1977	12.81	7.39	5.42	4.55	2.26	1.86
1976	12.47	7.13	5.34	4.53	2.18	1.71
1975	12.28	6.99	5.29	4.47	2.16	1.64
1974	12.36	7.05	5.31	4.51	2.15	1.62
1973	12.95	7.31	5.63	4.84	2.13	1.68
1972	12.69	7.02	5.67	4.92	2.07	1.52
1971	11.89	6.48	5.40	4.74	1.95	1.28
1970	11.66	6.47	5.19	4.57	1.91	1.24

[a]Revenue for each fiscal year is divided by personal income in the preceding calendar year.
[b]At least 95 percent of property tax revenue is raised by local governments, but some state governments also levy a property tax, usually on specific classes of property.
[c]Some figures for 1985 are preliminary estimates based on tax collections in the year ending June 1985.

SOURCES: Bureau of the Census, Governmental Finances (Washington, D.C.: U.S. Department of Commerce, various years); Bureau of the Census, State Government Finances (Washington, D.C.: U.S. Department of Commerce, various years).

per $100 of personal income has trended irregularly downward after peaking in 1972. The net result is that combined state and local taxes claim about the same proportion of personal income as they did in 1970. The relative increase in state tax revenue, compared with that raised by local governments, reflects a policy of fiscal centralization aimed at relieving the property tax and boosting the state share of the costs of elementary and secondary education. In the 1980s the main factor accounting for large tax increases other than general fiscal problems has been the desire to increase resources for schools. Arkansas, Missouri, South Carolina, Texas, and Vermont are among the states that boosted their sales taxes to support education in this decade.

What do these statistics (along with the history they encapsulate) suggest about the ability of state governments to raise taxes from their present level? As a proportion of personal income, state taxes are about 5 percent below their peak level of 1978. Recent experience suggests that it is politically feasible to boost taxes when a strong case can be made for the necessity of such action—because of either financial difficulties (provided that a period of "belt tightening" has occurred before the tax increase) or the need to improve elementary and secondary schools. If a strong political case is established, taxes can be raised. In most states there is room to increase taxes without raising them to a higher proportion of personal income than they were previously. On the other hand, recent history also suggests that it is not easy to raise taxes for one reason (for example, a short-term fiscal problem) and then to maintain the new rate once the original reason is no longer valid (as may have often occurred in the past). As discussed in the final section of this report, the legacy of the tax revolt and interstate tax competition both constrain the ability of states to raise taxes.

The situation appears different if local taxes are also considered. Local taxes are more than 20 percent below their highest level (in 1972) as a proportion of personal income. Combined state and local taxes are about 11 percent below their 1973 peak. Of course, it would not be easy to boost local taxes significantly, but that is one possible avenue for expanding state and local resources.

This discussion has focused on tax revenue because taxes are the most visible and important source of revenue. Part of the reason taxes have risen so little, particularly at the local level, is the increased reliance of governments on nontax revenue. In 1984, charges and miscellaneous revenue per $100 of personal income were $4.59 per $100 of personal income for state and local governments, a major increase from $3.19 in 1973 (the peak year for taxes). Total own-source state and local revenue in 1984 was slightly above its previous peak of 1978; tax revenue, on the other hand, was 10 percent lower. The increase in nontax revenue has been much greater for miscellaneous revenue (e.g., interest received) than for charges, and it has been considerably larger at the local than at the state level.[2] An

---

[2] Between 1978–1984, local general revenues rose 65.9 percent, with major components rising as follows: federal aid, 7.8 percent; state aid, 64 percent; taxes, 53.5 percent; charges, 104.7 percent; and miscellaneous revenue, 224.1

important part of this rise in nontax revenue, which did not support core services, was for nontraditional activities such as mortgage subsidy programs.

Federal Aid

The third outside influence on state fiscal conditions, in addition to the economy and the tax revolt, has been federal aid policy. Federal aid is commonly divided into two parts: grants for payments to individuals (e.g., as Aid to Families with Dependent Children [AFDC]) and all other grants. The first category has grown considerably over time, relative to the second category. In fiscal year 1986, for example, grants for payments to individuals were 46 percent of total federal aid, a significant increase from their 35 percent share in fiscal year 1980. This shifting composition of federal aid implies that aid to state and local governments that is not simply passed through to individuals has decreased much more than total aid has decreased. According to one estimate, federal aid to state and local governments, excluding grants for payments to individuals, was slashed 23.5 percent between 1980 and 1985 (Rymarowicz and Zimmerman, 1986). Federal aid cutbacks have affected local governments more than states, although the difference is hard to measure precisely. According to NIPA, between 1980 and 1984 federal aid to states rose 15 percent in nominal dollars whereas federal aid to local governments dropped 20 percent. These figures are somewhat misleading, however, because grants for payments to individuals are received primarily by states.

Census Bureau statistics, summarized in Table 6, provide additional detail about the changing shape of federal aid to states. Federal aid for public welfare jumped from 39.9 percent of the total in fiscal year 1980 to 46.5 percent in 1984. The major reason for this increase was rapidly increasing Medicaid costs, which are included in the welfare category. Aid for health and hospital programs also rose at an above-average rate, but aid for education and highways trailed behind. Federal aid outside of these four major categories decreased slightly, primarily because general revenue sharing for states was eliminated during this period. (Note that these statistics are for

---

percent. For states, the corresponding percentages were: total, 74.9 percent; federal aid, 51.7 percent; taxes, 73.8 percent; charges, 89.9 percent; and miscellaneous revenue, 203.3 percent (Bureau of the Census, 1980, 1985a).

TABLE 6 Federal Aid to States, Fiscal Years 1980 and 1984

Category	Percentage of Total Grants		Percentage Change, 1980-1984
	1980	1984	
Public welfare	39.9	46.5	43.5
Education	20.6	18.4	9.5
Highways	14.3	13.6	17.2
Health and hospitals	3.7	4.3	40.5
All other	21.5	17.2	-1.4
Total	100.0	100.0	23.0

SOURCE: Bureau of the Census (1981, 1985b).

state fiscal years; because the NIPA data in the previous paragraph are for calendar years, the total change in aid differs between the two sources.)

State expenditure policy has been relatively restrained. For the 6-year period 1979–1984, there were only 2 years when real general fund spending increased by more than 1.5 percent (Table 7). In 3 years there were decreases in real expenditures. Much spending was deferred during those years, and a significant amount of "catch up" spending occurred as state fiscal conditions improved. General fund spending jumped sharply in fiscal years 1985 and 1986 for this reason.

STATE AID TO LOCAL GOVERNMENTS

Aid to local governments is the largest component of state budgets. The Bureau of the Census reports that, in fiscal year 1984, states provided $106.7 billion of aid to local governments, accounting for more than one-third of total state general spending (see Table 10). This statistic, however, is misleading. On the one hand, it counts federal aid that merely passes through states on its way to local governments (e.g., financing for AFDC in states in which such aid is partially a local function). On the other hand, it gives no credit for some very significant increases in assistance provided by states to local governments over the past quarter-century.

The most important distortion arises from the fact that when a state assumes complete responsibility for a particular program, that program ceases to be a local responsibility; hence, the money spent by the state does not count as local aid. Consider, for example, two states: one of the states fully funds its $1 billion Medicaid program;

the other finances three-quarters of Medicaid and requires counties
to finance the other 25 percent. The first state is credited with no
local aid for Medicaid; the second state will normally be considered
to provide $750 million of aid in this area. This phenomenon is
most important for Medicaid and AFDC, two programs with large
expenditures for which many states have assumed complete financial
responsibility since the 1960s. As states assume these programs, total
state aid to local governments is reduced in Census Bureau statistics.

The composition of aid by function is shown in Table 8. Education is by far the most important function supported by state aid,
accounting for more than $5 out of every $8 of aid in 1984. This
proportion has been relatively stable over the past quarter century,
although state aid for elementary and secondary schools jumped 30
percent between 1983 and 1986. The increase in state aid was relatively larger than the increases in local funding and federal aid,
and state aid accounted for 50.1 percent of the costs of elementary
and secondary schools in 1986, compared with 47.9 percent in 1983
(National Education Association, 1986).

Public welfare spending (including Medicaid) has decreased considerably from 18.9 percent of the total in 1972 to 11.2 percent in
1984. Part of this decrease is due to the creation of the federal

TABLE 7 General Fund Spending Increases
(percentages), Nominal and Real, Fiscal Years
1979-1986

Year	Nominal Increase	Real Increase[a]
1986	9.5	4.3
1985	10.2	4.6
1984	8.0	3.3
1983	-0.7	-6.3
1982	6.4	-1.1
1981	16.3	6.1
1980	10.1	-0.5
1979	10.1	1.5

[a]Real increases were estimated using the implicit
deflator for state and local governments.

SOURCE: National Governors' Association/National
Association of State Budget Officers (1986:4).

TABLE 8 State Aid to Local Governments (percentage of total) by Function for Selected Fiscal Years

Function	1984	1980	1977	1972	1967	1962	1957
Education	63.3	63.7	60.5	57.7	62.2	59.4	56.6
Public welfare	11.2	11.2	14.3	18.9	15.2	16.3	15.3
General local govt. support	10.1	10.4	10.4	10.2	8.3	7.7	9.0
Highways	5.3	5.3	5.9	7.2	9.8	12.2	14.6
Other[a]	10.1	9.4	8.9	6.1	4.5	4.4	4.6
Total	100.0	100.0	100.0	100.0	100.0	100.0	100.0

[a]The largest categories of "other" aid are for health, transit, corrections, housing and community development, and sewerage.

SOURCE: Bureau of the Census (1959, 1968, 1979, 1981, 1985b); Advisory Commission on Intergovernmental Relations (1977:10, 16-17).

Supplemental Security Income program in 1974, which relieved both state and local governments of their welfare costs for the aged, blind, and disabled, but states' assumption of financing for local welfare programs also contributed. General local government support has been steady over the period 1972–1984, with slightly more than a tenth of local aid. Support for highways, however, has decreased sharply as a proportion, mirroring the decline in highway spending as a proportion of total state and local spending. The increase in miscellaneous aid, with its share more than doubling between 1967 and 1984, reflects the fact that states have become involved in some nontraditional areas. Aid for transit programs is a good example of an emerging focus of state aid. States gave local governments $1.5 billion of aid for transit in 1984, an increase of 143 percent since 1979 and 28 percent since 1982.

In view of the functional distribution of aid just described, it is not surprising that school districts and counties receive much more state aid than municipalities. In 1984 their shares of total state aid were 52.4 percent and 22.4 percent, respectively, as shown in Table 9. School districts, of course, provide most of the educational services, although cities and counties are important in the education function in a number of states. Counties traditionally are the major providers of welfare services. Municipalities receive only 16.3 percent of state aid.

Table 10 shows how aid to local governments has grown over

TABLE 9 State Aid to Local Governments (percentage of total) by Recipient Government, Selected Fiscal Years

Recipient	1984	1980	1977	1967	1957
School districts	52.4	51.8	47.6	50.2	48.1
Counties	22.4	22.2	22.6	24.9	27.6
Municipalities	16.3	15.2	19.3	21.3	20.2
Townships[a]	1.1	1.3	1.2	3.1	3.7
Special Districts	1.2	1.2	1.1	0.5	0.3
Combined and unallocable	6.6	8.5	8.2	0.0	0.0

[a]Includes New England "towns."

SOURCE: Bureau of the Census (1959, 1968, 1979, 1981, 1985b); Advisory Commission on Intergovernmental Relations (1977:10, 16-17).

TABLE 10 State Aid to Local Governments, Per Capita and as Proportion of Total State Spending, Selected Fiscal Years

State-Local Aid	1984	1980	1977	1972	1967	1962	1957
Total (billions of dollars)	106.65	82.76	61.07	36.76	19.06	10.91	7.44
Per capita (dollars)	452.75	365.54	278.70	176.07	96.43	58.92	43.64
Per capita (1972 dollars)	185.44	200.19	194.42	176.07	137.17	99.81	84.90
As percentage of total state spending	34.4	36.3	36.8	37.2	35.7	34.9	35.3

SOURCE: Bureau of the Census (1979:9-10, 1981:52, 1985b).

time. It was nearly 10 times as great in 1984 as it had been in 1962. Although the absolute amount of aid has grown impressively and continues to increase in per capita terms, per capita aid failed to keep up with inflation between 1980–1984, dropping about 6 percent over that 4-year period. Aid has also been remarkably constant as a proportion of total state spending, fluctuating between 34 percent and 37 percent since 1957.

OUTLOOK FOR STATE FISCAL CONDITIONS

The outlook for state finances over the next decade depends on the course of the economy, exogenous influences on tax policy (tax revolt sentiment and interstate tax competition), and trends in federal aid. Taking all of these factors into account, the prospects are not particularly rosy.[3]

The course of the economy certainly is the most important single factor affecting the outlook for state finances—both in the aggregate and for particular states. Currently, the farm and energy-producing states are the most economically depressed, and their fiscal conditions are also among the worst. As for the national economy, growth has not been particularly strong in this decade. In view of the problems arising from the federal budget and international trade deficits and Third World debt, the potential for serious dislocations appears significant.

The legacy of the tax revolt continues to restrict potential state revenues. As one review of the experience in California concluded, the tax revolt "is dormant, not dead" (Citrin and Green, 1985). Two Michigan senators were recalled in 1983 after they had voted for an income tax increase, and initiatives to repeal tax increases were defeated in Ohio in 1983 and Michigan in 1984 only after hard-fought campaigns. The widespread elimination in 1984 and 1985 of income tax (and some sales tax) increases that had been passed in 1982 and 1983 reflected the feeling of public officials that citizens did not want tax rates increased permanently.

The tax revolt also lives on in legislation and some state constitutions. Fourteen of the 40 states with personal income taxes have indexed them, at least partially. These provisions permanently reduce the built-in growth rate of this major source of revenue. Seventeen states have spending or revenue limits that place a lid on the growth

---

[3]This prognosis is somewhat at variance with the conclusions of a 1985 Treasury Department study based on a simple model of the state and local sector. That study argued that if state and local governments maintained their current tax systems and service levels and if the Reagan administration's federal aid projections and economic forecasts were accurate, large surpluses would develop in aggregate state and local budgets. State and local governments would not allow this to occur, however, and would therefore reduce tax levels, increase services, or enact some combination of these options (U.S. Department of the Treasury, 1985).

The Treasury study also showed that if economic performance is much poorer than predicted by the administration and most leading forecasters, the fiscal situation of state and local governments would be much worse. The study is also open to question on several technical grounds, such as its assumptions about the responsiveness of state and local tax revenue to economic growth (an issue on which most estimates are outdated) and the expenditures necessary to maintain current service levels.

of state fiscal activity, usually tying it to the rate of increase of personal income or to the sum of the inflation and population growth rates (Gold, 1984). Enacted between 1977 and 1982, nearly all of these limits have not been restrictive in their initial years because growth in tax revenue was relatively sluggish, in part because of tax cuts. The limits are likely to become more significant in the future, however. Michigan and California are very close to their limits, and some officials have concluded that they have exceeded them. Virtually none of these limitation measures has provisions that will allow some liberalizing of them if the state has to assume responsibilities cast off by the federal government.

Several other factors add to the problems facing state tax systems. Although difficult to measure, interstate tax competition appears to have intensified, manifesting itself in the proliferation of business tax incentives and in pressure for states with high personal income tax rates to lower them. Because virtually all states engage in this competition, each state's actions tend to be canceled out by the behavior of other states; the result is merely reduced state and local tax revenue, with little if any economic advantage for the states. Reductions of maximum income tax rates also reduce the built-in responsiveness of tax revenue to economic growth. In addition, tax bases are being eroded by economic trends: retirement income is often partially exempt from the income tax, and it is growing much faster than taxable income. Likewise, most services are exempt from the sales tax, and they are claiming a growing share of consumer expenditures. These developments dampen the growth of state tax revenue.

Federal tax reform is likely to exacerbate interstate tax competition because lower federal marginal tax rates imply that differentials in state and local tax rates will be more significant. Currently, "high" federal tax rates "shield" state and local governments to some extent with above-average tax rates because each dollar paid to a state or locality substantially reduces federal tax liability. After federal tax reform, however, the "federal offset" will be considerably smaller. Other effects of federal tax reform tend to offset each other. States with an income tax will benefit from a broader tax base to the extent that they conform to the federal definition of taxable income, but lower marginal rates will increase the cost of borrowing for state and local governments and perhaps result in a decrease in charitable contributions, which could increase the demand for state and local services that substitute for charitable activity.

Reductions in federal aid are a final negative factor for state finances. In view of the pressure to reduce the federal budget deficit, the major question appears to be the rate at which real federal aid decreases—not whether it will continue to fall. Excluding grants for payments to individuals, the Reagan administration projects a real decrease of 37 percent in aid to state and local governments between 1985 and 1991 (Office of Management and Budget, 1986). Future federal aid cuts will probably have greater fiscal effects on the states than past cuts have had because states will be under much greater pressure to replace lost federal revenue, given the nature of the programs affected. Reductions in such areas as transit and wastewater treatment will generally be too significant for states to ignore.

As a result of these forces—economic trends, constraints on tax policy, and federal aid cuts—many states will probably experience some degree of fiscal stress in the next decade. Such stress implies that it will not be easy for states to increase their urban aid by a large amount, a statement that seems particularly valid because urban aid will face stiff competition from other claimants on state budgets, especially school, infrastructure, and social service programs. (Of course, to some extent, each of these "rivals" has an important urban aspect itself.)

One of the most potent political forces in most state capitals is the education lobby—and appropriately so because education is widely viewed as the most important service funded by states and localities. The education lobby has become even more powerful since 1983 because of the educational reform movement that has sprung from dissatisfaction with the products of the nation's schools. Improving the educational system could be very expensive. For example, to implement fully the recent proposals of the Task Force on Teaching as a Profession for the Carnegie Forum on Education and the Economy would cost about $48 billion per year. Even if educational reform claims only a fraction of this amount, it would draw scarce state dollars from possible urban initiatives.

If fiscal stress develops as the preceding paragraphs suggest it may, how will state governments respond? One part of their response should be a thorough reexamination of existing programs to improve their efficiency and eliminate those of low priority; states should also consider new funding mechanisms (which in practice will often result in increased privatization). Furthermore, relations between state and local governments will probably change in important ways. States will recognize the need to reassess their existing policies toward local governments, and many restrictions currently in force will be relaxed, including restrictions on available taxes and some mandates. States will certainly replace some of the federal aid lost by local governments, but the mechanisms they use may not follow precisely the format used in federal programs. Much lost federal aid also will not be replaced by states.

The same forces causing fiscal stress at the state level during the next decade will tend to produce even greater stress for many urban governments. States will not be blind to this development, but their ability to respond with increased aid will be constrained by the restrictions on their fiscal capacity discussed in this report.

REFERENCES

Advisory Commission on Intergovernmental Relations
    1977   *The States and Intergovernmental Aids.* Report A-59. Washington, D.C.: Advisory Commission on Intergovernmental Relations.
Bureau of the Census
    1959   *Census of Goverments: 1957.* Vol. 4, No. 2. *State Payments to Local Governments.* Washington, D.C.: U.S. Department of Commerce.
    1968   *Census of Goverments: 1967.* Vol. 6, No. 4. *State Payments to Local Governments.* Washington, D.C.: U.S. Department of Commerce.
    1979   *Census of Goverments: 1977.* Vol. 6, No. 3. *State Payments to Local Governments.* Washington, D.C.: U.S. Department of Commerce.
    1980   *Governmental Finances in 1977-78.* Series GF80, No. 5. Washington, D.C.: U.S. Department of Commerce.
    1981   *State Government Finances in 1980.* Series GF80, No. 3. Washington, D.C.: U.S. Department of Commerce.
    1985a *Government Finances in 1983-84.* Series GF80, No. 5. Washington, D.C.: U.S. Department of Commerce.
    1985b *State Government Finances in 1984.* Series GF80, No. 3. Washington, D.C.: U.S. Department of Commerce.
Citrin, J., and D. P. Green
    1985   Policy and opinion in California after Proposition 13. *National Tax Journal* 38:15-35.
Gold, Steven D.
    1983   Recent developments in state finances. *National Tax Journal* 36:1-29.
    1984   State tax increases of 1983: Prelude to another tax revolt? *National Tax Journal* 37:9-22.
    1986a Developments in State Finances, 1983 to 1986. *Public Budgeting and Finance* 7(Spring 1987):5-23.
    1986b State Government Fund Balances, Financial Assets, and Measures of Budget Surplus. In Federal-State-Local Fiscal Relations: Technical Papers. Office of State and Local Finance. Washington, D.C.: U.S. Department of the Treasury.

Gold, Steven D., and Karen M. Benker
    1983   *State Budget Actions in 1983.* Denver, Colo.: National Conference of State Legislatures.

Gold, Steven D., Corina L. Eckl, and Max R. Price
    1985   *State Budget Actions in 1985.* Denver, Colo.: National Conference of State Legislatures.

Levin, David, and Donald Peters
    1986   Receipts and expenditures of state and local governments: Revised and updated estimates, 1959–84. *Survey of Current Business* 66(May):26–29.

National Education Association
    1986   *Estimates of School Statistics: 1985–86.* Washington, D.C.: National Education Association.

National Governors' Association/National Association of State Budget Officers
    1978   *Understanding the Fiscal Condition of the States.* Washington, D.C.: National Governors' Association/National Association of State Budget Officers.
    1986   *Fiscal Survey of the States: 1986.* Washington, D.C.: National Governors' Association/National Association of State Budget Officers.

Office of Management and Budget
    1986   *Budget of the United States Government, 1987—Historical Tables.* Washington, D.C.: U.S. Government Printing Office.

Rymarowicz, L., and D. Zimmerman
    1986   *The Effect of Federal Tax and Budget Policies in the 1980s on the State–Local Sector.* Washington, D.C.: Congressional Research Service.

U.S. Department of the Treasury
    1985   *Federal–State–Local Fiscal Relations: Report to the President and the Congress.* Office of State and Local Finance. Washington, D.C.: U.S. Department of the Treasury.

Urban Infrastructure:
Problems and Solutions

RICHARD R. MUDGE and KENNETH I. RUBIN

WHAT IS INFRASTRUCTURE, AND
WHY IS IT IMPORTANT?

Users of inadequate public works facilities bear significant costs. Every time a bridge is closed to traffic or subjected to weight restrictions because of deterioration, users' time and money are lost. For example, operating costs for small automobiles are almost one-third higher on poor roads than on well-maintained roads (Congressional Budget Office, 1983). In the worst cases, there may also be substantially increased safety risks.

The deterioration of existing facilities and their insufficient capacity to accommodate future growth will eventually constrain economic development. The nation's urban transportation network, water supply, and wastewater treatment facilities all provide vital services both for industries and individuals; where capacity is inadequate, growth will be stunted. Similarly, a community with badly deteriorated roads, bridges, or other transportation facilities is in a weak position to attract new businesses. Although difficult to quantify, the costs of lost opportunities are no less real. For example,

This paper is based in part on a series of reports on public works infrastructure prepared by Apogee Research for the National Council on Public Works Improvement.

according to a 1983 Transportation Systems Center report, halting deterioration (but not eliminating all deficiencies) in the nation's highway network would improve economic growth for the economy as a whole: national income would be 3.2 percent higher by 1995, employment would be 2.2 percent higher, and inflation would be 8 percent lower than if road conditions had continued to deteriorate as in the late 1970s (Transportation Systems Center, 1983).

Why Is It Infrastructure?

Infrastructure projects are not ends in themselves. Rather, their importance to the economy and to society as a whole derives from the services they offer: the opportunity to improve productivity or reduce costs. Although most easily thought of in a physical form—a bridge, a wastewater treatment plant, a subway train—the real output of infrastructure is service: the movement of people and goods, the provision of adequate clean water, and so forth (Apogee Research, 1986b).

Infrastructure generates additional investment or economic activity through a multiplier effect on private firms or other public agencies. This process occurs in several ways:

• by making better use of underutilized resources that previously were very costly or difficult to obtain;
• by enabling more efficient trade-offs among factors of production (for example, reduced transport costs versus a location closer to markets);
• by reducing costs and thus increasing economic efficiencies; and
• by expanding markets as improved efficiency results in more effective competition with other countries or regions.

In other words, infrastructure encompasses those activities without which there would be only limited economic activity. In particular, most public works infrastructure projects share several characteristics: (1) high fixed costs (they are capital intensive); (2) a long economic life; (3) the potential to dominate local markets; and (4) interaction with other infrastructure projects.

Because of their long time horizons and high construction costs, major infrastructure investments usually involve higher risks than the more typical industrial investment project. As a result, some public sector involvement is often required. Also, most infrastructure projects are part of a larger system—for example, a national road network or a regional water supply system. The coordination required for projects of this type means that some public involvement is needed even if the projects are financed privately. Also, because of the high costs of market entry, many infrastructure projects have near monopoly power in their local markets. As a result, economic and safety regulations are often required.

Facilities with these general characteristics—strong links to economic development, high fixed costs, long economic life, interaction with other parts of a system, and strong traditional public sector involvement—may be termed public works infrastructure. When applied to urban areas, this definition usually includes the following "modes": highways, public transit, wastewater treatment, water supply, solid waste, and airports.[1]

Despite these special characteristics, infrastructure has much in common with other sectors of the economy, particularly those that involve capital investments. By definition, all investments require deferring current consumption to achieve greater consumption in the future. As a result, infrastructure must compete for financial and human resources with other public and private activities. In this sense, even though they may generate important public benefits, proposed infrastructure projects require the same careful analysis as should be applied to other investment projects.

Why Is It Public?

Projects that can be characterized as infrastructure may be provided either by the private or the public sectors. Indeed, the division of responsibility between public and private bodies varies considerably by infrastructure mode, by country, and by historical period. For example, freight railroads are now almost completely private even though in the nineteenth century they received large public contributions. Also, telecommunications is a private sector responsibility in the United States, but in most other countries it is publicly owned.

A number of straightforward rationales help determine the degree of public sector involvement in providing infrastructure services.

---

[1] Except for the lack of strong current public involvement, such areas as communications and electric utilities would fit the public works infrastructure characteristics set out in the text. Other observers might cite a broader list: government buildings, housing, prisons, hospitals, education, and so forth.

The applicability of each rationale may change according to the location of infrastructure and its developmental stage. These rationales include:

reasons public involve

- *The public good nature of infrastructure.* The benefits of certain public activities are received by society as a whole. In these cases, individuals cannot be assessed the costs of the activities (this is sometimes called the "nonappropriability" problem). National defense provides the classic example of a public good.[2]

- *Externalities.* The full impact of some actions may not be borne directly by the individual or group responsible for the action. Because the benefits or costs are received or borne by others, there are incentives to under- or overinvest.[3]

- *Infant industries.* The potential rewards from developing a new industry may be so uncertain or removed in time that outside help is needed to share development risks.[4] The major economic effect of public aid for infant industries is to bring forward the time when society benefits from a mature industry—not to determine the industry's ultimate success or failure. The timing of such support is the key to its effectiveness and is not always obvious. Investments may be premature, as with Dulles Airport in suburban Washington, D.C.

- *Regional development.* Underutilized resources can justify public investment as a means to greater growth. In addition, infrastructure spending and the growth such projects may generate are sometimes used as mechanisms to redistribute income.[5] Further,

---

[2] Defense is also often closely linked with infrastructure development. Some examples include the development of ports and inland waterways by the Army Corps of Engineers in the last century, the construction of the interstate highway system over the past 30 years, and certain current port proposals.

[3] Examples of externalities include dirty water that affects downstream communities and extra peak-hour travel that increases the delay for all other travelers. Solutions to these problems usually involve regulatory or financial action by another level of government.

[4] The clearest examples concern interurban infrastructure; public support for railroads and canals in the nineteenth century and federal promotion of the aviation industry through mail contracts and the air traffic control system are two such instances.

[5] Using infrastructure to redistribute income ignores the primary consideration that applies to decisions on infrastructure projects: how productive is the investment relative to the benefits from greater productivity? The Appalachian Regional Commission is a good example. Despite substantial expenditures to repair and revitalize the old and decayed infrastructure of Appalachia, there is no indication that the area developed more rapidly than it would have without

regional competition for new development is a prime motivator for locally sponsored infrastructure projects.

Infrastructure's Role in Fostering Economic Growth and Employment

Functional View of Infrastructure

Infrastructure problems may be considered in two different contexts: (1) the physical (removing existing deficiencies, meeting recurring problems, or adding capacity for expansion), and (2) the functional (considering population-based needs versus those required to produce goods and services).

The physical view is the traditional approach to defining problems and framing solutions. The functional or economic view of infrastructure has two components: one based on population and the other on production. The first or core component of infrastructure demand depends on individual needs that, in turn, are a function of personal tastes, income levels, and location. Examples might include local travel needs such as trips for work, shopping, and recreation. These components change relatively slowly and depend on social and population makeup: for example, age distribution, family structure, disposable income, and residential location. The second component is oriented toward production; that is, what is needed to produce goods and services. Infrastructure needs under this portion change as the economic base shifts among agriculture, manufacturing, services, government, and foreign trade.

The functional view serves three purposes: (1) as an aid to understanding the role of public works infrastructure in fostering economic growth; (2) as one explanation for the development of different public and private roles; and (3) as a possible explanation for recent trends in infrastructure spending. These latter two points are discussed in more detail in the next sections.

---

the expenditures. The most successful infrastructure investments were not those linked to income redistribution but those designed to make resources more competitive and to lower costs. The Tennessee Valley Authority is a prime example of this kind of investment.

Caveats About Economic Growth

Although there is an obvious link between infrastructure in general and economic growth, this link generally must be taken on faith. There have been few attempts to measure the magnitude of the effect and how this link functions, except in the case of developing countries and for certain individual projects.

As with every economic sector, investing in projects with relatively low rates of return diverts resources from other potentially more productive economic investments. Investments of this kind may be made because of limited information on alternatives or because of financial incentives that distort investment decisions (e.g., overly generous matching grants); however, whatever the reason, if such a policy is pursued, overall economic growth will be smaller than would otherwise occur. This problem is not unique to the infrastructure sector but can also occur in housing, steel, defense, and other industries.

The effect of inefficient investment decisions can be seen in an economic simulation of the costs of removing all highway deficiencies that was carried out by the Transportation Systems Center (1983). This study found that the costs exceeded the expected economic gains from better roads. Thus, even if a particular infrastructure program stimulates economic growth, the question that must be asked is whether there are other investment packages (public or private) that might bring about even higher rates of social and economic return.

DIFFERENT PUBLIC ROLES

The relative incidence of benefits and costs is the key link in determining the proper infrastructure role for the public and private sectors and for the various levels of government. There are strong equity and efficiency arguments that those sectors receiving great benefits from a particular infrastructure mode should bear an equally large share of the financing responsibility. When an imbalance exists between benefits received and financial responsibility, there are strong incentives either to over- or underinvest. (For example, it is doubtful whether New York City would have pursued the development of the Westway highway project if the federal government had not been paying 90 percent of the costs.)

Public Versus Private

Combining the physical and functional definitions of infrastructure helps provide a framework for considering what the public and private infrastructure roles should be and how they have evolved in the United States. Table 1 summarizes the interaction between these two views.

Historically, the private sector in this country has been most actively involved in areas that increase capacity for production (see the lower right corner of Table 1). These are also areas in which the beneficiaries have been able to pay for the benefits received, in part because they faced growing markets. Examples of this phenomenon vary by historical period, however. For instance, in the early nineteenth century, canals were privately owned in large part because they were seen as an efficient way to serve the nation's growing industrial capacity. Similarly, this combination of growth and key economic ties explains why the communication portions of infrastructure—telephone, telegraph, and electronic communications—have been dominated by private firms from their inception.

Once a particular infrastructure mode receives public subsidies, it becomes more difficult for that mode to revert to an organization

TABLE 1 Comparison of Functional and Physical Views of Infrastructure

Physical Problems	Functional (Economic) Roles	
	Core or Population Based	Economic or Production Based
Maintain system	Intraurban	Interurban "older" systems (canals, highways)
	Public sector dominates	Public sector dominates
Increase capacity	Intraurban	Interurban
	Sunbelt	Communications, airlines
	Public sector dominates	Greater chance of profits Strong private role

SOURCE: Apogee Research (1986b).

having a strong private sector role. The larger the subsidies and the [*handwritten: role subsidies*] longer they are received, the more difficult this reversal becomes; witness the current efforts to restore a private role in urban mass transit.

The line between public and private involvement is sometimes difficult to draw. Pennsylvania now permits the establishment of independent transportation districts that are funded in part by assessments on local developers. For example, Upper Merion (near Philadelphia) is financing some $66 million in highway improvements, with one-half the funds from assessments on new development—the rate is $933 for each peak-hour auto trip generated, or one-half the estimated capital costs of $1,866 for each new peak-hour auto trip.[6] [*handwritten: private developers pay cost new roads*] Texas has a program whereby developers help defray the costs of new roads by contributing land for rights-of-way, thus speeding construction. Over the past 2 years, some $400 million of donations have been received under this program. As a result, there appears to have been a shift in priorities in state highway projects.

Many private infrastructure projects involve indirect public financial support. For example, tax-exempt industrial development bonds provide interest rates below those available to other corporate borrowers. As with other private capital investments, rapid depreciation schedules and investment tax credits are available as well, although this may change with the new tax bill.

Private involvement in infrastructure projects depends on the level of risk or uncertainty. Risk increases according to the size of the investment required and the degree of market uncertainty. Even massive projects can be financed privately if market uncertainty is low enough; the Trans Alaska and Trans Canada pipelines were privately financed and built, based on long-term contracts and take-or-pay agreements. At the other extreme, if market uncertainty is high because there are no commitments from end users, some form of public support or guarantee may be required for even modest projects (public transit is an example) (TELESIS, 1986).

---

[6] In some cases, developers find it less expensive to make their contribution in kind by contracting for the improvement work directly. Partly because of this, Upper Merion has volunteered to double its contribution for state–local highway projects to 50 percent if the state department of transportation will provide additional funds. For a discussion of other new approaches to financing urban infrastructure, see National League of Cities (1987).

State and Local Versus Federal

Current Roles

The existing division of responsibility among local, state, and federal governments derives largely from past history and political forces and only partly from a logical examination of the distribution of benefits and of financial and operational capabilities.

Beyond those areas of clear, overriding national interest—interstate highways, the network of inland waterways and canals, and the air traffic control system[7]—federal involvement depends on the importance of externalities and the strength of arguments to relieve local fiscal pressures.[8] For example, some federal role is called for in water and air pollution, a recognition of which has resulted in the Environmental Protection Agency (EPA) construction grants program and federal regulations. On the other hand, the major rationale for the federal transit program is a desire to help solve local fiscal problems, and most federal aid for urban water supply systems is targeted at fiscally stressed areas.

Yet any attempt to separate federal from other responsibilities does not mean that the condition of "local" infrastructure is not important to general economic growth. Because these areas are vital to regional growth as well, however, adequate incentives for local support should already exist.

Development Stages

The current roles of each level of government vary considerably according to the stage of the infrastructure development process. Five separate but related stages can be identified: (1) nomination, or the identification of candidate projects, including major new capital investments as well as routine replacements and maintenance options; (2) evaluation, in which potential projects are analyzed and those to receive funds are selected (this process can range from highly technical and formal to ad hoc procedures); (3) finance; (4) construction; and (5) operation.

---

[7]In fact, the federal government currently plans, finances, and operates both the inland wateray and air traffic control systems and provides 90 percent grants to construct interstate highways.

[8]Other traditional arguments for public roles are limited. Today, there are no new regions of underutilized resources, and infant industry arguments appear to be restricted largely to special cases such as space transport.

TABLE 2 Degree of Federal Involvement (percentage) by State in the Development of Public Works

Mode	Nominate[a]	Evaluate	Finance	Construct	Operate
Highways					
Interstate	50	0	91	0	0
Other federal	0	0	50	0	0
State-local	0	0	10	0	0
Transit	20	40	70	0	0
Airports					
Large	0	20	20	0	0
Small	0	0	50	0	0
Wastewater	0	0	55	0	0
Water supply	0	0	15	0	0
Solid waste	0	0	0	0	0

NOTE: These percentages are overall averages; rankings for particular facilities will vary considerably.

[a]Federal engineering standards often play a key role in identifying and evaluating projects. In addition, governmental economic, environmental, and safety regulations can influence any stage.

SOURCE: Based on data from the Office of Management and Budget (1986) and the Bureau of the Census (1986).

These stages are not of equal importance. Missed opportunities in the nomination and evaluation stages are costly to correct. Further, the steps are neither independent nor always sequential. Most importantly, the terms and availability of financing has a major effect on the number and types of projects that agencies nominate, on the rigor with which they are evaluated, and on the trade-offs made between capital-intensive and operating proposals.

For example, now that it is clear that a significant local contribution (50 percent or more for deep-draft ports) will be required for local port development, projects are being reevaluated. By changing its channel design, Baltimore will save about $100 million or one-third of the original cost projection. Similarly, Norfolk has cut the cost of its deep-draft development in half.

Table 2 summarizes how the current federal role varies across the five development stages and each of the major urban public works infrastructure "modes." The federal government plays a significant role in financing almost every area of infrastructure except solid waste and water supply. State and local governments dominate the nomination and evaluation stages of the process, including roughly 80 percent of the areas in which federal funds predominate. Except for a small (14 percent) proportion of mass transit, virtually all operating and maintenance funds for urban infrastructure are provided by state and local governments.

While considerable attention is being given to encouraging a greater private sector effort in financing public works infrastructure, the present level of private involvement is quite limited. Currently, this effort is most significant in water supply projects, for which private firms supply about 20 percent of total funding (Congressional Budget Office, 1987). Also, private firms make significant investments in port development facilities. Private involvement in other public infrastructure sectors, such as wastewater treatment, airports, and transit, is limited to 2 or 3 percent of spending. Of course, with the exception of mass transit, corporations and individuals provide most transportation rolling stock—such as buses, trains, cars, and airplanes.

Regulations

Federal or state regulations form an important "overlay" to this "normal" five-stage development process, even when no funding is involved. Environmental rules provide the most important examples. Federal clean water and clean air rules have forced localities to modify their investment plans quite significantly.

The costs of infrastructure projects are also influenced by federal labor rules. By setting minimum wage levels, the Davis-Bacon law increased the costs of virtually all construction projects that use federal monies. Similarly, because of the Urban Mass Transportation Administration's Section 13c rules, many transit operators do not use certain types of cost-effective service in order to avoid conflicts with labor unions.

The Development of Current Public Roles

Historical Background

There is a long history of federal financial aid to the states beginning with the federal repayment of state debts from the Revolutionary War. This early financial takeover in particular made it feasible for the states to play a more active role in supporting public works (Break, 1981).

Between 1820–1840 an estimated 11 percent of the federal budget was devoted to "internal improvements" of various kinds (Broude, 1959). This fraction is more than twice the level reached 50 years later and substantially exceeds the ratio today. By 1860 federal or state governments had provided 73 percent of the $190 million invested in canals and 24 percent of the more than $1 billion invested in railroads: a total of $413 million in public spending (U.S. Department of Commerce, 1980).[9] Much of this spending was provided by local governments to help foster local economic growth. In some cases, direct public investments were even made in the stock of private corporations (Tarr, 1984). The success of these private firms, in conjunction with the economic depression of 1839–1845, encouraged a laissez-faire view of the economy and resulted in reduced state and local spending on public works.

In the early 1900s, infrastructure programs began to proliferate (Congressional Budget Office, 1985c). The federal highway program began in 1916, the federal air traffic control system was instituted in the 1920s, grants for rural water supply systems began in the 1930s, and airport grants were first made in the 1940s. Federal grants for wastewater treatment and mass transit did not start until the 1960s, and the first federal aid for intercity transit rail passenger service was given in the 1970s.

The federal highway program represented an important landmark that, nearly 70 years later, still forms the basic model for most infrastructure programs: the federal government enters into a partnership with the states or local governments in which the states select, build, and operate projects for which the federal government provides funding in the form of matching grants. This partnership is typical of current federal programs for highways, mass transit, wastewater treatment, water supply, and airports.[10]

Highways

Although a federal role in highway construction dates back to the early days of the republic, the modern highway program had its beginnings in the Federal Aid Road Act of 1916 (Congressional

---

[9] This sum is in current dollars. Converting to 1984 dollars would increase it by perhaps 10 to 20 times.

[10] Water resources programs and intercity rail passenger services, however, are provided directly by the federal government.

Budget Office, 1978). This act established many of the basic provisions of federal highway policy that are still in effect today. The most important of these provisions is the federal–state partnership in which states retain ownership of the roads and the responsibility for their construction and maintenance and the federal government provides financial aid (in the form of matching grants) to the states for construction. These grants are apportioned according to formulas based on such factors as area, population, and road mileage.

This historic division of effort—federal support of construction and state and local responsibility for repair and maintenance—remained in effect until the late 1960s when the deteriorating condition of existing roads led to a gradual change in federal regulations to permit the use of federal funds for major repairs. Thus, the mid-1970s saw the first federal program dedicated to repairs on the interstate highway system and the creation of a federally funded program to repair bridges. Since then, an increasing share of federal spending for highways—now about 70 percent—has been for reconstruction and major repairs.

Water Supply

In 1926 Congress authorized a new program of water supply loans and grants to promote the growth of rural areas. Administered by the Farmers Home Administration, this program remains the major source of federal aid dedicated to water supply systems. Three more recent federal programs (administered by the Economic Development Administration, the Appalachian Regional Commission, and the Department of Housing and Urban Development) provide development grants that can be used to finance the construction of water supply systems, among other types of projects. In addition, although they do not build single-purpose water supply projects, both the U.S. Army Corps of Engineers and the Bureau of Reclamation have been authorized since 1958 to add extra storage capacity for public water supplies to ongoing water resources development projects.

Wastewater Treatment

Federal support for the construction of municipal wastewater treatment facilities now totals $3 billion a year. The federal involvement began in 1957 under the U.S. Public Health Service with about $40 million a year in federal grants that covered up to 30 percent of local construction costs. The program was transferred to the Department of the Interior in 1966 and then to the EPA in 1970. In the 1960s, a relatively small federal program ($100 million–$200 million a year) helped localities with grants for up to 50 percent of the cost of building treatment facilities. As public awareness and concern over water pollution escalated, federal spending for wastewater treatment rose dramatically.

The rationale for federal involvement in local wastewater treatment derives from the public aspect of clean water. A community that bears the responsibility and cost for resolving its immediate water quality problems also extends the benefits of its clean water to downstream communities that do not pay for it. Left to themselves, communities tend to spend less than the overall benefits would merit. But untreated or improperly treated wastewater also imposes costs on the downstream communities toward which it flows. Federal intervention, it was argued, would therefore be necessary to ensure the proper level of investment from the national point of view. This intervention took the form of regulations as well as financial aid (National Council on Public Works Improvement, 1987b).

The 1972 amendments to the Federal Water Pollution Control Act, now called the Clean Water Act, required that all publicly owned wastewater facilities meet minimum standards of secondary wastewater treatment in order to render navigable waters "fishable and swimmable" by 1983. To meet this goal, communities generally had to build new facilities. Federal assistance was provided to relieve the resulting financial burden on localities. The 1972 legislation authorized $18 billion for the first 3 years of construction grants and increased the federal share of costs from 50 percent to 75 percent.

Mass Transit

Early in this century, mass transit was dominated by private firms, among whose ranks were often found subsidiaries of firms in related businesses, such as land developers and electric power companies. With the proliferation of private automobiles following World War II, urban populations and employment—once concentrated in central cities—became more dispersed. As a result, transit ridership declined by about 65 percent between 1945–1965, and many privately owned transit companies failed. By the early 1960s the physical deterioration resulting from deferred maintenance had reached crisis proportions in most remaining private systems (Hilton, 1974). This crisis led to new state and federal programs for capital and operating aid. Indeed, during the 1970s federal aid to local transit was the fastest growing federal infrastructure program.

Aviation

In 1946 Congress, believing that an adequate system of airports was a matter of national concern both for defense reasons and because of the rapid growth expected for civilian aviation, authorized a program of federal grants to help finance the construction of airports. Today, these grants account for a modest fraction (less than 20 percent) of capital costs for large airports but are quite significant for air fields that cater to general aviation. User taxes finance federal capital spending on airports and air traffic control, as well as a portion of Federal Aviation Administration operating expenditures (National Council on Public Works Improvement, 1987a).

INFRASTRUCTURE PROBLEMS

The infrastructure problem is usually summarized simply: Are we spending enough? Although other ways of stating the problem can lead to more meaningful sets of policy options, a brief review of recent public spending trends for urban public works infrastructure provides a useful background.[11]

[handwritten margin note: ? Spending enough]

Recent Financial Trends

Conventional wisdom holds that public spending on infrastructure has declined steadily in recent decades, particularly when measured as a fraction of the gross national product (GNP) (Peterson, 1984). One policy proposal often drawn from this view is that infrastructure spending should simply be returned to its historical share of GNP. The premise behind this solution—a recent decline in public spending for public works infrastructure—is not entirely incorrect. A more complete, although still somewhat contradictory, picture emerges when we examine total spending for infrastructure,

---

[11]The following section uses a definition of public works infrastructure consistent with that established by the National Council on Public Works Improvement. It includes highways, transit, airports, water supply, wastewater treatment, and solid waste facilities. Water resources programs have been excluded because they are less oriented toward urban areas.

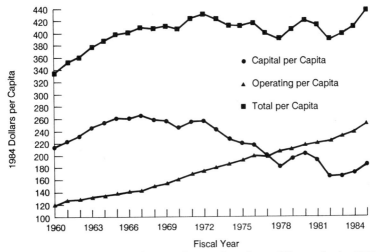

FIGURE 1 Total capital and operating outlays for public works in 1984 dollars per capita. SOURCE (Figures 1–9): Apogee Research's consolidated public works finance data base, which is based on data from the Office of Management and Budget (1986), Bureau of the Census (1986 and prior years), and published and unpublished data from the Farmer's Home Administration, Economic Development Administration, Appalachian Regional Commission, U.S. Department of Housing and Urban Development, Urban Mass Transportation Administration, Federal Highway Administration, U.S. Environmental Protection Agency, U.S. Army Corps of Engineers, and Bureau of Reclamation.

as well as its two major components: capital and operations (Apogee Research, 1986d).

Total public spending on infrastructure has grown steadily over the past 25 years, increasing by more than 50 percent even when measured in constant dollars. This rate of increase has kept pace with the nation's population, remaining at a remarkably constant $400 per capita (in 1984 dollars) since 1960 (Figure 1). Total spending has declined as a fraction of GNP, however, dropping from 3.6 percent in 1960 to 2.6 percent in 1984 (Figure 2). One possible explanation for these contradictory trends—steady spending relative to population growth but declining spending compared with the size of the economy—may be offered by the "functional" view of infrastructure introduced earlier in this paper.

The steady pace of overall spending just described camouflages two contradictory trends. Although funds devoted to capital investment have not kept pace with increases either in economic activity or population, public spending to maintain and operate the nation's

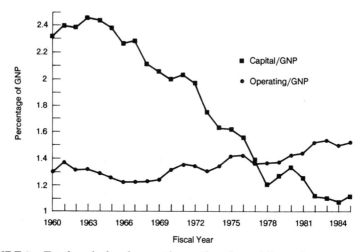

FIGURE 2   Total capital and operating outlays for public works as a percentage of the gross national product (GNP). SOURCE: See Figure 1.

infrastructure has grown in line with the growth of the economy as a whole and has increased almost twice as fast as the growth in population (see Figures 1 and 2). In 1960 capital outlays by all levels of government for public works infrastructure equaled about 2.3 percent of GNP versus about 1.1 percent in 1984. Expenditures for maintaining and operating public works infrastructure remained at roughly the same 1.4 percent of GNP over this period. In terms of population, capital investment in infrastructure fell from $220 per capita in 1960 to $170 per capita in 1984; spending for operations and maintenance, on the other hand, was increasing from $120 per capita to $240.[12]

Spending by Purpose

The internal composition of total government spending for public works shifted over the period 1960–1984 (Table 3). In 1960, for example, spending was dominated by outlays for highways (60 percent) with spending on water supply (11 percent) a distant second. Airports and wastewater treatment plants accounted for only 4 percent and 7 percent, respectively, of total government outlays for public

---

[12]Spending trends generally refer to all public works infrastructure.

TABLE 3 Composition of Public Spending by Purpose
(percentage of total) for Selected Years

Purpose	Year			
	1960	1970	1980	1984
Highways	60	57	43	41
Airports	4	87	6	7
Mass transit	4	5	12	14
Wastewater	7	8	13	12
Water supply	11	10	14	14
Solid waste	4	4	4	5

SOURCE: Apogee Research's consolidated public works finance data base, which is based on data from the Office of Management and Budget (1986), Bureau of the Census (1986 and prior years), and published and unpublished data from the Farmer's Home Administration, Economic Development Administration, Appalachian Regional Commission, U.S. Department of Housing and Urban Development, Urban Mass Transportation Administration, Federal Highway Administration, Environmental Protection Agency, U.S. Army Corps of Engineers, and Bureau of Reclamation.

works in 1960. In 1970 highway spending began to fall but not substantially. Airport spending almost doubled, however, to 7 percent of total public works outlays. Spending for the other purposes remained roughly in proportion to spending for these purposes of 10 years earlier.

Major shifts had taken place by 1980. Highway spending dropped to 43 percent of the total, and mass transit spending, as a percentage of the total, more than doubled, increasing from 5 percent 10 years earlier to 12 percent in 1980. Spending on wastewater and water supply projects also registered large increases, climbing to 13 percent and 14 percent, respectively. Spending for solid waste remained steady at 4 percent of the total.

Spending by Level of Government

Over the past quarter-century, local spending has driven total government outlays, with short-term peaks and valleys a result of similarly short-term bursts of federal spending. This pattern has resulted from steadily increasing local operating expenditures combined with spikes of federal capital outlays, which were primarily associated with the highway program in the 1960s, the wastewater treatment grants program in the 1970s, and mass transit capital grants in the 1980s.

Local outlays for public works (capital plus operating) has dominated total government public works spending from 1960–1984. In 1960 local public works outlays accounted for 40 percent of total government spending for public works. But the local contribution grew slowly to 41 percent in 1970, 44 percent in 1980, and 50 percent in 1984 (Table 4). Over the first decade of the period (1960–1970), the relative federal contribution to total public works outlays fell by about the same amount that the state contribution grew—that is, by 3–4 percent. This drop was due to the federal devolution in spending for highways and water resources in the late 1960s, combined with increased state spending in these areas.

The trend reversed between 1970–1980, however, with the federal contribution growing from 27 percent to 32 percent and the state share of spending falling from 32 percent to 24 percent. Most of this reversal is explained by large increases in federal wastewater treatment grants and even larger state cutbacks in highway spending.

Between 1980–1984 state contributions remained relatively steady, but local public works outlays grew rapidly to compensate for an equally rapid reduction in federal spending. Local utility spending—water supply, wastewater treatment, solid waste, and transit—accounted for the major increase in the local government share of outlays. Federal spending reductions appeared in almost all modes, primarily because of the pressures to reduce the federal budget deficit. This trend may reverse again as the increased highway authorizations following the 5-cent-per-gallon increase in federal fuel taxes (beginning in 1983) become outlays.

TABLE 4 Composition of Public Spending on Public Works (percentage of total capital spending) by Level of Government for Selected Years

Level of Government	Year			
	1960	1970	1980	1984
Local	40	41	44	50
State	29	32	24	23
Federal	31	27	32	27

SOURCE: See Table 3.

DETAILED SPENDING TRENDS BY PURPOSE

Highways

Total public spending for highways grew by about 3 percent a year from $36 billion in 1960 to a peak of $50 billion in 1971.[13] Following a period of declining investment during most of the 1970s, spending has again begun to rise as a result of the Surface Transportation Assistance Act of 1982. This act increased the federal tax on motor fuels from 4 cents per gallon to 9 cents, the first increase since 1961.

Once the major portions of the interstate highway system were built during the 1960s, federal outlays for highways declined as a percentage of total public highway spending. In 1960 federal spending accounted for 34 percent of total highway outlays, falling to 29 percent in 1970 and 27 percent in 1980. Since World War II, state spending for highways has accounted for the largest portion of total spending: 43 percent in 1960, increasing to 48 percent by 1970, and since falling off slowly to 43 percent in 1984. On the other hand, local governments accounted for only 24 percent of total highway spending in 1960, but that share grew to 30 percent by 1984. This growth, however, was due more to the decline in net spending by states and the federal government than to substantial increases in local outlays.

The total expenditure data tell a different story when viewed in terms of their capital and operating components. State and local operation and maintenance spending has doubled since 1960 whereas all capital outlays have dropped by roughly half since peaking in the early 1970s (Figure 3). Although fewer new roads (especially fewer interstate highway segments) have been built since the mid-1970s, maintenance requirements for existing roadways have steadily increased as roadway stock has aged and vehicle miles traveled have continued to grow.

Mass Transit

Total public spending for mass transit increased the fastest of

---

[13] All spending is expressed in 1984 dollars in this section. For more details on each mode, see the Categories of Public Works Series published by the National Council on Public Works Improvement (May 1987).

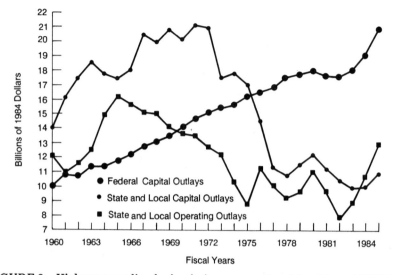

FIGURE 3   Highway spending by level of government and by object. SOURCE:
See Figure 1.

any public works mode between 1960–1984 (Figure 4). Total expenditures in this area grew by 445 percent in 24 years, registering a compound growth rate of over 7 percent per year. By comparison, total public works outlays grew at an annual rate of only 2 percent over this period. This growth is the result of two trends: (1) rapid growth in federal capital expenditures and (2) equally rapid growth in local operating outlays.

Prior to 1965, there was no federal support for local transit systems. Yet federal capital grants grew quickly from a modest $34 million in that year (about 5 percent of total capital outlays for transit) to $3.2 billion in 1984 (80 percent). State and local governments have provided little more than the minimum funds necessary to match federal capital grants since the federal government first began making them in 1965 (see Figure 5).

On the other hand, state and local expenditures to operate and maintain transit systems have grown rapidly, in rough proportion to the growth in transit capital stock. In 1960, for example, state and local operating expenditures totaled only about $2 billion. By 1984 these expenditures had more than quadrupled in constant terms, increasing to $8.5 billion. Federal operating assistance was first provided in 1975 in response to the burden that rapid growth in operating deficits placed on urban areas but also as a reflection of the public takeover of most remaining private transit systems. After

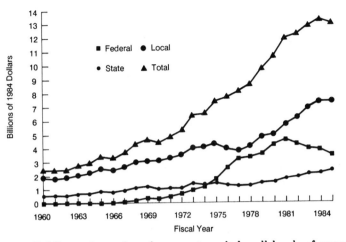

FIGURE 4   Public works outlays for mass transit by all levels of government.
SOURCE: See Figure 1.

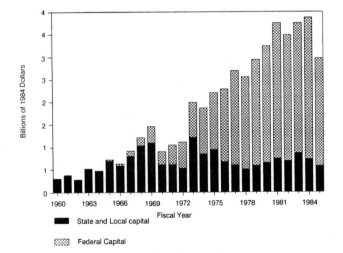

FIGURE 5   Capital outlays for mass transit by all levels of government.
SOURCE: See Figure 1.

peaking in 1980 at $1.5 billion, federal operating assistance began to drop off. The Surface Transportation Assistance Act of 1982 limited federal operating assistance to just $875 million a year through 1986, and the most recent congressional budget resolution calls for a further 10 percent cut.

Wastewater Treatment

Total public spending for wastewater treatment grew rapidly between 1970–1981 in direct response to an expanding federal grants program designed to help clean up the nation's waterways (Figure 6). Between 1972 and 1977, when federal funding was at its greatest, there was a clear substitution of federal spending for nonfederal spending. Prior to the onset of EPA's wastewater treatment construction grants program in the early 1970s, local capital spending ranged between $3 billion and $5 billion a year (spending by state governments was and is minor). But as federal capital grants expanded rapidly after 1972, local capital spending diminished by half to about $2 billion a year. After federal grants peaked in 1977 and declined rapidly through 1984, nonfederal capital spending picked up again, although not as rapidly as federal spending had fallen off. As a result, total public spending has dropped slightly because increased local operating outlays have failed to offset the reduction in federal grants.

As more facilities were built under the EPA program, the data show that local operating outlays continued to mount (Figure 7). In 1960, for example, local operating outlays were only about $1 billion, or approximately one-quarter of total state and local wastewater spending. At the beginning of EPA's program, local operating outlays had doubled, accounting for almost 30 percent of total nonfederal spending. In 1984, local operating outlays approached $6 billion a year, or more than two-thirds of all state and local wastewater treatment expenditures.

Water Supply

Municipal water supply has always been and continues to be primarily a local responsibility. Total public spending for water supply has more than doubled from about $6.5 billion in 1960 to about $14 billion in 1984. Local outlays are completely responsible for this trend, accounting for 90–95 percent of total government

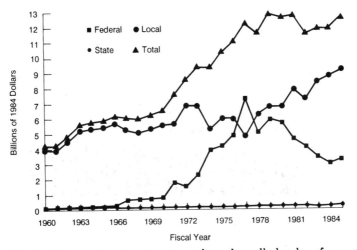

FIGURE 6 Wastewater treatment outlays by all levels of government. SOURCE: See Figure 1.

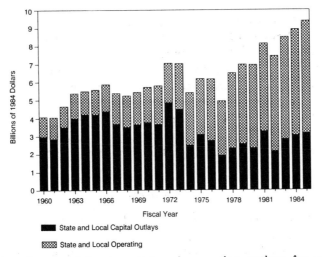

FIGURE 7 State and local capital and operating outlays for wastewater treatment. SOURCE: See Figure 1.

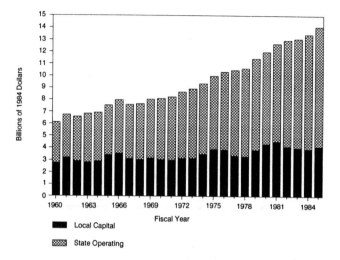

FIGURE 8 Nonfederal outlays for water supply by capital and operating expenditures. SOURCE: See Figure 1.

spending on water supply. Only recently—since about 1980—has state capital spending accounted for more than a token proportion of the total. State water supply assistance appears to be a direct response to decreased federal capital spending for this purpose.

Growth in local water supply spending has been due mostly to growth in operating outlays with only slight increases in local capital spending (Figure 8). Local operating outlays have grown from about $1.5 billion in 1960—about one-quarter of total local spending—to $9 billion in 1984, or about two-thirds of total local spending.

Airports

Public spending for airports[14] and airways grew at a very fast

---

[14]Public spending for airports includes the Federal Aviation Administration's capital and operating outlays for the nation's air traffic control system as well as federal grants and nonfederal direct spending to build, operate, and maintain the nation's airports.

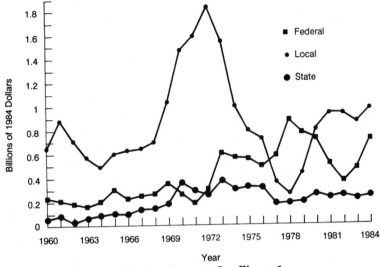

FIGURE 9   Capital spending for airports. See Figure 1.

pace—about 11 percent per year—between 1966 and 1973, peaking at almost $7 billion before dropping off to the $5 billion–$6 billion range in 1980 (Figure 9). Much of this increase was due to equally rapid spending by state and local governments (to build new and expand existing airports) and by the federal government (to modernize the air traffic control system). Since 1982 federal spending to operate the nation's air traffic control system has increased, in part because of the lifting of traffic restrictions imposed after the 1981 walkout by the Professional Air Traffic Controllers' Organization and to continued growth following deregulation. Both local airport construction and maintenance expenditures began to increase in the early 1980s. Although the majority of the nation's 16,000 airports are in low-density areas, commercial and general aviation airports in urban and suburban areas account for virtually all aviation travel.

Solid Waste

Local governments alone provide solid waste collection services and disposal facilities.[15] In 1960 local expenditures for these purposes

---

[15]Neither the Bureau of the Census nor the Department of Commerce's Bureau of Economic Analysis provides enough detail to disaggregate total local solid waste expenditures into capital and operating components. The Bureau

totaled about $2.2 billion and have since increased steadily to about $4.7 billion in 1984. This total is equivalent to a compound growth rate of about 3 percent per year. Urban solid waste facilities account for some three-fourths of total solid waste spending.

THE AGING OF INFRASTRUCTURE

The average age of fixed capital infrastructure stock depends on three factors: (1) the rate of construction of new facilities, (2) the depreciation rate of existing ones, and (3) the book (or expected) longevity of all structures. Age alone is an incomplete indicator of infrastructure condition and does not necessarily relate to the level of service (dams and bridges, for example, have much longer expected lives than do roads or buses). This factor notwithstanding, Figure 10 presents the average age of capital structures owned by federal, state, and local governments since 1925. These trends clearly show the rapid buildup of federal structures and the aging of nonfederal structures prior to and during World War II (including many war plants that had shorter lives than most public works). In the post-war years through about 1970, new state and local capital structures were built, forcing a decline in their average age. During this period, federal structures aged significantly from 10 years to 20 years old, on average. Since 1970 both federal and nonfederal capital structures aged at a relatively slow pace. It is interesting to note that although federal structures are older, on average, than state and local structures, all of these structures are saging at about the same rates, which are only modestly higher now than they were in years past.

It is apparent that the nation as a whole is not adding new capital stock as rapidly as it once did. In fact, the rate at which new capital stock is built now exceeds by only a small margin the rate at which existing stock depreciates. These data alone may not indicate a significant decline in the productivity of our existing capital structures. In fact, it would be inappropriate to assume that there is an optimum rate at which new capital should be added. It would not be possible to postulate such a norm without fully considering specific types of capital, the output equivalents of these types that might be available through nonstructural means, opportunities for

---

of the Census has agreed to reexamine its unpublished data in an attempt to make such a disaggregation but had not done so by the time of this writing.

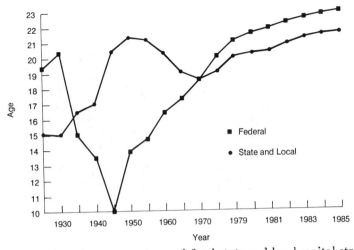

FIGURE 10   Age of government-owned fixed state and local capital structures. SOURCE: From data supplied by John C. Musgrave, Bureau of Economic Analysis, U.S. Department of Commerce.

technological advances in output returns to invested capital, and locational differences in capital productivity.

STATE AND LOCAL SOURCES OF PUBLIC WORKS FINANCE

States and localities finance public works from three sources of revenue: (1) intergovernmental aid, (2) debt, and (3) own-source funds (Apogee Research, 1986c). Own-source funds encompass all tax and nontax receipts including those from the operation of government-owned enterprises such as public utilities, liquor stores, and recreation facilities.

Intergovernmental Aid

Federal grants-in-aid as a percentage of total state and local capital expenditures for public works remained relatively stable at about 33 percent over the period 1960–1975 (Figure 11). This percentage increased rapidly in 1976 and again in 1977, however, peaking that year at about 50 percent. This sudden increase was due primarily to sizable federal wastewater treatment and mass transit grants. Be-

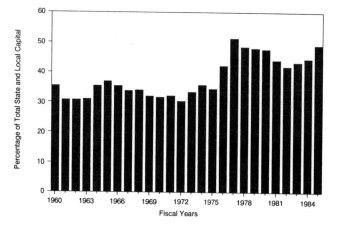

FIGURE 11   Federal grants as a percentage of state and local outlays for public works capital structures. SOURCE: From data in U.S. Department of Commerce (1980).

tween its 1977 peak and the present, federal grants have declined somewhat, ranging between 40–45 percent of total state and local public works capital expenditures. The major trends in these data are as follows:

- Federal grants have accounted for as little as 34 percent (in 1975) and as much as 51 percent (in 1984) of total state and local capital outlays for highways. Since its drop between 1965–1972, this percentage has generally increased over the 1970s and 1980s.
- Federal mass transit capital grants have grown steadily since they were first available in 1965. In that year, they accounted for only 5 percent of state and local capital outlays for transit. In 1984 federal capital grants accounted for 81 percent.
- Federal wastewater treatment grants peaked in 1977, both in dollar terms and as a percentage of nonfederal capital spending. That year, federal grants constituted 76 percent of nonfederal outlays for treatment plants. This percentage dropped steadily, however, reaching a low point of 46 percent in 1984, a level that was still about twice the federal share just prior to the passage of the Clean Water Act in 1972.
- Surprisingly, federal grants to construct state and local water supply facilities have averaged 23 percent of total state and local

capital outlays over the period 1960–1984. Conventional wisdom generally notes the federal contribution to this public works mode as much smaller than its actual amount.

- Federal grant contributions to total state and local capital outlays for airports have ranged widely but averaged about 30 percent. Federal capital grants contributed only 10–20 percent of the total construction costs of major airports and 70–80 percent of the costs of small airports.

Federal grants for all public works modes have remained surprisingly steady since 1960 at about $75 per person, more or less. The 1965 local peak in federal grants per capita was due chiefly to highway grants; a similar jump in 1977 was due to the combination of wastewater and transit grants.

Trends in the Issuance of State and Local Debt

According to the Bureau of the Census, new state and local long-term debt (maturities greater than 1 year) has grown from about $7 billion (in current dollars) in 1960 to $95 billion in 1984. Most of this growth, however, comes from uses that are not defined as public works for the purposes of this paper. For example, bonds for public housing, hospitals, and other "social welfare" purposes now account for about one-third of these new issues. Industrial pollution control bonds—industrial development bonds issued publicly and used to fund private investments—account for another 16 percent. Educational facilities claim another 8 percent.

Public works, as defined in this paper, accounted for about 20 percent of all new debt issued in 1984, which was about the same percentage as in 1980 but roughly a third lower than the comparable percentage in the 1970s and 1960s. As a result of the Tax Reform Act of 1986, this percentage is likely to increase as noninfrastructure areas such as industrial development bonds face new restrictions.

The data do not allow a detailed analysis of the role of debt within public works modes, but experience has shown that in recent years, debt accounted for about half of all state and local capital financing for public water supply systems, 10 to 20 percent of highway financing, about 20 percent of transit financing excluding New York or perhaps over 50 percent if New York is included, 90 to 95 percent of airport financing (100 percent for the major hub airports), and perhaps 60 to 70 percent of wastewater treatment facilities financing.

Trends in the Use of Own-Source Funds to
Finance Public Works

State and local own-source funds include tax receipts, user fees collected from government-owned or government-run enterprises, and other special charges assessed periodically. These sources generally fund current government operations, but in special cases they directly fund public works construction through "enterprise funds." An enterprise fund is a capital management technique that is used to finance the capital expansion of a particular public works system out of fees paid by users of that system. Some airports finance capital expansion this way by setting up a so-called "sinking" fund to siphon off the excess of current revenues over current expenditures and hold the balance until needed for a future capital outlay. Similarly, some port authorities allocate a portion of their current revenues to enterprise funds. The highway trust funds maintained by most states operate much the same way, with the exception that projects are built on a pay-as-you-go basis, with annual outlays equivalent to annual revenues. In a recent survey of 529 cities, common city enterprise functions included water and sewer utilities (when supported by user fees), electric and gas utilities, airports, parking lots, and local transit (Matz and Petersen, 1985).

Unfortunately, the use of own-source revenues to finance public works is not well documented historically. This is the case with the Census Bureau's and the Bureau of Economic Analysis' (BEA) series on sources of state and local receipts data; these series tabulate revenues by government and by type of revenue but not by use of those revenues. Some of the other data sets that are not centrally collected attempt to link sources of funds to uses, but most are limited in one way or another: they focus on one public works mode, data represent a small sample of all state and local governments, or data have been collected only over a short period of time.

This section briefly reviews the trends in the composition of overall state and local government receipts. It may not be appropriate to extend conclusions drawn from this section to the finance of strictly public works investments.

Aggregate State and Local Own-Source Revenues

Total state and local own-source revenues have tripled in real terms from some $150 billion in 1960 to $480 billion in 1984. This increase is equivalent to about 5 percent a year in real growth. The combined state contribution to this total roughly equals the combined local government contribution. Moreover, the rates of growth in each have been roughly comparable over the 24-year period. Interestingly, this 5 percent annual rate of growth in own-source revenues compares closely with the 4 percent annual growth rate in state and local operating expenditures for public works (Apogee Research, 1986d).

Trends by Source

Between 1960–1984 user fees and other user-based revenue sources accounted for an increasingly larger share of total state and local own-source revenues. That the share of state and local own-source receipts claimed by property taxes fell by about the same amount during the study period suggests a substitution of user-based revenue for property taxes. California's Proposition 13, passed in 1978, provides the most dramatic example, but this trend appears to have caught on in other states and localities throughout the nation.

Income and other taxes have also grown slightly as a proportion of total state own-source receipts; sales taxes, on the other hand, have remained relatively stable. The opposite is true at the local level, which has seen a small increase in relative sales taxes and steady property taxes.

ALTERNATIVE MODELS FOR INFRASTRUCTURE SOLUTIONS

The economic and financial costs of neglecting infrastructure problems can be substantial. These costs include higher long-term construction and repair costs for facilities that are not properly maintained, higher costs borne by users of inadequate facilities, and potential constraints on economic development.

Three alternative but related "models" for analyzing and solving public works infrastructure problems are presented in this section:

- a needs- or engineering-based approach that emphasizes the identification of facilities and services that do not meet engineering standards;
- a private sector model that considers the rates of return from public works improvement projects and compares these rates with returns available elsewhere in the economy; and

- a capital management model that focuses on improving the incentives for productive public and private action contained in the way in which federal, state, and local funds are provided.

Although distinctly different in philosophical approach, all three of these models are closely related. Thus, the needs-based approach can help define the physical problems of public works that are, in turn, a key input to estimating the economic returns from alternative projects. And correctly setting public and private incentives as called for under the capital management view depends on information assembled using tools that properly belong in one of the other two models.

Engineering-Based Model

An engineering-based needs assessment is the typical first step in evaluating the adequacy of public works (Apogee Research, 1986a). After identifying the scope and efficiency of available capacity in light of present and projected demands, needs assessments highlight two types of specific project investments: (1) those that meet current demand and (2) those that provide additional capacity to meet projected demand. Removing bottlenecks to meet current demand and improving existing levels of efficiency are usually assigned the highest priorities.

Many presentations of needs estimates amount to a picture of a technically possible optimum, an idealized goal measured without regard to economic feasibility and based principally on age, capacity utilization, or technical standards. Age alone is not a reliable indicator of the demand for repair or replacement; age-based estimates tend to ignore intensity of use, materials, and construction techniques— even the state of maintenance. Standards tend to be vague in the scope of their definitions and, in some cases, "gold-plated." Strong incentives to overestimate needs frequently offset the pressures for cost-effective solutions that budget limits tend to impose. Finally, the analysis is usually based on average standards instead of being site-specific.

Private Investment Model

If there were no limits on available resources (no budgetary constraints), the entire capital investment program identified by a needs assessment could be carried out without financing problems.

Yet resources are limited and budgets are constrained, forcing society to make difficult choices among competing investment projects, as well as among competing economic sectors. In the private investment model, the basis for the choice is rooted in the extent to which the project contributes to the economy—in effect, its economic efficiency. The private investment model applies the same economic criterion of efficiency to infrastructure investments as would be applied to any investment, public or private.

In economic terms, the project's contribution to the economy is measured by its return on capital investment. Rate-of-return analysis measures the rate at which current investments will be converted into future consumption (value).[16] As such, it is a key tool used by many private firms to help choose among competing investments. It has seen only limited use, however, as a tool for ranking and then selecting among alternative government investments.

A positive rate of return is not enough to justify the selection of a project, however; rather, the return should exceed the rate available on the last project to be invested in—the marginal rate of return. The most widespread use of rate-of-return techniques has been by private corporations in which the future stream of benefits is simply expected profits (or perhaps expected cash flow). The use of these techniques by the public sector obviously requires a broader definition of benefits.

This simple description begs a number of serious technical problems with the use of rate of return for government-sponsored projects. Some problems are largely technical and concern the availability of adequate data and estimating techniques: most importantly, what is the proper discount rate? Other problems are conceptual and concern the degree to which a technique designed for private, financial returns can be applied to public investments in which intangible outputs (income redistribution, for example) and returns to the public at large (national defense, for example) are often a key rationale for government involvement.

---

[16]Rate of return is closely related to a number of other techniques and concepts, including some in regular use by the public sector. These include benefit–cost analysis, in which the ratio of benefits to costs is used to rank projects; net benefits, which calculates the total dollar value of benefits minus the total costs; and the first-year benefit. Other cost-effectiveness approaches might use measures of physical output instead of financial return, calculating, for example, the number of new passengers per dollar spent on different transit strategies.

When applied to public rather than private projects, benefit–cost analysis attempts to quantify the economic returns to the community as a whole rather than merely the financial returns. This kind of emphasis represents a significant difference from the application of the same techniques to private sector investment decisions. More specifically, a project could generate great public benefits but still show up as ineffective in terms of its financial returns. This difference between public and private costs and benefits is a major justification for public investment in public works. For example, because a new or upgraded highway provides improved operating conditions, it thus generates savings in user time, operating costs, and reduced accidents. These savings eventually result in greater productivity and lower transport costs and could justify the project even if public financial support were required.

Capital Management Model

The capital management approach attempts to combine economic techniques from the private sector model, local data available through the engineering model, and the recognition that an attempt to apply either of these models in their pure form would be likely to run into impossible technical and political problems. A key assumption is that decision makers act in their own best interests. Thus, the goal is to find those financial and organizational incentives that, along with adequate data, will encourage actions that support an effective infrastructure.

Many of the options presented in the next section might be characterized as capital management, even though they have been debated for years (Congressional Budget Office, 1986).

SOLUTIONS

There are two general solutions to public works infrastructure problems: (1) increase funding, and (2) make more effective use of existing resources. These solutions are not mutually exclusive because no matter what the level of funding, there is a natural interest in seeing it used effectively. Given the fact that all levels of government will probably be faced with budgetary pressures for the foreseeable future, a significant increase in general funding for infrastructure is improbable. Infrastructure revolving funds may be one way to establish a new financing mechanism despite such budget pressures.

Revolving funds are currently used in several states, and at the federal level, they will probably replace the existing EPA wastewater treatment grant program during the 1990s (Congressional Budget Office, 1985b).

Thus, the most promising policy alternatives are likely to involve ways to improve the effectiveness of existing as well as any new resources devoted to infrastructure.

Managing Demand: Low-Capital Solutions

The purpose of infrastructure is to provide productive services. As such, there is no inherent reason why infrastructure solutions must be dominated by capital-intensive projects. In fact, ways of encouraging more productive use of existing capital often show greater rates of return than do new investments. For example, the 1968 decision by the Port Authority of New York and New Jersey to quintuple peak-hour minimum landing fees for general aviation (from $5 to $25) brought about an immediate decline in aircraft delays of 30 minutes or more (Federal Aviation Administration, 1976). A comparable improvement could have been achieved by adding new airport capacity but not without also incurring massive capital and operating costs.

The productivity of low-capital options has long been recognized. In the early 1970s, Congress even earmarked funding for low-capital urban highway improvements (this program was called TOPICS and included traffic signal coordination and high-occupancy vehicle lanes). Indeed, an analysis of recent state and local spending trends for public works infrastructure shows a shift away from capital spending and toward what the data classify as operations.

Better Incentives

The U.S. economy is governed by free market precepts, under which individuals, acting in their own best interests, increase the productivity of the economy as a whole. The parallel principle for the public works economy may be called "rational parochialism." Most of this nation's infrastructure has been built using one or both of these principles as the rationale for its construction. Thus, it is important that infrastructure programs contain incentives to channel this parochialism along productive lines.

The interstate highway trade-in program provides a good example of the influence of financial incentives. For more than 10 years,

states have been allowed to "transfer" local interstate highway segments back to the federal government and to use the released funds
either for transit improvements or alternative highway projects. Since
1980 projects worth some $3.7 billion have been withdrawn. Fully 71
percent of these projects turned out to have had low (often negative)
rates of return (Congressional Budget Office, 1986; Skrotzki, 1983).
Thus, when 90 percent funding was available only for new highways,
states acted quite rationally in trying to maximize the number of
segments that qualified for this level of funding. When trade-ins permitted states to keep these funds for other local purposes, they also
acted quite rationally in dropping road segments with low economic
returns.

At present, the federal government provides quite generous
matching rates for those programs in which it is active: 70 to 90
percent for highways, 75 to 85 percent for transit, 55 to 75 percent
for wastewater treatment plants, up to 90 percent for airports, and,
of course, close to 100 percent for most water resources programs.
These high ratios of federal to nonfederal dollars have a history
of encouraging capital-intensive projects. For example, a statistical
analysis of wastewater treatment plants found that dropping the basic federal matching rate from 75 percent to 55 percent would reduce
the overall costs of secondary treatment plants by some 30 percent
(Congressional Budget Office, 1985a).

The Shifting of Current Roles

There is always considerable inertia favoring the current division
of infrastructure responsibility, whatever it may be. At present, the
federal government dominates the funding of infrastructure capital
despite the fact that most of the direct benefits accrue to lower levels
of government. A realignment of responsibilities could be made based
on one of two different principles.

First, financial responsibilities could be adjusted to bring them
closer to the incidence of benefits shown in Table 1. This adjustment would be likely to shift considerable financial burdens to state
and local governments (and probably to the private sector as well).
Arguments against such a move have usually centered on the heavy
new financial responsibilities that would be imposed on state and
local governments. Given the significant level of federal user fee financing of public works infrastructure, however, there may be ways

to soften the transition (Advisory Commission on Intergovernmental Relations, 1986).

Second, the degree of responsibility for each of the major stages in the infrastructure development process could be realigned more equitably. Because the federal government is the dominant source of funding, this realignment might imply an increased federal role, particularly in the key nomination and evaluation stages (see Table 3). There would probably be increased costs as the decision process became further removed from the local level.

Better Information and Techniques

Good information is needed at several stages of the infrastructure development process:

- engineering and socioeconomic trend data are needed to help develop long-term plans for federal as well as state and local agencies;
- inventory-type data are required both to help formulate general policy options and to help identify and evaluate specific local project proposals; and
- performance measures are needed to help develop and evaluate a range of alternatives that includes low-capital options as well as more traditional approaches.

System performance measures could also play a valuable role in ex post facto evaluations of program effectiveness, but they are usually ignored. Such a use of performance measures would help greatly in the design of new infrastructure programs and in improvements to existing ones.

REFERENCES

Advisory Commission on Intergovernmental Relations
    1986   *Devolving Federal Program Responsibilities and Revenue Sources to State and Local Governments.* Report A-108. Washington, D.C.: Advisory Commission on Intergovernmental Relations.

Apogee Research, Inc.
    1986a   A Review of the Uses and Misuses of Infrastructure Needs Surveys and Inventories. Paper prepared for the National Council on Public Works Improvement. Apogee Research, Inc., Bethesda, Md.
    1986b   Infrastructure: Issues, Problems, and General Solutions. Paper prepared for the National Council on Public Works Improvement. Apogee Research, Inc., Bethesda, Md.
    1986c   Trends in Financing Public Works, 1960–1984. Paper prepared for the National Council on Public Works Improvement. Apogee Research, Inc., Bethesda, Md.

1986d   Trends in Public Works Expenditures, 1960–1984. Paper prepared
         for the National Council on Public Works Improvement. Apogee
         Research, Inc., Bethesda, Md.

Break, George F.
1981   Fiscal federalism in the United States: The first 200 years, evolution
         and outlook. Pp. 39–65 in Advisory Commission on Intergovernmen-
         tal Relations, *The Future of Federalism in the 1980's*. Report M-126.
         Washington, D.C.: Advisory Commission on Intergovernmental Re-
         lations.

Broude, Henry
1959   The role of the state in American economic development, 1820–1840.
         Pp. 4–28 in Hugh G. J. Aitken, ed., *The State and Economic Growth*.
         New York: Social Science Research Council.

Congressional Budget Office
1978   *Highway Assistance Programs: A Historical Perspective*. Washington,
         D.C.: U.S. Government Printing Office.
1983   *Public Works Infrastructure: Policy Considerations for the 1980s*. Wash-
         ington, D.C.: U.S. Government Printing Office.
1985a   *Efficient Investments in Wastewater Treatment Plants*. Washington, D.C.:
         U.S. Government Printing Office.
1985b   *Infrastructure Revolving Funds: A First Review*. Washington, D.C.: U.S.
         Government Printing Office.
1985c   *The Federal Budget for Public Works Infrastructure*. Washington, D.C.:
         U.S. Government Printing Office.
1986   *Federal Policies for Infrastructure Management*. Washington, D.C.: U.S.
         Government Printing Office.
1987   *Financing Municipal Water Supply Systems*. Washington, D.C.: U.S.
         Government Printing Office.

Federal Aviation Administration
1976   *Airport Quotas and Peak-Hour Pricing: Theory and Practice*. Washington,
         D.C.: U.S. Department of Transportation.

Hilton, George W.
1974   *Federal Transit Subsidies*. Washington, D.C.: American Enterprise
         Institute.

Matz, Deborah, and John E. Petersen
1985   Trends in the Fiscal Condition of Cities: 1983–1985. Report prepared
         by the Government Finance Research Center for the Joint Economic
         Committee of the U.S. Congress.

National Council on Public Works Improvement
1987a   Airports and Airways. Report prepared by Apogee Research, Inc.
         Washington, D.C.: National Council on Public Works Improvement.
1987b   Wastewater Treatment. Report prepared by Apogee Research, Inc.
         Washington, D.C.: National Council on Public Works Improvement.

National League of Cities
1987   *Financing Infrastructure: Innovations at the Local Level*. Prepared by
         Apogee Research, Inc. Washington, D.C.: National League of Cities.

Office of Management and Budget
1986   *Budget of the United States, 1987*. Historical Appendices. Washington,
         D.C.: U.S. Government Printing Office.

Peterson, George E.
1984   Financing the nation's infrastructure requirements. Pp. 110–142 in

Royce Hanson, ed., *Perspectives on Urban Infrastructure.* Washington, D.C.: National Academy Press.

Skrotski Associates
1983   Economics of Completing the Interstate Highway System. *Congressional Record,* 98th Congress, First Session, 1983, Vol. 129, No. 5, pp. 53533–53537.

Tarr, Joel A.
1984   The evolution of the urban infrastructure in the nineteenth and twentieth centuries. Pp. 4–60 in Royce Hanson, ed., *Perspectives on Urban Infrastructure.* Washington, D.C.: National Academy Press.

TELESIS
1986   Promoting and Financing Large Scale Infrastructure Projects in Europe. Report prepared for the Commission of the European Communities and the Roundtable of European Industrialists.

Transportation Systems Center
1983   Highways and the Economy. Report FHWA/PL/33/014, DOT-TSC-FHWA-83-1. Cambridge, Mass.: U.S. Department of Transportation.

U.S. Department of Commerce
1980   A Study of Public Works Investment in the United States. Report prepared by CONSAD Research Corporation. Washington, D.C.: U.S. Department of Commerce.

Urban Governance:
The New Politics of
Entrepreneurship

JOHN J. KIRLIN and DALE ROGERS MARSHALL

Perhaps for the first time in two decades of breathless announcements of a "new era" in urban governance, in national urban policy, or in intergovernmental relations, there is some evidence of important changes in city governance and in governmental roles in the federal political system.

Most fundamentally, the emerging changes in urban governance involve increases in the importance of local political and economic factors and policies. National policies are of less importance in part because the funding (and sometimes the scope) of such policies has been reduced. They are also less important because the policy approaches involved have not proven effective in addressing the issues of job creation and economic growth, issues that loom large on the policy agendas of most cities.

It is also very important to recognize that policies that address the pursuit of economic growth are being made in ways quite different from policies that address the delivery of traditional services. It is not much of an overstatement to argue that a bifurcation in policy processes is occurring, with two distinct sectors emerging. One sector is focused on traditional service delivery through tax-supported public employees (e.g., public education). The other sector is focused on economic growth/infrastructure provision/land use and increasingly achieves its purposes without the expenditure of tax funds and with less intensive use of public employees. The two sectors are not only

348

different in goals, resource base, and dependence on public bureaucracies. They also differ in participants, beneficiaries, and political styles. The two sectors are competitors for resources and space on the public policy agenda. They also complement each other and interact in several ways, so the conflict is not one of zero-sum.

Increasingly, the national government is reducing its direct policy involvement with local economic growth and job creation. National fiscal, monetary, tax, and defense procurement policies affect local economies but with much less place-specific intent than was the case with sewer grants, urban development action grants, or even community development block grants and grants from the Economic Development Administration. The national government remains involved in locally delivered programs that affect residents of cities as individuals, programs such as welfare, medical care, and education. But these policies should not be considered a "national" urban policy; they simply have too little direct impact on the economics, physical design, and politics of cities. States vary in the extent of their policy involvement with cities as political units and economies, but the same pattern of commitment to programs that benefit individuals (e.g., public education, welfare, or health) is often seen.

This paper looks at the changes strengthening urban governance capacity, examines some theoretical explanations of their causes, and explores the strength and consequences of the new patterns. To establish the setting, we first present an analysis of the dominant approach to urban policy of the 1965–1980 period. This analysis is followed by an assessment of the dimensions of the changes that are occurring and an exploration of ways to analyze those changes. These analyses provide a framework in which to conceptualize the major causes and features of the changes, emphasizing a shift in dominant theory from service delivery-focused "public administration" to economic growth-focused "public entrepreneurship." Public entrepreneurs try to maintain local business and employment growth—and thus local government revenues—by stimulating private sector involvement in local economic development projects and urban service delivery.

CONTINUITIES IN POLICY THEORIES AND PRACTICES

Despite some apparent changes in national urban policies, in approaches to federalism, and even in officeholders, the 1965–1980 period was characterized by substantial continuities. The persistent patterns are easiest to see in formal national urban or intergovernmental programs, but we believe they also existed at the local level. Challenges to these practices began to emerge in the later 1970s; such challenges have gathered momentum as the 1980s pass.

During the mid-1960s, a major expansion in the role of the national government occurred. This expansion took the form of greatly increased numbers of national intergovernmental grant programs, increased appropriations to grants, and increased national regulations placed upon state and local governments, either directly as mandates or as conditions on grants-in-aid (Advisory Commission on Intergovernmental Relations, 1980). The major elements of these urban programs—that is, their essential policy theory (definition of the problem and how to solve it) and political dynamics—remained virtually intact into the 1980s.

There is much diversity in the detail of the programs, and yet there is much similarity in the policy theory underlying them. Most share, for example, the following attributes, which are derived from the service delivery-focused public administration orientation to government:

- definition of the "problem" as requiring direct action by public employees, usually with little attention to the potential role of a private individual, firm, or organization;
- policy strategies that rely on service provision to achieve the desired ends;
- program designs based on implementation through highly formalized, functionally specific organizations supported by general tax revenues (i.e., public bureaucracies); and
- an emphasis on the distributive and redistributive elements of choices, as opposed to choices intended to change the available resources.

The national policies of the 1965–1980 period shared not only a common theoretical orientation but also similar origins. Individual members of Congress were overwhelmingly the most important factor in the origination of intergovernmental grant programs (Advisory Commission on Intergovernmental Relations, 1981:11–13). The institutional constraints on and incentives to the members of Congress and the institutional features of intergovernmental bureaucracies interacted to encourage the continuation of categorical grants (Chubb, 1985).

Urban governance also exhibited similar patterns. Local officials shared the policy theories enumerated above. As local governments became more dependent on federal funds, national policies and grants influenced their policy agendas, guided resource allocation, and shaped the structures of government. Cities defined problems as requiring direct action by public employees, emphasized service provision, and created highly formalized, functionally specific organizations.

A focus solely on national grants policy is too limiting, however; it misses many of the critical public policies and private actions that shape urban areas. "Urban governance," the subject of this paper, cannot be reduced to national grants policy. Similarly, the factors affecting urban governance range far beyond Congress and intergovernmental bureaucracies.

Before the 1965–1980 period, city politics was often studied in isolation from the larger political and economic context. But the growing local dependence on federal grants soon led some to see cities as only subordinate agents in a nationally dominated intergovernmental system, and important local dynamics were often ignored (Pressman and Wildavsky, 1984; Reagan and Sanzone, 1981). Today, a better balance is emerging in the study of cities. Cities are recognized as separate political jurisdictions with their own political and economic dynamics, jurisdictions that make genuine choices within significant constraints set by the intergovernmental system and by economic and demographic trends (Stone and Sanders, 1987:3).

After carefully reviewing research on the intergovernmental system in this nation, Anton (1984) concluded that the national government plays a much more limited role in the policies and politics of local areas than is often claimed. Specifically, Anton argued that the size of local governments (measured by budget or personnel) is not determined by national policies or grants, that local governmental structures are under virtually constant review and reformulation, and that national grants are both less stimulative and less constraining of local expenditures than is sometimes suggested. Anton carefully observed that national policies and grants do have some impact on local government activities, but those effects are neither determinative nor global. In this nation, and in the European nations he also reviewed (although less thoroughly), intergovernmental relations are characterized by mutual dependence and not by domination.

Urban gov.

This brief analysis suggests that three factors shape urban governance: (1) theories concerning problems and policies, (2) institutional constraints and incentives, and (3) individual leadership and policy entrepreneurship.

The 1965–1980 period was one of continuities in national urban policies and in urban governance because these three factors were coaligned. Dominant theories legitimated and gave force to actions by individual policy entrepreneurs operating within facilitative institutions. Kirlin (1984) calls this the period of "aggressive pluralism," when a new policy often created groups whose newfound interests could be variously served by government action. Browning et al. (1984) emphasize the importance of electoral success for minority groups in this period and, once elected, of participation in the dominant coalition. Individual leadership or entrepreneurship were central to the formation of both electoral and governing coalitions. The Advisory Commission on Intergovernmental Relations (ACIR) has advanced similar arguments. ACIR's analyses of changes in the federal political system (1981:Ch. 2) identified individual policy entrepreneurs operating within the constraints and opportunities of context as key factors in those changes.

CHANGES IN THEORIES AND CONSTRAINTS

Beginning in the mid-1970s (but more fully visible in the 1980s), changes occurred in all three of the factors identified in the preceding section. Theories concerning problems and policies have changed. Institutional constraints and incentives have changed. And, in response to those changes, the activities of individual policy entrepreneurs have changed.

Keynes ec.

Consider first the changes that have occurred in theories. Once-dominant Keynesian economic theory, which legitimated high levels of public spending and deficits and provided a nonmoral rationale for poverty, has been challenged by monetarism, supply-siders, and old-style conservatives. And even if none of these alternative economic theories has succeeded in dominating policy-making, taken together, they have broken the domination of Keynesian ideas, introducing variations and fluctuations into policy processes (Bosworth, 1980). In another instance, welfare policies and their undergirding theories are under similar attack (Lemann, 1986; Wiseman, 1985), although such news does not reach the front pages as often as do controversies concerning economic theories and policies.

TABLE 1 Trends in Median Personal Income (in 1984 Dollars) for Selected Years and for the Period 1960-1984

Year	Families	Men		Women	
		All	Full-time Only	All	Full-time Only
1960	19,711	14,311	19,060	4,424	11,558
1973	28,167	18,830	26,805	6,535	15,165
1984	26,433	15,600	24,004	6,868	15,422
Change (%), 1960-1973	42.9	31.6	40.6	47.7	31.2
Change (%), 1973-1984	-6.2	-17.2	-10.4	5.1	1.7

SOURCE: Calculated from Council of Economic Advisors (1986:286).

Policy makers, analysts, and citizens appear less accepting of the notion that any problem we encounter can be surmounted by a public policy. Consider, for example, the growth in self-help/support groups such as Alcoholics Anonymous, or the great expenditures made by firms to educate their employees.

The institutional context of policy-making is changing fundamentally. Much of the transformation that is occurring can be traced to changes in the structure of the economy. As service and trade employment increases more rapidly than manufacturing employment, the share of jobs in manufacturing declines relative to total employment. For example, in California, which remains the state with the nation's largest manufacturing sector (measured in employment or value added), about 340,000 net new jobs were created in the January 1984–January 1986 period. Yet only 5 percent of those jobs were in manfacturing; 85 percent were in the categories of trade, services, and government (Kirlin, 1986). Because median wages are lower in service and trade employment, the consequences of these shifts include pressure on the incomes of individuals and the erection of barriers to access to middle-class life styles. Table 1 reports changes in real personal income in the 1960–1984 period, showing increases from 1960–1973 and then decreases in the 1973–1984 period. Women are the exception to these trends, however; their income continued to increase but still lagged behind men's income.

These data suggest that fiscal limits on governments mirror the fiscal stress citizens are experiencing; far from being the work of "crazies," which was the initial reaction to California's Proposition 13, fiscal limits may be a rational balancing of citizens' private economies versus those of the public sector (Kirlin, 1982). More than three-quarters of the states have seen one or another form of fiscal limit imposed since the late 1970s, and the Gramm-Rudman-Hollings Act, if it is triggered by high deficits on the federal budget, may limit the expenditures of the national government. Whatever the explanation that is offered, growth in public sector revenues has slowed, as is shown in Table 2, which reports growth rates in total public expenditures by decade as a percentage of the gross national product (GNP).

Table 2 reveals the gradual slowing of the relative growth of the public sector vis-à-vis the total economy; yet the fiscal limits movement has also had major effects on particular jurisdictions. For example, in California, $86 billion in cumulative reductions of state and local taxes have occurred since June 1978, and Proposition 4, the Gann expenditure limit, is projected to reduce expenditures an incremental $20 billion over the next decade. The annual reductions are now approximately $18 billion and will increase to $25 billion within 5 years (compared with actual expenditures of $86 billion by all California governments in 1985–1986).

Another consequence of the changes in the structure of the economy is a shift in the location of jobs. Since the beginning of industrialization, most jobs were created in central cities, but in the past several years, more jobs have been created in suburban locations than in central cities. Table 3 illustrates this phenomenon with data on job creation in San Francisco, California, and in three adjacent

TABLE 2 Growth Rates in Government Receipts as a Percentage of Gross National Product

Decade	Growth Rate
1929–1939	55
1939–1949	29
1949–1959	21
1959–1969	18
1969–1979	0
1979–1984	0

SOURCE: Calculated from Advisory Commission on Intergovernmental Relations (1987:Table 3).

TABLE 3 Job Creation (percentage change in nonagricultural employment) in San Francisco and in Three Adjacent Suburban Counties, by Industry, December 1980-December 1984

| Industry | San Francisco | Adjacent Suburban Counties | | |
		Contra Costa	San Mateo	Sonoma
Total	0.8	13.1	4.0	15.1
Construction	3.8	16.5	0.0	7.5
Manufacturing	-5.2	5.4	-10.3	18.0
Transportation and public utilities	-4.5	9.2	5.1	10.9
Wholesale trade	-5.9	13.6	2.9	28.6
Retail trade	6.7	13.0	13.3	19.9
Finance, insurance, and real estate	-4.9	38.5	13.1	24.1
Services	7.7	23.9	12.1	20.1
Government	-2.2	-3.5	-4.4	-0.5

SOURCE: Computed from data provided by the California Economic Development Department.

suburban counties during December 1980–December 1984. As can be seen, San Francisco was stagnant overall, whereas Contra Costa and Sonoma Counties had high rates of job creation and San Mateo, a more mature economy that had grown rapidly in the past, grew modestly.

These changes in the structure of the economy are major shifts from the previous patterns on which much national policy was based, patterns that provided the context for the design of institutions of city governance. Changes of this magnitude provide new institutional incentives and constraints for policy makers. In particular, fiscal resources are often scarcer, although, as will be examined shortly, some cities have discovered ways to prosper even during these periods of economic change and fiscal limits.

PROCESSES OF MOBILIZATION, INCORPORATION, AND LEADERSHIP

These changes in theory and institutional context, as well as the increased importance of local political economies in supporting government services, have focused renewed attention on local governments. They highlight the fact that local governments make a difference. Local political dynamics are continually producing changes in leaders, institutions, and policies—changes that are quite significant.

Examining local governments in this larger context, we see that local politics is not issueless or groupless. Competition among cities for economic resources is important, as Peterson (1981) has effectively argued, but it does not eliminate intracity political controversies. Local politics involves continuing contention among different forces. It is the politics of coalitions, which involves periodic realignments over time at the local level as at the national level (Chubb and Peterson, 1985). New events, problems, or populations create opportunities for new coalitions to form and challenge more established groups (Fainstein et al., 1983; Shefter, 1985; Stone et al., 1986). Individuals play an entrepreneurial role in the mobilization of these groups.

Problems of equity, representation, and redistribution were the focus of insurgent coalitions from the 1960s through the mid-1970s. Fiscal crises moved to the top of many local agendas in the late 1970s. More recently, the emphasis of such coalitions is frequently economic development, job creation, and the generation of new revenues for the public sector. Redistribution issues have been associated with high levels of conflict, including protest demonstrations. Observing this conflict, analysts worried about the governability of the city, fearing that the social order was in serious danger and that disruption threatened the established political and economic mechanisms (Banfield, 1970; Yates, 1977). Others feared that there would not be enough conflict to transform these mechanisms (Piven and Cloward, 1971).

City fiscal crises, beginning in New York in 1975, changed the terms of the debate, and analysts found a new worry: the fiscal viability of the city. Bankruptcy, not group unrest, appeared to present the greatest threat to social order. City officials chose a variety of cutback strategies to bring expenditures into balance with revenues. According to Shefter (1985:220), these strategies were shaped by "the composition of the political coalitions they depend on for support and the structure of political organizations and institutions in their cities." Policy entrepreneurs who played leadership roles in the reduction of fiscal strain chose adaptive mechanisms and strategies that were influenced by their ideologies, that is to say, their policy theories. Shefter has shown that in New York, periodic fiscal crises have resulted in political reorganization that allows new social forces to be integrated into the city's political makeup, often changing the balance of power. After the 1975 crisis, city banks, unions, fiscal monitors, and the mayor became the major centers of power. The new dominant coalition was weighted toward creditors and against broad citizen participation.

In the 1980s, attention has focused on the economic vitality of cities. The changes in the structure of the economy reviewed earlier are one reason for this shift in focus. In addition, President Reagan's domestic policies and the 1980–1982 recession have increased city interest in local economic development and the generation of local revenue. Yet, although there may be a broad consensus on the desirability of development, there is often also disagreement on which developments are in the city's interest. Specific proposals may generate controversy concerning location, scale, or environmental impacts. Developments often have differential effects, unevenly distributing benefits and losses. In turn, the fact that benefits and losses are distributed unevenly provides opportunities for policy entrepreneurship (Stone and Sanders, 1987).

These changing urban issues are associated with the processes of change in urban governance—with the mobilization of interest groups, their representation, and their incorporation into and effects on urban political processes. The processes and policies of cities, like those of organizations, depend on the way differences are resolved; that is, on the political arrangements by which coalitions are formed and conflict is managed. Thus, attention must be paid not just to rational policy choice but also to internal political relationships, ideologies, and interests, all of which are important in shaping the choices of each interest group and, through their interaction, the public policies that ultimately develop. In this process of mobilizing interests and melding disparate elements into effective political forces, individual policy entrepreneurs play important leadership roles. They are critical in identifying, attracting, and organizing individuals into interest groups and shaping the group's theory base, including its rationale for existence, its image of the world, and its agenda.

How have these patterns of city political coalitions and leadership changed in the recent past? How have the political structures of cities been changing to adapt to new leaders and issues? It is noteworthy that available data on council members and mayors do not include information (e.g., partisan affiliation or links to various interests) that would help identify changes in coalitions. We can, however, see increases in minority (blacks and Hispanics) and female elected officials and changes in political structures. These political changes were facilitated by the "aggressive pluralism" and larger societal trends in the 1965–1980 period and are now being institutionalized in ways that interact with the other changes taking place in urban governance.

Increases in the Number of Black and Hispanic Elected Officials

The number of black and Hispanic municipal officials has continued to grow in the 1980s as it did in the 1970s. In 1985 there were 2,898 blacks in municipal office, including 286 black mayors, 27 of which were in cities with populations of over 50,000. The number of black local officials has almost doubled since 1975 when there were only 1,513. A majority of black elected officials are in the South, with 196 mayors and 1,780 other municipal officials (Joint Center for Political Studies, 1985). In addition, blacks are mayors of several large central cities, including Los Angeles, Chicago, Oakland, Detroit, Philadelphia, Atlanta, Newark, and Washington, D.C., among others.

In 1985 there were 1,025 Hispanics in municipal office, including 3 Hispanic mayors in cities with populations over 50,000: San Antonio, Denver, and Miami. Hispanic officials are found primarily in the Southwest. Texas has 897 Hispanic municipal officials, New Mexico has 188, California has 165, and Arizona has 104 (National Association of Latino Elected Officials, 1986).

These trends suggest that blacks and Hispanics are continuing to mobilize, to form coalitions, and to achieve representation in city government as they did in the 1960s and 1970s, although they are still underrepresented (blacks constitute 11.7 percent and Hispanics 6.4 percent of the population) (Browning et al., 1984). The significance of race and ethnicity in local politics is not declining. Local conditions and structures, however, shape the political mobilization of minorities and governmental responsiveness to them. Comparisons of cities show great variation in the amount of power minorities have achieved, how it was obtained, and what difference it makes for policy. The variations depend on differences in history, population, economics, political structures and processes, and leadership exercised by individuals (Browning and Marshall, 1986).

Minority politics reveals the importance of electoral organizing and coalition formation in city politics. Variations in minority incorporation and political power are shaped by the ability to win local elections. Successful leaders of insurgent coalitions are those who can capitalize on available resources and who identify common interests among disparate groups, getting them to work together to win the necessary votes for a given candidate or slate of candidates (Browning and Marshall, 1986).

Minority political achievements are not linear, however; they can be reversed, and the groups themselves can lose cohesion. Fiscal constraints can reduce support for minority-oriented programs and favor other, more conservative coalitions. In cases in which minority political participation is heavily linked to national grant programs, cuts in those programs may reduce the groups' influence. Browning et al.'s (1984) study of 10 California cities found wide variations among them. In those cases in which minorities had achieved the most political power, cities responded to fiscal problems with the most sensitivity to minority interests: when cutting expenditures and generating new revenues, they minimized the detrimental effects of those policies on minorities. When promoting economic development, they included strong requirements for minority contracting and employment.

Black and Hispanic elected officials make strong efforts to gain the support of major business interests, as can be seen in Los Angeles, Atlanta, Miami, Denver, and Philadelphia. This dependence on established economic interests limits the extent to which minority political power can be translated into redistributive policies. It also subjects minority officials to criticism from minority groups. Yet the accommodations minority leaders make are likely to be more responsive to minority concerns than those made in cities in which minorities have less political power.

So, under the more economically adverse conditions of the 1980s, minority interests are still being institutionalized. Earlier concerns about equity and redistribution have not disappeared, however, and they continue to shape the responses of some cities to their new problems and their diminished shares of national grant funds (Browning and Marshall, 1986).

Increases in the Number of Female Elected Officials

Women now constitute more than 14 percent of mayors and municipal council members. A decade ago, women held fewer than 5 percent of these posts; now, there are 14,672 female council members and mayors out of the total 102,329 municipal officials. In general, states in the Midwest and West have the highest percentages of women serving in municipal office: Michigan (27.5 percent), Alaska (23.1 percent), Oregon (22.2 percent), Washington (19.3 percent), Connecticut (18.7 percent), Wyoming (17.8 percent), California (17.8 percent), Arizona (17.6 percent), Delaware (17.5 percent), and Ohio (16.5 percent) have the highest percentages of female municipal officials. Hawaii and the District of Columbia, with only one incorporated municipality each, have 30 percent and 50 percent female council members, respectively.

Of cities with populations of over 30,000, almost 10 percent (85) have female mayors. Among the 100 largest cities in 1986, there are currently four female mayors: Houston (Kathy Whitmire, a Democrat); Sacramento (Anne Rudin, a Democrat); San Francisco (Dianne Feinstein, a Democrat); and Toledo (Donna Owens, a Republican). Fourteen other cities among the 100 largest have had female mayors, including Chicago and Austin (Center for the American Woman and Politics, 1986).

As the proportion of women on local councils grows, we will begin to see more clearly how the presence of women might make a difference in the way government works and the kinds of policies that are adopted. Initial studies of female elected officials reveal that their attitudes are different from those of men on current issues, and the gap is greatest on women's issues. Concerning the dominant urban policy issue of the 1980s, the ability of the private sector to solve economic problems, women were less optimistic than men (Center for the American Woman and Politics, 1986).

There are a number of explanations for this difference in attitude between men and women. Women have been absent from the higher positions in the corporate sector and are less socialized into these values. Women voters are more sympathetic to the Democratic party and less sympathetic to Republican candidates than are men (Chubb and Peterson, 1985; Lipset, 1986:224–225). In many cities, white female council members are more supportive of minority concerns than are white men (Browning et al., 1984).

The increase in the number of female elected officials, like the increases in minorities, suggests the emergence of new coalitions at the local level that might approach the issues of the 1980s differently than would be the case in the absence of these new leaders.

Changes in Urban Political Structures

The changes in urban political structures that are now receiving the most attention are district elections, directly elected mayors, and other actions to strengthen elected city officials, such as greater pay or larger staffs. In a broad context, these changes represent departures from the reform model of city politics, which was characterized by nonpartisanship, weak elected officials, strong professional administrators, and professionalized public bureaucracies operating under civil service systems.

The reform model was the product of the political mobilization of the Progressive era, a mobilization of the middle class to focus city government on the effective and efficient delivery of the core urban services that were required by rapid industrialization and urbanization. Today, as the pressing policy issues move away from basic service delivery (in good part because basic municipal services are usually delivered adequately) and other groups mobilize and seek to direct the political agenda toward their needs, efforts are being made to change the structures of city politics. In short, new dominant coalitions seek to institutionalize their power by changing political structures, and challenging coalitions seek to change the same structures to enhance their power.

Since 1970, 6 percent of the nation's cities have changed their electoral systems, with changes most common among the larger cities and particularly prevalent in cities of the South. The pace of such changes increased during the last half of the 1970s, during which the Southern cities typically changed from at-large to district elections. The civil rights movement, increased black population and political strength, and new neighborhood interests all contributed to the changes. The change from at-large to district elections has also occurred in the West, including municipalities such as Long Beach, Sacramento, San Jose, Stockton, and Oakland, California; and Tacoma, Washington. A study by the International City Management Association (1982:185) concluded that "growing council-manager cities may adapt to large size by altering their scheme of representation while maintaining the values and norms of professional local management." In addition, pressure through private lawsuits charging exclusionary electoral systems and through similar Justice Department actions have spurred some of these changes, particularly in the South but also in other parts of the nation.

Heilig and Mundt's (1985) study of approximately 500 cities with populations of over 10,000 sheds more light on the shift to district elections. Larger cities have been more likely to change to district elections. In the 1970s, cities with populations that were more than 15 percent black were more likely to shift to district elections; in addition, the rate of change was greater in southern than in northern cities. Cities with substantial Hispanic populations were less likely to make the change, partly because Hispanics' residences are less concentrated geographically than those of blacks. Litigation and Justice Department intervention played a role in the change to district elections in San Antonio, Richmond, Dallas, and Mobile. In Fort Worth and Montgomery, local leaders, apparently wanting to avoid racial strife and fearing legal actions, proposed district elections. In other cities, such as Charlotte, Raleigh, and Sacramento, the pressure to change to district elections came from middle-class groups, which in most cases mobilized around neighborhood desires to have more influence on city policy choices.

New dominant coalitions have also sought to institutionalize their power by changing governmental structures to decrease the power of professional administrators and to increase that of elected officials. A study of 10 California cities (Browning et al., 1984:201) found that the formal powers of elected officials had been increased in more than half of the cities (Berkeley, Oakland, San Jose, Sacramento, Stockton, and San Francisco). Some had instituted direct, popular elections of mayors. Moreover, city managers were increasingly seen less as neutral administrators and more as instruments of the dominant coalition. This perception led dominant coalitions to seek to control the actions of city managers more closely and newly dominant coalitions to replace the city manager of the prior regime with their own selection, apparently in the expectation of greater responsiveness to their political agendas.

These changes are not all unidirectional, however. Reversals of direction and changes in direction are particularly possible in a federal political system in which different coalitions may dominate the different arenas. In the California election of June 1986, for example, voters approved Proposition 49, amending the state constitution to prohibit political parties from endorsing, supporting, or opposing a candidate for judicial, school, county, or city offices. In other instances, those in which a few California city elected officials have made frontal attacks on the council–manager form of government and proposed its abolition, such officials have been defeated.

The three trends in urban governance we have been discussing in this section affect who makes policy choices, how they are made, and the likely outcomes. While arguments continue about the extent of realignment in national politics (Chubb and Peterson, 1985; Lipset, 1986), forces at the local level can go against the national direction and serve as counterbalances. One indication of this phenomenon is the continuing control by Democrats of state and local politics (Cavanagh and Sundquist, 1985; Lipset, 1986:223). The growing presence of minorities, especially blacks, and women at the local level—two groups that are an important part of the Democratic constituency—suggests that this situation is likely to persist even though the local issues and responses by those coalitions are changing.

PUBLIC ENTREPRENEURSHIP AS AN ALTERNATIVE POLICY THEORY

When most individuals concerned with city policy choices accepted the theory that the urban problem was ineffective service provision and graft and corruption, and that the solution was the delivery of municipal services through functionally specific professionalized public bureaucracies supported by tax revenues, urban governance was greatly affected. This impact occurred during the Progressive era, roughly between 1880–1920, during which machine-based city political systems were displaced. Virtually the entire gamut of contemporary public services and regulation, from police and fire through parks to land use planning, was established during this period, all following the same basic theory concerning effective policies. The central elements of this Progressive era–public administration theory of politics dominated policy processes through the 1970s (Kirlin, 1984).

Although data on urban finances and policy design demonstrate the emergence of a new theory of public entrepreneurship that rivals the older public administration theory of urban governance, the most important evidence of that challenge is that a wide variety of urban officials appear to accept the new theory. The evidence concerning the emergence of a new theory of public entrepreneurship reveals that its progress is uneven but that it is most advanced at the local level. Some states are using tax abatements and public investments to attract industry, but they appear to fall short of cities in their current use of public entrepreneurial policy strategies. The national government is focusing its resources on direct service delivery and income redistribution. Meanwhile, cities are expanding beyond their traditional role of the delivery of municipal services to a wide range of entrepreneurial activities that are designed to stimulate economic activities, create jobs, and generate revenues. It is this pattern that leads to the conclusion that a bifurcation in policy arenas is occurring.

Table 4 presents data on the revenue sources of all governments—the national, state, county, and city. Changes in the composition of fiscal-year revenues between 1976–1977 (just before Proposition 13) and 1983–1984 (the latest data available) are reported. The table is selective, including only intergovernmental grants (with national and state grants separated), taxes, current charges, and utilities revenues; it shows that overall, and for each type of government, taxes decreased as a revenue source. Additionally, for state, county, and city governments, intergovernmental grants from the national government declined as a percentage of total revenue. State intergovernmental grants increased in importance as revenue sources for counties and cities, however. Although taxes and grants from the national government declined, current charges and utility revenue increased in importance as revenue sources for every type of government.

These patterns illustrate a shift from a tax-supported, grants-lubricated policy system toward a more entrepreneurial policy system based on charges and fees. All types of government demonstrate some entrepreneurial elements in their public finances. Even the national government received 12.1 percent of its revenues from current charges in 1983–1984, mostly from the postal service. Counties received 15.3 percent of their revenues in the same period from current charges, mostly for hospitals.

Cities and states provide an interesting contrast. Cities have experienced much greater constraint on their revenues than have states, as illustrated by growth rates of 79.9 percent versus 95.4 percent in total revenues, respectively, in the 1976–1977 to 1983–1984 period. States derived 58.5 percent of their revenues in 1984 from taxes, down very slightly from 58.7 percent in 1977. In contrast, cities received 33.8 percent of their revenues from taxes in 1983–1984, down more substantially from 36.8 percent in 1976–1977. Current charges generated 11.9 percent of city revenues in 1983–1984 versus 7.7 percent of state revenues in 1984. In this period of fiscal stress, states have fared comparatively well and made the fewest changes in their fiscal systems. Total state revenues increased faster than any other type of government, tax revenues were constant as a percentage of total revenues, and the increase in current charges was the smallest

TABLE 4 Changes in Components of Revenues (expressed as percentages of total revenues) by Type of Government

Type of Government	Total Revenue[a]	Revenue Component				
		National	State	Taxes	Current Charges	Utilities
All						
1976–1977	523.5	N.A.	N.A.	80.1	10.8	2.7
1983–1984	1,015.9	N.A.	N.A.	72.4	13.1	3.7
Percentage of change (growth)	90.0	N.A.	N.A.	75.0	134.6	163.4
National						
1976–1977	285.0	N.A.	0.5	85.6	8.8	N.A.
1983–1984	531.1	N.A.	0.3	78.1	12.1	N.A.
Percentage of change (growth)	86.3	N.A.	16.0	70.1	156.4	N.A.
State						
1977	172.1	26.7	N.A.	58.7	7.0	0.4
1984	336.1	22.6	N.A.	58.5	7.7	0.7
Percentage of change (growth)	95.4	65.9	N.A.	94.7	113.1	281.2
County						
1976–1977	41.9	12.9	34.2	37.9	11.8	0.7
1983–1984	78.2	7.3	35.3	35.7	15.3	1.1
Percentage of change (growth)	86.6	5.9	93.0	75.9	140.3	175.6
City						
1976–1977	71.8	15.7	19.8	36.3	9.6	14.9
1983–1984	129.2	10.0	20.4	33.8	11.9	18.6
Percentage of change (growth)	79.9	14.2	85.2	67.7	123.4	125.4

NOTE: N.A. = not available.

[a]These figures exclude trust funds and are expressed in billions of dollars.

SOURCE: Calculated from Bureau of the Census (1978-1985).

of all governments. Intergovernmental transfers from states have increased modestly as a percentage of county and city revenues, but this increase has occurred mostly because of reduced total revenues available to those local governments and not because of the increased largess of states. Increases in grants from states to counties lag slightly behind increases in total state revenues (93 percent versus 95.4 percent); by the same measure, the states are less generous with cities, a fiscal area in which state grants increased only 85.2 percent.

Strong evidence of the decline in the fiscal importance of intergovernmental grants from the national government to cities is clear in Table 4. Such grants declined from 15.7 percent of total revenues in 1976–1977 to 10 percent in 1983–1984. By 1983–1984, current charges were a larger revenue source to cities than grants from the national government. Utility revenues were smaller than national grants in 1976–1977 but nearly twice as large by 1983–1984. Cities have had strong incentives to become more entrepreneurial public financiers, and it appears they have done so reasonably successfully. Many of the most entrepreneurial activities of cities, in which the private sector now often finances an activity that would have been funded publicly a decade ago, do not appear in any available statistical series. (Some attention is given to this phenomenon later in this paper.)

It is also important to understand the changing composition of the intergovernmental grants provided by the national government. Grants for infrastructure purposes, such as wastewater treatment facilities, have been reduced (Congressional Budget Office, 1985:5). Increasingly, the grants systems of both the national and state governments focus on income transfers and service provision in the areas of health, education, and welfare.

For example, consider the shifts within categories Kirlin (1979) used to analyze changes in grants through the mid-1970s. Those national grants categorized as focusing on structural weaknesses in the economy (for example, economic development assistance, community development block grants, or the Jobs Training Partnership Act) declined from 10.1 percent of all grants in 1976–1977 to 7.9 percent in 1984–1985. More strikingly, grants that focused on remedying negative externalities (e.g., sewerage treatment facility grants) decreased from 6.1 percent to 2.7 percent of grants in the same period. Grants focused on countering cycles in the performance of the economy, which represented 6.9 percent of the total in 1976–1977, did not even exist in 1984–1985. At the same time, welfare state grants, including income security, health, and a variety of targeted education and social services grants programs, increased from 55.9 percent of all grants in 1976–1977 to 61.9 percent in 1984–1985.

Available statistical series do not include many forms of entrepreneurial public finance, especially cases in which costs previously borne by the public sector are shifted to the private sector. No aggregation of these expenditures is available, to the best of our knowledge, even for a single state. In California, a state in which such public–private bargains are well established, some observers believe that this is the primary method of financing public works projects, outstripping direct financing, grants, or public debt (Kirlin and Kirlin, 1982). New institutions are also being created to enable the private financing of infrastructure within public policy frameworks, a trend with considerable effects on land use patterns because the new financing instruments influence decisions in that arena (Misczynski, 1986).

Hard evidence on the spread of the theory of public entrepreneurship is difficult to find. It is important to note that there are also other contenders to replace the policy orthodoxy of the last few decades. One is "privatization," commonly defined as turning many government functions over to the private sector, sometimes through contracts and sometimes simply by terminating the public policy or program (Savas, 1982). The Reagan administration has advocated privatization, and this term has now taken on highly partisan overtones.

In contrast, public entrepreneurship encourages the broadest use of public powers but has no preconceived attachment to achieving public purposes through tax-supported public bureaucracies. Most of the literature on public entrepreneurship has emphasized infrastructure and new development, although attention is also paid to alternative forms of service delivery (Committee for Economic Development, 1982; Kirlin and Kirlin, 1982; Leavitt and Kirlin, 1985; Moore, 1983). The major associations concerned with urban management, land development, and economic development, including the Urban Land Institute, the National League of Cities, the Public Securities Association, the International City Management Association, and the Municipal Finance Officers' Association, have all sponsored program sessions, training workshops, and publications concerning public entrepreneurship.

To succeed, political leaders must address problems within the constraints and opportunities of their time. Policies are an instrument in their task of mobilizing supportive interests, of incorporating those interest groups into governing coalitions, and then of influencing urban governance. In the contemporary context, public entrepreneurship is attractive to urban public officials and to those who aspire to influence the course of urban governance. It addresses important problems of economic performance and job creation and does so within the fiscal constraints imposed on the public sector. A mayor of the 1960s, such as Richard Lee in New Haven, could build a coalition in which grants from the national government played a large role (Kotter and Lawrence, 1974), but today's mayors do not have that option. Instead, they are more likely to follow the path of Tom Bradley, whose approach to governing Los Angeles has emphasized building coalitions with private interests around development projects that will stimulate economic growth, job creation, and increased public revenues (Sonenshein, 1986).

Two very important factors encourage mayors and other urban leaders to embrace public entrepreneurship: the alternatives are few, and public entrepreneurs can achieve dramatic results. Concerning the latter point, Frieden and Sagalyn (1984) studied downtown shopping centers and concluded that the new public–private entrepreneurial style succeeded in the completion of such projects far more frequently than old-style (i.e., grants- and regulation-oriented) redevelopment efforts. Frieden and Sagalyn are cautious regarding the long-term economic effects of the projects they studied (most of the projects are only recently completed) and are not convinced such projects always warrant the substantial public investments made. But they are certain that the projects do not have the negative impacts of old-style redevelopment and that they are popular politically with the public officials involved.

CHALLENGES OF PUBLIC ENTREPRENEURSHIP

The changes in urban governance and the interplay among interest groups, dominant political theories, and the policy choices examined earlier in this paper all underscore the continued governability of cities. Cities have emerged from the recent period of fiscal limits, recession, and decreases in grants-in-aid with strengthened, not diminished, capacity. Although their share of total governmental revenues has fallen, cities have diversified their revenue bases and have shifted financing responsibility for parts of their historic activities to the private sector. They continue to incorporate new groups into their political processes.

Cities have adapted to complex, unforeseen changes in their circumstances; they play an increased role in economic development;

and city officials have discovered opportunities for successful leadership in apparent adversity. A theme running through all of these successful adaptations is public entrepreneurship. Cities have not succeeded by passively awaiting the manna of grants, mandates, or even policy ideas from the national or state governments. Instead, they have succeeded through strong, purposeful action. Most importantly, those actions have involved much more joint action with the private sector (including, among others, firms, developers, neighborhoods, and nonprofit organizations). The greater focus on the economic functions of cities is also appropriate: cities are critical locations of economic activity (Jacobs, 1984), and their role in economic growth warrants greater attention.

Although the emergence of public entrepreneurship and the consequent bifurcation of policy arenas into one focused on economic growth and development and another focused on the delivery of services are positive developments, they do not answer all questions. One set of questions that continues to call for answers derives from the differences between the two sectors. Service providers and entrepreneurs face different constraints and opportunities; they may not work effectively together even in those cases in which they can be complementary (e.g., the contribution that quality primary and secondary education can make to economic growth). A major challenge to public entrepreneurship arises from the structures and routines of city government. The structures commonly fragment authority needed for successful entrepreneurship, and administrative routines (especially of personnel, finance, and procurement), which consume so much of the attention and energies of city officials, are focused on service delivery activities rather than entrepreneurship.

Yet another set of challenges arises from perceived (and real) inequities and corruption that are possible in public entrepreneurship. A dominant definition of equity in our society is "treating equal cases alike," a definition easily met by service-delivering public bureaucracies (if you are in this category, you get these services) but often violated in the more particularistic practices of public entrepreneurship (the freeway interchange financed by the developer will not equally improve the traffic circulation of all parts of an area). More bargaining between the public and private sectors affords the opportunity for corruption, in either the form of personal graft or of ceding concern for any public interest in the scramble for jobs or revenues. But most political systems have proved open to some level of corruption, and any evaluation that is made of public entrepreneurship in this regard should be against real alternatives and not against an abstract standard.

Moreover, public entrepreneurship is unlikely to solve the needs of all locations or all groups. San Diego is likely to have more entrepreneurial opportunities than Des Moines because the former is growing. Both may do better following that strategy than any alternative, however. The problem of the underclass has not been solvable and continues to be a critical issue in many cities, an urban-area time bomb. Economic growth, the objective of public entrepreneurship, has not helped reduce urban poverty, despite Banfield's (1970) hopes. Lemann (1986) argues that poverty has worsened among poor blacks, not so much because of the failure of national programs, as Murray (1984) suggests, but because of deep-rooted cultural patterns made more visible and given freer rein by the movement of successful blacks out of central-city ghettos. That movement occurred in part because of successful public policies to provide economic opportunities and access for housing to blacks.

Thus, the governability of cities has been demonstrated, at least in part, by redefining public policy objectives. Problems of poverty, or of equality of access, remain. These problems are unlikely to disappear from the national political arena, despite efforts by the Reagan administration to shift responsibility for them to the states.

REFERENCES

Advisory Commission on Intergovernmental Relations
1980   *In Brief: The Federal Role in the Federal System: The Dynamics of Growth.* Washington, D.C.: Advisory Commission on Intergovernmental Relations.

1981   *An Agenda for American Federalism: Restoring Confidence and Competence.* Report A-86. Washington, D.C.: Advisory Commission on Intergovernmental Relations.

1987   *Significant Features of Fiscal Federalism, 1987 Edition.* Report M-151. Washington, D.C.: Advisory Commission on Intergovernmental Relations.

Anton, Thomas J.
1984   Intergovernmental changes in the United States: An assessment of the literature. Pp. 15–64 in Trudi C. Miller, ed., *Public Sector Performance: A Conceptual Turning Point.* Baltimore, Md.: Johns Hopkins University Press.

Banfield, Edward C.
1970   *The Unheavenly City.* Boston: Little, Brown.

Bosworth, Barry P.
1980   Economic policy. Pp. 35–70 in Joseph A. Pechman, ed., *Setting National Priorities: Agenda for the 1980s.* Washington, D.C.: Brookings Institution.

Browning, Rufus P., and Dale Rogers Marshall, eds.
    1986   Minority power in city politics: A forum. *PS* 19(Summer):573–640.
Browning, Rufus P., Dale Rogers Marshall, and David H. Tabb
    1984   *Protest Is Not Enough: The Struggle of Blacks and Hispanics for Equality in Urban Politics.* Berkeley: University of California Press.
Bureau of the Census
    1978   *Governmental Finances in 1976–1977.* Series GF80, No. 5. Washington, D.C.: U.S. Department of Commerce.
    1979   *Governmental Finances in 1977–1978.* Series GF80, No. 5. Washington, D.C.: U.S. Department of Commerce.
Cavanagh, Thomas E., and Thomas L. Sundquist
    1985   The new two-party system. Pp. 33–68 in John E. Chubb and Paul E. Peterson, eds., *The New Direction in American Politics.* Washington, D.C.: Brookings Institution.
Center for the American Woman and Politics
    1986   *Women Municipal Officers.* New Brunswick, N.J.: Eagleton Institute of Politics, Rutgers University.
Chubb, John E.
    1985   Federalism and the bias for centralization. Pp. 273–306 in John E. Chubb and Paul E. Peterson, eds., *The New Direction in American Politics.* Washington, D.C.: Brookings Institution.
Chubb, John E., and Paul E. Peterson, eds.
    1985   *The New Direction in American Politics.* Washington, D.C.: Brookings Institution.
Committee for Economic Development
    1982   *Public–Private Partnerships: An Opportunity for Urban Communities.* New York: Committee for Economic Development.
Congressional Budget Office
    1985   *The Federal Budget for Public Works Infrastructure.* Washington, D.C.: Congressional Budget Office.
Council of Economic Advisers
    1986   *Economic Report of the President.* Washington, D.C.: U.S. Government Printing Office.
Fainstein, Susan S., Norman I. Fainstein, Richard Child Hill, Dennis Judd, and Michael Peter Smith, eds.
    1983   *Restructuring the City: The Political Economy of Urban Redevelopment.* New York: Longman.
Frieden, Bernard J., and Lynne B. Sagalyn
    1984   Downtown Shopping Malls and the New Public–Private Strategy. Department of Urban Studies and Planning, Massachusetts Institute of Technology.
    1986   Downtown shopping malls and the new public–private strategy. Pp. 130–147 in Marshall Kaplan and Peggy L. Cuciti, eds., *The Great Society and Its Legacy: Twenty Years of U.S. Social Policy.* Durham, N.C.: Duke University Press.
Heilig, Peggy, and Robert J. Mundt
    1985   *Your Voice at City Hall: The Politics, Procedures, and Policies of District Representation.* Albany, N.Y.: State University of New York Press.
International City Management Association
    1982   *Municipal Yearbook, 1982.* Washington, D.C.: International City Management Association.

Jacobs, Jane
    1984   Cities and the wealth of nations. *The Atlantic* (March):41–66.
Joint Center for Political Studies
    1985   *Black Elected Officials: A National Roster.* Washington, D.C.: Joint
            Center for Political Studies.
Kirlin, John J.
    1979   Adapting the intergovernmental fiscal system to the demands of an
            advanced economy. Pp. 77–104 in Gary A. Tobin, ed., *The Changing
            Structure of the City.* Vol. 16, Urban Affairs Annual Reviews. Beverly
            Hills, Calif.: Sage Publications.
    1982   *The Political Economy of Fiscal Limits.* Lexington, Mass.: Lexington
            Books.
    1984   Policy formulation. Pp. 13–24 in G. Ronald Gilbert, ed., *Making and
            Managing Policy.* New York: Marcel Dekker, Inc.
    1986   Fiscal context. Pp. 15–32 in John J. Kirlin and Donald R. Winkler,
            eds., *California Policy Choices,* vol. 3. Sacramento: University of
            Southern California Press.
Kirlin, John J., and Anne M. Kirlin
    1982   *Public Choices–Private Resources.* Sacramento, Calif.: Cal-Tax Founda-
            tion.
Kotter, John, and Paul Lawrence
    1974   *Mayors in Action.* New York: Wiley.
Leavitt, Rachelle, and John J. Kirlin, eds.
    1985   *Managing Development Through Public–Private Negotiation.* Washington,
            D.C.: The Urban Land Institute.
Lemann, Nicholas
    1986   The origins of the underclass. *The Atlantic* (June):31–55, (July):54–68.
Lipset, Seymour Martin
    1986   The anomalies of American politics. *PS* 19(2):222–265.
Misczynski, Dean
    1986   The fiscalization of land use in California. Pp. 73–105 in John J.
            Kirlin and Donald R. Winkler, eds., *California Policy Choices,* vol. 3.
            Sacramento: University of Southern California Press.
Moore, Barbara, ed.
    1983   *The Entrepreneur in Local Government.* Washington, D.C.: International
            City Management Association.
Murray, Charles
    1984   *Losing Ground: American Social Policy, 1950–1980.* New York: Basic
            Books.
National Association of Latino Elected Officials
    1986   *The National Roster of Hispanic Elected Officials.* Washington, D.C.:
            National Association of Latino Elected Officials.
Peterson, Paul E.
    1981   *City Limits.* Chicago: University of Chicago Press.
Piven, Frances F., and Richard Cloward
    1971   *Regulating the Poor.* New York: Pantheon Books.
Pressman, Jeffrey L., and Aaron B. Wildavsky
    1984   *Implementation,* 3rd ed. Berkeley: University of California Press.
Reagan, Michael D., and John Y. Sanzone
    1981   *The New Federalism,* 2d ed. New York: Oxford University Press.

Savas, E. S.
  1982 *Privatizing the Public Sector.* Chatham, N.J.: Chatham House.
Shefter, Martin
  1985 *Political Crisis/Fiscal Crisis: The Collapse and Renewal of New York City.*
        New York: Basic Books.
Sonenshein, Raphe
  1986 Biracial coalition politics in Los Angeles. *PS* 19(Summer):582–590.
Stone, Clarence N., and Heywood T. Sanders, eds.
  1987 *The Politics of Urban Development.* Lawrence: University Press of Kansas.
Stone, Clarence N., Robert K. Whelan, and William J. Murin
  1986 *Urban Policy and Politics in a Bureaucratic Age,* 2d ed. Englewood Cliffs,
        N.J.: Prentice-Hall, Inc.
Wiseman, Michael
  1985 The welfare system. Pp. 133–202 in John J. Kirlin and Donald R.
        Winkler, eds., *California Policy Choices,* vol. 2. Sacramento: University
        of Southern California Press.
Yates, Douglas
  1977 *The Ungovernable City.* Cambridge, Mass.: MIT Press.

Index